Ideas and Realities of Emotion

When people (including psychologists) talk about emotions, they usually assume that they are describing something that goes on simply inside the individual mind or body, and that can be easily isolated, pinned down and dissected. Brian Parkinson shows that the relationship between ideas and reality, or words and things, is far more complex. He gets to 'the heart of emotion by denying that the personal heart has much to do with it' and looks at emotion in real-time encounters between people, expressed in gesture and movement, talk and silence.

Ideas and Realities of Emotion presents a clear and concise overview of state-of-the-art research into emotion, focusing on cognitive appraisal, bodily changes, action tendencies and expressive displays. The book challenges the idea of emotion as an individual intrapsychic phenomenon, and formulates a new and distinctive conceptual framework based on the idea of emotion as interpersonal communication – a social practice influenced by culture and language. *Ideas and Realities of Emotion* will prove invaluable to all those approaching emotion from a social psychological perspective, whether at advanced undergraduate or graduate level.

Brian Parkinson is Lecturer in Psychology at the University of Leicester.

D1059115

International Library of Psychology
Edited by Anthony Manstead
Universeit van Amsterdam

Ideas and Realities of Emotion

Brian Parkinson

London and New York

First published 1995
by Routledge
11 New Fetter Lane, London EC4P 4EE

Simultaneously published in the USA and Canada
by Routledge
29 West 35th Street, New York, NY 10001

Typeset in Times by LaserScript Ltd, Mitcham, Surrey
Printed and bound in Great Britain by
Mackays of Chatham PLC, Chatham, Kent

British Library Cataloguing in Publication Data
A catalogue record for this book is available from the British Library

Library of Congress Cataloguing in Publication Data
A catalogue record for this book has been requested

ISBN 0–415–02858–2 (hbk)
ISBN 0–415–02859–0 (pbk)

Contents

Illustrations

Preface

A fact that is difficult to deny about the word 'emotion' is that it connotes a certain set of ideas. The question of how these ideas relate to any kind of reality, however, often seems an intractable, even metaphysical one. When I first started out in research psychology, a sceptic about anything and everything, I thought that at least it would be possible to investigate the *idea* of emotion, and take it from, or leave it, there. I rapidly came to the conclusion that most of the social psychological studies of emotion, although they purported to account for a set of real phenomena, actually had more to say about what people believe about emotions than how they actually worked (whatever 'they' actually were).

For example, Valins (1966) found that people were willing to base their judgements of the attractiveness of erotic slides on false feedback of heart-rate change, showing, as I believed, that people will (in certain special circumstances) define their reactions in affective terms when presented with supposedly objective information of bodily reaction. In other words, people appeared to assume that internal responses are symptomatic of emotion and attempted to act accordingly. This, so it seemed to me when I was writing my PhD thesis on this topic back in 1982, did not actually mean that real emotions were sometimes *caused* by beliefs about heart-rate change, but simply that people were willing to apply an idea of emotion to themselves whenever certain aspects of that idea were made available. Of course, the fact that the idea itself apparently led to some quasi-emotional effects should even then have brought me to the realization that the idea was less separable from the reality than I had at that time naively assumed.

To take a more recent instance, Smith and Ellsworth (1985) tried to find out what evaluative dimensions determine the quality of emotion by asking students to remember pure emotional experiences and rate their recalled appraisals. The findings of this research, I immediately assumed when I read about them back then, told us only that people *define* different emotional states based on evaluative dimensions: the idea of anger implies that someone else is blamed for something bad happening and so on.

Both these studies (and most others in the psychology of emotion) make an implicit assumption that emotion is out there (or in here) somewhere in psychological reality waiting to be isolated, pinned down and dissected. They try to conjure up the phenomenon within the 'subjects' of their investigations so that they can get a better look at it. And the participants in the experiments are usually willing to cooperate with these intentions, wanting to put their emotions (or what they too believe to be their emotions) on the table for all to see. But all that they ever come up with is something conforming to a shared idea of emotion, rather than the thing itself (whatever that might have turned out to be if their initial assumptions happened to have had any chance of being correct).

My reaction to all this at the time was, for a self-professed professional sceptic, predictably extreme. I suppose I thought either that there was no such thing as emotion, except insofar as people believed it existed and made it happen in this way, somehow deluding themselves, or that maybe there was some phenomenon roughly corresponding to what people were talking about, but that their talking about it would never get them any nearer to what it was really like. Around that time, I planned a book outlining this argument and applying it to amenable examples from the empirical psychology of emotion. The book was to be called *The Idea of Emotion*; a good title, I still think, but one that no longer meshes with the confused developments in my subsequent musings about 'emotion'. This book is not (or at least not quite) the same one, and I think I am obliged to say why it is not, if only to appease that earlier would-be author still lurking somewhere in the back of my 'mind'.

My opinions have changed, at least a little. Now I realize that the relationship between ideas and reality, or indeed words and things, is not nearly as simple as I had originally supposed. Ideas are expressed and have an impact; realities are not as static, substantial or unidimensional as I had imagined. Emotion is more than a way of talking about behaviour, and talking is not always simply talking *about* anyway. At some point, I must have stopped being a straightforward relativist and admitted at last that there was an intractable real world out there (containing, among other things, ideas as well as utterances), a world that kept moving on and in which our little attempts at understanding it had at least some minor impact. The problem, of course, lies in finding any sensible way of getting at that world except through our ideas of it.

Specifically, in the case of emotion, I now accept that a real set of processes exist in the social world that correspond (though inexactly) to what people mean when they talk about emotion, and to what people are doing when they say emotional things to one another. Sometimes the real world of emotion is actually manufactured through the medium of talk in the course of a conversation. My scepticism is now restricted only to specific aspects of the idea of emotion: that it is purely intrapsychic, private, that personal feelings are all-important. In contrast, I want to look for emotion in real-time encounters between people, expressed in gesture and movement, talk and silence.

The upshot of all this is that although I believe that the existing social psychological literature on emotion, which incidentally is the general topic of this book, tells us something, it does not always tell us exactly what it purports to tell us. Because of an unquestioning shared acceptance of the idea of emotion as an individual phenomenon, the reality of emotion as a real-time communicative social process tends to go missing. 'Emotion' as a concept achieves a certain reality in mutual understandings of psychological phenomena, but the psychological idea of emotion fails to touch on the actual emotional episodes that unfold regardless in the actual social world.

This book will be about the ideas and realities surrounding emotion talk and emotional interaction. I want to get to the heart of emotion by denying that the individual heart has all that much to do with it. Having said all this, much of the coverage of this book will be fairly traditional. I think it is worth considering the results of recent (and some not so recent) experiments into emotion, which adopt the usual common-sense assumptions. My argument will be not that these studies tell us nothing, but that they often miss the wider picture by treating individual variables in isolation. After reviewing the literature on individual emotion, I want to examine how well the relevant theories stand up to the realities of emotion in the sociocultural world (or rather, the interpersonal and institutional worlds).

My book, like any other, will be a partisan one. I want to present a particular view of emotion and of social psychology in general. Basically, I consider the idea that emotions happen and are played out in an essentially private intrapsychic arena to be misguided, even dangerous. I believe that such a notion is close to the centre of our individualistic ideology which often takes personal freedom and responsibility as basic values and hence allocates blame and credit apparently even-handedly according to individual outcomes. Hence capitalism; hence disregard for *society* in its complex and ever-changing variety.

Having said all this, the book will by no means be just a dogmatic piece of polemic. I am sufficiently interested in the psychology of emotion, with all its present weaknesses, warts and all, to want to do justice to the work that has gone before, without which I could have made no start on the present undertaking. This will be a critical account of an existing literature, rather than a merely theoretical speculation (although that too will have its place). I want what I say to make contact with the material practices of emotion investigation which currently go on in laboratories and other research sites around the contemporary world. Too often, I have read critical accounts that are persuasive in general terms but offer no alternative methodology with which to proceed. I hope I can avoid that trap in this book.

Finally, confession time: I have been torn between two sets of external and internal demands which cannot be resolved in any putatively final version of what will eventually pass for my book: I want to educate and I want to say what I think. I want to review a literature and also to say that that literature does not do what it ought to. I want to make value judgements and still claim to be doing science (whatever meaning remains in that activity). Thankfully, it will not be up to me to say how close I come to succeeding.

ACKNOWLEDGEMENTS

It is of course customary in contexts such as this to offer acknowledgements and dedications. I have had neither the time nor the inclination to pass draft chapters of the manuscript around to colleagues for comments so for once the author can in all honesty and without false modesty take full blame for all the misunderstandings and confusions contained in the text (and there certainly are instances of both). Nevertheless various kinds of credit, as always, go to people too numerous to mention, but especially to Tony Manstead, John Wearden, Andrew Colman, John Downes, Rainer Reisenzein, Steve Evans, Nico Frijda, Rob Briner, Peter Totterdell, Shirley Reynolds, John Bowers and Ludwig Wittgenstein, but not always nor necessarily in that order. Although many of these would likely be surprised or dismayed to know that they had any hand in what I have done, each in different ways made some kind of contribution. However, at least one or two were probably at the time in no fit condition to register fully the insights or otherwise that they had imparted, especially, of course, Ludwig himself. As for dedications: the book is for my parents, for my brother, sister and niece, and for Gillian. But most of all, it is for me.

Part I
Individual emotion

1   Conceptualizing emotion

OVERVIEW

Because all of us know what emotion is from the outset, or at least believe that we do, it might seem as if the ground is already clear for development of a scientific analysis in this area. In this chapter, I consider whether the common understanding of emotion provides firm foundations for construction of a psychological framework of investigation. More generally, I attempt to introduce the topic of emotion by discussing how the domain should be conceptualized, taking common-sense thinking into account. My concern, as in the rest of the book, is with how ideas and realities of emotion overlap and how they are separate from one another. In the first part of the chapter, I argue that the everyday delineation of emotion provides at best a provisional demarcation of the field of interest rather than well-defined theoretical boundaries for psychological exploration. In other words, common sense allows us to section off some phenomena that are clearly irrelevant to emotion, and to capture others that are of more obvious direct concern. Developing this approach in the second section, I show how psychologists have staked out a scientific territory by sharpening and tightening the everyday idea of emotions as evaluative mental states directed at intentional objects. Unfortunately, however, common sense is a source of confusion as well as clarification concerning emotion and how it works. In the third part of the chapter, I examine in general terms how the concept is currently operationalized in scientific practice and call attention to the restrictiveness of this research focus. Three levels of phenomena have been distinguished in studies of emotion, relating to its individual experience, interpersonal communication and consensual representation. The traditional assumption, derived from common sense, is that the primary source of emotion knowledge comes from private experience and that communicative and representational emotional phenomena are derivative and secondary. I shall argue that this view is oversimplistic. The three varieties of evidence are neither as diverse nor as distinct as commonly assumed, and by fixing attention singlemindedly on each in isolation, researchers are missing out on the broader picture. Finally, I question the traditional assumption that private experience provides the only direct access route to emotion, and suggest instead that the relevant phenomena can often be interpreted in interpersonal rather than individual terms. Although this revised approach is directed at conceptual objects picked out and partly constituted by common sense, it adopts a radically different perspective with respect to these objects.

ORIENTATION

One thing that is certain about 'emotion' is that it is not an entity or substance in the world in the same way as, say, a thunderstorm or rainbow, milk or honey. It is not something that you can easily put your finger on. 'Emotion', to be sure, is a word used in psychological discourse as well as in everyday conversation, but this does not mean that there is a simple object, event or process that is referred to whenever the word is used. Then again, it is not just a word either. Emotion is a concept, a social practice, a way of being-in-the-world. All this and more. In this book, I want to explore some of the things that emotion is and is not in order to try to get a clearer sense of how phenomena relating to the concept fit in with our ways of speaking when we speak emotionally. In short, I will be concerned with emotion as an idea and as an individual as well as interpersonal reality. My conclusions will not provide a simple or complete answer to the question of what emotion is, but rather may help to understand why, despite its deceptively straightforward wording, this is actually not such a good question in the first place.

One thing needs to be made clear before I begin. Many people assume that emotions are just intact and uncomplicated internal feelings which are immediately distinguishable in terms of their felt quality. In this case, not only would definition be no problem, but also there would be little interest in studying emotions in psychology because the only thing to do with phenomena of this nature would be to catalogue meticulously their variety (cf. James, 1898). Unless emotions are bound up in cognitive, motivational or more general psychological processes, they can only be of peripheral interest to analysts of human action. There are a number of reasons why the idea of emotions as individual feelings does not bear up to close scrutiny, many of which should become clear in the course of the chapter. For now, I only want to point out that whatever is usually connoted by the term 'emotion' is something more intricate, involved, and involving than directly felt qualities of consciousness. Whatever else they might be is the specific concern of this chapter and much of the rest of the book.

STATUS OF EMOTION AS TOPIC

The traditional and obvious way to begin a discussion of the present topic would be to attempt to answer the question 'What is emotion?' Indeed, the modern psychological approach to emotional phenomena started with an article written over a hundred years ago which had as its title a very similar question (James, 1884). As yet no one has been able to come up with a completely satisfactory answer (one paper on this topic listed ninety-two distinct definitions organized in eleven separate categories; Kleinginna and Kleinginna, 1981). Much of the content of the present book addresses this fundamental conceptual (as well as practical) issue in one way or another, but before confronting the question head on, I think it is first worth asking a shorter and possibly simpler question: namely, 'Is emotion?' (alternatively, 'What emotion?'). To be more explicit, I shall start by considering whether whatever phenomena are picked out by the ordinary language word 'emotion' have any necessary common defining features, and if it is correct from a scientific view to use the concept of 'emotion' as part of a general analysis of how human beings act in the real world. Does emotion actually exist, in a psychological sense?

Common-sense concepts have an ambiguous status within psychology. On the one hand, several theorists argue that ordinary language contains a psychological category system that has evolved into a powerful and sensitive descriptive instrument over the course of cultural history. In this case, the fact that people talk about each other's and their own psychological functioning in emotional terms is ample reason for taking the idea of emotion seriously (e.g. Harré and Secord, 1972). On the other hand, there are also psychologists who believe that the cultural evolution of common-sense categories follows a quite different logic from that of proper scientific development, and that it would be unwise to import a vernacular idea such as that of emotion with all its associated baggage whole-sale into our scientific accounts of behaviour. As Mandler (1975) reasoned: 'It seems useful not to fall into the trap of trying to explain what an emotion *is*, that would be to follow the error of trying to explicate the common language' (p. 2). Some of the more extreme proponents of this critical view have even suggested doing away completely with explanations phrased in terms of emotion, and relying instead on more 'objectively' defined concepts. Duffy (1941), for example, argued as follows:

> I am aware of no evidence for the existence of a special condition called 'emotion' which follows different principles of action from other conditions of the organism. I can therefore see no reason for a psychological study of 'emotion' as such. 'Emotion' has no distinguishing characteristics. It represents merely an *extreme* manifestation of characteristics found in some degrees in all responses.
>
> (p. 292)

Imagine Admiral Nelson as a latterday psychologist wearing a misplaced conceptual eyepatch and remarking 'I see no emotion'.

More commonly, theorists begin their analyses with a relatively undefined and off-the-peg common-sense version of the emotion concept but reserve the right to adjust or tailor its fabric to suit their scientific needs should this become necessary. In this third view, 'emotion' is accepted provisionally as a valid scientific concept, in order to get the analysis under-way.

I too believe that there are good reasons for taking the common-sense concept of emotion seriously, but I also feel that many of its intuitive connotations are unhelpful for constructing a complete psychological picture of what goes on when people 'get emotional'.

Taking the plus side first, it can easily be claimed that the workability of the common-sense concept is continually reasserted by its apparently successful everyday usage. However, this article of faith is of little practical use without guidelines for deciding which aspects of the idea map directly onto the psychological phenomena of concern and which do not. In any case, when people actually use emotion representations, the psychological process never ends with a simple descriptive characterization of an independent emotional world. This is because deployment of emotion ideas always exerts some effect on the way that psychological reality is formulated: even if consciousness actually provided a neutral running commentary on what was going on, such a process would have little point unless it changed the ways that people reacted to and dealt with the objects and events characterized in this internal monologue. Thus, thinking about emotion in certain ways is bound to affect as well as reflect the conduct of emotional life in the real world. The consequence of this conclusion is that the common sense of emotion cannot be assessed in a simple way in terms of its correspondence with a separable realm of application. Rather, common sense helps to define and constitute the very reality with which it is compared.

This analysis of how emotional ideas intrude into emotional reality does, however, suggest a different reason for making use of the common-sense concept in psychological analysis. As attribution theorists have argued, the fact that people use certain psychological concepts when describing and accounting for their own and other people's behaviour is itself a phenomenon of interest (e.g. Heider, 1958; Kelley, 1992; and see Chapter 9). In other words, even if there were no such thing as 'emotion' in 'scientific' terms, people's usage of the idea might still make some kind of difference to the way they acted on the social world. Indeed, to the extent that the idea of emotion helps to constitute a set of relevant phenomena, it may prove helpful in theory development.

The impact of common-sense ideas of emotion on the realities of psychological functioning becomes even more obvious when the conceptual focus is broadened to encompass the interpersonal world. Emotion concepts are part of the accepted currency of social transactions and their value is difficult to undermine. Our relative interpersonal positions are culturally predefined in emotional terms, and can be reproduced (deliberately as well as automatically) in any ongoing encounter. For example, when a lover betrays us, we know from countless books and films what our reaction should be and how other people are supposed to deal with us when we are like this. We play out the preformulated roles, sometimes in a quite self-conscious way, and construct emotional realities between us during the course of our interpersonal encounters. More generally speaking, I want to claim that the cultural availability of interpersonal identity positions based on emotion, where, for example, one person gets angry and another is thus encouraged to apologize, makes it likely that in some circumstances people will actually take on the relevant roles with the requisite level of identification. In certain social situations, then, believing in emotion can make it real.

Moving to the disadvantages of the common-sense idea of emotion, it is obvious that not *all* of our common-sense ideas about emotion are entirely accurate, even when evaluated as simple one-way descriptions, mapping onto a putative independent psychological reality. Words and concepts are shaped by ideological rather than perfectly realistic forces, and serve to justify and mystify interpersonal relations as well as directly describe them. For example, Sampson (1977) has argued that much of psychological theory and experimentation is misguided by a cultural prejudice that individual functioning is primary. Because in Western capitalist society, every person is taught to take responsibility for his or her own actions, and to account for himself or herself as an origin of intentions, personal causes come to be seen as all-important. A similar situation emerges from the ideology of emotion. The emphasis of common-sense as well as scientific accounts of emotion tends to fall on private and intrapsychic aspects of the phenomenon, often at the expense of interpersonal factors. One of the main aims of the present book is to redress this misemphasis.

To summarize this section, I have argued that it is reasonable to start out by accepting with due scepticism the existence of a divisible portion of psychology loosely bounded by the common-sense category of emotion. The aim is to extend this analysis so that we can find out what factors underlie the manifestations that we call emotion, and revise our analysis accordingly. Furthermore, it is important to see the everyday idea of emotion as part of the phenomenon in which we are interested rather than as a separable categorization of an independent psychological reality. In this book, I shall consider common-sense ideas as topics as well as resources for investigation.

It may turn out, over the course of history, that the present idea of emotion becomes redundant and unnecessary or simply misguided. In this case, it is possible to foresee a time when psychologists as well as other people (assuming that such a distinction also continues to hold) cease to speak in emotional terms. For now, however, the idea serves its scientific and everyday purposes.

In much the same way as common-sense ideas influence everyday realities of emotion, the traditional psychological concept of emotion (itself derived partly from common sense) also shapes the practice of psychological research in this area, and partly determines how the events and episodes that count as emotions are constituted in laboratory and naturalistic settings. The main focus of this chapter will shift from common-sense to psychological ideas of emotion in the sections that follow (although, as it turns out, the division between these two areas is far from clear-cut). In the next section, I show how the implicit theory of emotion suggested by the ordinary language concept can be translated into a working definition for the psychologist. This discussion also serves the purpose of making clear what phenomena fall under the general heading of emotion in traditional psychological research into the topic.

Although I believe that the realities of emotion are complex and multifaceted, the basic idea of emotion that underlies most psychological research is at heart a simple one. As in common sense, it is assumed that emotion is an individual experience typically caused by something that has happened to the person in question. Much of the existing research on emotion which I review in subsequent chapters implicitly accepts this common-sense definition of emotion, although it is rarely spelt out in detail by investigators. To repeat, the view of emotion offered in the next section should in no sense be taken as a final and definitive analysis, but rather as a way of getting a fix on the kinds of things that psychologists and other people mean by emotion. As the book progresses, I will be drawing attention to the way that this limited individualistic and representational view of what emotion is fails to tell the whole story.

COMMON-SENSE DEFINITION OF EMOTION

It has often been remarked that everyone knows perfectly well what emotion is, but no one can define it (e.g. Fehr and Russell, 1984). In fact, as with many paradoxes, this is not entirely true. On the one hand, not everyone agrees about what emotion is. Although people have their own intuitive understanding of emotion, there is nevertheless some uncertainty about what counts as an emotion, and even how various different emotional conditions such as anger, embarrassment, pride, and so on are manifested. People from different cultures and different eras sometimes have very different conceptions of emotions (e.g. Heelas, 1986; Lutz and White, 1986) and their lists of individual states that come under the general heading may differ quite substantially. Indeed, in some cultures, there is no word that directly translates as 'emotion' at all (Lutz, 1988). Furthermore, the same person can adopt different and incompatible formulations of emotion at different times and in different circumstances, at one moment characterizing emotion as distorting presentation ('I wasn't myself') and at another as providing a direct and heartfelt access to the authentic self ('No matter how it seems to you, this is how I really feel'). It appears that the implicit unanimity about emotion is an illusion, and even if everyone does know what emotion is, they often still disagree about it sometimes even with themselves (cf. Billig, 1987).

On the other hand, there are at least some words, such as 'happiness' and 'anger' (or their respective translations), that few people in Western culture would leave outside the category of emotion names. Similarly, there is some degree of consensus about how to define the phenomenon in question. When we look at the phenomena that most people (including psychologists) want to call emotions, it becomes clear that they share certain common features to a greater or lesser extent and this certainly allows some sort of provisional demarcation of what kinds of things fall under this general heading. What, then, do these conditions that people think of as emotional have in common with one another?

First, people tend to see emotions as characteristically *intentional* states. In other words, emotions are assumed to take an object of some sort, whether this object is a state of affairs, something that has happened, will happen, or might happen, another person, oneself, a physical object, event, relationship or whatever. For example, it is hard to imagine a pure state of pride, anger or love without the state being directed at something: you are proud of your success, angry with someone who has insulted you, in love with a particular person, rather than just proud, angry, or in love *per se* (e.g. Averill, 1980). This characteristic has been termed the 'aboutness' of emotion (Gordon, 1974). The apparent exceptions to this rule are conditions such as 'free-floating anxiety', which is a clinical phenomenon where people supposedly just feel generally anxious without it having a specific direction. However, here too it is possible to argue that the experience only becomes properly emotional when it crystallizes around some object or event, so that the person is now anxious about his health, now about the direction her life is taking, now about existence itself, and so on. At any rate, it is certainly unusual for emotions not to be about anything.

According to this reasoning, then, emotions imply a certain relationship between an individual and an object or another person. A complementary feature of our common understanding of emotion is that the relation with the object is an intrinsically evaluative one. When emotional, we feel good or bad, approving or disapproving, relieved or disappointed about some state of affairs. Third and finally, this evaluative attitude is not seen as a permanent and enduring aspect of our way of relating to the world, but as a disruption or break away from our background position. Even the derivation of the word 'emotion' suggests a *move away* from normal functioning, something that takes us out of ourselves for a while. Thus, emotions are states that are more or less transient and short-lived. Of course, here again there are possible exceptions to this general rule. For example, the condition of grief can apparently persist for months or even years. When we think about grief in terms of the feelings it causes, however, it may be that the actual emotional component ebbs and flows over the course of a protracted grief episode, focusing in turn on different, aspects of the loss that has been experienced. In this case, the emotion may be experienced repeatedly, but each individual phase of the reaction does not last too long. Again, in most cases at least, emotions are relatively short-lived.

To summarize, although it is not easy to come up with a thoroughgoing definition which includes all the phenomena that laypeople might want to call emotion (and excludes all those that they would not), it is still true that certain characteristics are agreed to be fairly central defining features. The chances are that if someone is considered to be emotional, they will be seen as having a positive or a negative evaluative position with respect to some definite object (whether imagined or real), and this position will not be a constant or permanent one. In other words, emotions are conceptualized as evaluative, affective, intentional, and short-term states.

This preliminary demarcation of emotion allows us to distinguish emotions from related conditions such as moods (Batson *et al.* 1992; Clark and Isen, 1982). Like emotions, moods have an evaluative component that is felt as good or bad (i.e. they too are *affective* states); unlike emotions, moods do not usually take a definite or specific object (you can just be grumpy as a result of 'getting out of bed the wrong side' without any particular focus to the feeling); and unlike emotions, moods can persist for relatively long periods of time. Moods are therefore often described as *tonic* states (they set a background level or tone of experience which remains relatively stable), whereas emotions are thought to be *phasic* (they imply a temporary move away from the relatively stable baseline).

To give a few examples of states that might fall into these two categories: embarrassment is an emotional condition which is rarely just a mood; it usually reflects a relatively intense and often quite temporary reaction to a specific kind of situation. 'Happiness', on the other hand, can refer either to a mood or to an emotion, although the *emotional* experience of happiness is more likely to be called joy or euphoria because of its power and focus. As a final illustration of this distinction, you can be in an anxious mood, but 'terror' is a word that can only describe an emotional state. It would be unusual, for example, to claim that you had been feeling terrified for the whole day, whereas anxiety-prone individuals can sometimes be in an anxious mood for weeks on end.

Despite these distinctions, however, it is also worth remembering that emotions and moods are related concepts. For example, note that terror could easily be seen as an intense kind of anxiety that was focused on a particular object. Furthermore, some theorists have suggested that mood-states may sometimes arise as a result of emotional experiences: you can still feel generally good or bad, long after the direct cause of the reaction has ceased to affect you directly (Isen, 1984; Ruckmick, 1936). There is no need to prejudge the issue by claiming that moods and emotions are under the control of different explanatory systems.

Emotion as a common-sense category

The common-sense idea of emotion can be clarified further by considering examples. It seems reasonable to assume that once we know what items are included in the common-sense category of emotion, we will have a pretty good idea of how emotion is conceptualized. Unfortunately, even this is not quite as easy as it seems because there is less than universal agreement about what conditions count as emotions. Psychologists as well as laypeople differ in their opinions of whether certain phenomena are or are not emotional.

However, it does seem that certain emotions are better and clearer examples than others. Fehr and Russell (1984) asked Canadian college students to rate a series of emotion terms on the basis of how closely they represented the category. *Love* was rated as the best example of an emotion overall, followed by *hate*, *anger*, *sadness*, and *happiness*. These same words also tended to be the ones that most readily sprang to mind when the participants were asked to list emotions (see Table 1.1 for a list of the most commonly mentioned examples of emotion).

Other words were rated as relatively poorer examples of emotions, such as *pride*, *hope*, *lust*, *pain*, and *hunger*. Some participants thought that these conditions were emotional and others did not. Fehr and Russell concluded from their research that the category of emotion is not one around which any sharp dividing line can be drawn, separating emotions on the inside from other, non-emotional states on the outside. Rather, there are many states that might be labelled as emotions in some circumstances but not others, and by certain people but not everyone. The class of emotional phenomena, in such a view, is bounded by fuzzy rather than distinct edges, and is best represented by its most central examples (love, anger, hate, and so on).

Table 1.1 Two 'top tens' of representative emotions

Common-sense chart*	Psychologists' chart**
1 Happiness (152)	1 Fear (9)
2 Anger (149)	2 Anger (7)
3 Sadness (136)	3 Disgust (6)
4 Love (124)	4 Sadness (5)
5 Fear (96)	5 Joy (5)
6 Hate (89)	6 Surprise (5)
7 Joy (82)	7 Rage (4)
8 Excitement (53)	8 Love (3)
9 Anxiety (50)	9 Happiness (3)
10 Depression (42)	10 Interest (3)

Notes: Numbers in parentheses reflect number of selections of the emotion names by members of relevant group of contributors.
* Based on free listings of emotion names by 200 subjects (Fehr and Russell, 1984).
** Based on lists of 'basic emotions' produced by fourteen representative basic emotions theorists (Ortony and Turner, 1990).

This approach to the structure of categories is known as the *prototype approach* (Rosch, 1978; Russell, 1991), because the category is considered to be defined by its most central and characteristic example, or prototype. Membership of the category then depends upon degree of similarity to this prototype: the more features a particular item shares with the prototype, the more likely it is to be included in the category, but all-or-none judgements are often difficult. Indeed, according to this account, it might be possible for two instances of emotion to have no common features whatsoever as long as both were related to the prototype itself. In other words, the prototype view assumes that emotions are linked only by *family resemblances* with one another (Wittgenstein, 1953).

The alternative 'classical' view of categories is that it is possible to draw up a list of defining features which allow an exact determination of what belongs inside a category and what belongs outside. For example, some concepts have very tight and precise definitions which allow us to make incontestable decisions about what counts as a member of the category and what does not. For example, a square *is* a quadrilateral with sides of equal length and vertices of 90 degrees. The most obvious problem with a classical approach to the category of emotion is that it is hard to think of characteristics that all emotions have in common, but which other non-emotional states do not also share. Even apparently central characteristics such as evaluation, intentionality, and impermanence do not permit an all-or-none demarcation (see Clore and Ortony, 1991, for an alternative point of view). However, as I shall suggest later in the book, emotions may be more reliably specifiable according to their *functions* rather than their structural content.

When psychologists have drawn up their own lists of emotions, they too have often disagreed with one another. Some theorists have suggested that there are a set of basic or primary emotions, based on the genetic inheritance of the species or the commonalities in human development (see Table 1.1). For example, Ekman and his colleagues (e.g. Ekman and Friesen, 1971) have suggested that there are six basic biologically programmed emotions: *happiness, sadness, fear, anger, surprise,* and *disgust,* each with its own distinctive facial expression. Other theorists, however, would argue with the claim that surprise and disgust are states that are necessarily even *emotional* in the first place (Ortony and Turner, 1990). For example, if emotion implies an evaluative relationship with an object, then *surprise* does not count as a proper emotion because the experience of surprise may be either pleasant, unpleasant, or evaluatively neutral (surprise that every single car stopped at the traffic lights is a Volkswagen).

According to the basic emotions view, other non-primary emotions are thought to be blends of the basic ones (e.g. Plutchik, 1980). Unfortunately, the fact that psychologists have disagreed about which emotions are basic, about whether basic emotions exist, or even about whether basic emotions are emotions at all tends to detract from the credibility of the view that certain states are basically, irreducibly, and inescapably emotional. Indeed, some psychologists have denied that there is any good reason to suppose that there are *basic* emotions at all (Ortony and Turner, 1990; Turner and Ortony, 1992; see Chapter 10).

Clore, Ortony, and Foss (1987) proposed a simple and useful test for deciding whether a word refers to an emotion or not. They reasoned that certain terms are used to describe emotions only in certain particular circumstances and therefore do not constitute proper emotion names. For example, you may describe an emotional state in terms of 'feeling excluded' but few people would argue that 'exclusion' is always the name for an emotion. You could say 'I am being excluded' and this would not necessarily refer to an emotion at all. A proper emotion word, according to Clore, Ortony, and Foss, is one for which you can say that *feeling* it and *being* it are both equally considered to be emotional conditions. So 'feeling excluded' is usually an emotional condition but 'being excluded' may well not be. On the other hand, 'feeling angry' and 'being angry' both clearly refer to emotional experiences. In other words, emotion terms already include some notion of feeling in them, whereas to make other terms refer to emotion you have to add the idea of feeling.

What I have tried to do in this section is draw a vague and provisional line around phenomena that would be of interest to analysts of emotion. I have tried to do this without taking on too many of common sense's embedded and often contradictory *theoretical* claims about the phenomenon. My analysis so far has avoided considering, for example, whether emotions are really mental states, feelings, motivational processes, communications, or whatever. In fact, a case can be made for seeing them as all of these things at once. I think that by accepting common-sense ideas about emotion at face value, there is a danger of prejudging essentially contestable issues. The historical and narrative processes of developing theory and delineating a coherent area of investigation are continually recursive processes. Therefore, what I want to do in this book is to see how well the provisional demarcation of emotion offered in this chapter holds up to conceptual analysis and empirical development and suggest revisions as becomes necessary. In the final chapter, I will offer a more precise and restrictive demarcation of an emotional research site, for future workers to develop and then move on.

To summarize, psychologists' ideas of the nature of emotion are not that different to what people mean by emotion in their everyday lives. Indeed, researchers have often tried to understand what emotion really is by asking people what they think it is (Fehr and Russell, 1984; Shaver *et al.* 1987; see Chapter 9). The shared idea of what counts as an emotion allows psychologists to proceed with their investigations of the topic, but the common-sense, often implicit, working definition that they adopt clearly has its limitations. One of the most important of these, as I shall be arguing in this book, is the assumption that emotion is essentially an individual and private experience.

THREE LEVELS OF EMOTIONAL PHENOMENA

The discussion of the idea of emotion in the previous section allows us to orient ourselves to relevant research areas and directions. However, looking at the common sense of emotion is no substitute for investigation of real emotional phenomena. Although it is now clearer what kinds of events can be seen to count as emotions, we cannot depend solely on our everyday understanding to *explain* these events. Having explored what psychologists and other people understand by emotion, I now want to consider what they actually do to investigate it. I will be arguing that in practice the common-sense idea of emotion as an essentially individual phenomenon becomes difficult to sustain when the full range of emotional evidence is considered. Because personal experience cannot in practice simply be prised apart from its interpersonal and cultural context, it becomes necessary to take a broader view of what emotion really is.

When we consider what psychologists actually do when they claim to be investigating emotion, it becomes apparent that they are missing out on a whole range of relevant phenomena. In this section, I want to present a preliminary classification of existing emotion research to show in general terms where the obvious omissions lie, and where we might look to fill in the details of an integrated and comprehensive picture. This framework serves as an orienting scheme which I hope will provide an overview of the terrain of emotion research. In presenting this orientation here, I am able to introduce some of the areas covered later in the book and highlight some of the key landmarks that we will come across along the route to my conclusion.

In order to understand how emotion research has organized itself into separate and independently investigated topics, it is again necessary to consider the view of emotion provided by common sense, which marks out separate territories for explorers of this area.

According to one of the *theoretical* claims of common sense, emotions are essentially intrapsychic. No one else ever really knows how you feel. An individual experiences something pleasant or unpleasant in relation to something that happens and apprehends its personal emotional meaning completely: end of story (or at least end of first episode). As Descartes (1649) once wrote concerning the passions: 'They are so close to, and so entirely within our soul, that it is impossible for it to feel them without their being actually such as it feels them to be' (p. 343).

How is it then, in this common-sense account, that emotions ever get out? Some feelings are thought to be so strong that they leak into the social world. For example, you may not be able to help yourself from laughing in church no matter how hard you try to suppress the reaction. Emotion is 'expressed' and other people become aware of it. Much of this nonverbal communication of emotion is apparently spontaneous and involuntary: in relaxed situations, there is little perceived need to control how emotions are displayed on the face, or in gesture and tone of voice. However, certain people in certain circumstances are still thought to be able to disguise completely their true feelings, to mislead their unwitting public into believing that their emotional state is quite different than it appears. The common thread of these related common-sense interpersonal narratives of emotion is that the individual intrapsychic emotion comes first as an instantaneous and fully formulated experience and then is either expressed or not, but in both cases never quite completely.

Finally, and on another separate conceptual level, people, including psychologists, including me at this moment, talk and write about emotions. This chatter concerning emotion is assumed to come *after* it has been experienced personally and often after it has been registered in other people. We already know about emotion from personal and interpersonal experience before we try to articulate this knowledge. Further, whatever is said in the various communal discourses is considered somehow to miss part of the point of emotion: words never quite get to the heart of the phenomenon, which is somehow ineffable and inexpressible. You cannot completely put your feelings into words.

Thus, according to common sense, there are three apparently separate levels of phenomena relating to emotion, the individual (experience of emotion), the interpersonal (communication of emotion), and the representational (ideas about emotion), but its essence is still popularly considered to lie at the first level inside a private psyche. Each of the upper levels in some sense is considered as dependent upon this basic level and to give only a degraded and inaccurate picture of what goes on there. To get to the bottom of emotion, it is considered necessary to look at personal experience.

Although no academic analysis of emotion would import wholesale such a theory of emotional functioning, the intuitive conceptions still get smuggled into psychological discourse somehow. Delineation of research areas, for example, depends on common-sense distinctions between emotional experience, communication, and conceptual knowledge. Investigation focuses on problems relating to each of these topics separately rather than looking for interconnections between levels. The question of what causes individual emotion is treated as independent of the question of how an already existent emotion gets communicated, and of how our knowledge about the experience and communication of emotion is organized. This, of course, makes it difficult to develop a theoretical understanding of emotion across levels. Furthermore, psychology like common sense tends to assume that emotion is primarily an individual phenomenon. Whatever is found out about emotion in the interpersonal and cultural spheres does not alter the view of emotion as essentially personal. The relevant phenomena are thought to be secondary and dependent on the prior experience of an intact individual feeling.

Now if emotion really operated as the common-sense analysis suggests, then the three-level approach would be an appropriate one. Unfortunately, however, the separation of levels is by no means as hard and fast as it might seem. There are not three stages in the propagation of emotion into the cultural world moving from internal experience, through public display to cultural understanding. Instead, the stages feed back and forward into one another and the levels overlap and interpenetrate over time. For example, the way that we experience emotion personally is partly constituted by our idea of what emotion is or should be which derives from everyday discourse (see Box 1.1). Thus, self-attribution of emotion implies buying into a cultural representational system of some kind. Further, emotions do not burst ready-made into personal consciousness, but are manufactured out of ongoing, usually interpersonal processes, or negotiated during the course of an encounter. People do not always immediately and directly know how they feel.

BOX 1.1: WITTGENSTEIN'S (1953) PRIVATE LANGUAGE ARGUMENT

Conventional ways of speaking about emotions as internal entities lead us to believe that we know how we feel directly on the basis of introspection. In this view, private experience is the primary reality of emotion, and cultural conceptions are attached after the fact. A basic logical problem facing such a view is that there is no way of establishing a reliable connection between a supposed private experience and a linguistic name. This means that we cannot know, for example, what anger or pain are purely on the basis of internal observation. Further, the supposed existence of private experiences could make no difference to the way we talked and theorized about emotions, because we could never translate this purely internal knowledge into communicable terms. Wittgenstein first demonstrated these points in his *private language* argument by using a concrete metaphor based on the common-sense idea of minds as containers for mental entities such as emotions (cf. Lakoff and Kövecses, 1987). To work through his analogy, you should imagine a more mundane situation than that of a metaphysical emotional state contained within an abstract mental system. Think instead of a beetle inside a matchbox, with the beetle standing for the emotion, and the matchbox for the mind. Mapping the rules set up by our idea of private experience onto this analogic situation, assume that a guessing game is being played where everyone is holding their own personal matchbox and can look inside that particular one but not into anybody else's. The aim of the game is to find out what everyone has in their matchbox without anyone actually showing the relevant object to anyone else. The first thing you might do if actually taking part in this game, of course, is to say that you have a beetle in your box, but this is clearly ruled out because we must also assume that you do not possess any word that *already* has a conventional relation to the object. Nor can you characterize the item in terms of other *externally* observable features because the beetle is supposed to be an essentially private object and defining characteristics are always things that can be observed by others and agreed upon. After all, if the entity in the box was really a completely private emotion, there would be no recognizable independent criteria available for identification. How can you possibly solve the problem? Wittgenstein argues that whatever is in the box cannot in principle have any effect on actual language use. Because the object is not measurable against any external and independent yardstick there are no reference points for others to use in making sense of it ('Imagine someone saying: "but I know how tall I am!" and laying his hand on top of his head to prove it', p. 96). It would even be impossible to give the internal object a *private* name, because you would have no way of knowing when the same thing came along again without some testable criteria for recognition. The only way round this problem is to say that the private object has definite and reliable connections with something that can be matched up against publicly available standards. For example, you may know that you are experiencing the same emotion because it is connected with a situation when someone insults you, and insults are things whose occurrence can be argued about with others on the basis of what actually went on during a *shared* situation. This may be a plausible solution (e.g. Skinner, 1953), but it should be noted that the private aspect of the phenomenon then drops out of the analysis ('A wheel that can be turned though nothing else moves with it, is not part of the mechanism' p. 95). If the emotion is characterized according to its relation to an external situation, then the internal feeling plays no role in identification ('The box might even be empty – no, one can 'divide through' by the thing in the box, it cancels out, whatever it is', p. 100). Thus, defining emotions *purely* in terms of private experience is a non-starter.

When we examine individual, interpersonal, and representational manifestations of emotion as they occur in the experimental laboratory and life outside, it becomes obvious that a rigid conceptual separation between these levels cannot stand up in practice.

WHAT TRADITIONAL EMOTION RESEARCH LEAVES OUT

In the common-sense individualistic view, emotion may be expressed to other people, but is not necessarily communicated in any way. Such a position is not only difficult to sustain conceptually (see Box 1.1) but also makes things difficult for psychologists who want to investigate emotions, because it means that they must either rely on their own experiences for data, or else depend on the outward manifestations of emotion and on the ways that other people describe them. If we are dealing with something that is in essence a private phenomenon then these are necessary compromises.

Psychological research into emotion, having no independent idea of what emotion might be, typically follows the common-sense assumption that emotions are first and foremost reactions of individual subjects. The paradigm case of emotion is taken to be a single person who is affected by something that happens to him or her: we see a bear, are frightened, and run (cf. James, 1884). Correspondingly, in the laboratory, stimuli are presented to passive participants who then rate their reactions, or have their emotional responses measured in some other way (using facial movements, physiological reactions, and so on). It is imagined that this approach somehow isolates the distilled essence of emotional response, away from the self-presentational distortions that are characteristic of everyday social life, and the complications brought on by confounding variables of all kinds.

However, if we look closer at the standard experimental situation in which intrapsychic emotion is studied, it becomes clear that more than individual emotion is involved even here. Most crucially, when the respondent provides some judgement or description of his or her emotional state (or even if it is expressed nonverbally), this is never just a simple readout of an internal state, but a communication of emotion to some real or imagined audience. Furthermore, this communication necessarily depends upon a set of social conventions about how emotions are described or expressed. In other words, even when investigators try to look at individual emotion, the phenomenon is already permeated with interpersonal and cultural processes.

The conventional solution to this problem is to try to minimize the supposedly distorting effects of communicative intent and cultural prejudice by purifying measures and making the experimental setting as simple and controlled as possible. I want to argue instead that the idea of an emotion as something that could exist as a private phenomenon is wrongheaded, and that it is better to analyse emotion in terms of the three levels together. This is what I try to do in this book.

A first step in this attempt to devise an integrated approach to emotional experience, communication, and representation is to consider what factors are specifically excluded by the research practices that are currently deployed at each of these levels of investigation. I shall therefore now consider each level in turn.

Limitations of traditional research into individual emotion

Traditional research into individual emotion prioritizes a particular interpretation of emotional experience: that it consists of a momentary personal reaction to specific external stimuli and that it is imposed on the person by the situation. Just about every aspect of this view of the essential nature of emotion is questionable. Three key assumptions of the individual approach to emotion deserve particular scrutiny:

1 *Instantaneous emotions* Emotions are typically measured at a single point during an experimental procedure, as if they were momentary one-shot reactions to events (Ekman, 1984, for example, has argued that emotions last for between half a second and four seconds). It seems more realistic to consider emotions as unfolding over time rather than switching on and off in this binary fashion. Emotions are not self-contained stories beginning with the onset of a particular stimulus and ending with a felt experiential reaction, and ought not to be treated as such. Rather, we should try to understand how objects and events attain emotional significance by their contextualization in people's ongoing projects (which, as it happens, are often interpersonal projects).

2 *Passive emotions* A second and related point concerns the supposed passivity of emotional experience. In psychological studies, experimental 'subjects' are treated as victims of their emotions. However, in everyday life we often make more or less successful attempts to control what we are feeling, when we want to get ourselves out of a bad mood, for example (Catanzaro and Mearns, 1990; Mayer and Gaschke, 1988). Importantly, many of our attempts to change our feelings are conducted quite deliberately and consciously, and are based on commonly held ideas about how emotion works. Thus, representations of emotion can feed into individual experience rather than being simply separable and derivative phenomena.

3. *Impermeable emotions* Finally, and most importantly, the individual experimental approach looks at emotion outside its everyday social context. In reality, many emotions are explicitly directed at other people and arise out of interactions with them. Anger, for example, does not usually make sense without someone else with whom to be angry. Despite the practical problems of interpersonal research (see Chapter 7), I believe that the psychology of emotion urgently needs to look at the way that emotions arise during ongoing interactions with other people.

Limitations of traditional research into interpersonal emotion

Investigators of interpersonal emotion also make attempts to purify the phenomenon in question by separating out communication from individual experience. It is assumed that an emotional experience needs to be created in one individual, so that it can then be transmitted to another person. For the sake of control, these two roles are usually kept separate. For example, a common form of experiment in this area involves a judgement task in which videotaped emotional reactions of one individual (the 'sender') are subsequently observed by a second person (the 'receiver'), who makes assessments about the sender's emotional state (e.g. Buck, 1979a; Wagner *et al.* 1986). Clearly this paradigmatic experiment into emotion reception systematically excludes certain kinds of real emotional phenomena from the analysis:

1 *Removal of interaction* Because senders and receivers in these studies never actually interact with each other, emotion communication occurs as a one-way process of information transmission (where the relevant information is considered as some kind of readout of a pre-existing emotional experience; Buck, 1984, and see Chapter 7). In everyday life, emotions may not usually arise as full-blown reactions within an individual consciousness, to be subsequently delivered out into the social world. Rather, emotions often emerge over the course of an unfolding interpersonal episode.

A possibility specifically precluded by the traditional approach to emotional communication is that emotion typically arises as a function of real-time *negotiation* between people about the meaning of the current social situation, rather than any intrapsychic evaluative process. This negotiation may go on partially at a nonverbal level, with interactants responding directly to posture and gesture, rather than depending on interpretative mechanisms. Thus, emotion can arise quite spontaneously out of social interaction without the need for complex transformations of cognitive inputs. More research is needed into the generation and perception of emotion in ongoing social interactions.

2 *Removal of relationships* A second point concerns the relationship between the experimental participants: in emotion judgement studies, the sender is almost always a stranger to the receiver, whereas in everyday life people who communicate emotionally usually already have some relationship with each other. Obviously what we know about another person's characteristic interpretations and expressions of emotion and about their current projects will help us to understand what they are feeling. It therefore seems worth investigating the different ways that emotions are formulated and expressed within the context of different kinds of pre-existing relationships. More radically, rather than assuming that interpersonal emotion depends upon the separate and independent subjective experiences of participants in an interaction, emotion might be seen as emerging from dialogue over the course of real-time encounters between involved participants (see Chapter 7 for further development of these points).

Limitations of traditional research into emotion representation

Research into emotion representation is also typically sectioned off as a separate area. Rather than looking at how emotion representations are deployed in everyday situations, psychologists have instead tried to study an abstract and decontextualized grammar of emotional language. Explorers in this area triangulate the semantic distances between emotion terms in an attempt to map out the logical geography of affective space (e.g. Osgood *et al.* 1957; Russell, 1980).

Unfortunately, there is no deep structure to emotion, only words and sentences as they are actually used in and out of emotional contexts. In my view, a representation is usually something that is made by someone to somebody else, and not something that exists as a hard-wired yet still abstract mental category.

Of course, what psychologists study when they study emotion representations is closely related to what I have called the common sense of emotion above. Earlier, I considered representations as a *resource* for psychological investigation, whereas now I am taking another angle and considering them as a *topic* for research. As with emotion communications, I want to suggest that it is not always so easy to separate out representational aspects of emotion from the experience itself. One reason for this is that emotional experience may be partly constituted out of our emotional representations.

An illustration of how representational factors might feed into emotional experience is suggested by a modified self-attribution analysis (cf. Bem, 1972) which reverses the traditional priorities relating to emotion experiences and emotion conceptions. In this example, the representation of emotion rather than the individual experience is primary, with ideas about what emotion involves causing the person to register certain information as symptomatic of an emotional state, and then to act out and express this assumed state according to the prescriptions contained in the representation. To see how this might work, consider the following scenario. Under certain special circumstances, probably best contrived in a psychological laboratory, people may *decide* that they feel emotional (and act accordingly) on the basis of supposedly objective information about their own reactions, information that corresponds exactly to that which they would use in their judgements of other people's emotions. These judgements in turn may be derived from their common-sense theories of the constitution of an emotional response. It may be, then, that processes of emotion attribution, to oneself and others, are based partly on common-sense representations of what it means to be emotional.

Research by Valins (1966) has provided limited evidence for such a view, showing that people are willing to adjust their inferences about their own emotional state on the basis of bogus information about the speed of their own heartbeat (see Parkinson, 1985, for a review). If they can be led to believe that their bodies have reacted to a plausibly emotional event, then they may conclude that they feel emotional about it, and conduct themselves in accordance with this conclusion. Correspondingly, research on representations of emotion shows that heart-rate and other kinds of internal bodily reactions are also relatively central features of people's everyday descriptions of emotional experiences (e.g. Parkinson, 1990; Rimé *et al.* 1990).

In this section, I have tried to show some of the ways in which real emotional phenomena might not neatly fit into the categories of emotion research that have evolved out of the implicit common-sense model of emotion as private. In contrast to the traditional common-sense view, I want to argue that emotion does not belong in any one of the levels of phenomena that I have outlined, but crosses them all. By focusing on conceptually separate levels of emotion, investigators have failed to catch sight of the complete picture. By constructing theories based on artificially delimited phenomena, they have failed to tell the whole story. I would argue that an individual emotion is not something basic and essential that could sensibly exist apart from its interpersonal manifestations or the cultural categories that allow it to be interpreted. (Even if it were, we could find no access to it.) We should instead see emotions as always already communications (sometimes addressed to internal or imaginary audiences; Fridlund, 1992) formulated in languages that derive from shared representational resources. There may be a private aspect to emotion, but it should not be considered independently of its other manifestations.

What is neglected about emotion by investigating the phenomenon as if it were a private experience and then attempting to ensure that no extrinsic factors contaminate its supposedly pure form, is the essentially social dimension of the concept. In the laboratory, an isolated individual rarely experiences anything more than an artificial and decontextualized version of emotion. When we think of the emotional situations that genuinely involve us in real life, they usually concern someone else, often someone with whom we are engaged in some kind of relationship. Indeed, love, hate, and anger, which are considered by people to be the best examples of emotions (Fehr and Russell, 1984) are all intrinsically relational states: they are inconceivable without the real or imagined presence of another person. To go further, I would suggest that when we think of emotional situations in general, the most common ones that come to mind take place in interpersonal settings. By systematically excluding real-time interpersonal processes from the psychology of emotion, previous investigators have missed out on many of the factors that add the sense of involvement and reality to emotional reactions. Real emotions normally emerge and develop over the course of an ongoing dialogue, not as momentary and intact internal responses to external stimuli, and they should be investigated accordingly.

In this section, I have given an overview of previous psychological approaches to emotion and their limits. Recurrently in this discussion, I have relied on the simplifying assumption that emotion is the name for a descriptive category of experience which is used in common sense as well as psychology. In later sections of the book, I want to broaden this analysis by suggesting that people are doing things in addition to just characterizing their own and other people's 'states of mind' when they employ emotional discourse in their everyday lives (e.g. Austin, 1962; Bedford, 1957). Specifically, they are presenting themselves in a particular way to a specific audience, and their self-presentation partially constitutes their emotion rather than neutrally describing it. If this is true, then arguing about the relative accuracy of common-sense ideas of emotion partly misses the point because emotional concepts are not intended as neutral representations anyway. A full theory of emotion should be directed at the real-life contexts for the use of emotion discourse and the effects that such discourse may have on the conduct and formulation of ongoing relationships between people. Psychological research into emotion has been mainly directed at a narrower range of phenomena circumscribed by a neutralized and rigorized descriptive category derived from common sense. In this book, I will consider the results of such an approach and their limitations before trying to extend the analysis beyond individual and representational aspects of emotion.

STRUCTURE OF THIS BOOK

In the remaining chapters of the book, I will develop a critique of the individualistic approach to emotion, in Part I by focusing on research conducted within the single-subject tradition and drawing attention to its constraints, and in Part II by discussing the broader interpersonal, institutional, and cultural factors that impact on emotion. The basic plot of the book, then, is as follows. In Part I, I consider what psychologists currently say and have recently said concerning emotion as a *personal* phenomenon. My review of this literature focuses on four factors of individual emotion experience: cognitive appraisal, bodily changes, action tendencies, and expressive displays. In my discussion of each of these components, I show how existing approaches tend to minimize the importance of social variables in the causes, content, and consequences of emotion. After providing this review and critique of research on individual emotion in Part I, I broaden the analysis in Part II to the interpersonal world of social interaction, and finally to the realms of institutional and cultural roles and representations, showing how incorporation of social and societal considerations extends and deepens understanding of the ways in which individual emotion is constituted and manifested in everyday life.

The route I shall be taking through the social psychological literature in the direction of my conclusion about emotion as a set of interpersonal phenomena is a somewhat indirect one. I want to start by discussing theory and research that follows an individualistic tradition before moving on to my revisions of the standard view. This is partly because the assumptions made in this body of work are worth examining closely in order to determine their weaknesses, and also partly because the concepts and ideas about emotion developed over recent social psychological history will help to lay the foundations for a more interpersonal theory. For example, the concept of appraisal (see Chapter 2) which has been central to individualistic emotion research since the 1960s has been developed by Lazarus (e.g. 1991a) into a transactional entity which comes close to explaining how different emotions might arise in ongoing interactions.

Having said all this, the first chapters on individual emotion depend on a somewhat simplified version of how the concept functions which will need to be revised before the theory can be extended. I will occasionally make claims in these first few chapters that will need to be modified as the argument progresses. The advantage of this approach is that Part I of this book can serve as an introduction to the existing social psychological literature on emotion, largely unencumbered by theoretical speculations from my side. Of course, I will be presenting a view of my own, but it is not one that I believe is particularly prejudiced or extreme in the main body of this text. The disadvantage of my approach is that I may mislead the reader into believing that a certain delimited view of how emotion operates is workable, when in fact I do not think that this is the case.

Chapters 1–6, then, cover individual emotion. Each of the subsequent chapters is devoted to the role of one of four basic components in the evolving individual experience of emotion. I will review the evidence relating each component to emotion as potential cause and effect. The first and most basic emotion component (discussed in Chapter 2) relates to cognitive appraisal of the situation. Individuals apparently react emotionally to stimulus events to the extent that they are perceived as relevant to their current central goals and interests (Lazarus, 1982). In Chapter 2, I conclude that appraisal may be seen as a logically defining central aspect of emotion rather than as an independent cognitive event in the causal sequence leading to emotion. The next three chapters reconsider the role of the other components in the constitution of emotional experience.

The second component of emotion relates to overt behaviour (Chapter 3), often considered in terms of approach or avoidance tendencies, which may be intensified as a result of the presence of emotion. For example, the typical reaction to a frightening event is considered to be fight or flight. Some investigators even define emotions in terms of action tendencies with felt control precedence (Frijda, 1986). In this chapter I consider how emotions might reset action priorities in social situations as well as how they might be a function of failures or successes in ongoing action plans (e.g. Mandler, 1984).

The third component is the body's internal reaction (Chapter 4), which is usually thought of as a generalized sympathetic arousal response in emotionally provocative situations (Cannon, 1927). Such a factor underlies familiar sensations of pounding heart and dry mouth when one is intensely afraid or angry. The psychophysiological approach to emotion uses measures such as heart-rate, muscle tension, and skin conductance as indices of emotional response, all of which relate to the body's mobilization of energy in preparation for response. In Chapter 4, I review this research on bodily changes as symptoms of emotion, before considering the reverse causal sequence suggested by James (1898) and later by Schachter and Singer (1962) who argued that in some circumstances perception of unexplained physiological arousal can lead to emotional experience via a self-attributional process. I conclude that bodily changes enter into the emotion process in a number of different ways but that the implicit connection between emotional meaning and gut reactions is often metaphorical and symbolic rather than material (cf. Averill, 1974).

Finally, researchers have examined the facial expressive response to emotional events (Chapter 5) in accordance with the widely recognized association between happiness and smiling, anger and scowling, and so on. A great deal of debate has centred on the extent to which emotions and facial displays are directly connected at a neural and innate level (e.g. Ekman, 1994). The case for this basic link between intrapsychic emotion and facial display is conceptually confused and generally overstated (see Russell, 1994). I argue that facial movements serve communicative rather than simply expressive functions in everyday interpersonal interactions (e.g. Fridlund, 1992). I also consider the evidence for the role of facial movements as causes of emotion (e.g. Laird, 1974) and evaluate some of the possible mechanisms for such a linkage.

All four of these emotion components have been viewed by different theorists as both cause and effect of emotion, and in each chapter I focus on both these possible roles before concluding that a less determinate temporal sequence characterizes the structure of individual emotional experience. The picture of individual emotion that should emerge from these chapters is of a multilevel syndrome that unfolds over time in a variety of ways.

In Chapter 6, I describe some of the theoretical attempts to integrate analyses of individual emotion by incorporating all four of the factors of emotional experience into a unified model. A basic problem with all the theories I shall discuss is that they assume a relatively deterministic sequence of cause and effect, or input and output specifies the way that an emotional episode unfolds. Furthermore, I argue that their emphasis on internal generative mechanisms artificially isolates emotional experience from the ongoing social context within which it is often intrinsically embedded.

Having tried in Part I to understand emotion from the inside, by dismantling it into component mechanisms, I move on in Part II to an attempt to make sense of emotion by contextualizing it in broader social and cultural processes, and explaining the phenomenon from the outside. Chapter 7 extends the analysis of emotion by moving into the interpersonal sphere. In this chapter, I try to make a start at developing a theory of how ideas and realities of emotion are produced in actual ongoing social life. At this point, some of the simplifying assumptions made in the earlier discussion of individual emotion will need to be modified and extended. My conclusion will be that emotions typically arise as a function of interpersonal interactions rather than encounters between a single individual and an independent reality, and that the ongoing negotiation of emotional experience is fundamental to the phenomenon.

Interpersonal interactions never take place entirely in a cultural vacuum and we bring to our encounters shared suppositions about appropriate conduct as well as institutional baggage relating to our relative social positions. In Chapter 8, I discuss how cultural and institutional factors impact on the experience and expression of emotion in real-time social encounters. My argument is that emotions are used to make claims about one's identity within an ongoing relationship in a particular institutional context. For example, on a trivial level, we get angry because we think that someone is not treating us with the respect we deserve. The social function of getting emotional is thus to reconfigure the relative identity positions of participants in an interchange. In some contexts, emotional techniques of identity assertion or abasement are used quite self-consciously to produce role-prescribed effects. On these occasions our experience can be of denying a 'genuine' and authentic emotional reaction and superimposing upon it one that is artificial and simulated. A better account of such experiences, I suggest, refers to the varying levels of identification that are attached to the roles on which emotions depend, and to the different alternative audiences available for our self-presentations.

Not only are emotional realities shaped interpersonally but also the way we talk about emotions and express them in conversations depends crucially on interpersonal communicative factors. In Chapter 9, I will develop the arguments begun in the present chapter about emotion as a common-sense category of experience by suggesting that words never only describe reality, they also construct or reproduce it. Furthermore, when we speak emotionally, we are often doing something other than characterizing our state of mind; we are appealing for help, complaining, thanking or chastising, and so on. The performative (cf. Austin, 1962) content of emotional talk forces us to adapt the model of emotion as a descriptive category of experience. Chapter 9 will describe research into how emotion is represented in language and point to limitations of these studies as well as future directions for investigation.

In the final chapter, I will attempt to bring together the themes of the book and map out the ways in which an integrative three-level approach to emotion might proceed. I shall propose that, at the present stage of psychology's development, an interpersonal rather than individual conceptualization of emotion brings clear theoretical and practical benefits.

SUMMARY AND CONCLUSIONS

In the book, I will not be offering a definitive theory of how emotion works but instead trying to sketch out an approach that does full justice to the real-life phenomena associated with the common-sense concept. What I hope that I have done in this chapter is to call attention to some of the problems of accepting received wisdom about emotion too uncritically. Although we can never entirely escape from our implicit conceptual frameworks, it is as well to be aware of their existence and to watch out for their possible impact on theory development and on the constitution of objects of study in empirical practice. Emotion as an idea is socially and culturally manufactured, as also is emotion as a reality. However, this does not mean that the processes that lead to the formulation of an emotional idea are always identical to those that generate the realities of emotion. Instead, there are clear distinctions between the ideological content of the common-sense concept of emotion, on the one hand, and the interpersonal and institutional construction of emotion as it is lived out in the real world, on the other. The idea is that emotion is private and internal; the reality is that it is intrinsically interpersonal and communicative or performative. However, ideas about emotion can also contribute to the way that emotion is played out and regulated in everyday life. To the extent that we take our ideas about emotion seriously, they are bound to influence the way that we react to our own and other people's actual emotions. Indeed, we may decide that we are emotional on the basis of information that our ideas imply is diagnostic of emotion, and act accordingly. This is exactly what can happen in laboratory investigations of emotion. Experimenters manipulate variables with some obvious implicit connection to emotion in order to assess their causal impact. Experimental participants, sharing the investigators' idea of what emotion is, react to the information offered by manipulation of the emotionally relevant variables and draw appropriate emotional conclusions. In the next four chapters, I will focus on four sets of variables that psychologists and other people believe are directly relevant to emotion and review the empirical evidence about their connections to ideas and realities of emotion. In each case, I will be arguing that existing research has adopted too unreflective a notion of what emotion is and of how different levels of evidence concerning experience, communication, and representation are distinguished and interrelated.

2   The appraisal factor

OVERVIEW

According to the common-sense definition formulated in Chapter 1, emotions are characterized by evaluations of intentional objects. The evaluative factor is central to what most people mean by emotion. Unless we are experiencing the situation as positive or negative, in a good or a bad light, it seems to make little sense to claim that we are emotional. Current psychological theory translates the evaluative relation implicit in emotional meaning into a real-time cognitive process of *appraisal* which is thought to determine the nature and intensity of the resulting experience. For example, Lazarus's (1968, 1991a) model implies that cognitive appraisal is the sole factor explaining how emotion is initiated, sustained, and differentiated. In this chapter, I argue against putting so much explanatory weight on a single causal factor, and suggest that a more interactive view of the production of emotion is more helpful.

The chapter is organized into the following sections. First, I introduce the idea of appraisal as developed by its most influential proponents. Second, I consider the different possible interpretations of the nature of the association between appraisal and emotion. Third, I review the evidence for appraisal theory and conclude that it only supports the limited proposition that representations of emotions are linked to representations of appraisal rather than the existence of any empirical or causal connection. Fourth, I examine the conceptual justifications offered for appraisal theory and find them similarly wanting. Finally, I focus on the concept of appraisal itself and what implications it has in terms of information-processing mechanisms. It turns out that theorists have defined appraisal largely in terms of cognitive content rather than process. I will suggest that the real role of appraisal is not as a distinct stage in the causal sequence leading to an emotional experience, but as a logically necessary condition for attribution of emotion. As such, appraisal theory is true by fiat rather than because of a contingent and empirically established generative relationship.

WHAT IS APPRAISAL?

Emotion would not be emotion without some evaluation at its centre. If we think about our experience of any particular emotional state, it seems to consist mainly of good or bad feelings about something that has happened, is happening, may happen, or is about to happen to us. During emotion, our perspective on the personal world changes and things look different: bleaker or more appealing than usual. The psychological concept of appraisal provides a means of organizing these basic common-sense observations about emotion into a causal account of the phenomenon. According to most versions of appraisal theory, the evaluations that contribute towards emotional feelings actually represent a definite stage in an information-processing sequence that leads to these experienced reactions.

Arnold (1960) was responsible for introducing the appraisal idea to the psychology of emotion, taking as her starting point the phenomenological insight that the perception at the heart of emotion involved more than a simple registering of the cold facts of the situation. If emotion typically occurs in reaction to an object or event, she reasoned, what is it that makes the reaction an emotional one? Apparently, something extra needs to be added to simple objective perception to make it into emotional perception: according to Arnold, this something is appraisal. In her view, appraisal was the process whereby the personal relevance of an emotional event is apprehended: 'To arouse an emotion, the object must be appraised as affecting me in some way, affecting me personally as an individual with my particular experience and my particular aims' (p. 171).

In other words, whenever you feel emotional, this implies that whatever you are emotional about is appraised as being in some significant relationship to you within the current context, as being good or bad, beneficial or detrimental, morally outrageous or admirable, as the case may be, otherwise you would not *care* about the situation and consequently no emotion would be felt. Arnold believed that the process of appraisal involved an instinctive, intuitive, and immediate evaluation of the emotional object. In most subsequent theories (e.g. Lazarus, 1968, 1991a), the appraisal process has come to be seen in more protracted, articulated, and above all, more cognitive terms.

According to Lazarus (1968), appraisal is a relatively complex evaluation of the current or impending transaction between the person and the environment. This evaluation has two basic facets. *Primary appraisal* refers to the issue of whether the situation has relevance for personal well-being. During primary appraisal, individuals can be considered to ask themselves 'Does this situation affect me personally?' or, more specifically, 'Am I in trouble or being benefited, now or in the future, and in what way?' (Lazarus and Folkman, 1984, p. 31). *Secondary appraisal*, on the other hand, focuses on the possible ways of *coping* with the situation, and evaluates the extent of available personal and environmental resources for dealing with the encounter. The secondary appraisal process can be translated into the implicit question 'What, if anything, can be done about the situation?' (p. 31).

For example, if someone loses their job, depending on the personal importance of the various perceived benefits of employment, they are likely to evaluate this event in mainly negative terms. Primary appraisal will lead to the person concluding that the event has unwanted implications and experiencing unpleasant emotions as a consequence. However, it may be that there are ways of correcting this problem. It is possible, for instance, that the job loss occurs during an economic era when employment is easy to come by (*environmental* coping resources). Alternatively, the newly unemployed person may possess valued skills which make finding new work straightforward (*personal* coping resources). Secondary appraisal is the process whereby the individual weighs up from a personal perspective these ameliorating considerations, or the lack of them.

In addition to evaluating how well they are able to deal practically with the situation (*problem-focused coping*), Lazarus (e.g. Folkman and Lazarus, 1980) suggested that individuals also consider the extent to which they are equipped to deal with the way that the situation will make them feel. In the process of *emotion-focused coping*, individuals are thought to act on the experience itself and try to make themselves feel better about what has happened. The process of secondary appraisal evaluates the person's *potential* for emotion-focused coping as well as problem-focused coping (e.g. Smith and Lazarus, 1993).

It is less easy to apply Lazarus's concept of secondary appraisal to situations where positive rather than negative emotions occur because in these cases there is usually no problem or difficulty to deal or cope with. This weakness partly arises because Lazarus's theory was originally devised to explain phenomena relating specifically to stress (e.g. Lazarus, 1966) and was only subsequently extended to cover all emotions. In general, like many other theories of emotion, Lazarus's account seems more convincing when applied to unpleasant reactions.

A further conceptual unclarity is that the distinction between primary and secondary appraisal is not a hard and fast one. In fact, Lazarus argued that these two mechanisms are actually aspects of a single integrated process (e.g. Lazarus and Folkman, 1984). This is because even initial evaluations of how good or bad a situation is depend on the existing context of personal or environmental re-sources. For instance, losing a job when the economic climate is favourable is not usually as traumatic or stressful an event as losing a job when the employment outlook is bleak in the first place. In other words, people do not experience job loss as a distinct outcome and afterwards think about how they can cope; rather, they experience a particular job loss which already implies a series of coping options. Indeed, they may anticipate the bad news and develop preparatory strategies before the event actually occurs. To give another less complex and more traditional example, confronting a poisonous snake is rarely as frightening when it is displayed behind aquarium glass. Depending on whether the object of appraisal is seen as the snake itself or the snake behind glass, the protective barrier can be conceptualized either as a coping resource or simply as one part of an unfeared stimulus complex.

Together, the processes of primary and secondary appraisal are thought to determine both the quality and the quantity of the emotional reaction: 'Secondary interpretations of coping options and primary appraisals of what is at stake interact with each other in shaping the degree of stress and the strength and quality (or content) of the emotional reaction' (Lazarus and Folkman, 1984, p. 35).

Finally, in a process Lazarus termed *reappraisal*, the individual may revise initial evaluations based on changes in the situation and success or failure of implemented coping strategies. For example, if none of the available ways of combatting an unpleasant situation are successful, the individual may decide that the unpleasant facts should be denied rather than confronted. It is therefore possible that after engaging in emotion-focused coping, the person reappraises the situation as not being as bad as was originally thought.

Despite the details he offered concerning the *content* of the evaluative judgements involved in the appraisal processes, Lazarus has rarely been precise about the *process* of appraisal. The theory specifies what conclusions an individual must reach in order to be emotional but not how the individual reaches those conclusions. About the closest Lazarus ever came to characterizing exactly what happens during appraisal is captured in the following quotation from Lazarus and Folkman's (1984) book:

> Cognitive appraisal can be most readily understood as the process of categorizing an encounter, and its various facets, with respect to its significance for well-being. It is not information processing per se . . . , although it partakes of such processing. Rather, it is largely *evaluative*, focused on meaning or significance.
>
> (p. 31)

According to this account, appraisal is a partly cognitive process resulting in the situation being classified according to its evaluated personal meaning. In his later writings (e.g. 1991a; 1991b), Lazarus explicitly broadened his idea of appraisal to include a range of possible cognitive and perceptual mechanisms. In the final section of this chapter I shall return to the question of what appraisal processes might involve in terms of cognitive (or emotional) activity.

APPRAISAL AND EMOTIONAL DIFFERENTIATION

The relationship between evaluation and emotion operates at the level of particular emotions as well as emotion in general. Different emotional states seem to imply characteristic judgements and appraisals. When you are experiencing guilt, for example, what you think and feel about what is happening to you is very different from what you think and feel when you are in love. Indeed, we often assume that the way in which we evaluate something can *determine* how we react to it emotionally. For instance, attention from someone to whom we are attracted produces a contrasting set of feelings to those produced by attention from someone we dislike or find disturbing. Like common sense, appraisal theory also assumes that different emotional states are at least partly determined by different patterns of appraisal.

Following early work by Roseman (1979, 1984), Smith and Ellsworth (1985), and Weiner (1985), there have been several formulations of the particular appraisal patterns that are associated with different emotions. For example, one of the most comprehensive and theoretically sophisticated of these models was devised by Smith and Lazarus (1993; see also Lazarus and Smith, 1988), who suggested that differences in profiles along just six basic appraisal dimensions can account for the differentiation of the full range of possible human emotional experience (see Table 2.1).

According to the Smith and Lazarus scheme, *all* emotions are characterized by primary appraisals of *motivational relevance*. This means that unless the individual *cares* about what is happening (or has happened, or might happen), it will have no emotional significance for them. The primary appraisal of motivational relevance, then, does not distinguish between different emotions, but rather is a precondition for the occurrence of any emotion at all.

A second primary appraisal dimension relating to *motivational congruence* differentiates between positive and negative emotional states. Motivational congruence depends on whether events further personal aims and intentions or conflict with them. If the situation is concordant or beneficial to the individual's current goals and concerns, the experienced emotion is pleasant, whereas if what is happening interferes with, or otherwise impedes, ongoing projects and plans, then the emotional experience will be an unpleasant one.

Secondary appraisals further distinguish positive and negative emotions according to evaluated coping potential (problem-focused and emotion-focused), accountability, and future expectations. For example, the emotion of sadness is thought to depend on a secondary appraisal pattern in which the individual feels unable to cope with the motivationally incongruent situation, and has low expectations about possible future improvements in this situation.

Smith and Lazarus also suggested that the distinctive pattern of primary and secondary appraisals associated with each particular emotion can be summarized in terms of a *core relational theme*. For example, sadness is represented by the core relational theme of *irrevocable loss* or helplessness about such a loss, while anger is characterized by the core relational theme of *other-blame*. A possible implication of this idea is that people may not need to piece together different sources of appraisal evidence before an emotion can be generated, but instead may simply experience the overall emotional meaning codified in the theme all in one go.

To restate an earlier point, it is worth noting that the secondary appraisal structure of positive emotions is generally less articulated than that of negative emotions. For example, no secondary appraisals whatsoever are thought to be associated with happiness, which simply reflects primary appraisals of motivational congruence and relevance. This is partly because of the difficulty of applying the concept of coping potential to situations where there is nothing negative to cope with.

Although a number of competing models of the appraisal patterns associated with different emotions are available (e.g. Frijda, 1987; Lazarus, 1991a; Roseman, 1991; Scherer, 1993; Smith and Ellsworth, 1985; Smith and Lazarus, 1993; Weiner, 1985), disagreements between them generally refer to points of detail rather than reflecting major substantive controversies. Empirical evidence for dimensional schemes of appraisal will be reviewed in later sections of this

Table 2.1 Appraisals associated with some common emotions

EMOTIONS	Happiness	Hope	Sadness	Fear	Anger	Guilt
PRIMARY APPRAISALS	Motivational relevance					
	Motivational congruence		Motivational incongruence			
SECONDARY APPRAISALS		High problem-focused coping potential	Low problem-focused coping potential	Low or uncertain coping potential		
		Positive future expectations	Negative future expectations		Other-accountability	Self-accountability
CORE RELATIONAL THEMES	**Success**	**Potential for success**	**Irrevocable loss**	**Danger**	**Other-blame**	**Self-blame**

Source: based on Smith et al. (1993)

chapter. For now, I want to draw attention to the alternative possible interpretations of the apparently obvious connections between different appraisals and different emotions.

NATURE OF THE APPRAISAL–EMOTION CONNECTION

Appraisal theory, as I have just presented it, seems an eminently reasonable codification of some basic common-sense distinctions between different emotional meanings, and between emotion and non-emotion. It is hard to believe that anyone would want to argue with the general claim of dimensional appraisal schemes that emotions as defined in common sense imply characteristic evaluations and judgements about what is going on in the personal world. The only difficulty of interpretation then lies in determining what this uncontroversial fact tells us about emotion as it actually happens in everyday life.

In this chapter, I want to argue that the main problem with appraisal theory is not that it is false, but that it is true in a different way than is commonly supposed by its proponents. Rather than containing propositions about empirical realities of emotion, appraisal theory is mainly a formalization of common-sense cultural *definitions* of emotion. One of the ways that we know that someone (including ourselves) is emotional is by reference to the evaluative and judgemental aspects of their talk and action. For example, we recognize anger partly on the basis of expressed judgements about blame for an untoward act, and we say someone is in love when their behaviour, words, and gestures lead us to believe that they put a high value on someone else. Engaging in certain patterns of appraisal is part of what it means to call someone emotional; it is not something that psychologists have discovered goes on independently when people happen to be emotional. In other words, I am suggesting that appraisal theory mistakes the logical necessity that appraisal should accompany emotion, for causal necessity.

Below, I review the empirical evidence for appraisal theory. My point will be that most of these findings are more directly relevant to emotional representations (level 3) than individual emotion generation processes (level 1): They concern ideas rather than realities of emotion. However, appraisal theorists typically discuss the model as if it made definite and falsifiable predictions about the way that emotions work in the real world. It does not (at least not directly). Where appraisal theory is correct, it is true *by fiat*, not because of contingent relationships established between independent variables.

Although I am claiming that the basic relationship between emotion and appraisal is at the representational level, the interdependence of ideas and realities of emotion means that this representational link also has consequences for the way that emotion is formulated, negotiated, and acted out in the real social world. To the extent that emotional realities are constituted by emotional ideas, the propositions contained in appraisal theory may actually have some relevance to the on-line production of emotional experience. Nevertheless, it is still important to maintain a conceptual distinction between emotion as conceived and emotion as lived out. In the present section, I want to explore the range of claims made by appraisal theory about ideational and real connections between appraisals and emotions, in order to be clear about what significance the empirical evidence actually has. To repeat, I will be suggesting that appraisal and emotion are conceptually rather than causally connected. Appraisal is part of the idea of emotion, and only secondarily part of its reality.

In order to understand where appraisal theory goes wrong and how it over-states its conclusions, it is helpful to break the model down into a hierarchically arranged series of propositions about the way that emotion works. Not all of these claims are made by every proponent of appraisal theory, but it would be difficult to be an appraisal theorist and not subscribe to any of them. What then, does appraisal theory say about emotions? Lazarus's (1991a) theory implicitly or explicitly makes the following claims (here presented in order of increasing inclusiveness and contention):

1 The meaning of 'emotion' is represented partly in terms of appraisal (*definitional* connection).
2 Emotion is associated *empirically* with appraisal (*descriptive* connection).
3 Emotion is *caused* by appraisal (*explanatory* connection).
4 Emotion is *always* caused by appraisal (*dependency* connection).

These claims also have their corollaries concerning the way that *different* emotions are related to *different* appraisal patterns:

1a Different emotional meanings are represented partly in terms of different appraisal patterns (definitional connection).
2a Different emotions are associated *empirically* with different appraisal patterns (descriptive connection).
3a Different emotions are *caused* by different appraisal patterns (explanatory connection).
4a Different emotions are *always* caused by different appraisal patterns (dependency connection).

Note that in both of these two series, each subsequent claim implies a closer relationship between appraisal and emotion, and that acceptance of later claims presupposes that earlier ones are also correct. However, it is perfectly legitimate to accept earlier claims in the series but reject later ones.

Most of the available evidence for appraisal theory (reviewed in the next section) is directly supportive only of propositions 1 and 1a which relate to emotional ideas rather than emotional realities. However, many theorists draw stronger conclusions from this evidence, implying that they confirm empirical and sometimes even causal relationships between appraisals and emotions. Part of the reason that appraisal theorists go beyond the evidence in this way is that there is a well-integrated theoretical rationale for appraisal as an emotion-generation system (see pp. 58–61). However, the main basis for overgeneralization is simply conceptual confusion about important distinctions between ideas and realities of emotion.

I shall now consider the status of the graded claims of appraisal theory one by one.

Definitional connection

The almost self-evident core of appraisal theory is that if someone is described as being emotional, this fact carries implications about general appraisal (1), and, secondarily, that if someone is described as being in a particular emotional state, this fact carries more specific implications about the way that person is interpreting and evaluating what is happening (or has happened or might happen, 1a). In other words, the definitional connection states that the common-sense *idea* of emotion is closely related to judgemental concepts. For example, saying that an individual is emotional implies that they are taking some evaluative position relative to some intentional object (see Chapter 1), saying that an individual is angry implies that they are taking offence at something that someone else has done or failed to do, and saying that you are in love with someone means that they have a special personal value for you. Indeed, if we think about sentences such as 'I am angry with you, but I don't blame you for anything you have done' or 'I am in love with you but my relationship with you doesn't matter to me at all', they seem to be almost self-contradictory and would certainly require further explanation before any sense could be made of them.

None of this is seriously contestable. The real issue is how central the evaluative aspect is to the emotion itself. According to several theories of emotion (e.g. Armon-Jones, 1986; Solomon, 1976), emotion and emotions may be *defined* mainly in terms of moral and value judgements about states of affairs. In this case, finding out that when a person says someone is angry they also judge that this angry individual finds someone else's action (or inaction) insulting only demonstrates that the person in question is a competent language user who understands the common-sense meaning of the word 'anger'. In this case, it makes little sense to say that emotion on the one hand is *empirically* associated with appraisal on the other, because the two concepts are logically interrelated by definition. You simply would not call an experience emotional unless it contained a characteristic evaluative judgement.

Descriptive connection

Instead of taking emotion words as *conventionally* and logically related to appraisal concepts, many theorists assume that these terms reflect a separate emotional reality whose actual internal structure they accurately capture. The fact that people employ emotional distinctions in their everyday conversation is taken as confirmation that they have *valid knowledge* about the real differences between emotions, and it just happens that one of these differences relates to appraisal. For example, according to this view, people believe that when angry, a person blames someone else for some insult, and people are correct to hold such a belief.

Put this way, the descriptive connection seems almost self-evidently true. Of course people know what it is like to be emotional in a variety of ways and what usually happens on these occasions. Unfortunately, however, people's supposed 'beliefs' about appraisal–emotion relations, although correct in one way at least, are not actually empirical conclusions at all. People do not in fact observe natural examples of pre-labelled emotions and then notice that these emotions tend to be linked to particular evaluations (Wittgenstein, 1953). Rather, the evaluative aspects are precisely what differentiate the various emotions in the first place. The main problem with the descriptive view, in other words, is that there are few obvious and workable criteria for distinguishing different emotions *apart* from appraisal characteristics. (Possible sources of additional evidence will be considered in subsequent chapters.)

The trouble is that unless emotion in general, and specific emotional terms in particular, can be defined independently of appraisals, none of the sensible predictions about empirical associations between emotion and appraisal turn out to be falsifiable. Common-sense propositions about emotion-appraisal relations become circular. On an operational level, as long as investigators continue to depend on self-report measures of emotions that reflect common-sense definitions of the experiences in question, then their results are bound to reflect the connections built into these shared representations, including the intuitively held connection between appraisal and emotion.

Of course, if the shared definition of emotion specifies factors other than appraisal, then there certainly are valid hypotheses to be formulated about the empirical relations between appraisals and other emotional components. Knowing that someone appraises a situation in a certain way may allow us to predict contingent facts about bodily changes (e.g. Smith, 1989), facial movements, action tendencies, or the future course of interpersonal relations. Unfortunately, this fact still does not make it reasonable to claim that the connection between appraisal and emotion itself is an empirical one. To the extent that appraisals are seen as diagnostic of emotions, these two broad categories of experience become difficult to differentiate from one another definitionally or operationally, and empirical claims about relationships between appraisal and emotion as separate variables start to seem hard to sustain.

Explanatory connection

Most appraisal theorists assume not only that appraisal characterizes emotion in general and that particular appraisal patterns characterize different emotions, but also that the relationship between appraisal and emotion is a causal relationship, with appraisal being one of the most important determinants of emotional experience. If we appraise the situation in sufficiently personally significant terms then this is highly likely to lead to an emotion of some kind. If we appraise the situation as personally significant, discrepant with our goals, and intentionally caused by someone else, then this pattern of appraisal will tend to lead to anger.

Clearly, this account is also perfectly concordant with the common-sense idea of how emotions are caused. People certainly do assume that if someone blames someone else for something significant that befalls them, they are liable to become angry at that person, so that blaming can lead to anger, and more generally, distinctive patterns of appraisal can lead to different emotions.

It also seems sensible to assume that if you can change the way that someone appraises the situation, then this can also change their emotion. For example, your anger at your loved one's lateness disappears when you are told that they have been hurt in a car accident. So, by working on people's cognitive beliefs and evaluations, it seems that we can have some influence on the way they react emotionally (e.g. Abramson *et al.* 1978; Beck, 1976).

Again, I want to say that people's common-sense accounts of how emotion works are correct in at least one sense, but not actually in the sense that psychologists have typically supposed.

The main way in which I take issue with the causal account is that it postulates a two-step process whereby first an appraisal takes place and then consequently an emotion happens. As is clear from my earlier discussion, I do not believe that it is so easy to distinguish the two concepts of appraisal and emotion. The fact that there is conceptual overlap between appraisal and emotion means that it is not so easy to imagine how one could occur cleanly without the other.

In order to specify what actually happens in the dynamic process leading to an emotion, it seems that it is necessary to find out exactly at what moment the emotion begins, and then work backwards in time from this instant. In practice, it is very hard to draw this line. Once we have got to the point of judging and evaluating things in accordance with a core relational theme, for instance, it is hard to say that we are not actually yet emotional. For example, it is very difficult to envisage a situation in which a person has reached the appraised conclusion that someone else is to blame for something seriously bad that has happened to them with the requisite level of personal involvement but is not yet emotional. It seems to me that the complete appraisal pattern, including the primary appraisal of caring about the situation at a high enough level, is itself already an emotional experience. The appraisal pattern, then, does not explain the anger, it defines it. Appraisal is a criterion for emotional experience, not its cause.

If I am correct that you cannot have a full-blown emotional appraisal pattern without also having the emotion defined by that pattern, then we must abandon the idea that the appraisal precedes emotion as a cause leading to a subsequent effect. However, it is possible to imagine another explanatory kind of relationship between appraisal and emotion which depends on a generative structure rather than causal mechanism. We might want to argue that appraisal patterns are underlying grammars that give emotions their meaning and distinctiveness (cf. Ortony *et al.*, 1988). However, this is not really an empirical claim in the usual sense.

In this book, I want to make a different claim about how emotions and appraisals are related. I want to say that in reality what we call emotions are means of *conveying* appraisals. In this view, appraisals are messages rather than private interpretations of situations, and they are always addressed to some real or imagined audience. People get emotional in order to make particular appraisal claims about shared situations. The appraisal represents the content of the emotional communication and thus defines the quality of the emotion. However, the emotion, insofar as it incorporates the mode of transmission of the appraisal as well as the appraisal itself, is not wholly identical with the appraisal.

With respect to the explanatory connection, I accept that there are some situations where appraisal implications can lead to emotions in a causal sense, but appraisals as such are certainly not the *only* way in which emotions are caused. For example, if someone insults us, our judgement that this is a personal offence leads us to get angry in order to defend our moral identity against this other person. Note that in this case the appraised situation is one of the grounds for getting emotional rather than its direct cause in a temporal sequence. In fact, the emotion is activated in tandem with the appraisal, or, to be more precise and less scientific, the two interconnected activities of emoting and appraising run completely in parallel throughout the emotional episode.

Even though appraisal cannot usually be seen as a separable precedent for emotion, the fact that appraisal representations are associated with emotional representations does have implications for how emotion is caused under certain special circumstances. It can happen that an emotion arises from contact with a situation and the way that situation is subsequently interpreted and evaluated. For example, someone might make a remark to me that I do not at first completely understand, but which is subsequently reinterpreted to me by someone else who tells me that the comment was in fact intended as an insult. An apparent compliment, for example, may contain concealed sarcasm, whose presence needs an independent interpreter. The interpreter's judgement may well in turn make me angry at the original remark. In this case, my anger certainly follows the interpretation and evaluation because they were supplied by someone else after the fact.

What seems to be happening in this example is that the person providing the subsequent interpretation is suggesting that the earlier situation was a proper occasion for justified anger, or that the original opportunity for expression of this anger has been missed. This appraisal interpretation relies on a shared cultural understanding of the kinds of social transaction that carry identity-threatening implications and are thus appropriate scenes in which people are expected to get angry. In other words, I am conforming to shared expectations about how I should act which are based on a common-sense model of a morally binding relationship between appraisal and emotion. I get angry because I understand that the situation ought to have demanded such a reaction in the first place, and replaying the original encounter before my mind's eye, I can work up the relevant appraisals quite easily in imaginary rather than real time. I think to myself something like: 'So when he was talking to me he was really saying *that*' and the actual cause of my anger is the fact that as socialized moral agents we have been taught to believe that people should not easily get away with such transgressions. In other words a representational connection between appraisal and emotion results in a represented appraisal causing a real emotion.

It is instructive to compare this secondary emotional situation with what would have happened if the emotion had arisen during the course of the ongoing interaction itself. Had I understood the significance of the comment immediately during the original encounter, I would have found it insulting and this apprehension would have corresponded precisely to the process of getting angry.

My reaction would be locked in and entrained to the ongoing structure of the interpersonal episode. It is an open question how often such real-time emotional episodes are also based on shared moral assumptions about duties and rights in social interactions. It may be that a substantial part of our emotional lives reflects socialized appraisal representations. However, the appraisals are not usually something separate from the emotions because we act out the corresponding presupplied emotion roles to convey these appraisals just as unselfconsciously and just as directly. The cultural logic of appraisal completely interpenetrates the cultural logic of emotion.

I have argued that there are possible occasions when an appraisal precedes an emotion in time and may contribute to its causation, but that these occasions depend on shared representations relating to emotions, appraisals, and personal rights and obligations, rather than direct deterministic linkages between a separate emotion and an appraisal. In a sense, we decide that we are, or should be, emotional on these occasions on the basis of the appraisal-relevant evidence that is offered us. In some situations, we only recognize a situation as one in which anger is an appropriate reaction by reference to an explicit appraisal. In more everyday on-line situations, emotions are partly constituted out of appraisals and it is usually difficult to make a rigid separation between the points at which one process ends and the other begins.

Dependency connection

The final and most extreme claim made about the relation between appraisal and emotion is one that has only been made explicitly by Lazarus (1991b) who argues that not only do appraisals characterize emotions, and not only does appraisal determine emotion, but also that appraisal is the central and sole cause of any instance of emotion; that appraisal is in all circumstances emotion's necessary and sufficient condition. According to Lazarus (1991b), without appraisal, emotion is impossible, and with appraisal of the correct sort, emotion is inevitable. Appraisals of certain kinds always lead to particular emotions, and these emotions never occur without the required appraisals. For example, not only does blame always lead to anger, but it is only via an appraisal of blame that anger can ever be produced.

I will consider Lazarus's theoretical position in more detail later in this chapter, but for now I want to point out that in one way at least, it is perfectly consistent with my argument that appraisal is constitutive of emotion in a definitional sense. Lazarus's model also sees the connection between appraisal and emotion as so close that it is impossible to separate the two variables in practice. Furthermore, Lazarus (1984) incorporated appraisal in his definition of what counts as an emotion. Finally, Lazarus (1991b) accepted that the putative one-way temporal sequence leading from appraisal to emotion is oversimplified and that the real relationship is bidirectional and mutually reciprocal (appraisal causes emotion which in turn causes appraisal and so on, see pp. 65–7).

All these supposed 'facts' about emotion fit in neatly with the view that I have offered that appraisals are at the heart of our common-sense definitions of what it means to be emotional. In my view, given that the relevant concepts are so closely related at a representational level, it is no surprise that appraisal is a necessary and sufficient condition for emotion, that you cannot separate the two processes in practice, and that any temporal and causal sequence is overlapping. The trouble is that despite all these agreements between the present position and that of Lazarus, there still remains a fundamental difference in at least the rhetoric of the presentations. Lazarus's theory interprets the relationship between appraisal and emotion as empirical and causal, rather than simply logical and representational. However, given all his qualifications about the impossibility of isolating the relevant variables and stringing them out into a causal series, it becomes difficult to see how the supposedly empirical content of Lazarus's model actually makes any difference in practice (see pp. 65–7).

As I have said, Lazarus's view that the empirical relation between appraisal and emotion is as close as it could possibly be is not one that is shared by many other appraisal theorists. Most would concede that other factors can also contribute to the causation of emotion (e.g. Parkinson and Manstead, 1992). By taking such a position, investigators are able to maintain an empirical distinction between emotion on the one hand and appraisal on the other. Emotion and appraisal can then be sensibly separable things. However, if, as Lazarus has claimed, it is only appraisal that always leads to emotion, then through trying to explain everything about emotion, appraisal theory paradoxically ends up explaining nothing.

If what I have said in this section is correct, that appraisal is constitutive of what it means to be emotional, and only serves as a cause when representations of emotion are brought into play, then the questions that should be addressed in future research are rather different to those posed by current appraisal theory. I would suggest that instead of simply trying to determine the content of judgements that supposedly lead to different emotions, investigators need to focus on the real-time, often interpersonal processes that actually cause emotion and appraisal in everyday life. Emotions should not be seen as direct and momentary reactions to appraised situations but as developing communicative syndromes. It is the course of this development of emotions that should be the topic of empirical research. In the following sections of the chapter, I will criticize much of the existing appraisal research for investigating emotion as if it were something easily detachable from its ongoing interpersonal context.

Another related problem of the appraisal paradigm is its tendency to see emotions as always simply reactive events that are undergone by the individual experiencing them rather than being actively constructed in the course of social life. I would argue that emotional meaning is sometimes tactically or strategically imposed on an interpersonal encounter by someone getting emotional. For example, a person might get upset during an argument when other means of persuasion have failed (e.g. Biglan *et al.*, 1985). In this case, it is not that a specific incident triggered an emotion, but that the emotion is formulated as part of an ongoing interpersonal dynamic. The unrealistically passive and reactive view of how emotion works in everyday social life implied by appraisal theory (and emotion theory in general) will be a recurrent theme in this chapter (and this book as a whole).

In the next section, I will consider the empirical evidence relating to appraisal and emotion before turning to the conceptual justifications that have been offered for the appraisal concept. I will argue that current formulations of appraisal theory are difficult to defend using either experimental data or theoretical arguments.

EMPIRICAL EVIDENCE FOR APPRAISAL THEORY

Four kinds of study have produced evidence directly relevant to appraisal theory: the first assesses experimentally the impact on emotion of manipulating appraisals (e.g. Lazarus and Alfert, 1964); the second seeks to relate individual differences in appraisal styles to individual differences in emotionality (e.g. Smith and Pope, 1992); the third collects reports of appraisals associated with specific emotional events (e.g. Smith and Ellsworth, 1985); and the fourth considers judgements about the emotional reactions of characters in short stories that specify theoretically relevant patterns of appraisal information (e.g. Roseman, 1991). I shall consider each of these sources of data in turn, and draw attention to some of the main limitations of existing findings.

Manipulating appraisal strategies

Research conducted by Lazarus and his colleagues in the 1960s provides the classic demonstration of how appraisal processes are thought to influence emotion. In a ground-breaking series of studies, participants were shown short films depicting unpleasant situations under conditions designed to encourage different appraisal strategies. Several of these studies used a movie showing adolescent males from the aboriginal Arunta tribe undergoing an apparently painful operation on their genitals as part of the ritual of 'subincision'. Unsurprisingly, a preliminary experiment demonstrated that the silent version of this film was emotionally unpleasant to watch, producing autonomic and self-report reactions of stress in viewers (Lazarus *et al.*, 1962). Subsequent studies succeeded in modifying viewers' stress responses to the movie by presenting various soundtracks and orienting passages intended to affect the way that the stimulus was appraised.

For example, in an early study (Speisman *et al.*, 1964), participants' heart rate and skin conductance were recorded while they watched the subincision film coupled with one of three alternative soundtracks. The first two soundtracks were designed to reduce stress reactions by encouraging viewers to reappraise the visual stimuli either by intellectualizing or denying what was happening on screen. The intellectualization soundtrack described the episode from a scientific anthropological perspective in detached unemotional terms whereas the denial soundtrack suggested that the operation was an occasion for joy rather than pain. In contrast, the third 'trauma' soundtrack emphasized rather than minimized the unpleasant aspects of the procedure. It was found that stress as indexed by skin conductance was greater for the trauma soundtrack condition but reduced in the intellectualization condition and also, to a lesser extent, in the denial condition. Lazarus and Alfert (1964) obtained similar results concerning the effectiveness of denial by prefacing the silent film with an orienting passage containing the same information as the soundtrack in the earlier study. In this experiment both self-report and physiological indices of stress were reduced by the denial passage. The authors argued that the soundtracks and orienting passages used in these studies modified participants' ongoing appraisal of the emotional content of the movie, allowing them to interpret the material as less threatening and thus experience less stress, but there are reasons for doubting their confidence in this conclusion.

What do these studies tell us in terms of the appraisal theory claims listed on p. 34? First, the results clearly have little bearing on issues relating to emotional differentiation because they focused on a single variety of emotion. The logic of the experimental design suggests that the findings support a causal claim roughly equivalent to proposition 3, that emotion in general is dependent on appraisal processes. However, looking at the actual procedure, it is clear that there was no *direct* manipulation of appraisal in these studies, and no attempt to assess whether any appraisal changes had actually taken place as a result of the different instructional and soundtrack conditions. These facts open up the possibility that the effects of the manipulation may have been mediated by some mechanism other than appraisal.

The different soundtracks probably affected respondents' information processing in a number of ways apart from their postulated influence on evaluation and interpretation. First, the pattern of presented information itself was quite different in the different experimental conditions. Second, the different instructions may have selectively emphasized different aspects of the stimulus complex as the depicted stressful episodes unfolded, with consequences for the registration and encoding of emotional information. In other words, the soundtracks and orienting passages may have affected the direction of attention rather than the interpretation and evaluation of the presented material. Because the experimental situation involved vicarious rather than actual stress, it is also possible that participants may have deliberately diverted their attention from certain unpleasant aspects of the film as a function of the different conditions. They may even have closed their eyes or looked away on occasion.

This analysis of the differences in the social situation being responded to by participants in the different conditions, and in the aspects of that situation to which they paid attention, means that the supposed appraisal manipulation may actually have changed the nature of the emotional situation itself rather than the way that this situation was appraised. In this case, the obtained group differences may not have been due to manipulated appraisal at all.

Another reason that the implications of Lazarus's early appraisal research may be limited concerns external rather than internal validity. Specifically, it is not at all clear how relevant these results are to the way that emotion normally occurs in everyday interpersonal interactions. A possibly important factor in the results obtained by Lazarus and his colleagues is the nature of the film stimulus used. Note that the subincision film depicted a situation that was likely to be unfamiliar to the Westerners viewing it. This fact allows a certain degree of flexibility of interpretation concerning what is really going on. A subsequent study (Lazarus *et al.*, 1965) demonstrated similar reduction of stress using an industrial safety information film depicting in graphic detail various accidents at work, such as the amputation of fingers in a milling machine. In this study, however, the denial orientation passage did not attempt to suggest that the accidents were not in fact painful but instead drew viewers' attention to the fact that the accidents were staged rather than real. As the authors themselves admitted at the conclusion of this paper: 'In real-life stressful situations, as opposed to vicarious ones such as watching a film, credible directions for reappraisal of the situation may not be so readily available' (p. 634).

In other words, the fact that the stimulus material was presented as a film rather than in a real-life situation in which the person was actively involved, meant that subjects' interpretations of the situation were more flexible and their emotional reactions more manipulable. It is possible therefore that in everyday episodes emotional reactions are more fully determined by the actual ongoing context and less dependent on mediation by appraisal.

Lazarus and Folkman (1984) argued that real-life episodes are open to reinterpretation just like the films used in the studies described: 'Much of our social existence is ambiguous . . . and personality factors can play a large role in perception and appraisal' (p. 47). My contention, in contrast, is that social life is rarely as difficult to define as the emotional stimulus from Lazarus and Alfert's (1964) appraisal study, which consisted of a silent film showing people from an alien culture performing a mysterious ritual. Interpersonal roles and cultural conventions structure our encounters (see Chapter 8), and meanings are often intersubjectively available to involved participants as real-time events unfold in the social world (Chapter 7). In this case, recognition of the personal significance of transactions that lead to emotional experience may often require relatively little by way of cognitive processing.

Lazarus's early experiments may offer some support for the idea that different cognitive perspectives can alter the strength of a developing emotional reaction. By working on one's involvement in the action, it is possible to stand back emotionally from what is going on. Whether this actually constitutes an appraisal strategy as such is another matter. It might instead be seen as directly keeping one's emotional distance.

In summary, these studies clearly showed that changes in the course and strength of emotion can be brought about by changing the nature of the social situation, but they provided no hard evidence that the reported changes in emotional intensity were dependent on appraisal *per se*. Furthermore, the fact that emotional reactions were alterable in this artificial laboratory context does not mean that similar processes generally apply in real-world situations. Certainly, there are everyday circumstances where people's emotions can be modified using interpretational or evaluative hints about what is going on, but it is an open question how commonly these circumstances occur, and how representative they are of emotion at large.

Appraisal style as a personality factor

A second line of evidence marshalled in support of appraisal theory concerns people's characteristic interpretational and evaluative tendencies and the ways that these may relate to their emotional experience. Clearly if appraisal theory is correct in assuming that the ways in which we evaluate and deal with stimuli can affect our emotional reactions, then people with different characteristic styles of appraisal or coping are likely to be prone to different emotions.

Research has investigated the emotional reactions of individuals with different dispositional concerns and cognitive styles (Smith and Pope, 1992). For example, a few studies have attempted to uncover the personality variables that predispose people to appraise things divergently. For example, in Lazarus and Alfert's (1964) experiment described in the previous section, reactions to the stimulus film were found to depend upon personality factors in addition to the recommended appraisal strategies. Specifically, participants diagnosed as high in their disposition to respond to emotionally unpleasant events with *denial* rated their emotional reactions to the silent subincision film as less unpleasant than those less prone to denial. Furthermore, in Speisman and colleagues' (1964) study, air executives scored higher on denial than students and also tended to exhibit less pronounced stress reactions to the film.

The usual interpretation of studies such as these implies that different modes of cognitive evaluation characterize different individuals, and that these evaluative styles in turn determine their emotions. The problem is that it is almost impossible to untangle the direction of causality between appraisal and emotion. Few people would argue with the conclusion that certain people are dispositionally more likely to display particular emotional reactions more strongly, and that this predisposition might be associated with certain cognitive factors, but there is no reason to prefer an explanation prioritizing the causal influence of the cognitive factors over an account that explains cognitive styles in terms of emotional or temperamental predispositions.

The limited available evidence concerning dispositional propensities for certain appraisals and emotions seems to support a general descriptive connection (proposition 2, p. 34) and to suggest that appraisal is empirically related to emotion. However, the problem of distinguishing appraisal from emotion at an operational level also applies to personality measures relevant to appraisal and emotion. It is hard to develop a dispositional measure that assesses tendencies towards certain appraisals but does not at the same time index tendencies towards certain emotions. Like the state variables of emotion and appraisal, the corresponding trait variables are difficult to isolate empirically one from the other.

This means that data from studies finding relations between trait appraisal measures and state emotion measures may in fact only reflect a definitionally implied connection between appraisal and emotion (proposition 1, p. 34). This problem applies more or less to any study of personality influences on appraisal and emotion.

A more sophisticated attempt to show how dispositional factors may be implicated in emotional appraisal and hence determine emotion was reported by Smith and Pope (1992). In this study, students high or low in mathematical ability were exposed either to a series of consistently easy arithmetic puzzles or to a series of puzzles that suddenly became difficult half-way through. Participants defined as low in mathematical ability faced with the second series of puzzles rated their problem-focused coping potential (how well they thought they could deal with the situation) as lower after they had tried to solve the more difficult problem than after they had worked only on easy problems. Their ratings of problem-focused coping potential were also lower than either high-ability participants working on the same puzzles, or both groups of participants working only on easy puzzles. Similarly, ratings of emotional reactions to these puzzles showed a corresponding pattern, with low-ability participants rating resignation and hopelessness as higher, and effortful optimism and determination as lower than the other groups when faced by the suddenly difficult puzzles. In short, participants who were bad at maths felt less able to cope with more difficult puzzles and also felt less optimistic while trying to solve them. Thus, changes in emotion and appraisal were predictable on the basis of a dispositional ability-related measure in conjunction with a situational manipulation.

Smith and Pope's results clearly demonstrate that different people can have different emotional reactions to an objectively similar situation, but what does this imply for appraisal theory? At first sight, the findings are certainly encouraging for views suggesting a causal role for appraisal in emotion since the appraisal was predicted using a dispositional dimension that has no obvious emotional component (mathematical ability). However, Smith and Pope incorporated a self-rating of mathematical competence into their subject allocation criterion which opens up the possibility that the obtained differences in reported emotion were due to differences in dispositional emotional reactivity to difficulties in solving mathematical puzzles rather than the appraisal-based problem-focused coping variable *per se* (bearing in mind that this distinction is not an easy one to draw anyway). Of course, a similar but more indirect process could also explain the results even if the measure of mathematical ability actually had been a pure performance measure, because experience of failure at maths puzzles is in any case likely to diminish confidence in settings where difficult puzzles are faced.

As for the effects on appraisal and emotion, the relations between these two sets of measures in Smith and Pope's study are unsurprising given the overlapping semantic content of items (reflecting the conceptual overlap of appraisal and emotion). For example, it is only to be expected that people who say that they find a puzzle more difficult to deal with also report feeling more resignation and hopelessness, and less optimism and less of a sense of challenge, when faced with this puzzle.

Smith and Pope's interactional approach to predicting emotion on the basis of a combination of situational and personal variables remains a promising one, despite the difficulties of finding a clear interpretation of their results so far. Whether appraisal theory as it is currently formulated provides the best rubric for interpreting results produced by such an approach, however, remains to be demonstrated.

Appraisal dimensions and the differentiation of emotion

The third source of evidence concerning the relation between appraisal and emotion is intended to bear on the issue of how different emotions may be associated with different appraisals (descriptive connection, 2a: p. 34). The basic methodology as pioneered by Smith and Ellsworth (1985) and Weiner (1985) involves asking participants to rate a series of emotional experiences along presupplied dimensions of appraisal. The different patterns of appraisal that are associated with each rated emotional experience are then determined using sta- tistical procedures such as discriminant and principal components analysis. The target emotional experiences may be based on imagined (e.g. Weiner, Russell, and Lerman, 1978), recollected (e.g. Smith and Ellsworth, 1985), or real-time (Smith and Ellsworth, 1987) episodes.

For example, in one of the earliest and most influential of these studies, Smith and Ellsworth (1985) asked students to think of occasions in the past when they had experienced fifteen specific emotional states such as pride, anger, and so on. These participants then answered various questions about their evaluations of these remembered situations, using a series of rating scales. The questions concerned how enjoyable the situation had been, what had caused the situation, how expected it was, how fair it had seemed, and so on.

Smith and Ellsworth found that characteristic patterns of ratings were associ- ated with the different emotions. For example, anger was associated with judgements that the situation was unpleasant, and that another person was responsible for this situation, whereas guilt was related to ratings of unpleasantness and self-blame. Other experiments (e.g. Frijda *et al.*, 1989; Manstead and Tetlock, 1989; Tesser, 1990) have produced broadly consistent findings for a wide range of emotions and appraisal dimensions, whether the target emotion was remembered, imagined, or experienced in real time (Smith and Ellsworth, 1987). Furthermore, when participants were asked to recall episodes when they *appraised* the situation in the way associated with a certain emotion, they also tend to report that they actually did experience the theoretically specified emotion on that occasion (e.g. Ellsworth and Smith, 1988).

The results of these many experiments are largely uncontroversial and unsur- prising. They show that people describe particular emotional experiences in predictable appraisal terms, and describe their appraisal experiences in cor- responding emotional terms. For example, people say that when they are angry, someone else is responsible for what happened to them, and that when they are evaluating a situation as one in which they are helpless they tend to feel sad.

To what extent does this impressively consistent mass of evidence provide substantive support for appraisal theory? The obvious and avowed interpretation of the data is that different emotions are associated with different appraisals (descriptive connection, 2a: p. 34). Clearly, however, nothing in the findings bears on the issue of whether appraisal precedes and causes emotion (explanatory connection, 3a: p. 34), and indeed the appraisal questions asked in these studies are typically directed at situational interpretations and evaluations taking place *during* rather than before the emotional experience (Parkinson and Manstead, 1992).

In fact, given what I have said above, there is reason to doubt whether the results of the dimensions of appraisal studies are supportive even of an empirical descriptive connection. Looking more closely at what happened in these studies, it becomes clear that their results only have direct relevance to a definitional connection between appraisals and emotions (1a: p. 34), showing that people's emotional representations are closely related to their appraisal representations, but saying nothing directly about links between the realities of appraisal and emotion.

The interpretational ambiguity arises because in all these studies participants themselves were allocated the responsibility of deciding when a satisfactory instance of a particular emotion had been generated. No independent criterion of the identity of the emotion was used in addition to these participants' self-characterizations. This point applies whether the target emotional states were recalled, imagined, or concurrently experienced. In all cases, the investigators allowed participants to self-select target emotional episodes for rating on the basis of their own criteria for what counted as a relevant and representative example.

The problem with such a procedure is that whatever common-sense criteria participants used for generating the emotion examples, it is unlikely that they did not involve some implicit reference to the appraisal structure of the episode. If, as I have argued above, people define the differences between emotional experiences at least partly in terms of their associated appraisal representations, then it is hard to see how the selection task could be achieved without using appraisal-related information. For example, when participants tried to think of a pure instance of anger, their selection criteria would necessarily have been dependent on their understanding of the conventional meaning of the word 'anger', which itself is largely defined in terms of characteristic appraisals. Their memory search consequentially would have been attuned to situations when they blamed someone else for something bad that had happened. Unless the assumption is made that people possessed some extraneous source of information about their own emotions that made no reference to evaluative features of the situational context (introspective reference to a distinctive private experience, for example), then there is no way that they could have avoided using appraisal criteria for target selection.

In short, if the main differences between the meanings of different emotion terms are appraisal-based, then it would be unsurprising that appraisal criteria were used in this way, when trying to think of examples of appropriate distinct emotions (Smith and Ellsworth, 1985) or trying to characterize the quality of current emotional state (Smith and Ellsworth, 1987).

Of course, if participants actually used appraisal-based criteria to select or characterize their target emotions, then the finding that these emotions were then rated as being related to distinctive appraisal patterns is completely explained without any reference to an actual empirical connection between appraisal and emotion. In other words, the basic conclusion that can be drawn from these studies is that the conventional meanings of emotion words ensure that we all know what we are talking about when we use them, and what we are talking about is mainly appraisal (definitional connection, 1a: p. 34). The dimensions of appraisal findings therefore seem to concern the correspondence of participants' common-sense criteria for emotion and appraisal judgements, rather than any empirical relation between emotion and appraisal.

Appraisal theorists have overinterpreted their results because they make the mistake of accepting the common-sense idea that an emotion is really an intact experience which is somehow separable from the evaluative judgement at its centre. In this case, people who are thinking about their emotions are thinking about something private that is essentially independent of appraisal. However, as theorists such as Solomon (1976) have argued, emotions get their distinctive identities and their characteristic feelings directly from their appraisal content and the way that this is expressed in action or action readiness (Frijda, 1986). Saying that you are proud rather than happy necessarily implies a characteristic evaluative relationship to the situation. To test whether such a relationship occurs empirically seems to miss the point: without some independent (e.g. non-linguistic) criterion of what counts as an example of the emotion in question it is impossible to make the empirical claim. But in any case the only real way of getting at the quality of emotional experience is by looking at how the individual appraises the situation.

A very similar point was made by Ossorio (1981) when he argued that the supposedly scientific finding that frustration leads to aggression 'represents neither an empirical discovery nor a stipulative definition. Instead, it is a partial formulation of our familiar four-thousand-year-old concept of anger' (p. 49). Appraisal researchers have managed to mystify the nature of a connection that was already well understood by everyone on an implicit level. Of course, the particular content of the appraisals conceptually associated with different emotion qualities is of interest to researchers who want to develop models of how emotions are categorized by people and dimensions of appraisal research offer some useful details about how such emotion representations are structured. Unfortunately, however, the results have no direct implications concerning the empirical content of emotion, nor how it is caused.

Vignette studies

The final methodology that has been used to investigate the connection between appraisal and emotion involves presenting participants with written narratives describing the predicament of a protagonist, and then asking them to make judgements about the emotion experienced by that protagonist (Weiner *et al.*, 1978). The short stories or vignettes presented in these studies are constructed so that they vary systematically in their appraisal implications for the protagonist. Thus, the technique has the advantage of allowing quite precise manipulation of appraisal themes and components. Also, because the appraisals are actually manipulated in the stories rather than simply retrospectively measured, the data produced using this technique seems to have some potential for assessing the possible causal role of appraisal in emotion (explanatory connection, 3a: p. 34; Roseman, 1991).

There have been two relatively comprehensive attempts to investigate emotion-appraisal connections using the vignette method (Roseman, 1991; Smith and Lazarus, 1993; see also Smith *et al.*, 1993), and in this section I will review each of these in some detail, because I think that they help to illustrate some of the conceptual confusions made by appraisal theory concerning ideas and realities of emotion (see Parkinson and Manstead, 1993, for a more detailed review).

In Roseman's experimental procedure, participants read vignettes describing eight different scenarios in which a protagonist underwent an emotionally rele-vant outcome. The actual content of each of these stories was varied so that the outcome was either pleasant or unpleasant; caused by someone else, the protagonist, or impersonal circumstances; so that the protagonist was described as either deserving a positive or a negative outcome; and so on in a range of permutations.

For example, in one story a student called Susan obtained her exam results. Different versions of this story were constructed in which Susan did well or did badly, deserved to do well, or deserved to do badly, and did badly or well because of her own efforts, because of help from someone else, or because she was just lucky. Forty-eight different versions of each story were constructed representing all possible combinations of Roseman's proposed appraisal distinctions. Participants were asked to rate the protagonist's emotional reactions on a series of dimensions and it was predicted that different appraisal patterns would lead to differences in judgements about these emotions in theoretically specified ways. For instance, when Susan was described as getting the good grade that she deserved due to her own personal efforts, her predicted emotional reaction was pride, but when she failed to get a good grade and deserved not to get it, the predicted emotional response was guilt.

Roseman obtained substantial confirmation for most of his predictions about how different stories conveying different appraisal patterns would lead to differ-ent judged emotions. Thus, the description of different outcomes and different evaluations of these outcomes was interpreted by participants as implying differ-ent emotional reactions.

What do Roseman's results tell us about the appraisal–emotion connection? Although the experimental design contained an appraisal manipulation of sorts, the findings actually only show that readers are able to infer emotions on the basis of the appraisal-related information represented in the stories. In other words, the study shows that people think that different emotions are related to different appraisals of environmental contingencies, or, in other words, that there is a consensual implicit theory linking emotions with the ways that situations are evaluated (definitional connection 1a: p. 34).

Rather than limiting his conclusions to emotional representations (cf. Russell, 1987), however, Roseman suggested that his study provides data directly relevant to the issue of how ongoing emotions are actually determined by different appraisal patterns. Despite admitting that his experiment provides a *simulation* of emotion rather than manipulating emotion directly, he interpreted the obtained connections between linguistic representations of situations and linguistic representations of emotional reactions as evidence of a causal relationship between the corresponding real-world, real-time phenomena (explanatory connection, 3a: p. 34).

Roseman was perfectly explicit about this causal claim:

> Although it is possible, there is no particular reason to believe that subjects would in fact respond differently from what is indicated by these data if they were actually in the vignette situations. For example, is there any reason to believe that subjects would not respond with joy if they got the grade they wanted in an exam, with sadness if they did not, or with anger if they blamed the teacher for low grades?
>
> (Roseman, 1991, pp. 196–7)

Certainly, it is incontestable that once a person has got to the point of defining the situation as one in which he or she has got something they wanted (that they care about enough), then it is likely that they would also describe themselves as feeling joy, and when they had reached the conclusion that someone else was to blame for something that had gone wrong they would also say that they were angry about it. The problem, however, is that this supposedly empirical analysis in fact only tells us about the relations between the appraisal and emotion concepts we use to interpret behavioural episodes (whether they relate to ourselves or to other people) and nothing directly about appraisal and emotion in reality. Once someone has got to the stage of representing a situation in appraisal terms then it is likely that they have already drawn the appropriate emotional conclusions. The question that emotion theory needs to address is not how the appraisal representation leads to the emotion representation but how either of these representations is activated in the first place.

By taking as given the specific representation of the emotional situation and the protagonist's evaluation of the personal significance of this situation, Roseman managed to evade the issue of how real-time situations are dynamically encoded in ongoing emotional experience. Moreover, his implication that subjects could actually be 'in the vignette situations' reflects an unsupported assumption that the version of social reality presented in a conventional narrative can serve as a workable representation of all the factors that are functionally relevant to the real-time causation of emotion. In short, Roseman's analysis denied the important conceptual distinction between ideas and realities of emotion.

BOX 2.1 HOW TO MAKE A STORY REALLY EMOTIONAL

Let's say that you wanted to write a story that would really create an emotional reaction in your readers, that would encourage them to go through the actual causal process that leads to an emotion. How would you do it? First of all, you would need to establish a certain level of identification with the leading character, to make them appear sympathetic but not perfect, perhaps as someone who seems something like readers might like to see themselves. Then you need to describe the emotional situation itself and give it a sense of real impact. What is the best way of achieving this in words alone? Not, it would seem, by specifying particular patterns of information corresponding to agreed-upon appraisal dimensions. Rather, you should probably try to construct bit by bit the ongoing situation and its important interpersonal relationships that formed the basis for the emotional reactions. You might attempt to specify concrete evocative details and to incorporate some of the rhythm of the relevant reality into your prose. Say someone walks up to you softly, step by step, on the balls of his poised feet, caressing the carpet with the crepe of the soles of his hundred-dollar loafers. Now, anything can happen and it will get you involved, assuming that you are in the right mood for immersing yourself in this kind of story. The literary effect depends on who *you* are, who the character is, and the mesh between. At any rate, the sights, sounds, and smells, the texture of the tangible dynamic reality are the crucial aspects in the production of the emotion.

Verbal texts about emotion automatically translate the episode into representational terms so it is unsurprising that reactions to texts should reflect representational connections between appraisals and emotions (Parkinson and Manstead, 1993). If the episode were unfolding in real time and real life, however, the informational basis for the emotion would be presented dynamically to the participant and require little by way of re-presentation to make sense. It is not the case in everyday life that people always confront a situation, then evaluate it, then react emotionally. Rather, evaluations and prescribed (but negotiable) emotional responses are bound up together in the dynamic structure of what is really going on in the social world.

Of course, none of this is intended to negate the fact that sometimes people get emotional as a function of applying appraisal representations to a situation. For example, on discovering broken glass on the floor of the swimming pool changing room, I may infer that someone has carelessly dropped a bottle and failed to clear away all the pieces. I may think that someone might have got hurt due to this person's thoughtlessness, and hence feel angry with them (especially if I have a particular idea of who it might be). In this hypothetical episode, my interpretation of what happened and the apparent intentions behind it seems to shape my feelings. However, even in this case, the appraisal interpretation is embedded in an emotion script (e.g. Fischer, 1991) which prescribes the appropriate response, rather than being an independent cause of emotion. Furthermore, it is clear that emotion does not always occur in this way as a function of relatively explicit reasoning processes. More usually, emotions seem to arise spontaneously out of the real-time course of an interaction. Indeed, if we take emotions to be means of conveying appraisal messages, then it might be said that it was communicative intent that really caused the emotion: it may be that I resolve to tell off whoever I believe has caused the accident and failed to deal with it. My anger is directed at them, and the appraisal represents the lesson that I want them to learn from my being angry with them.

The assumed equivalence between ideas and realities of emotion, or more specifically between linguistic representations of emotional events, and the real-time processes themselves, was taken a stage further in another vignette study by Smith and Lazarus (1993), which was based specifically on the appraisal theory presented in Table 2.1 (p. 32). This experiment followed a similar procedure to Roseman's except that the stories were written in the second person rather than the third person, and participants were asked to project themselves into the described situation then rate their own emotional reactions, rather than those of the story's fictional protagonist. Thus, Smith and Lazarus changed the kind of simulation procedure used by Roseman into a 'directed imagery task', where participants were supposed to make their own appraisals in accordance with the information contained in the story, and experience genuine emotional reactions as a consequence.

In order to understand what actually went on in this experimental procedure, it is helpful to look at a specific example of one of the vignettes: the appropriately named 'cancer scenario'. In two different versions of this narrative, Smith and Lazarus tried to activate the patterns of appraisal theoretically associated with guilt and anger. To produce *guilt*, according to the theory, there must be primary appraisals of motivational relevance and motivational incongruence (the person must care about what is happening and it must conflict with what he or she would like to happen) in conjunction with a secondary appraisal of self-accountability (the person must believe that he or she is personally responsible for the bad thing that has happened). To produce *anger*, the primary appraisals must be the same but the secondary appraisal should be other-accountability rather than self-accountability (someone else is responsible for the bad thing that has happened). In fact, as Lazarus (1991a) has argued, the actual appraisals associated with guilt and anger representations are probably slightly more complicated than this model suggests, and possibly depend upon different kinds of ego-involvement, but in any case the critical distinction between self-accountability for guilt and other-accountability for anger still holds.

In the first part of the story, participants were instructed to imagine that a favourite relative was in hospital with lung cancer. This situation was intended to conflict with their desires while identifying with the protagonist of the story (motivational incongruence), in a way that was personally significant (motivational relevance), and hence to produce a negative emotional reaction.

The second part of the vignette contained the manipulation of the secondary appraisals of self-accountability or other-accountability. The text proceeded as follows in the former version:

> You blame yourself for what has happened. You believe that you've let your relative down – that you weren't insistent enough in trying to get him (her) to stop smoking. If only you had made your relative realise how much you cared about him (her) and how important it was to you that he (she) quit smoking, then maybe this whole situation could have been avoided.
>
> (Smith and Lazarus, 1993, p. 268)

To convey other-accountability, the story finished using the following alternative passage:

> You can't understand why your relative let this happen to him(her)self. You don't understand why he (she) kept on smoking even though he (she) knew it was dangerous, and even though you'd begged him (her) to quit. You also can't understand why he (she) waited so long before seeing a doctor. His (her) behaviour seems irresponsible and thoughtless of others.
>
> (p. 268)

As predicted by the authors, the first passage increased participants' ratings of both self-accountability and guilt and the second passage increased ratings of other-accountability and anger. Furthermore, ratings of other-accountability were correlated with ratings of anger, and ratings of self-accountability were correlated with ratings of guilt. What do these findings imply about the connection between appraisal and emotion?

First of all, the correlational findings have exactly the same implications as those obtained in the dimensions of appraisal studies discussed in the previous section. They show that when someone's experience is characterized in terms of emotion it is also likely to be judged as implying relevant appraisals. When we describe someone's experience (including our own) in terms of guilt, for example, we also imply that they are blaming themselves for something. In other words, common-sense emotion definitions contain appraisal implications (definitional connection, 1a: p. 34). The specific content of the appraisal-emotion correlations may at least be useful in clarifying some of our shared conceptualizations of emotion.

A potentially more interesting finding, however, concerns the obtained effects of story content on emotion ratings. In Roseman's study, the corresponding results concerned detached ratings of third-person emotions: participants were asked to judge how the character in the story felt. In Smith and Lazarus's vignette study, on the other hand, participants were told to imagine themselves in the story situation and rate how they themselves felt. Thus, the obtained effects of described situations on self-rated emotion seem to reflect a causal process whereby manipulated real-time appraisals patterns determined actual ongoing emotional experience.

Unfortunately, when Smith and Lazarus's procedure is examined more closely, the difference between the implications of their findings and those of Roseman turn out to be more apparent than real. Although participants were rating their own emotions in Smith and Lazarus's procedure, this was done as part of a procedure where they were imagining that they were in a particular situation. It would not therefore be too far-fetched to suggest that the judged emotions were also imagined emotions, or perhaps real emotions attributed to an imaginary version of themselves.

More seriously, Smith and Lazarus's dependent measures were based on participants' characterizations of their emotional state rather than on any representation-independent assessment. For this reason, all that can be concluded directly from the findings is that the way that people *represented* their emotional state was related to the way that the situation was formulated in the representation provided by the story. Any causal link demonstrated is only between a situational representation and an emotional representation rather than between the realities of appraisal and emotion.

How then did the narrative representation of the situation convey emotional meaning to the participants? Even at this limited level, it is not clear that appraisal information was all that differentiated the contrasting emotional ratings obtained in this study. For example, the obtained correlations between ratings of appraisal and ratings of emotion reveal that a substantial proportion of the variance in emotion as measured remained unaccounted for by appraisal as measured. Furthermore, comparing the different versions of the vignettes, there are obvious differences in their narrative content apart from those necessary to convey appraisal information. Indeed the passages quoted above designed to produce guilt and anger are rather long and complex if their only purpose is really to manipulate a single secondary appraisal component relating to the allocation of responsibility. This leads us to the conclusion that each passage contains more than this simple accountability idea.

For example, focusing on the other-accountability version of the second half of the cancer scenario, three out of its four sentences begin with phrases about not being able to understand the victim/culprit's actions ('You can't understand why your relative let this happen . . . You don't understand why he kept on smoking . . . etc.'). It is hard to see what relevance this repetition has to the secondary appraisal of other-accountability that it is supposed to be manipulating. Rather, the text seems to represent a familiar speech pattern observed during anger (repetition and emphasis of the point), whose purpose is presumably *communicative* when it occurs in real life, rather than simply evaluative or interpretational. Furthermore, the specific linguistic content of the text is designed to convey a sense of incomprehension, suggesting that the person's actions are not interpretable within a reason-based framework and are thus an occasion for emotion (see Chapter 10). Some of this extra meaning might be captured by using extra appraisal distinctions such as Roseman's *legitimacy* dimension, but the basic narrative device seems to be designed as an attempt to influence emotion directly rather than via appraisal. In this case, the impact of the story on emotion ratings appears less surprising.

In short, Smith and Lazarus's 'directed imagery' task seems to assess participants' ability to make sense of stylized depictions of emotional episodes, and the relationships between their appraisal and emotion ratings may be almost completely determined by the semantic similarity between the various questionnaire items.

The fact that people make certain implicit connections between appraisal and emotion representations (definitional connection, 1a: p. 34) when making sense of stories does not necessarily imply that these connections reflect empirical connections between appraisal and emotion in reality (descriptive and explanatory connections, 2a and 3a: p. 34). However, it is of course perfectly possible that part of our understanding of the way that stories work derives from our experience with real-life situations and that we sometimes make sense of real life in a similar way to the way that we make sense of a story – but certainly not always (Parkinson and Manstead, 1993).

The basic confusion in interpreting the results of vignette studies reflects the fact that the appraisals and emotions are manipulated as well as measured at the representational level, but conclusions are drawn concerning the realities of emotional experience. The finding that a representation of an appraisal can be interpreted as implying a represented emotion is insufficient grounds for claiming that appraisal and emotion are really linked by a descriptive or explanatory connection. In order to understand fully the significance of these results, we need to investigate how emotional and appraisal representations are actually deployed by people in their everyday encounters with other people.

Summary

To summarize the results of appraisal research, none of the lines of evidence concerning relations between appraisal and emotion leads to definitive conclusions about empirical rather than conceptual connections between appraisals and emotions. Nevertheless, supporters of appraisal theory suggest that the convergence of findings from the different approaches somehow supports the existence of deterministic appraisal–emotion linkages (e.g. Roseman *et al.*, 1990). My interpretation of this convergence, on the other hand, is that appraisals are bound up in our common-sense definitions of different emotional states, so that when people characterize their own or someone else's experience in emotional terms, this makes it likely that they will also endorse characteristic appraisal judgements.

Of course, to the extent that people deploy their emotion and appraisal representations when interpreting ongoing interpersonal situations and when formulating action possibilities, ideas of appraisal may impact to some extent on emotional reality. But this is not the only way in which emotion can be produced, nor are the appraisal representations typically activated independently of their associated emotion representations. In most ongoing interpersonal situations,

emotions convey appraisals and appraisals are the main part of the communicational content of the emotions. This is a theoretical view that I will be
developing in further detail in subsequent chapters.

So much for the empirical basis for appraisal theory. Although it seems clear
that different appraisals characterize our conceptions of different emotions, it
cannot be conclusively argued that appraisal typically precedes or causes
emotion. Why then have theorists such as Lazarus (1991a) placed so much
emphasis on appraisal in their explanation of emotion? The answer is that they
believe that there are good *theoretical* reasons for assuming that appraisal is the
key determinant of emotion. In the next section I evaluate the theoretical rationale
for appraisal.

THEORETICAL BASIS OF APPRAISAL THEORY

Support for appraisal theory depends not only on empirical evidence but also on
its coherence with broader conceptual frameworks. In the present section I will
consider some of the theoretical arguments that have been used in defence of the
appraisal position.

Appraisal as mediator of response to emotional stimuli

One set of reasons for believing that appraisal is a necessary condition for
emotion depends on some generally agreed assumptions about when and how
emotion occurs. The first of these assumptions relates to difficulties in explaining
emotional reactions as direct unmediated responses to stimulus situations.

Early theories often assumed that emotions were simply based on innately
programmed reflex mechanisms. For example, the startle reaction which is produced by sudden and intense stimuli can be understood as an unconditioned
response much like the knee-jerk reflex. If some emotional reactions were based
on this kind of pre-wired genetic mechanism then they might be conditionable to
other stimuli by association and reinforcement. Watson (1929), for example,
argued that there were just three basic innate emotional responses, each of which
could be triggered automatically by specific stimuli: *fear* by loud noises or loss
of support; *anger* by restraint on movement; and *love* by stroking and caressing.
He argued that other stimuli attained their emotional power by being associated
with these biological elicitors (e.g. Watson and Rayner, 1920), and that the whole
range of adult emotions were based on combinations of the three states.

Another view which suggested that stimulus features have rather direct effects
on emotion dates back to Wundt's (1897) early psychological theories. Wundt
argued that the relative intensity of stimuli determines what kind of experience
they will produce, with moderately weak stimulus events tending to elicit positive
feelings, and intense stimuli causing more negative affect. Tomkins (1962)
modified this proposal by suggesting that the determining stimulus factor is
intensity combined with suddenness of presentation. This conclusion was based
on the results of studies of reported feelings in connection with simple sensory

stimuli like sounds, tastes, and smells, which seemed to show that feelings change from positive to negative once the stimulus passes a certain degree of strength. However, it is much more difficult to apply this analysis to emotional responses to complex event sequences, where the variable of intensity cannot meaningfully be specified independently of the emotional significance of the situation.

A basic problem with stimulus theories is that emotions (as conventionally defined) generally seem to be more flexible response patterns than simple reflexes, and are not associated with simple and consistently definable stimuli. For example, Ekman, Friesen, and Simons (1985) argued that the startle response does not count as an emotion in the same way as, say, anger or happiness, because startle can be produced reliably in *all* subjects by exposing them to a sudden and unexpected intense stimulus such as a gunshot. According to Ekman and his colleagues, no *bona fide* emotion shows such inflexibility.

Thus, emotions, according to most contemporary theorists, cannot be seen as fixed action patterns that are run off in an unchanging sequence, but instead as adjustable modes of dealing with classes of situations. For example, Smith and Ellsworth (1987) argued as follows:

> Emotions represent an evolutionary step beyond innate releasing mechanisms and fixed-action patterns in that they provide a way of motivating behaviour that allows a measure of flexibility both in the eliciting conditions and in the form of the behavioural response.

> (p. 475)

Most current versions of appraisal theory similarly see emotions as sets of behavioural strategies (backed up with physiological support) for dealing with a complex and changing environment. In certain unpredictable situations of challenge or threat, so the argument goes, the individual needs to be prepared to respond quickly but not in an entirely indiscriminate way. Evolution has therefore provided humans with a cognitive-evaluative system for recognizing when these broadly defined situations arise, and for selecting the appropriate behavioural option for dealing with them. This system corresponds to the mechanisms underlying appraisal.

Thus, assumptions about the causal role of appraisal in emotional production (explanatory connections 1 and 1a: p. 34) derive partly from the assumed flexibility of emotional response which makes it seem unlikely that emotions are direct responses to stimulus configurations. Because stimuli apparently do not lead directly and consistently to particular emotions, it is assumed that there must be some mechanism that mediates between stimulus registration and emotional reaction. Appraisal, defined as a process whereby the adaptational agenda of a situation is apprehended, appears to be an ideal candidate for such a mediator.

Differential susceptibility to emotions

A second generally accepted supposition supporting appraisal theory is that different people have different emotional responses to apparently identical situations. Correspondingly, the same person may react differently to the same event on different occasions. Again the obvious conclusion that can be drawn from this is that situations cannot lead directly and automatically to the emotional response. Therefore, some variable relating to personal emotional significance must in some way mediate each individual's response to potentially emotional stimuli. Clearly, appraisal fits the bill for such a mediator.

Appraisal theory assumes that people have habitual ways of evaluating and dealing with situations which determine their differential reactivity to them (Smith and Pope, 1992; and see pp. 44–6). In other words, people's characteristic styles of appraisal shape their emotional lives. For example, someone who typically explains misfortune in terms of personal and unchangeable factors is thought to be more prone to depression (Abramson *et al.*, 1978).

The fact that people may show some stability in their characteristic styles of appraisal does not, of course, mean that evaluations are applied by individuals completely consistently: at certain times, people may evaluate their resources for dealing with a given difficult situation (coping potential) in more favourable terms than at others, thus changing their appraisal and hence their emotional reaction to the situation. For example, when we are tired and lacking in energy, our problems can assume exaggerated proportions, making us worry about them more. However, the same problems may seem more like exciting challenges after a good night's sleep, or a relaxing holiday.

Evaluating the theoretical rationale for appraisal

Summarizing the last two sections, the idea of appraisal helps to explain why the same stimulus has different emotional effects on different people or at different times, why different situations are responded to with the same emotion, and more generally why emotional response is more flexible than a direct reflexive connection. In addition, an evolutionary analysis offers a functional explanation for the existence of the mechanism. This is a tidy package justifying the appraisal concept. However, in reality things are not quite so neat.

The central point of the rationale is that stimuli cannot lead directly to emotion because otherwise reactions to the same stimulus would always be the same for different individuals and at different times. The main problem with this argument is that it depends on a restricted idea of the nature of stimuli in the real world and of the way in which they are actually structured. Certainly if we take the impetus for emotion to be a simple momentary and local information change, then the same stimulus can be followed by different emotions. However, if we make the more realistic assumption that emotional reactions relate to already contextualized objects or events that unfold over time (cf. Lazarus, 1991b) then it is less clear that the same pattern of meaningful information could produce different emotions.

In fact, emotions are not usually based on single momentary stimuli that confront the individual. Often, the emotionally provoking situation is something that has been developing for a while, and its personal significance derives (at least partly) from the nature of unfolding events rather than the way that any specific event is evaluated intrapsychically. For example, consider what happens when you first meet someone and have a conversation with them. First of all, there may be some initial evaluative feelings based on your impression of the person's demeanour, appearance, and style of dress, as well as your current mood-state. More definite affective judgements, however, do not usually depend on weighing up all the cognitively available information at any given moment, but emerge in real time as the conversation unfolds. The dynamics of your interaction build up expectations which are disappointed or fulfilled; the co-ordination of your responses determines the development of your mutual liking or loathing, or something in between.

The main point I want to make here is that the other person is not just a stimulus configuration for your evaluation but an active object offering niches or affordances (Gibson, 1979) for your mutually negotiable projects. You do not necessarily engage in a specific evaluative process to register these affordances. Instead they are picked up on-line as the encounter proceeds. In many examples of emotional reactions, dynamic and interpersonal factors are crucial to the causation of the associated feelings. Unfortunately, an emphasis on intrapsychic appraisal mechanisms tends to draw attention away from these factors.

This point is part of a more general claim that emotional stimuli often attain emotional meaning by dynamic contextualization rather than intrapsychic processing. In short, the idea of a simple momentary stimulus is itself a theoretical abstraction of a time-point in an ongoing transaction between the individual and the physical or social environment. Similarly, what we mean by emotion cannot be a simple momentary response, but is instead part of an evolving relationship with the world.

Of course it is also important to remember that some people may be predisposed to respond emotionally to certain themes or objects and that this fact will make a difference to the way that responses unfold. However, whether this differential reactivity is due entirely to differences in characteristic appraisals is another matter.

Another way of putting this point is that whatever appraisal theory says about differences in reactions to equivalent stimuli, in fact no two stimuli are ever exactly the same. Some of the apparent variations in response depend on contextual differences rather than intrapersonal evaluative judgements. The same situation is different depending on your relative position within it. The stimulus situation has a dynamic dimension and when this is included the need for cognitive mediation diminishes. Naturally, it is possible to argue that developing situations affect emotions by setting up intrapsychic expectations against which specific stimulus events are evaluated. Even in this case, however, the causal factors that make a difference are the situational dynamics rather than the intrapsychic expectations that they are assumed to set up automatically.

Of course none of my argument should be taken to imply that an internal evaluative process never changes the emotional meaning of an object or event, only that when the true nature of the information leading to emotional reaction is considered the need for such cognitive mediation becomes correspondingly less.

Another problem with the intrapsychic appraisal account of emotion is that anticipations may sometimes emerge from on-line *interpersonal* negotiation rather than private calculation. Furthermore, the argument above presupposes that the natural beginning of an emotional episode is when something happens in the external or personal world. In fact, it is also possible to think of instances of emotion that are adopted deliberately as ways of affecting other people's interpretation of what is going on. For example, people sometimes get upset because this serves the function of getting attention or sympathy rather than because some specific event has caused them to be emotional.

The second aspect of the theoretical justification for the appraisal concept depends on a natural selection account of how the relevant mechanisms have evolved over the history of the human species. The problem with this evolutionary analysis of the functions of appraisal is that it works better for some emotions than for others. For example, although it is relatively easy to imagine how a system for appraising fear-relevant situations might have survival value, the evolutionary advantages of embarrassment are harder to isolate. Of course, the appraisal–emotion system need not serve only survival goals. Human beings characteristically use their biological capacities in spheres of activity other than those that natural selection intended. My view is that it is over-restrictive to suggest that all emotions, or all examples of any particular emotion relate to evolutionary imperatives (cf. Averill, 1974). The function of such social emotions as pride, embarrassment, and guilt is not simply species survival, and there are occasions when fear and anger are based on socially constructed rules and roles rather than biological ones.

My conclusion from this section is that the need for an internal appraisal mechanism to mediate emotional response lessens when the dynamic and interpersonally constructed nature of emotional information is recognized. Although I do not deny that interpretative and evaluative work is often (and maybe always) *part* of the way that emotion emerges from any given encounter, I think it is a mistake to consider appraisal the sole causal factor in producing emotion.

I have argued that appraisal might not always be a necessary mediator of emotional responses to dynamic situations in the real (social) world. However, I have also implicitly accepted the notion that individual emotions are typically based on personal meanings of events. This latter assertion is traditionally assumed to be sufficient grounds for treating appraisal as the crucial causal factor in emotion because personal meaning is thought to be only apprehendable via cognitive processes. I question this necessary link by drawing attention to the existence of dynamic perceptual and interpersonal processes (e.g. Gibson, 1979) which allow the direct pickup of meaningful information from the environment. But perhaps these real-time dynamic processes to which I have alluded can themselves be seen as constituting appraisal processes. In this case, we might see that any process whereby personal meaning is apprehended counts as appraisal by definition. This, as far as I can tell, corresponds to Lazarus's (1991b) position which is reviewed in more detail in the following sections.

DEFINITIONAL BASIS OF APPRAISAL THEORY

In the previous sections, I have suggested that appraisal studies so far have failed to provide convincing evidence confirming appraisal's supposed causal role in emotion. Instead, most of the reported findings are only directly relevant to a definitional rather than empirical connection between appraisal and emotion. Furthermore, I have suggested that the conceptual rationale for appraisal theory is not as solid as has been generally supposed. In the present section, I consider a possible final line of defence offered by the specific version of appraisal theory suggested by Lazarus (e.g. 1991a).

Lazarus's argument is that emotion must be caused by appraisal because emotion necessarily involves a recognition of personal significance, and the only way that such significance can be recognized is via appraisal:

> Cognitive activity is a necessary precondition of emotion because to experience an emotion, people must comprehend – whether in the form of a primitive evaluative perception or a highly differentiated symbolic process – that their well-being is implicated in a transaction, for better or worse.
>
> (Lazarus, 1984, p. 124).

Zajonc (1984) suggested that Lazarus employed circular reasoning by *defining* emotions on the basis of appraisal, then inferring the presence of appraisal directly from the occurrence of an emotion as defined. If we accept Lazarus's formulation of what emotion is, then any evidence that emotion has occurred without appraisal can immediately be dismissed on the grounds that it was not real emotion after all because no appraisal preceded it. Correspondingly, if it is agreed that a real emotion has occurred, then it must be that some process of appraisal has preceded it by definition, even if there is no obvious evidence for this conclusion.

This is not as facetious a point as it might sound: Lazarus (1991a; 1991b) in fact has used arguments similar to this when defending his claim that appraisal is a necessary condition for emotion. Responding to the point that emotion cannot depend on appraisal because babies and animals who have relatively low-level cognitive capacities still seem to get emotional (e.g. Izard *et al.*, 1984), Lazarus (1991a) employed the following reasoning. First, he assumed that the information-processing potential of animals and children has been underestimated, and that to the extent that these creatures are in fact capable of making appraisals (although perhaps relatively undeveloped or instinctive ones), they can also experience genuine emotion; and second, he supposed that some of the events taken to be emotional are not in fact *real* emotions, but just 'expressive behaviour', which therefore does not require appraisal (see, for example, p. 181). Since we have no independent criterion of what counts as emotion, except that it must, according to

Lazarus's definition, depend upon prior appraisal, such an argument is easy to sustain. If it is real emotion, there must have been appraisal even if we did not realize it. If there is no appraisal then it cannot be an emotion, according to the definition.

In fact, Lazarus's formulation of the appraisal–emotion connection goes beyond this apparently circular definition. Lazarus's idea of emotion, like the common-sense definition proposed in the previous chapter, only specifies a cognitive-evaluative *content* to emotion, rather than making any direct claim about how this content arises. Emotion, as I have also suggested, implies certain characteristic evaluations, but this does not in itself necessarily mean that the evaluations are real-time processes preceding the emotion. It is this second claim about process that makes Lazarus's appraisal theory an empirical theory. According to Lazarus, appraisal is the real-time intrapsychic process whereby personal significance is apprehended, and this process always occurs before emotion arises.

In the next section of the chapter, I try to unpack the substantive content of appraisal theory by asking what actually goes on when appraisal takes place. Exactly what kind of process is assumed to take place before emotion occurs? Lazarus's later writings (e.g. 1991b) provide some clues about possible answers to this question.

The process of appraisal

What happens when an individual is supposedly appraising a situation prior to getting emotional about it? Appraisal theory, surprisingly, is usually almost completely silent on the issue of process (Scherer, 1993). The questions that those about to experience an emotion supposedly ask themselves are in no sense asked in a conscious, or even stage-wise, manner. Rather, they are merely the abstract representation of the conclusions a person logically needs to reach in order to be considered 'emotional'. How the path from cold, non-emotional cognition to hot, appraisal-drenched emotion is actually negotiated is largely uncharted territory, but it seems likely that a range of possible mediators and mechanisms may be brought into play in connection with any instance of a given range of emotional reactions. In other words, there may be several possible alternative routes to an emotional conclusion of any particular variety.

Lazarus (1991b; Lazarus and Smith, 1988) tightened his definition of appraisal by contrasting it with a related cognitive factor, that of knowledge. Essentially, Lazarus claimed that both kinds of cognition are implicated in the causation of emotion, but it is appraisal that provides the direct and proximate cause of emotion. His distinction ran as follows:

> *Knowledge* consists of what a person believes about the way the world works in general and in a specific context . . . *Appraisal*, on the other hand, is an evaluation of the significance of knowledge about what is happening for our personal well-being. Only the recognition that we have something to gain or

lose, that is, that the outcome of a transaction is relevant to goals and well-being, generates an emotion.

(p. 354)

According to this account, knowledge reflects the basic categorization of the situation, whereas appraisal refers to an evaluation and interpretation of the situation's personal impact. Although it remains an open question to what extent we categorize and internally represent situations independently of our judgements of their personal significance, there is at least a possible logical distinction between these two processes. Two things seem to distinguish appraisal from knowledge: first, appraisal reflects *personally significant* considerations rather than cold facts about the world; second, appraisal directly produces emotion whereas knowledge can only ever be a distal cause.

In fact, these two suggested criteria reduce to one. Since emotion is defined by Lazarus as an apprehension of personal significance, to say that appraisal is directed at personal significance simply means that it is linked to emotion, so criterion 1 is simply a more limited aspect of criterion 2. In other words, all Lazarus seems to be saying about the distinction between appraisal and knowledge is that the former is whatever directly produces emotion, or leads to the recognition of personal significance that defines emotion. Unfortunately, such a circular formulation makes it near impossible to evaluate the claim that appraisal is a necessary and sufficient condition of emotion.

Having attempted to define appraisal on the basis of content, Lazarus (1991b) further clarified the concept by detailing the kinds of cognitive process that it might involve. According to Lazarus, the appraisal process may be automatic or deliberate (e.g. Kihlstrom, 1987), direct or mediated (e.g. Baron and Boudreau, 1987), tacit or explicit (e.g. Polanyi, 1958), developmentally primitive or advanced (e.g. Werner, 1956), syncretic or analytic, schematic or conceptual (e.g. Leventhal, 1984), subcortical or neocortical, repressed or manifest (e.g. Freud, 1900), inarticulate or articulate, and so on, and it will still be appraisal. In other words, appraisal need not be conscious (but it may be), need not be abstract (but it may be), need not imply a mediational process (but might), and so on. In fact, Lazarus seemed to be saying that you need a very wide category of cognition in order to understand appraisal as a cognitive process. The breadth of Lazarus's category of possible appraisal processes makes his supposedly empirical claim that emotion is necessarily preceded by appraisal extremely difficult to disconfirm.

Lazarus argued quite sensibly that if there are several different forms of appraisal, it becomes more likely that at least one of them will precede any emotional experience:

> If . . . one takes seriously that there is more than one kind of cognitive activity in emotion, the automatic and the deliberate, one would no longer need to equate cognitive processing with the relatively slow, progressive, stepwise generation of meaning from meaningless stimulus bits, or with the deliberate, volitional, and conscious reasoning that is often found in the garden variety of emotion processes, but would recognize that emotional meanings can be

generated in more than one way. I believe this possibility strengthens my position that appraisal is a necessary and sufficient condition for emotion.

(p. 359)

Clearly, Lazarus's references to appraisal are not intended to refer to any specific cognitive process. Instead, Lazarus is defining appraisal in terms of content or meaning. Any of a range of cognitive and perceptual processes might lead to a conclusion that counts as an appraisal in Lazarus's terms, as long as it results in the apprehension of personal (i.e., emotional) significance.

In many ways, the differences between Lazarus's position and the view developed in this chapter are merely semantic. I have argued that appraisal is a defining criterion for recognizing emotion, whereas Lazarus argues that appraisal is a necessary and sufficient condition that must be met before emotion occurs. However, Lazarus is not saying that any *specific* appraisal process needs to take place before emotion can occur, but rather that any of a variety of routes might be taken to the conclusion that an event is of personal significance. The real substantive difference between our approaches, however, is that I want to claim that emotion is not always a passive recognition of the emotional power of a situation; rather, sometimes emotion is an active strategy for conveying an appraisal claim about what is going on. Emotions are not necessarily simply *reactions* to events or interpretations of events. Furthermore, I do not think that a full explanation for claims about the personal significance of some object or event can be provided simply by reference to processes going on inside an individual's head, however these processes are conceived.

APPRAISAL AS A CONSEQUENCE OF EMOTION

The theory and research discussed so far in this chapter is based on the assumption that appraisal is the natural starting point of an emotional episode and functions as a cause of the emotional experience itself. However, common sense would also suggest that there is a reverse causal relationship between emotion and appraisal, with emotion influencing judgement rather than vice versa. Popular wisdom holds that affective state is reflected in the way that the world is perceived and the way that we respond to it ('smile and the world smiles with you'). Similarly, a range of psychological evidence suggests that moods of various kinds influence perception, interpretation, and evaluation (e.g. Forgas, 1992; Isen, 1987). It seems likely that similar effects occur with emotions as well as moods (e.g. Ellsworth, 1991).

Common sense would suggest that being in a good mood makes the world look better, and being in a bad mood makes it worse. This general tendency of affect to push thinking into line with its general evaluative tone is termed the *mood-congruence* effect. An illustration of a mood-congruence effect on judgement is provided by Johnson and Tversky's (1983) study, in which it was found that bad moods brought on by reading about various disasters left subjects thinking that other kinds of disaster were more likely, and more likely to happen to them in particular. So, after reading the latest upsetting news in the paper, you may be put into a generally unpleasant affective state which leads you to over-estimate the chances of bad things happening, including accidents to yourself or getting a serious illness. Note that the judgemental effects are not limited to the cause of the mood-state but also generalize to other aspects of the current situation.

One possible reason for mood-congruence effects concerns the way that mood may activate related material in memory (Bower, 1981). According to this affect-priming model, a positive mood triggers off chains of pleasant associations which set the conscious context for any judgement. Support for this view was obtained in an experiment by Forgas and Bower (1987) concerning the effects of mood on impression formation. In this study, mood congruence caused partici-pants in a pleasant mood to generate more positive, and subjects in an unpleasant mood more negative, judgements of a fictional target person. Evidence con-cerning the processes underlying this effect was provided by response latencies to the computer-presented information about the target. It was found that positive-mood participants spent longer reading positive than negative statements before making their judgements, suggesting that the material was being linked to material primed in memory by the positive mood. However, when it came to the decision task, positive-mood participants made their mood-consistent judge-ments quicker, suggesting that they were able to access the relevant mood-congruent information more easily when in a corresponding affective state.

Most of the evidence concerning the effects of mood on judgement relate to general evaluative effects. Emotions are cognitively more complex than moods and carry interpretative implications about specific intentional objects, sug-gesting that any effects that they might have on cognition would be more focused, and perhaps restricted to their salient object. In fact, there has been little research into how emotions might impact on interpretation and evaluation, but an exploratory study by Keltner, Ellsworth, and Edwards (1993) found that anger, induced by imagining being unfairly awarded a low examination grade, tended to increase the likelihood with which unrelated events were judged to be caused by a human rather than situational agency. Clearly, it is worth pursuing the idea that emotions may have general effects on appraisal that are not just limited to the original object of the emotion (Ellsworth, 1991).

CAUSAL PRIORITY OF APPRAISAL AND EMOTION

According to Lazarus's (1991b) theory, too, appraisal plays the role of effect as well as cause of emotion. Not only did Lazarus refrain from specifying the exact nature of the appraisal process, but also he refused to restrict its function in the emotional process to a single unidirectional causal role. According to Lazarus (1991b), the relationship of appraisal and emotion goes both ways: 'The functional relationships between cognition and emotion are bidirectional' (p. 352).

Lazarus's apparently definitive statement about appraisal as the complete and direct cause of any emotion becomes less clear when he discusses the ongoing relationships between the two sets of processes: only if we treat emotion as an 'effect or dependent variable' is appraisal its necessary and sufficient condition. On the other hand, treating emotion as a 'cause or independent variable', it influences cognition: 'How we view the direction depends on where in the psychological process one chooses to stop the action to identify the variables that precede or follow each other' (p. 353). In other words, at any given time we may be able to tease out an appraisal that will subsequently lead to emotion, but this appraisal may easily have been caused immediately before by emotion anyway. Because this transaction between appraisal and emotion is constantly ongoing, Lazarus's apparently definite statement about appraisal's causal role now becomes somewhat arbitrary. We can see appraisal as a cause of emotion, but only if we choose to start with appraisal.

Furthermore, the emotion that the appraisal is supposed to produce is not seen as a separate, theoretically intact entity anyway:

> Emotion is a superordinate concept that includes cognition, which is its cause in a part-whole sense. Cognitive activity, A, about the significance of the person's beneficial or harmful relationships with the environment, is combined in an emotion with physiological reactions and action tendencies, B, to form a complex emotional configuration, AB.
>
> (p. 353)

So, not only is the causal sequence arbitrary, but also the separation of the two phenomena is not complete. In short, Lazarus's claim that appraisal causes emotion really means that appraisal continues as emotion occurs and is part of that emotion. In other words: 'We are simply saying that what has happened earlier affects everything afterward, including the appraisal process that follows and the emotional state it produces, in a complex causal time series' (p. 354).

Lazarus's conclusion, then, is that appraisal is the cause of emotion but also continues into its effect: although it is hard to know where the emotion is actually supposed to start in time, whenever it does, it must always be preceded by an appraisal. In explaining emotion this way, by direct and complete reliance on the concept of appraisal, Lazarus forces psychological analysis back one step and encourages us to ask the more fundamental question: 'What causes appraisal?' The apparent answer is one or more of the following: (a) appraisal causes appraisal – it just goes on all the time; (b) emotion causes appraisal, according to the principle of bidirectional causation; or (c) real-life encounters cause appraisals, in which case we are still left with the original question of how particular real-life situations lead to particular emotional appraisals, which is in essence exactly the same as asking how events cause emotions – the starting issue for a causal theory of emotion in the first place. In short, such an account of the emotion process does not seem to get us very far with our explanation.

Lazarus was perfectly aware that there is a way of reading his theory that makes it appear empirically empty:

> To say that emotion influences cognition, which is also its cause, seems at first

to be a meaningless tautology, particularly if we do not specify very clearly what the emotion includes or does not include and the thoughts or feelings it causes.

(p. 353).

Unfortunately, Lazarus fails to provide a workable operationalism for the concepts of appraisal and emotion.

To summarize Lazarus's theory, 'appraisal' is the 'cause' of 'emotion', as long as we define 'emotion' as a recognition of personal significance, and 'appraisal' as a process whereby personal significance is recognized, and if we also accept that 'causation' is actually only a simplification of the real empirical relations involved between appraisal and emotion processes.

APPRAISAL IN CONTEXT

My argument in this chapter is not intended to lead to the conclusion that appraisal is a redundant concept, only that it needs to be used more carefully, without making grand claims about its centrality to emotion. The main problem with appraisal theory is that it encourages an individualistic view of emotion based on representations rather than reality. The concept needs to take its place in the real world among the various other related factors that feed into the emotion process, at different times and on different occasions. Much of the remainder of this book will consist of an attempt to find a more realistic context for appraisal.

To recapitulate, despite my criticisms, I do believe that appraisal is an important principle in the understanding of individual emotions. No one would want to argue with the conclusion that evaluations of the situation are a central aspect of what we normally mean by emotional experience, nor with the fact that under some circumstances our judgements about the personal significance of a situation can lead to emotion. However, this does not necessarily mean that appraisal is the sole determining cause of emotion, nor that emotion is always caused by appraisal. Given the way that Lazarus defined appraisal and emotion, it is hard to separate the two concepts in practice, and thus the empirical problem of explaining emotion is never entirely solved by his theory, only translated into the equally difficult problem of explaining appraisal.

If we want to develop our understanding of what happens when someone gets emotional, it is not very helpful to rely on a concept whose central defining characteristic seems to be that it leads to emotion. To attain empirical content, appraisal theory needs to be more specific about what appraisals actually consist of, and how they interact with other causal factors.

THE REAL ROLE OF APPRAISAL IN EMOTION

In this chapter I have argued that appraisal should be seen as a central criterion for defining someone as emotional rather than as an empirical factor contingently associated with the process of getting emotional. I have also suggested that appraisals should be viewed in more interpersonal terms. Dimensions of appraisal research has been useful in cataloguing the various evaluations and interpretations that help people to differentiate abstract emotional meanings, but it is necessary to explore the ways in which these meanings are applied in everyday contexts. My view of how appraisals are actually deployed is based on the idea that emotions are communicative rather than reactive. I believe that appraisal theory provides a good way of characterizing the message content of conventionally defined emotional positions. (However, whether these conventional emotional positions exhaust the possible range of emotions is another question; Averill and Nunley, 1992). For example, getting angry with someone is a way of conveying blame (secondary appraisal), and of showing that you care about what you are blaming the person for (primary appraisal). More generally, getting emotional is a way of showing and telling someone: *'this matters to me'*. This does not mean that deciding that something matters to you causes emotion because sometimes the emotional position makes the something matter rather than vice versa. Often, emotion is adopted as a way of endorsing culturally and institutionally specified values, and of accepting society's view of what really should matter (see Chapter 8).

In summary, appraisal may be seen as an interpersonal demarcation criterion distinguishing emotion from non-emotion (and distinguishing different conventionally defined emotions from one another). In order to make a claim emotionally and to show that it matters, involvement typically has to be expressed in more than words. Claiming that something matters to you implies that you are willing to act on the expressed concern. Emotions, therefore, are often indications of predispositions for engaging in certain directed forms of behaviour concordant with the content of the appraisal. Psychological research into these actions and action tendencies associated with emotion are discussed in the following chapter.

3 The action factor

OVERVIEW

Appraisal theory as reviewed in the previous chapter assumes that emotions serve specific motivational concerns which are activated by cognitive-evaluative processes. The point of appraisal, according to this view, is to determine priorities for adaptive action. In the present chapter, I turn to these motivational aspects of emotion and look at the ways that emotion has been seen as affecting action, as well as the ways that action might affect emotion. Emotion is not usually thought to lead directly to specific action but rather to put the individual in a state of readiness for focused behaviour that is appropriate to the adaptational agenda activated by appraisal. For example, anger seems to involve a felt urge to hit out at someone, either literally or metaphorically, which may be expressed in a variety of different behaviours, or alternatively may be held back. In this chapter I consider the evidence that different emotions are characterized by different patterns of action readiness and discuss the possible links between action readiness and appraisal. Action variables can be causes as well as consequences of emotion, and in the final section of the chapter, I look at some of the ways that emotions might result from the successful or unsuccessful implementation of behavioural intentions.

COMMON-SENSE IDEAS ABOUT ACTION AND EMOTION

The association between emotion and action implied in common sense is not a straightforward one. To the extent that we think of emotions as private experiences that nobody else can completely share, it seems that emotion and action have little relation. However, we also imagine emotions to exert a kind of pressure on us to vent our feelings. Emotions in some sense seem to want to get out and find expression in action. To illustrate this intuitive idea of emotion, Lakoff and Kövecses (1987) analysed some of the metaphors that we use when talking about anger. One of the basic narratives underlying many of these linguistic expressions compares the anger experience to what happens when heat is applied to liquid in a sealed container. As more heat is applied, the pressure increases until ultimately there is some outlet or explosion. For example, you get *het up* or *simmer* with anger, you may try to *bottle it up* but you need to *let off steam*, and if you don't you may *flip your lid* or *blow your top*. Thus, we seem to think of anger as something inside struggling to escape, that we can either restrain or unleash (rather like a wild animal, as suggested by a second common metaphor also discussed by Lakoff and Kövecses).

To take another perspective on the intuitively indeterminate relation of action and emotion: on the one hand, we assume that certain actions are performed 'in the heat of the moment' and arise rather directly and impulsively from our emotions, such as when we hit out wildly at somebody or something out of anger. Because the relationship between intense emotion and action is seen as almost automatic under these circumstances, we sometimes use our emotion as an excuse for what we have done, saying perhaps that we could not stop ourselves, or were not thinking straight. In accordance with such ideas, sentencing in felony cases is often less severe when the violent action in question is unpremeditated and can be interpreted as a crime of passion. On the other hand, such outbursts are often seen as failures of self-control, and people tend to believe that it is possible to experience emotion up to a certain level without acting on it at all. You can keep it all inside. However, the restraint that this is thought to require is still an indication of the same general idea that emotions involve an impulse to action of some kind, whether or not this impulse actually finds direct expression.

Of course, the above intuitive analysis works better for some emotions than others. Certain kinds of sadness or grief are thought to be contemplative and quiet rather than energetic and active. These emotions seem to make us want to refrain from, rather than engage in, action. As a general rule, we might argue that common sense sees emotion as provoking an urge to *change* the way that we are behaving (cf. Frijda, 1986). In inner-directed emotion, this often means stopping what we are doing; in more outward emotions this typically means that we feel an impulse to engage in focused activity of some kind.

In summary, many emotions are commonly thought to contain the impulse to act (or refrain from acting) in certain ways appropriate to the quality of the particular experience. When angry, you may feel a strong urge to hit out at someone in some way; when in love, you may wish to seek out the company of your loved one and get as close to them as you possibly can; and when you are afraid, you may experience the desire to run away, literally or metaphorically. Correspondingly, when sad, you may want to withdraw from social contact and be quiet or to talk things over with a close confidant who will just listen.

APPRAISAL THEORY AND ACTION TENDENCIES

The common-sense connection between emotion and action readiness also has a place in more formal theories. This link was emphasized especially by Arnold (1960) who defined emotion as 'the felt tendency toward anything intuitively appraised as good (beneficial), or away from anything intuitively appraised as bad (harmful)' (p. 182). Such a view suggests a close relationship between evaluative appraisals of liking and disliking, the urge to approach or withdraw from whatever is appraised in these terms, and pleasant or unpleasant feelings about this object. Appraisal, action tendency, and emotion are seen as all of a piece.

More recent theories have similarly considered action tendencies to be important aspects of emotion, but without restricting their content to a single approach-withdrawal dimension. Frijda (1986), for example, assumed that different emotions can be distinguished according to the specific changes in action readiness that they bring about. Likewise, Lazarus (1991a) argued that each emotion is represented by a core relational theme summarizing the key *motivational* concerns implicated whenever that emotion occurs. Anger, for example, is said to be characterized by the theme of a *'demeaning offence against me or mine'* (p. 222) leading directly to a tendency towards attack or retaliation. In addition, according to Lazarus's theory, anger and other emotions may result in attempts at *coping* with the situation or with the emotion itself, which may also involve action of some kind. In this section of the chapter, I will consider some of the available evidence for these views about the impact of emotion on action and action readiness.

According to most versions of appraisal theory, the connection between emotion and impulses to action is determined by evolution. In this view, different emotions serve different survival-related goals and therefore prepare the individual for adaptive behavioural response to the current situation. Emotions, therefore, should be seen as inherently motivational states, serving particular functions which are thought to be defined by natural selection. For example, the evolutionary goal of anger might be to protect oneself from antagonists, so the angry state prepares the organism for aggression and retaliation. Similarly, fear has obvious survival relevance in preparing for rapid escape from a dangerous situation.

The survival implications of emotions such as happiness, embarrassment, sadness, and so on, however, are a little harder to determine. It may be that the behaviours associated with these emotions serve interpersonal or cultural rather than evolutionary functions. For example, we may get embarrassed to distance ourselves from a potential negative evaluation in public, and the urge to hide or become inconspicuous at such times may reflect the socially produced need to avoid being a focus of other people's attention (cf. Modigliani, 1971).

In summary, the general implication of the motivational view of emotion implied by appraisal theory is that different emotions are characterized by different states of action readiness. For example, anger is a state that impels the individual towards attack, fear a condition associated with the urge to run away, and so on. Note that this appraisal account of emotion implies a relatively fixed sequence of response in which the emotional state is preceded by an appraisal of prevailing concerns and followed by an increased likelihood of acting in accordance with the conclusions of the appraisal. First we interpret the situation as problematic (or beneficial), and then we get ready to do something about it, just like in the common-sense view of rational action which moves from contemplation through intention to action. At any rate, where appraisal is usually considered as a cause of emotion or as part of its content (e.g. Lazarus, 1991b), action readiness is typically conceptualized either as emotional content (Arnold, 1960; Frijda, 1986) or as a consequence of emotion. Thus, although there is possible overlap between the two factors, appraisal in most cases is thought of as being causally and sequentially prior to the action factor.

Differentiation of emotional action tendencies

The specific associations of different emotions with action tendencies have been investigated in experiments by Frijda and his colleagues (e.g. Frijda, 1987). Like the dimensions of appraisal studies described in the previous chapter, this research has generally taken its data from people's ratings of remembered emotional experiences. In a representative study (Frijda *et al.*, 1989), participants were asked to recall a series of emotional experiences and to complete questionnaires detailing the extent to which various action tendencies had accompanied these experiences.

The investigators found that different emotions were recalled as being accompanied by distinctive patterns of action readiness as well as distinctive patterns of appraisal. For example, anger was rated as involving wanting to engage in action against someone or something (antagonism) together with excitement, and love was described as involving general excitement along with a desire to approach or make contact with someone. Other emotions were less tightly specified by action readiness but showed at least some relations with one or more of Frijda and colleagues' rating items (for a list of action-readiness dimensions and some of their emotional associations as suggested by Frijda and colleagues, see Table 3.1).

Frijda's action-readiness experiments share many of the interpretational problems of the dimensions of appraisal studies reviewed in the previous chapter. Since the experimental procedure involved participants' self-generating examples of the particular emotions, then it is very likely that the described experiences reflected their intuitive ideas about the characteristic features of the relevant emotional state. As well as implying distinctive appraisals, different emotion names tend to be implicitly linked with ideas about likely modes of action. Furthermore, appraisal and action readiness themselves have intuitive connections. Indeed, if we take appraisal to mean an evaluation that something is significant to the person in question (e.g. Lazarus, 1991a), then it would be surprising if the presence of an appraisal did not tend also to imply distinctive modes of action readiness. For example, if you care about someone's insult against you then you are likely to be predisposed to think badly of that person, to act against them in particular ways, and to characterize your reaction in angry terms. Thus any self-reported relationships obtained between emotions, appraisals, and modes of action readiness may be explained simply by reference to common-sense semantic connections between these three concepts rather than contingent empirical associations between three sets of separate real-world phenomena.

Table 3.1 Some action-readiness modes and associated emotions

Action-readiness mode	Definition	Associated emotions
Approach	Tendency to get closer	Desire, happiness, love
Being-with	Tendency to stay close	Enjoyment, confidence
Attending	Tendency to watch, or think about	Interest, energy
Excitement	Tendency towards undirected action	Restlessness, nerves
Exuberance	Generalized action readiness	Happiness, elation
Rest	Acceptance of absence of action readiness	Relaxation
Apathy	Generalized absence of action readiness	Depression, sadness
Passivity	Absence of goals for action	Disinterest
Inhibition	Action readiness in the absence of action	Fear, anxiety
Helplessness	Uncertainty about direction that action readiness should take	Desperation, confusion
Submission	Tendency to submit to control	Resignation, humility
Avoidance	Tendency to avoid, flee, or protect oneself	Fear, anxiety
Rejection	Tendency to reject or break contact	Disgust, gruffness
Antagonism	Tendency to remove obstacle, hurt, oppose, or resist	Anger, irritation
Dominance	Tendency to control	Distrust, arrogance
Interruption	Tendency to interrupt ongoing action	Shock, surprise

Source: adapted from Frijda (1986) and Frijda *et al.* (1989)

In short, it is not particularly surprising that our descriptions of emotions are linked to reports of wanting to do something or make something happen given that emotions, as commonly conceived, imply involved evaluative responses towards intentional objects. If we like what is happening then we are also likely to want to do what we can to keep it happening, and correspondingly if what is going on is evaluated unfavourably, we will probably want to do something about it. To a substantial extent, this is simply what liking and disliking mean in practice. Similarly, if we appraise something as dangerous to us, then this also implies that we would like to escape from it, and if we blame someone else for something, this strongly suggests that we think that person deserves punishment.

Another weakness of the questionnaire studies of action readiness in emotion concerns the operationalization of the specific action tendencies. Many of these do not conform to our intuitive idea of what it means to have an impulse to act in a certain way. For example, one of Frijda's action-tendency items depended on agreement with the statement 'I boiled inside', a description that supposedly reflected what happens when anger is held back or turned inwards. Clearly, self-report responses to such a question do not necessarily reflect states of action readiness, but may instead refer to bodily changes (see Chapter 4), or indeed emotional feelings of other kinds. In Frijda's (1986) theoretical view, all these aspects of emotion are directly interrelated: the experience of an emotion is based on the felt state of action readiness which may also manifest itself in physiological changes. Nevertheless, for the purposes of an experiment designed to demonstrate connections between different aspects of the emotion process, it still seems important to try to preserve conceptual distinctions between bodily change, emotional experience, and action readiness at least at an operational level. Similar arguments can be applied to the items 'I blushed, or was afraid to blush' and 'I cried, had to cry, or wanted to cry' (among others) which seem to cross the tenuous logical boundary between action and expression (see Chapter 5).

Other items used by Frijda and his colleagues are difficult to see as impulses to action simply because it is implausible that anyone could ever actually implement them. For example, the item 'I wanted to sink into the ground, disappear from the earth, not to be noticed by anyone' was found to be associated with the emotion of shame. The problem here is that it is very difficult to see this as a functional mode of action readiness since it is unlikely that anyone who is ashamed would ever really act in any of the ways suggested. What the item seems to be is a metaphoric representation of what it feels like when people are ashamed, rather than a reflection of a felt tendency towards action.

According to appraisal theory, emotions are relatively *flexible* strategies for dealing with functional (often survival-related) goals. If this is true, the tendencies towards action that each separate emotion includes necessarily reflect abstract themes rather than specific behaviours. For example, the state of fear is not considered to lead to a direct tendency to run away or else there would be no need for *emotional* mediation of the response; a simple reflex mechanism would serve the purpose more efficiently. Instead, fear is thought to be associated with a *general* motivation to do something to alleviate the fearful situation. Put in these broader terms, it becomes difficult to imagine what such a state of action readiness might consist of, in distinction from the emotional state itself. Indeed, Frijda (1986) essentially *defines* emotions in terms of felt changes in action readiness: '*Emotions . . . can be defined as modes of relational action readiness, either in the form of tendencies to establish, maintain, or disrupt a relationship with the environment, or in the form of mode of relational readiness as such*' (p. 71, emphasis in original). Clearly, if experimental participants share such a definition, even on an implicit level, the connections established between action readiness and emotion become self-evident.

To summarize this section, questionnaire studies of appraisal, emotion, and action readiness demonstrate that these three concepts, insofar as they can be independently operationalized, are still implicitly interlinked. When people talk about emotions, they are also usually talking about appraisal and about changes in modes of action readiness. With respect to distinctions between emotions, the experimental results seem to confirm that there is substantial continuity between ideas relating to certain modes of action readiness (conceived in broad terms) and ideas relating to specific emotion terms. As with the dimensions of appraisal research, the particular implicit content of distinct emotion categories is of general interest to researchers concerned with operationalizing measures or investigating representations of emotions, but tells us little about empirical relations between emotion and action (Russell, 1987).

Control precedence and personal significance

According to Frijda (1986; see also Arnold, 1960), the feeling of action readiness is one of the main factors that makes emotions emotional. Without the urge to engage in particular kinds of behaviour (or at least some change in action readiness), the person's mental state would be cold and rational, unmotivated. According to Frijda's theory, new emotional priorities for action are experienced as compelling and unchosen by the individual undergoing the emotion. The pressure to behave (or to stop behaving) in a certain way seems to come over the person, rather than reflecting a conscious decision or deliberate intention. Frijda calls this intuitively plausible idea *felt control precedence*, meaning that, when emotional, our change in action readiness is experienced as intrusive and interrupting, so that emotion seems to take the reins of behaviour away from reason.

It is interesting to compare Frijda's idea of emotions as characterized by felt control precedence of changes in action readiness with Lazarus's (1991b) notion that emotion necessarily implies appraisal of personal significance (see Chapter 2). The obvious difference is that the emphasis of the former account is placed on *motivational* aspects of emotion whereas that of the latter apparently lies on *cognitive* factors. However, both authors have explicitly acknowledged that emotions are both cognitive and motivational: Frijda suggested that changes in action readiness are based on appraisals and Lazarus argued that appraisals have direct and necessary motivational implications. In fact, the concept of felt control precedence can be seen as continuous with the idea of appraised personal significance. If we feel the urge to change our action priorities with respect to a situation, then it goes without saying that we care about it. On the other hand, caring about something (however intensely and personally) does not in itself necessarily imply that action readiness change comes over us in an unpremeditated way. Sometimes situations about which we care deeply are so familiar and so bound up with our conscious identities that our reactions come as deliberate and considered rather than spontaneous and overwhelming. For example, it is unlikely that an experienced surgeon undergoes serious emotion during every heart operation undertaken. This suggests that the condition of felt control precedence is more restrictive than that of personal significance *per se*. The advantage of Frijda's criterion for distinguishing emotion from non-emotion, then, is that it fleshes out and makes more precise the notion of emotional significance. However, this still only provides a plausible definition of emotion rather than a practical theory of how emotion works.

Emotions as signals for action

Another related theory that has implications for how emotions alter action readiness was proposed by Oatley and Johnson-Laird (1987). These authors suggested that emotions provide an evolutionary solution to the problem of adjusting to changing goal priorities in a complex environment. Because social and cultural animals like humans have to keep track of a wide variety of concerns simultaneously during everyday life, an adaptive system has developed to attune them to events that require attention, and to reset the cognitive system appropriately to cope with these events. Oatley and Johnson-Laird argued that there are five genetically programmed emotions (happiness, sadness, anxiety, anger, and disgust) which correspond to common occasions when goal priorities and action readiness modes need to be changed. Each of these emotional experiences is thought to provide a distinctive signal which automatically reconfigures attentional attunements and action tendencies. For example, you may be relaxing alone at home when you hear an unexpected noise. This may trigger the emotion of anxiety, which sets the system in a state prepared for escape or caution, and maintains attentional vigilance, along with all the associated physiological accompaniments. Similarly, anger is thought to be triggered by the frustration of a current intention, which sets information-processing mechanisms in a mode that prepares for aggression and active response.

Oatley and Johnson-Laird's theory suggests that emotions are triggered fairly directly by biologically relevant situations, and that the initiation of the emotion then has consequences for the interpretation and appraisal of what is going on. Thus, appraisal is seen as beginning before the emotion starts but as developing after the emotion has been initiated. In other words, appraisal is considered to be a consequence as well as cause of emotion (Ellsworth, 1991; Frijda, 1993; Parkinson and Manstead, 1992).

Like Frijda (1986), Oatley and Johnson-Laird also saw emotions as involving changes in action readiness. However, according to the latter model, the emotion itself is something quite distinct from the action tendency and something that definitely precedes it in time. Indeed, one of the *functions* of the emotion signal is to change action readiness. However, a second possible relation between emotion and action suggested by the theory works in the reverse direction, with interruptions in ongoing action plans providing many of the occasions for elicitation of basic emotions (cf. Mandler, 1984; see pp. 82–4), so action feeds into emotion as well as resulting from it.

One of the advantages of Oatley and Johnson-Laird's theory is that it provides an analysis of *interpersonal* emotions which is a direct extension of the intrapsychic account. According to the model, emotions serve as messages informing the cognitive system about the adaptational priorities implied by the prevailing situation. Similarly, one person's emotional display may inform other people about the potential significance of what is happening (see Oatley, 1992). For example, in a meeting with your boss you may pick up facial expressions of anger from one of your colleagues which attune you to any potentially insulting content in what is being said. Thus, an emotion signal can also reset the cognitive processing of other people present. The exact mechanism for such effects is not discussed explicitly by Oatley and Johnson-Laird but certainly opens up interesting research questions about emotional contagion (e.g. Hatfield *et al.*, 1992).

Unconsidered in the model, however, is the way in which such an emotional display might impact on the emotion and information-processing of an antagonist rather than peer, for example the boss in the example above, who presumably would also adjust her presentation in response to any detected anger, one way or another. In Chapter 7, I consider these aspects of interpersonal emotion more directly.

ACTION AND THE COMMUNICATIVE MODEL OF EMOTION

In the previous chapter, I suggested that emotions are often adopted to convey appraisals to other people rather than being directly determined by these appraisals in real time. In these communicative cases too, it seems possible that actions of certain kinds would be involved. When people are delivering appraisal messages about evaluative objects that *matter* to them, they are also highly likely to express commitment to engage in certain kinds of action with respect to those objects. The extent of their avowed involvement in the emotional concern determines the degree of this commitment.

For example, if someone is making the angry claim that someone else is to blame for something seriously bad that has happened, then the personal significance of this concern, the extent to which it matters to the person who is angry, will be communicated in their apparent willingness to act in order to seek reparation from the transgressor. Indeed, this readiness to act in accordance with the appraisal claim made by the emotion may be physically communicated to others in a characteristic antagonistic posture with clenched fists (see Chapter 5). This stance can be seen both as expressive of the emotion and appraisal and as an early stage in a mutually definable action sequence (cf. Mead, 1934). In any case, action readiness may be intimately related to the *message content* of the emotion. According to this analysis the distinction between action and expression in emotion becomes an increasingly blurred one (see Chapter 5). Actions as well as expressions *both* communicate *and* are directed towards instrumental ends.

Verbal action tendencies

As another example of how communication and action shade into one another in emotion, it is worth considering a category of behaviour to which emotion researchers have paid a surprisingly small amount of attention: that of *verbal* action in conversation. Obviously, one of the ways in which you can perform an interpersonal action is by saying something to someone else, and by moving your vocal chords rather than another part of your voluntary musculature. Thus, spoken words clearly belong within the conceptual category of action (e.g. Austin, 1962), even if they are not always recognized in these terms. For example, anger may involve a tendency to hit out at someone either using your fists or by saying something hurtful to them. It seems, therefore, that emotions are associated with tendencies to speak as well as to move in certain distinctive ways.

Treating conversation as action makes the distinction between appraisal and action readiness even less clear-cut. Feeling the urge to make a certain kind of remark to someone is very close to what we mean by appraisal. The semantic distance between evaluating the situation as one in which problem-focused coping potential is low and feeling the urge to express helplessness, for instance, is not very great. Indeed, many of the questionnaire items used to measure 'core relational themes' supposedly summarizing the appraisal structure of emotions (Smith and Lazarus, 1993) actually correspond very closely to the kinds of things that a person might actually say to someone else when emotional (see Chapter 10). When saying these things, the person is not simply characterizing their state of mind or intrapsychic evaluative stance relative to the emotional object, but rather they are acting to influence their audience in some way. Saying that you are helpless is not simply describing an appraisal but making an appeal for help or support (e.g. Coyne, 1976), or at least defining yourself to another person as needing help. To put this another way, making an appraisal claim is itself an emotional action (see Box 3.1).

BOX 3.1: EMOTION, APPRAISAL, ACTION TENDENCY AS OVERLAPPING SETS

Some of the following questionnaire items are designed to assess appraisal dimensions, some are intended to evaluate states of action readiness, and some are supposed to measure emotions. Can *you* tell which are which? (Answers at foot of box.)

1 I don't see anything I can do to improve this bad situation.

2 I feel helpless.

3 I wanted to do something but I did not know what, I was helpless.

4 I shut myself off from the surroundings.

5 Things going on did not involve me, I did not pay attention.

6 This situation is totally irrelevant to my concerns.

7 Interested.

8 I stood above the situation, I felt I was in command, I held the ropes.

9 I feel powerful.

10 I boiled inside.

11 I was excited, restless, could not sit still.

12 I feel that things are going to get better in this situation.

13 If I try hard enough, I can get what I want in this situation.

14 Hopeful.

1. Appraisal; 2. Appraisal; 3. Action readiness; 4. Action readiness; 5. Action readiness; 6. Appraisal; 7. Emotion; 8. Action readiness; 9. Appraisal; 10. Action readiness; 11. Action readiness; 12. Appraisal; 13. Appraisal; 14. Emotion. All appraisal items are taken from Smith and Lazarus (1993) except 9 which is from Roseman *et al.* (1990). All action-readiness items come from Frijda *et al.* (1989). Emotion items are from Smith and Lazarus (1993).

Conversely, as suggested above, when we engage in physical actions, this too has a message content for others, so actions as well as statements can convey appraisals. For example, think of a parent spanking a preverbal child as a way of showing and telling them that what they are doing is wrong. The physical action can be used to give emotional emphasis to a message even when delivered in conjunction with words. Thus, in reality, emotion, appraisal, and action are intimately interrelated.

EFFECTS OF MOOD ON BEHAVIOUR

Apart from the self-report studies considered earlier, there is little direct evidence available concerning the relation between emotion and changes in action readiness, let alone the felt control precedence of these changes. As for research into the actual consequences of emotion for action, it is virtually non-existent (but see Berkowitz, 1993, for findings relevant to aggressive behaviour). However, as with the question of how emotion influences appraisal, potentially relevant data concerning this issue are available from the mood literature.

A range of studies have investigated how being in either a good or a bad mood can make a difference to the way that people respond to social situations. One of the most consistent findings in this area is of a mood-congruence effect, which occurs when affect tends to influence judgement and behaviour in a direction concordant with its valence. In other words, people in good moods tend to think and act in a positive manner, whereas people in bad moods tend to think and act more negatively and pessimistically.

For example, it has been found that people in a good mood generally seem more likely to act in a helpful way towards other people. In an early study, Isen and Levin (1972) found that subjects who found a dime in the coin-return tray of a telephone kiosk were subsequently more likely to assist a stranger who had dropped a pile of papers in their vicinity. The fact that such a low-value positive event had reliable effects on action confirms the power of the impact of pleasant mood.

Explanations for mood-congruence effects usually suggest that affective states influence the retrieval of information from semantic memory, making evaluatively related material more accessible (e.g. Bower, 1981; Isen, 1987; see Schwarz and Clore, 1983 for an alternative mechanism). However, people do not always respond to affective states in ways that are directly congruent with mood, suggesting that other less automatic processes may also play their part in determining the influence of affect on behaviour.

For example, more recent research suggests that there are limits to the extent to which a person in a good mood will help someone else. Specifically, it has been found that if helping is likely to detract from good mood, then people are less predisposed to do it. In Isen and Simmonds' (1978) study, for example, good moods increased the chances of participants helping someone by reading statements that they were told would improve their mood, but *decreased* the likelihood of them agreeing to read similar statements described as inducing bad mood. The probable reason for this result is that people experiencing pleasant affect typically want to keep their good mood going, and so engage in *mood-maintenance* and *mood-protection* strategies (Clark and Isen, 1982; Isen, 1984). In this view, helping is more likely if it improves or does not interfere with current good mood, but may be avoided if there is a chance that mood will worsen as a consequence.

In order to explain the findings concerning the impact of positive mood on behaviour, then, it seems to be necessary to postulate the existence of two kinds of process, one exerting a direct effect on judgement and behaviour in accordance with mood congruence, and the second arising from people's deliberate responses to their perceived mood-states. In other words, people are not simply passive recipients of their affect, but make attempts actively to adjust and control them (e.g. Parrott, 1993; Salovey *et al.*, 1993).

The effects of *unpleasant* mood on behaviour also seem to be mediated by both controlled as well as automatic processes (cf. Shiffrin and Schneider, 1977). Negative affect has been found to distort thinking in a mood-congruent manner and at the same time to encourage people to try to *improve* their mood by doing things that will make them feel better (*mood-repair strategies*, Clark and Isen, 1982). Thus, although unpleasant mood can intensify aggressive behaviour towards other people (e.g. Berkowitz and Turner, 1974), it also increases helping in certain circumstances (Isen, Horn, and Rosenhan, 1973). Sometimes mood-repair and mood-congruence pressures seem to cancel each other out and unpleasant mood fails to affect behaviour at all, even though the corresponding pleasant mood seems to make a big difference (e.g. Isen, 1970). In summary, the evidence suggests that when people are able to counteract the mood-congruent effects of bad mood on behaviour, they will often do so.

As an example of how mood-repair strategies might work in practice, Forgas (1991) allowed people in different mood-states to choose partners both for themselves and for another subject for the purposes of a decision-making task. Forgas found that subjects who had watched a sad movie selected a socially rewarding partner in preference to a task-competent partner. This choice appeared to be specifically intended as a mood-improvement strategy, because a similar selection bias did not occur when participants were asked to choose a partner for someone other than themselves.

The mood literature suggests that affect can influence behaviour in at least two ways: one a direct and spontaneous way reflected in simple mood-congruence effects, and the other mediated by more deliberate attempts to deal with the affect-inducing situation or the affect itself. In short, emotions and moods imply impulses to actions and secondarily make us want to deal with the situation we are in.

Another important conclusion from these findings is that affect not only influences behaviour towards the specific object that caused the affect, but also exerts more general effects on action (Berkowitz, 1993). For example, feelings about finding a coin in a phone-box (Isen and Levin, 1972) had demonstrable effects on actions towards someone who clearly had nothing to do with this piece of good luck. Similarly, it may be that getting emotional about something in particular leads to modes of action readiness that are directed at objects other than those at which appraisal was originally directed.

SECONDARY EFFECTS OF EMOTION ON ACTION

The insight derived from mood studies that affect can have direct as well as indirect influences on action is also applicable to the area of emotion. In previous sections, I have considered how emotions change priorities for action due to their intrinsic content. However, it also seems likely that awareness of emotional state can lead to active attempts to improve it in some way.

Lazarus (1991a) distinguished some of the different ways in which emotions might have consequences for action. First, he argued that certain emotional states may be accompanied by biologically provided action tendencies which automatically lead to urges for flight in fear or fight in anger, for example.

Second, Lazarus suggested that appraisal of the emotion-provoking situation can lead to actions undertaken deliberately to deal with the difficulty or challenge it presents (*problem-focused coping*). Such actions arise not from the emotion itself but from the appraised demands of the situation, for example, when we try to avert an impending catastrophe. Successful *anticipatory* problem-focused coping may even circumvent the experience of emotion, since the stressor may be effectively dealt with before it exerts any influence on appraisal. More commonly, problem-focused coping probably arises in tandem with the development of the emotion.

The third kind of action implied in Lazarus's analysis is based on his idea of *emotion-focused coping*. Lazarus suggested that when individuals appraise their capacity for dealing directly with a stressful event as inadequate (low problem-focused coping potential), they may redirect their efforts to working on the emotion itself. For example, when depressed about a concern that will not go away, people may try to distract themselves by engaging in displacement activities (e.g. Rippere, 1979). Although Lazarus saw emotion-focused coping as a mainly cognitive process, it is clear that there are also ways of trying to change emotions that involve more than simply intrapsychic activity (e.g. drinking in order to forget). Emotion-focused coping therefore suggests one way in which people might act in response to a perceived emotion in distinction to simply acting emotionally.

More generally, people do not just experience emotions about situations but they also have feelings about, and attitudes towards, their emotions themselves (Mayer and Gaschke, 1988; Mills, 1993; Sommers, 1984). These secondary affective states may motivate actions designed to adjust or improve the primary emotion. For example, anger may be directly associated with the urge to hit out at someone, but also may in some people lead to actions intended to reduce the anger itself, such as counting to ten (Tavris, 1984), or engaging in vigorous exercise in an attempt to dispense with the energy non-aggressively. These strategies arise because many people have also been taught that anger is a bad or socially inappropriate thing to feel (Stearns and Stearns, 1986). The topic of emotion regulation will be considered in more detail later in the book. For now, the general point is simply that emotion and action are related in many different interrelated ways, and more research is needed to untangle their intricate mutual influences.

ACTION AS A CAUSE OF EMOTION

The discussion so far has focused on the role of action and action readiness as a consequence of emotion, or as part of the content of emotional experience. However, connections between action and emotion work in both directions, with action-related factors leading to emotions as well as vice versa.

In common sense, emotions are often considered to be closely related to goals, plans, and intentions. When we are frustrated in our attempts to attain something we want (or avoid something we do not want) this is usually an unpleasant emotional experience, and when we are successful in attaining our ends, we tend to feel good about it. Similarly, a wide range of psychological theories have proposed that success and failure in personal projects are occasions for emotional experience (e.g. Carver and Scheier, 1990; Lazarus, 1991a; Mandler, 1984; Weiner, 1985). There is a large area of overlap between many of these accounts, and in this section I will focus on the basic ideas rather than the detail of the theories.

Goal attainment and emotion

There is a general consensus among many psychological theories that emotions can be dependent on completion of plans and progress towards goals. One particular version of this proposal has been developed by Carver and Scheier (1990), who argued that affect does not depend directly on the proximity of goals, but rather on the *speed* with which the individual is approaching them. Specifically, Carver and Scheier suggested that positive emotions occur when the individual is moving faster towards a goal than anticipated, and negative emotions arise when the rate of progress is slower than expected. This proposal implies the existence of certain intrapsychic monitoring machinery whose operation Carver and Scheier attempted to spell out in detail.

Carver and Scheier saw the cognitive system in cybernetic terms, organized as a hierarchy of negative feedback loops. Each feedback loop serves a specific goal, and the purpose of the loop is to reduce the discrepancy between the actual state of the organism and the ideal state represented in the goal. For example, if the goal is to reach a certain geographical destination, then progress is monitored by cognitively comparing current position with intended end position. In more concrete terms, you might look at a map to see how far you have travelled on your journey. According to Carver and Scheier, simply being a long way from where you are going is not sufficient in itself to produce an emotional response; rather, it is only when you are nearer or further away than anticipated, given the time that has passed, that you experience frustration or elation.

In other words, Carver and Scheier proposed that superimposed upon each simple feedback loop which directly monitors discrepancy reduction, is a meta-monitoring loop which monitors the rate of discrepancy reduction taking place in the first loop. Changes in the rate of goal approach are registered in this meta-monitoring system as emotion.

Carver and Scheier's analysis works relatively well for simple satisfaction-and disappointment-related emotions which are specifically related to goals, but fares less well for more complex social emotions (grief, guilt and so on). It seems clear that the kinds of goal implicated in emotions such as these are not always things that can be approached at a measurable rate. For example, the emotion of embarrassment apparently reflects worries about how one is perceived by others, suggesting that the associated goal is about *maintaining* a positive public impression. However, it seems a little far-fetched to argue that embarrassment reflects the recognition that you are not approaching this goal of maintenance of a positive public impression as fast as you would have liked. Rather, the emotion is more likely to reflect directly the actual perceived discrepancy between desired public impression and actual public impression.

The general problem with Carver and Scheier's theory is that in order to interpret all human behaviour as goal-directed, it is necessary to adopt a rather broad conception of goal, and if one adopts such a broad conception to include goals that are about maintaining states of affairs rather than approaching them, it becomes difficult to imagine how *rate of progress* toward these goals could be directly measured by any hypothetical meta-monitoring system. The concept of goal ultimately seems like a simple translation of what is really going on during action rather than a genuinely explanatory concept.

Interruption of plans

A general assumption of many theories is that the interruption of plans is a common occasion for emotion (e.g. Hebb, 1949; Lewin, 1935; Mandler, 1984; Oatley and Johnson-Laird, 1987). From a phenomenological point of view, what seems to happen is that when people strive towards a goal, expectations are built up about attaining it. When the plan fails and reality ceases to match these expectations, there is inevitably disappointment arising from the comparison of what actually happened with what ought to have happened or was expected to happen.

Interruption is also thought to have direct physiological effects based on the orienting reflex (Sokolov, 1963). When perceptual anticipations are confounded, the body automatically becomes activated (see Chapter 4) and attention is reattuned to the source of the discrepant information. This process also applies when the anticipations in question are based on the predicted outcomes of an intended course of action, so disruption of plans may lead to arousal by a similar mechanism. The bodily responses to interruption may in turn themselves have emotional consequences (Mandler, 1984; and see Chapter 4).

Differentiation of emotions resulting from action variables

The perceived cause of plan interruption, or of success or failure, is one determinant of the kind of emotion that is likely to result (Weiner, 1985). For example, if you trip over while running an important race, the resulting emotion is likely to be simple disappointment, but if someone else trips you up, you will probably get angry. A second variable affecting the kind of emotion experienced, as suggested by appraisal theory, is the nature of the goal that is implicated in the transaction (Lazarus, 1991a). For example, if someone beats you to making a date with someone towards whom you are romantically attracted, your anger may be mixed with jealousy.

It is not always simply a cognitive appraisal or attribution process that determines the nature of the emotion arising from plan interruption, however. Assuming that emotions often carry communicative content, they may be adopted in achievement-related contexts to convey particular messages to an audience. For example, we have all played competitive games with people who characteristically get angry when they are losing, whatever the actual apparent cause of their lack of success. Of course, it is perfectly possible that these people genuinely blame some external factor for whatever is going wrong as a result of some dispositional attribution style (cf. Abramson *et al.*, 1978), but it is often hard to avoid the conclusion that their emotional display is specifically intended to avert the interpretation that their own performance is somehow wanting (cf. Weiner *et al.*, 1987). Relatedly, getting emotional during personal projects may not always be directly responsive to the progress towards the end but also may serve the function of signalling commitment to the goal to others who are present. The kind of emotion communicated depends crucially on the nature of the audience and of the message that is intended.

Self-perception theory

A final way in which action might affect emotion arises from the fact that different emotions are implicitly connected with certain kinds of action tendency according to common sense. This means that when we see someone behaving in a particular way this implies to us that they are emotional, or to put it another way, certain actions are diagnostic of emotion. According to Bem (1972), we occasionally recognize emotions in *ourselves* on the basis of the same kinds of information that we use to recognize emotion in others: 'Individuals come to 'know' their own attitudes, emotions, and other internal states partially by inferring them from observations of their own behaviour and/or the circumstances in which this behaviour occurs' (p. 2). According to Bem, the conclusions we draw about our own current emotion may in turn lead us to act in accordance with the self-attributed internal state. Thus, action may affect emotion in an indirect way, by leading us to believe that we are emotional, so that we then act on the basis of this belief.

The results of an experiment by Bandler, Madaras, and Bem (1968) offer some support for this argument. In this study, the investigators administered electric shocks to participants and told them either to endure them for as long as possible or escape from them as soon as they wanted, depending on the colour of a displayed signal light. It was found that equal intensity shocks were rated as more uncomfortable when subjects escaped from, rather than endured them, even though their escape behaviour was actually entirely under the control of the light signal rather than the physical voltage of the shocks. These results suggest that people are willing in certain circumstances to make inferences about their affective experience on the basis of their self-observed behaviour (see also McAllister, 1980).

Other results consistent with Bem's analysis have arisen from cognitive dissonance experiments. For example, in Festinger and Carlsmith's (1959) classic forced compliance study, participants who were given only a small reward for saying that they had enjoyed performing a series of boring tasks apparently came to believe that these tasks were in fact not so boring after all. In other words, liking of an object can depend partly on how one has observed oneself behaving with respect to that object: we may change the way we feel about something in response to the way we act towards it.

Bem's analysis seems to suggest that we consciously decide that we are emotional and then act out the implications of this decision. Certainly, this implied sequence of events does not conform to the way that emotion is usually seen as coming about. As Frijda (1986) has argued, our awareness of emotion is not typically selfconscious; rather, our attention tends to be directed towards the emotional situation which is perceived as coloured by emotion, rather than to the emotional state itself. According to this analysis, emotion in most cases involves *irreflexive* rather then *reflexive* experience in Sartre's (1962) terms.

Although the self-attributional sequence does not seem to account for the full range of emotional experiences, it may be plausibly applied in certain specific circumstances. For example, the explicit conclusion that we are emotional, based on self-observation of behaviour, may in turn direct our attention towards aspects of the situation that support its emotional definition, so that we ultimately lose conscious track of the deliberative process that had originally induced the state. Thus, in testing out whether your intense conversations with a new acquaintance were really symptomatic of love, you may become attuned to available confirmatory evidence for such an emotional attachment in the way that things develop when you are next together (cf. Snyder, 1984). More generally, even if we assume that our self-attributions typically start out as conscious (and many theorists would resist such a conclusion), this does not mean that the awareness of these initiating processes necessarily stays in place when their implications ultimately take effect.

The self-attributional view of emotion suggests that people may draw conclusions about emotional state on the basis of any relevant information that is available. For example, if we notice internal body symptoms, facial expression, or a particular kind of behaviour in the context of a situation, this may lead us to draw inferences about our emotional state (the impact of facial and bodily feedback on emotion is discussed in the next two chapters). However, such an account fails to confront the issue of how bodily changes or actions are initiated in the first place (see Chapter 6): if we catch ourselves reacting internally or externally in an emotional situation, the most likely reason is that we are genuinely emotional, and that an underlying emotional process has produced these effects (cf. Frijda, 1986). Nevertheless, as I shall claim later in the book, feedback explanations based on self-perception ideas do have some role to play in the general theory of emotion.

CONCLUSIONS

Emotion is related to action in a variety of different ways. Not only do emotions arise directly as a result of success and failure of actions, but also we may use our self-observed behaviour as information about our current emotion. Moving to the consequences of emotion for action, appraising a situation in emotional terms may lead directly to distinctive modes of action readiness in addition to activating various problem-focused coping attempts. Furthermore, the influences of affect on action may generalize to objects other than the specific target of the emotional state. Finally, our awareness of emotion may lead to us deliberately attempting to adjust or improve it using affect-regulation strategies that may also depend on some kind of action.

A communicative model of emotion similarly suggests several ways in which action and emotion are related, although the connections implied in this case tend to be less direct and automatic. Taking the effects of action on emotion first, expressed emotions may provide a commentary on our own actions, for example when we get angry with someone else or with ourselves as a way of showing that expectations have been frustrated, and that we would normally be more successful. On the action readiness side, the fact that emotions communicate the claim that the situation matters implies also that the emotional person must be prepared to act on its consequences: emotional involvement in a situation is manifested partly in the apparent readiness to respond to it. Actions carried out in support of appraisals may themselves serve communicative as well as instrumental functions, for example, when we smack a child to punish as well as to inform it that what it has done is wrong. Similarly, adopting a posture that corresponds to the beginning of a familiar and predictable emotional action sequence provides a clear and often directly apprehended message that the person is ready to respond with the rest of the sequence (Mead, 1934), so we may also display action readiness as part of our communication of emotion (see Chapter 5).

Of course, all of these connections imply that emotion is something that takes place separately from action. In fact, emotions and appraisals are communicated in real time and this process itself is a form of action. The feeling of being ready to act in a certain way or the feeling of carrying through an emotional action with full involvement is apparently a central part of what people mean by emotion.

4   The activation factor

OVERVIEW

Our intuitive idea of emotions as subjective feelings seems to imply that they involve internal bodily disturbances of some kind (e.g. Averill, 1974). The heart is the metaphoric seat of emotion, and it is thought to 'skip a beat' when a person falls in love. Your 'blood boils' and you get 'hot under the collar' when angry (Lakoff and Kövecses, 1987), whereas various coarser visceral symptoms are thought to accompany intense fear, and you need to have 'guts' to deal with such reactions. Psychologists as well as laypeople have tended to assume that emotion involves internal upset, specifically focusing on changes in heart rate, respiration, general arousal, and so on. In this chapter, I consider the evidence concerning the role of bodily reaction in emotion. Like other components of emotion, the bodily factor can be seen as cause as well as index of emotion, and I review theories and research relating to both these hypothetical roles. I argue that body changes typically occur in emotion as part of more integrated actions (including also appraisals) and that the activation system can provide inputs as well as outputs to emotion.

COMMON-SENSE IDEAS ABOUT BODILY CHANGES AND EMOTION

According to common sense, emotion, especially intense emotion, tends to involve bodily changes of some sort. We often seem to be aware of these changes when we get emotional. Furthermore, different emotions are apparently accompanied by different kinds of bodily symptom: we feel hot and tense when angry; our heart sinks in disappointment; we get a lump in our throats during sorrow; we experience palpitations or a cold sweat in intense fear; and have butterflies in our stomachs when going through certain forms of love. Although these particular responses are not consistently related to the respective emotions in everybody, there is a general tendency to believe that distinctive patterns of bodily symptom accompany different emotions.

The association of body change with intuitive ideas about emotional states was confirmed by data from one of my own unpublished studies (Parkinson, 1983). In this experiment, I asked forty-five psychology students to imagine a situation in which they would experience a clear and typical instance of several different emotional states, then write down the defining features of the experience of the corresponding emotion (see Chapter 9). Roughly two-thirds of the definitions of emotional states offered in this study mentioned some kind of bodily change. Specific symptoms also tended to be reported in connection with particular emotions. For example, anger was often defined as being associated with tension, arousal, and feeling hot, while fear was thought to be characterized by feelings of nausea and stomach upset, cold sweat, and increased heart rate. Mention of bodily symptoms was less common, however, in definitions of the emotions of happiness and sadness, suggesting that bodily changes may not feature equally strongly in our ideas of all emotional states.

Other research into people's everyday ideas of emotion also supports the existence of these perceived connections between emotions and internal body symptoms. For example, Nieuwenhuyse, Offenberg, and Frijda (1987) asked respondents to report where the symptoms of specific remembered emotional experiences were located by marking their position on schematic diagrams of the front and rear of the human body. The researchers found that most of the ten emotions investigated were implicitly associated with localized body symptoms. For example, disgust was thought to be felt mostly in the stomach and throat, whereas the symptoms of fear were assigned mainly to the anal area and abdomen (although sometimes also to the stomach). Anger, on the other hand, was said to be experienced over the whole body. Some of the specific results of this study may be questioned due to the imprecise instructions to participants which apparently did not distinguish between bodily symptoms, consequences of emotions for action (see Chapter 3), and expressive components of emotional response (see Chapter 5). Despite this limitation, however, the findings do still support the conclusion that people believe that the bodily symptoms of different emotions tend to have different locations.

Further confirmatory evidence comes from a study conducted by Rimé, Philippot, and Cisamolo (1990). In their experimental procedure, remembered examples of four different emotional states were rated according to the presence of several commonly perceived physical symptoms. It was found that joy was thought to be characterized by muscular relaxation, but anger and fear were considered to involve muscular tension. Further, respondents reported that they felt hot during anger, but warm during joy. Broadly comparable results concerning people's ideas of the differences in bodily responses associated with different emotions have also been obtained by Shaver, Schwartz, Kirson, and O'Connor (1987), Shields (1984), and Wallbott and Scherer (1986).

In summary, there is consistent evidence that people's implicit definitions of different emotional terms involve distinctive patterns of bodily accompaniments as well as distinctive appraisal and action-readiness profiles. But what relation do these ideas have to the realities of emotional experience? In the next section, I move on from discussion of common-sense characterizations of emotions to a consideration of what really happens inside the body when someone gets emotional.

AUTONOMIC RESPONSE PATTERNS

Before discussing theories and research relating to the bodily accompaniments of different emotions, it is worth making a few remarks about the physiological response systems usually implicated in emotional reactions. Psychologists have devoted most of their attention to the activity of the *autonomic nervous system* (ANS) in this regard. The main function of this system is to control the mobilization and conservation of energy within the body: for example, the ANS influences heart rate, blood flow, gastric activity, and so on. Activation of the *sympathetic division* of the ANS increases metabolic function and mobilizes energy, whereas its *parasympathetic division* controls energy conservation by slowing metabolic activity. Although there is evidence that many of these functions can be put under voluntary control as a result of biofeedback training and related procedures (Miller, 1969), they are nevertheless usually considered to be largely involuntary systems. People do not normally have to devote any attention to keeping their hearts beating, or reminding themselves to breathe, for example.

The sympathetic system is thought to become activated in a relatively unified manner in certain circumstances (e.g. Duffy, 1962), producing the following responses: increase in heart rate and blood pressure, increased respiratory volume, constriction of the blood vessels in the skin (pallor), dilation of the pupils, inhibition of gastro-intestinal activity, decrease in salivation (dry mouth), and increased action of the sweat glands. This pattern of changes is known as generalized *sympathetic activation* (or arousal). The response system is partly mediated by increased adrenaline (epinephrine) secretion, which may also result in trembling and feelings of cold. When sympathetic activation is particularly high, the parasympathetic system may also come into play, causing increased peripheral blood flow (flushing), decrease in blood pressure, enhanced intestinal action, and lowered heart rate.

Although parasympathetic and sympathetic activation represent the two basic peripheral response patterns commonly assumed to be associated with emotion, they very rarely occur in such pure forms. This is partly because muscular activity, the direction of attention, and several other factors have their own independent effects on separate aspects of the physiological response. Furthermore, different individuals show their own characteristic response patterns (e.g. individual response stereotypy; Lacey and Lacey, 1958).

Measurement of autonomic activity may be achieved relatively simply using electrodes attached to the surface of the skin. A common index of autonomic change is electrodermal activity (EDA) which depends on the level of electrical conductance of the skin, which in turn is related to the amount of perspiration taking place. To measure this, two electrodes are placed on the palm of the hand and a small electrical current is passed between them. Changes in skin conductance are charted on a moving roll of paper using a *polygraph*. Increases in skin conductance tend to be associated with increased arousal and therefore this simple technique can provide a crude but relatively reliable measure of autonomic activation.

Similarly, respiration, heart rate, and so on can be measured. Although these variables tend to show positive correlations with one another, these correlations are not usually very large (e.g. Ax, 1953). This is partly because the different response components are differentially affected by different psychological and physiological factors. This fact suggests that activation or arousal may not actually exist as a unified and generalized reaction in many real-life circumstances (e.g. Johnson and Anderson, 1990). Researchers who continue to endorse the activation concept despite these difficulties often argue that it is necessary to use more than one psychophysiological index in order to get an accurate and triangulated measurement (e.g. Wenger and Cullen, 1958).

Arousal is typically believed to be an accompaniment of excited emotions such as fear and anger (e.g. Cannon, 1929), and its presence is often taken as an index of degree of emotional reaction. However, sympathetic activation also occurs in connection with high levels of attention and with physical exercise, so even if we can be confident from the pattern of physiological changes that arousal is present, it still remains to be determined whether this arousal is emotional arousal.

PERIPHERAL DIFFERENTIATION OF EMOTIONS

The question of whether emotions are accompanied by distinctive bodily changes has been a recurrent issue throughout the history of psychology. William James's (1884) theory of emotion suggested that the matrix of internal bodily processes provided a hypersensitive 'sounding board' that resonated in specific sympathy with each particular tone of emotion that might occur:

> The various permutations and combinations of which these organic activities are susceptible make it abstractly possible that no shade of emotion, however slight, should be without a bodily reverberation as unique, when taken in its totality, as is the mental mood itself.
>
> (James, 1898, p. 1066)

Furthermore, James argued that our awareness is tightly attuned to the pattern of concurrent internal reaction: '*every one of the bodily changes, whatsoever it be, is* FELT, *acutely or obscurely, the moment it occurs*' (p. 1066, emphasis in original). According to James's theory then, not only can emotions be distinguished according to body states in principle, but in fact as conscious subjects we are able to recognize our own emotions at the time that they happen on the basis of our sensitivity to internal state. (The final stage of James's reasoning was that the awareness of distinctive bodily reactions actually *determined* emotional experience, but I will defer discussion of this last *causal* claim until a later section.)

James's theory was developed at a time when there had been relatively little rigorous research into physiological response systems. As soon as investigators began to measure actual bodily changes such as heart rate and blood flow during emotion, it turned out that the pattern of response tended to be more integrated and much less differentiated than James's theory seemed to imply. For example,

Cannon (1927) pointed out that for a range of widely different emotional conditions, the body's reaction is actually rather consistent. In both fear and anger, for example, adrenaline is released, heart rate increases, the pupils widen, and so on. According to Cannon, then, the body response accompanying many emotions is undifferentiated sympathetic arousal, which provides metabolic energy to mobilize the organism for possible urgent action in emergency situations.

Over the years, several studies have explicitly addressed the issue of whether there are measurable differences in the body's reactions under various emotional conditions. One of the first systematic investigations was a classic, though ethically dubious, experiment by Ax (1953) into the differences between anger and fear. In Ax's procedure, participants were recruited for a study supposedly addressing physiological differences between people with and without symptoms of hypertension. The experimental task was described as involving lying down on a bench and listening to personally selected music for an hour while various physiological measures were taken using electrodes attached to the surface of the skin. In reality, rather more dramatic incidents had been prepared for the unwitting participants. Ax stage-managed what happened in the laboratory with the intention of creating intense and involving anger and fear experiences in his experimental participants.

In the fear condition, one of the electrodes attached to the participant's finger started to deliver gradually increasing intensities of detectable but painless electric shock. As soon as the participant mentioned feeling these shocks, the experimenter expressed surprise and pretended to check the wiring connections. While doing this, he flicked a switch that resulted in sparks flying from the circuitry. On this cue, the experimenter became openly alarmed, remarking that there was a dangerous high-voltage short circuit in the equipment. A full five minutes of apparent panic later, the shock wire was removed and the experimenter attempted to reassure the participant that the danger was now over. Unfortunately for this hapless volunteer, however, the anger condition was still to follow.

In the anger condition, a bad-tempered polygraph operator entered the scene from the adjoining equipment room under the pretext of needing to check the wiring. Under protest, the experimenter withdrew to the equipment room ostensibly to monitor the recording. The technician then turned off the music, and remarked sarcastically that it would have helped things if the participant had been on time for the experiment. While checking the electrodes, the operator roughly moved the participant on the bench. This manhandling was accompanied by criticism and continual rudeness. After five minutes of abuse, the experimenter returned and apologized for the polygraph operator's bad behaviour.

These experimental manipulations were apparently quite convincing and emotionally involving for participants as demonstrated in comments made when the investigator questioned participants about the incidents afterwards, as well as their responses to the incident at the time. For example, in the anger condition, one of the participants reported that he had been ready to throw a punch at the ill-mannered polygraph operator. During the fear condition, one participant pleaded:

'Please take the wires off! Oh! Please help me', another prayed to be spared, and a third participant subsequently remarked 'Well, everybody has to go sometime. I thought this might be my time.' In short, some participants were apparently in fear for their lives during this experimental procedure. Despite this, Ax found it necessary to exclude six other participants from his analysis because he judged, on the basis of their demeanour during the incidents and their remarks in the interview afterwards, that the manipulations had not made them sufficiently angry or afraid.

The results of Ax's study suggested that the patterns of physiological response associated with the experiences of fear and anger were different from each other. For example, in the anger condition, blood pressure rose more than in the fear condition, heart rate decreased to a greater extent, and muscle tension reached generally higher levels. However, the fear condition showed higher values than the anger condition for increases in skin conductance and quickening of rate of respiration. Ax concluded that the pattern of response in fear was similar to that produced by an injection of adrenaline (sympathetic activation), whereas the reactions accompanying anger corresponded to the effects of adrenaline together with noradrenaline (sympathetic and parasympathetic activation).

However, there are problems of interpretation with Ax's experiment which highlight some of the difficulties of investigating the physiological differentiation of emotions. The first and most obvious problem relates to the assumed connection between the body changes and the particular emotions manipulated. Although it seems likely that many of Ax's participants really did experience the stipulated emotions, we cannot be certain that the reported body changes were associated specifically with these emotions rather than the conditions used to produce them. For example, the 'fear' situation involved the threat of electric shocks via the skin, encouraging a probable tendency to try to withdraw from the electrodes, and possibly to brace the body against potential pain. It seems possible that part of the pattern of changes reported by Ax depended on postural adjustments related to the specific situation of the threat of shock rather than the emotion of fear *per se*. A more general point to be made in this connection is that any specific technique for producing an emotion may bring about particular physiological changes that have no necessary relation to the emotion in question. Given only one set of reactions from each participant, the investigator has no way of determining which responses are due to particular characteristics of the situation (or of the behavioural tendencies it encourages), and which are actually symptomatic of the emotion itself. Clearly, studies are required that employ more than one method of producing each emotional state under consideration, so that the investigator is able to determine which aspects of the reaction are common to all instances of the emotion in question. In practice, such a procedure has rarely been implemented.

A second problem of interpretation relates to the intensity of the emotion produced (Levenson, 1988). Intuitively, stronger emotions are more likely to be associated with more pronounced symptoms. However, the relationship between any given physiological index and emotional intensity is not always a simple monotonic one. For example, it has been observed that weak emotion is often associated with activity of the sympathetic nervous system, whereas stronger emotion may also recruit parasympathetic activity which to some extent counters sympathetic activation. Consequently, more intense forms of the same emotion may result in different patterns of physiological response. If an investigator is trying to compare the bodily changes associated with different emotions, therefore, it is important that an attempt is made to match the intensity of the different states, otherwise any reported distinctions may be due to differences in emotional intensity rather than quality. Unfortunately, the issue of how to compare different emotional states along a common intensity dimension is one that is by no means straightforward to resolve (Frijda *et al.*, 1992).

Many of the studies investigating the physiological differentiation of emotions are subject to these above-mentioned problems of interpretation (e.g. Averill, 1969; J. Schachter, 1957), making it difficult to draw any firm conclusions about the results that they have produced. Furthermore, the emotional manipulations used in later studies have rarely been anything like as powerful as those originally employed by Ax, mainly for obvious ethical reasons. Despite these difficulties, studies do tend to show physiological differences between different emotions, and these differences are often consistent (though not always; see Zajonc and McIntosh, 1992).

A more recent study by Ekman, Levenson, and Friesen (1983) corrected one of the main problems of previous research by using two separate tasks to produce each of six emotions. The first task involved instructing the professional actors and emotion researchers who served as participants to adjust their faces, muscle by muscle, until their expression corresponded to the theoretically defined pattern for each of the emotions. Several theorists have argued that such a procedure tends to produce the associated emotional experience (e.g. Izard, 1971; Tomkins, 1962; and see Chapter 5). In the second task, participants were asked to relive previous experiences corresponding to each of the specified emotions in their imagination.

Only three of the possible differences between the six emotions on five separate physiological indices were obtained consistently in both tasks (see also Zajonc and McIntosh, 1992): heart rate increased more in the anger and fear manipulations than in the happiness manipulations, and finger temperature also increased more for anger than for happiness. One possible interpretation of these findings concerns the relative ease of imagining and recreating different kinds of emotional experience. It may be that anger is more readily reconstructed than happiness because of its commonness. If this were the case, then the imagined examples of anger may have been at a generally higher intensity than the happiness experiences, and any differences obtained between the emotions may have resulted from this fact rather than qualitative considerations. Other distinctive physiological patterns emerged in each induction procedure separately but not consistently across both, suggesting that these results too were due to task characteristics and not intrinsic emotional differences.

In a series of later replications of the face movement procedure from their earlier study, Levenson, Ekman, and Friesen (1990) confirmed that different autonomic patterns were associated with the different facial positions, especially when the displays actually produced corresponded closely to the usual spontaneous expressions associated with the specified emotions. It does seem therefore that the adoption of facial expression of particular emotions itself tends to induce distinctive autonomic response, even though it is hard to know what implications this fact has for naturally occurring emotional experiences, where the facial display occurs in reaction to an affective stimulus or as part of a broader communicative process.

Despite the problems of interpretation considered above, and the limitations inherent in the data, it seems reasonable to conclude that certain different emotional states may often be associated with distinguishable bodily responses. However, the significance of these differences remains in question. For example, it is not clear whether the distinctive changes relate to tendencies towards action (see Chapter 3), to expressive or postural factors (Chapter 5), or to general intensity differences between the manipulated emotions. Furthermore, the differences between physiological symptoms associated with different emotional states seem generally less obvious than James's theory implied, and certainly not as pronounced as suggested by our intuitive ideas about the distinctive symptoms of anger, fear, and so on.

COMPARING IDEAS AND REALITIES OF EMOTIONAL BODILY CHANGE

Why is it that psychological research has failed to find evidence of the clear and salient differences between the bodily changes associated with distinct emotions, which common sense tells us ought to be obviously apparent? There are a number of possible reasons for this apparent discrepancy between the ideas and realities of emotional reaction, which I will consider in this section.

The first set of reasons concerns possible limitations of the experimental findings relating to physiological differentiation:

1 *Potency of laboratory manipulations of emotion* It may be that intense emotions as experienced in everyday life actually do have distinctive bodily accompaniments, but the weaker reactions that have been evoked in the laboratory since Ax's study (for practical as well as ethical reasons) are less clearly differentiated. In this case, people's beliefs about distinctive bodily accompaniments may still be correct despite the apparent weaknesses of the experimental evidence.

2 *Quality of laboratory manipulations of emotion* A second problem with many of the experimental studies concerns the way in which different emotions are operationalized. Although the situational manipulations employed to produce distinctive emotions such as fear and anger usually seem like plausible occasions for the intended reactions, it is difficult to say exactly how effectively and precisely the required experiences were created. It seems possible that the

fact of taking part in a study would tend to lead to a set of characteristic emotions in and of itself which would provide a common affective background in all experimental conditions. Thus, the addition of the actual emotional manipulation would probably result in a complex blend of mixed feelings, rather than the single pure emotion needed for a clean test of the differentiation hypothesis. Furthermore, in practice the pattern of reaction generated would likely vary to some extent from person to person and from occasion to occasion. All of these factors would reduce the consistency of distinctions between emotional conditions. Even when self-report manipulation checks have been incorporated in experimental procedures as attempts to assess participants' actual emotions, we cannot say to what extent participants would *spontaneously* characterize their experience as predicted, nor how involved they might have been in the staged situation. In many cases, ratings on these scales might well be based on second guesses from respondents about the kind of emotion that the investigator wanted to elicit rather than readouts based on introspection. Experiments using self-generation of specified emotions (Ekman, Levenson, and Friesen, 1983) provide a partial solution to this problem because here participants implement their own criteria for achievement of the emotional differentiation task. However, in these studies, it is unclear how completely and convincingly participants can construct each of the distinct emotional experiences.

3　*Adequacy of psychophysiological measures* A further way in which implicit theories about body changes in emotions might actually be more accurate than psychophysiological findings depends on the idea that people pick up information from their bodies during emotional experience that has never been adequately assessed using conventional measurement procedures. Psychophysiological research tends to focus on variables that can be easily indexed using simple transducer devices, but it is conceivable that the actual changes that people believe they feel during emotion simply do not correspond to the kinds of energy variations that would register on the commonly used response measures. For example, there is no standard psychophysiological measure that directly corresponds to symptoms such as butterflies in the stomach or 'sinking feelings'.

4　*Sampling of different emotions* Few studies have sampled a wide enough array of emotions to find out for sure whether or not there are real differences between all those that common sense suggests should be different. This is partly because many commonly occurring everyday emotions are difficult to produce in the laboratory. Although the weakness of the findings for intuitively distinctive states such as anger and fear seems surprising, there are no available comparable data for emotions such as embarrassment, guilt, pride, love and so on. Perhaps if a study were able to create deep embarrassment, for example, and compare the associated responses with those produced during extreme sorrow, support for physiological differentiation might be more forthcoming. Of course, there would still be the problem of determining whether any distinctive patterns were *intrinsic* to the emotional experience rather than consequences of other related components.

To summarize these points, the best way of testing the physiological differentiation hypothesis would be to look explicitly for the particular bodily changes that common sense implies are associated with different emotions in genuinely involving and convincingly distinctive emotional situations. As yet, no such comprehensive study has been conducted, but with recent advances in telemetry (remote recording techniques) and the increasing availability of more rigorous appraisal-based criteria for attribution of different emotional conditions, it may not be long before more definitive data are available.

Three other possible reasons for the discrepancy between implicit and psychological ideas about body change in emotion depend on the common-sense ideas rather than the psychological findings being distorted:

1 *Influence of implicit theories on emotional representations* It is possible that cultural stereotypes about what symptoms are supposed to be associated with different emotions bias people's retrospective reports about these connections. For example, Rimé, Philippot, and Cisamolo (1990) argued that people possess socialized cognitive schemata which specify distinctive physiological patterns for each emotion. In this case, it is possible that enquiries about emotional differentiation may be answered by reference to these schemata rather than by reference to actual experience. The obvious question raised by this analysis concerns where the intuitive emotion-symptom associations came from in the first place, if not from experience with the relevant factors in real time. Possible answers to this question are suggested under points 2 and 3.

2 *Influence of implicit theories on encoding of emotional experiences* Ideas about emotion may not only affect the way that these experiences are represented and recounted but also the way that emotional episodes are encoded in real time (e.g. Pennebaker, 1982). For example, if a person becomes aware of feeling embarrassed, the content of their implicit theory for this emotion may direct attention towards particular symptoms that are specified in the cognitive script for this emotion (Fischer, 1991; Shaver *et al.*, 1987), such as flushing and warmth of the face. Even if there is only partial evidence for such a symptom available, and even if this evidence is part of a more general activation response, the perceptual attunement engendered by script-based processing may still be taken as confirmatory support for the original script. Similarly, Cacioppo, Berntson, and Klein (1992) have suggested that learnt perceptual schemata determine which aspects of the pattern of internal response are consciously registered during different emotional experiences. These schemata may be based on intense and pure examples of the relevant emotions during which bodily changes actually were distinctive.

3 *Influence of content of emotional episode on symptom attunement* Instead of assuming that *representations* of emotions affect registration of bodily information, it is possible to argue that the particular situations themselves that are associated with different emotions draw attention to relevant aspects of bodily state. For example, it may be that the actual occasions for embarrassment, which typically involve making some kind of *faux pas* in public, by their very

nature tend to focus awareness on the part of the body to which other people are most likely to pay attention, namely the face. Embarrassment actually may involve a generalized activation reaction but exaggerated consciousness of the face may lead to the embarrassed person only noticing the facial aspect of this reaction. Thus the perceived connection between emotions and specific bodily responses may be based on perceptual attunements engendered by the associated ongoing situation rather than any intrinsic connection.

In summary, the available data relating to physiological differentiation are inconclusive, but it still seems possible that different emotions are often associated at least with the perception of distinctive bodily symptoms. It is clearly important to maintain a distinction between these felt bodily symptoms of emotion, and the actual physiological changes which may or may not underlie them.

Like the research into appraisal and action readiness, the autonomic differentiation literature suffers from a failure to provide a precise operational definition for the different emotions studied. The research question of whether emotions on the one hand are related to bodily changes on the other, presupposes that emotions can be defined quite independently of the way that they are physically manifested in the body. In fact, bodily changes are part of what people usually mean by emotion, and awareness of such changes may even represent one of the criteria used in self-attribution of emotional state (Schachter, 1964; Valins, 1966; and see pp. 101–13). Rather than exploring relations between emotions and bodily changes then, it seems more sensible to focus on the way that bodily changes and the perception of these changes relate to the other components considered central to common-sense ideas of emotion, namely appraisals (e.g. Smith, 1989), states of action readiness (e.g. Frijda, 1987), and facial displays (e.g. Levenson *et al.*, 1990).

AUTONOMIC PERCEPTION

The assumption that common-sense ideas about distinctive emotional bodily symptoms are accurate is given a further blow by evidence that suggests that we are not in fact as aware of our current physiological condition as we think. For example, Pennebaker (1982) asked participants to give self-reports of pulse rate, hand temperature, and depth of breathing during the performance of a range of different tasks. Objective psychophysiological measures of relevant variables were recorded at the same time. It was found that self-reports showed small and often nonsignificant correlations with the objective measures. Similarly, in another study, Pennebaker asked participants to press a button in time with the rate of their heartbeat and again found that correspondence between estimated and actual heart rate was poor.

These findings help to explain why manipulations of false autonomic feedback (e.g. Valins, 1966; see pp. 108–11) are generally convincing: because people simply do not know how fast their heart is actually beating, it is relatively easy to convince them that it is beating faster or slower than they think. Of course, there are likely to be limits to such an effect, for example when palpitations make people directly aware of their heart rate (Parkinson, 1985). It may be that autonomic awareness only occurs when symptoms are quite extreme and salient but that most of the time people do not register internal bodily reactions. Because investigators have usually assessed autonomic perception during quite low levels of response, the effects of stronger internal stimuli would not show up in their studies. At any rate, the balance of evidence suggests that in many everyday situations, we do not really know how our bodies are reacting, so our perceptions of bodily symptoms during emotion are at least sometimes likely to be incorrect.

BODILY CHANGE AS A CAUSE OF EMOTION

James's (1898) theory did not only suggest that distinctive body symptoms *accompany* different emotions, but also claimed that the perception of these symptoms *determined* the experience of emotion. On this point, James's theory explicitly contradicts the common-sense idea of emotion by arguing that intuition gets things backwards – see Figure 4.1(a) and (b):

> Our natural way of thinking . . . is that the mental perception of some fact excites the mental affection called the emotion, and that this latter state of

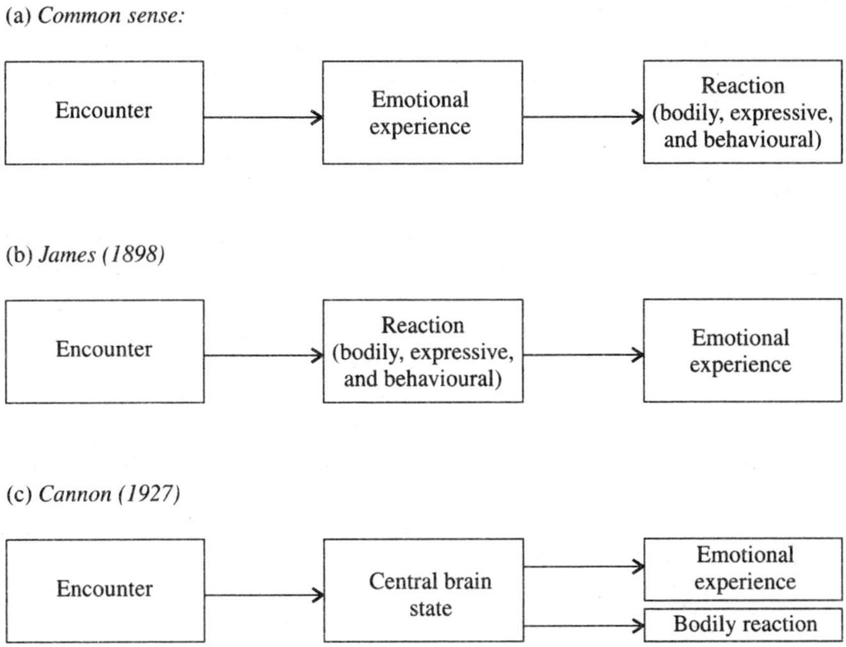

(a) *Common sense:*

(b) *James (1898)*

(c) *Cannon (1927)*

Figure 4.1 Early theories of the emotion sequence

mind gives rise to the bodily expression. My thesis, on the contrary, is that *the bodily changes follow directly the perception of the exciting fact, and that our feeling of the same changes as they occur* IS *the emotion.*

(p. 449, emphasis in original)

James argued that the differences between emotions are a direct result of the different patterns of physiological response associated with them. According to James, seeing something frightening instinctively triggers an integrated set of reactions in our bodies. The specific pattern of these reactions is felt by us consciously and experienced as the particular emotion of fear. For example, our fear feelings might be based on the perception of raised blood pressure, a tightening of our muscles, and a certain sensation in our guts.

Given what I have already said about the lack of obvious and consistent distinctions between physiological changes in different emotions, and our apparent lack of awareness of bodily changes when they do occur, this causal hypothesis of James now seems like a non starter. In a famous critique of James's theory, Cannon (1927) marshalled together the physiological evidence against it.

The essence of Cannon's argument was that the characteristics of autonomic response simply did not match up with the characteristics of subjective emotional response, so that it would be hard to conceive of the former as a direct source of the latter. His five specific points were as follows:

1 *Insensitivity of receptors* Internal organs are mostly too *insensitive* to provide the differential feedback necessary to produce the variety of emotional experiences: neural receptors tend to be located close to the surface of the body and do not closely monitor changes at deeper levels.
2 *Response latency* Body response is usually too *slow* to underlie rapid emotional reactions. The time taken before a change in autonomic response can occur and be registered using existing efferent and afferent neural pathways respectively adds up to more than a full second, and many theorists believe that urgent emotional reactions necessarily arise more quickly than this.
3 *Irrelevance of feedback* When 'sympathectomies' were performed on animals so that their viscera were completely separated from their central nervous system, the animals still continued to manifest 'emotional' behaviour (e.g. Sherrington, 1900), suggesting that peripheral feedback was not even a *necessary* condition for emotional responding.
4 *Lack of differentiation* As mentioned earlier, the *same* kind of autonomic pattern seemed to accompany each type of emotional reaction, as well as certain non emotional states, so that autonomic differentiation was insufficient to account for the various emotions that occur.
5 *Insufficiency of body response* Artificial induction of the kind of autonomic pattern that characterized emotions, using direct injections of adrenaline for example, did not usually, in itself, produce emotion (Marañon, 1924), effectively ruling out this factor's direct causal role in the emotion generation process.

Although some of these arguments are inconclusive taken alone, and in fact parts of the evidence cited by Cannon are questionable, the critique as a whole convinced most investigators that the peripheral theory was untenable at least in its specifics. This conclusion still holds true today.

Cannon's (1927; 1929) alternative theory represented a slight return towards the common-sense view of emotion. His idea was that emotional encounters were emergency situations which directly triggered a central brain process in the thalamus, which had two simultaneous and independent outputs, one to the arousal system which prepared the body to cope with the emergency, and the second to the cortex where the conscious experience of the emotion was registered – see Figure 4.1(c). Thus, the symptoms of quickened pulse, sweating and so on were simply side effects of energy mobilization in preparation for emergency response, and were irrelevant to the subjective awareness of emotion. Bodily changes, in Cannon's view then, were consequences rather than causes of emotion.

If we do not know what we are feeling on the basis of internal bodily symptoms, then how do we know how to characterize and describe our current emotional feeling? Cannon's theory suggests that we know emotions directly from hard-wired brain processes, but such a notion implies that an unrealistic degree of inflexibility characterizes emotional experience. An obvious alternative possibility suggested by appraisal theory as detailed in the previous chapter is that we recognize different emotions based on our evaluations of the current situations. Schachter's (1964) two-factor theory was the first account of emotion to emphasize the importance of *both* physiological and situational factors in determining emotion.

Two-factor theory

Schachter (1964) revived and revised James's idea that emotions are dependent on feedback from bodily changes. Although accepting Cannon's points about emotions generally sharing the same bodily response of generalized sympathetic arousal, Schachter still believed that this response was an important determinant of the experience of emotion. Correspondingly, Schachter rejected Cannon's argument that emotion was possible in the absence of autonomic response (point 3 above), and criticized the evidence on which this conclusion was based because it derived purely from animal experiments where questions concerning the *experience* of emotion are practically unanswerable. In comparable studies using humans (e.g. Hohmann, 1966; and see pp. 110–11), loss of autonomic feeling apparently did lead to some loss of emotional feeling. Furthermore, more recent animal studies than those considered by Cannon demonstrated that although autonomic feedback was not required for the maintenance of emotional responding, *acquisition* of the relevant behaviours was much slower after animals had been sympathectomized (e.g. Wynne and Solomon, 1955). Thus, even in animals, autonomic responses seem to make a vital difference to emotion-related phenomena.

Schachter's conclusion was that autonomic arousal provided the energy and warmth of emotion. The problem then was that arousal by itself could determine the quantity but not the quality of emotion that was experienced. Because the same state of arousal seemed to accompany a wide variety of emotional states, there had to be some other variable which gave each emotional state its distinctive feeling. Schachter argued that this extra emotional information concerning quality came from the situation in which the arousal was experienced.

According to Schachter, the kind of emotion felt depended on how arousal was interpreted and explained by the person experiencing it. For example, if someone believes that their state of arousal is caused by a wild animal that is chasing them, then they are likely to experience the state as fear. If, on the other hand, they think that their internal activation is triggered by the close presence of an attractive person, they might well come to feel their reaction as love, or at least as lust, for that person. In other words, emotion consists of an *attribution* of the arousal response to an emotionally relevant situational cause (see Figure 4.2).

In this view, messages from the body only tell us that we feel something, not that it is necessarily an emotion, nor what emotion it is. It is our interpretation of the situation that leads to these last two specifications. For example, if we have just had a strong cup of coffee we might assume that our symptoms are caused by this, whereas if we are lost in a jungle and there are ominous growling noises, we would be more likely to decide that we are experiencing the emotion of fear.

Schachter and Singer's (1962) experiment

If Schachter's theory is correct, then it is possible to change the emotions that people experience simply by modifying the way that they interpret their arousal reactions. This is exactly what Schachter and Singer (1962) attempted to achieve in their much-cited and celebrated experiment. In order to test the viability of

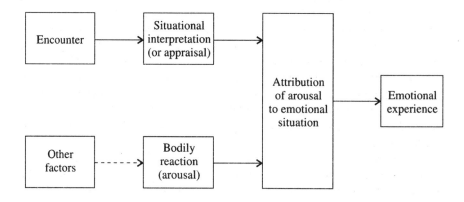

Figure 4.2 Schachter's two-factor theory (1964)

Note: Broken lines represent linkages that are possible rather than necessary

two-factor theory, the first requirement was to manipulate arousal independently of emotion. This was accomplished by injecting experimental participants with adrenaline, under the pretext that it was a new vitamin compound called Suproxin, whose effects the experimenters were testing (in a control condition, the Suproxin injection was actually a saline placebo). Second, it was necessary to manipulate whether the experienced arousal was attributed to an emotional or non-emotional cause. Accordingly, Schachter and Singer accurately informed some participants that the injection would have side effects corresponding to the usual symptoms of arousal (heart-rate increase, a rise in body temperature, and so on), but deceiving other participants about the bodily effects of the injection. These latter misinformed participants, therefore, were intended to experience arousal symptoms without knowing their source, and consequently should have sought to explain these symptoms by reference to the current situation.

Finally, Schachter and Singer manipulated participants' emotional explan- ations for arousal by putting them into one of two different situations. This was done while participants were supposedly waiting for the vitamin compound to be absorbed. Each participant waited with another supposed participant who was actually an accomplice of the experimenter and who acted in one of two different ways, contrived to convey contrasting emotional possibilities.

In the first condition, the accomplice messed around with the pieces of paper, pencils, and rubber bands lying around in the untidy waiting room and tried to create a general atmosphere of *euphoria*. For example, he improvised a basket- ball game with screwed up pieces of paper and a waste-bin, made a paper plane and tried flying it, aimed a makeshift catapult at a tower he had built from some folders, and finally discovered some conveniently concealed hula hoops and started playing with one of these, leaving the other within easy reach of the participant.

In the second condition, the situational manipulation was intended to provide an appropriate setting for the emotion of *anger*. This time, the real participant and the accomplice were asked to fill in a questionnaire while waiting for the Suproxin to be absorbed. The content of this questionnaire became increasingly personal and insulting. For example, the final item asked: 'With how many men (other than your father) has your mother had extra-marital relationships?' The only response alternatives available were: '4 and under', '5-9', and '10 and over'. The accomplice carefully timed his answering of the questions so that he was always at roughly the same place as the participant, and made irritated comments about the questionnaire as he completed it. In the end, his acted annoyance reached such a pitch that he tore up the questionnaire and stormed out of the waiting room in a huff.

The extent to which the participant got caught up in the general emotional atmosphere of these two contrasting situations was assessed by observers who watched the behaviour of the accomplice and the participant from behind one- way glass. In addition, all participants made self-ratings of their emotional state. According to the experimental predictions (see Figure 4.3), the only participants who should have got emotional as a function of the accomplice's behaviour were

MANIPULATIONS	CORRESPONDING CONDITIONS AND THEIR PREDICTED EFFECTS			
Manipulation 1: injection	*Adrenaline*			*Placebo*
Predicted effects of 1	Arousal			No arousal
Manipulation 2: explanation	*Pre-warned of side effects*	*Misled about side effects*		
Predited effects of 2	Arousal explained non-emotionally	Unexplained arousal		
Manipulation 3: emotional situation	↓	*Euphoric accomplice*	*Angry accomplice*	↓
Final prediction of emotional state	No emotion	Euphoria	Anger	No emotion

Figure 4.3 Predictions of Schachter and Singer's (1962) experiment

those who had been injected with adrenaline but incorrectly warned about its effects. Participants given an accurate warning about symptoms would have a perfectly good nonemotional explanation of their felt reaction and therefore would not take on the mood of the accomplice. Correspondingly, participants who had been injected with a placebo should have experienced no arousal and therefore no emotion. In effect, if either arousal or an emotional explanation for arousal were missing, then no emotion should have resulted. On the other hand, participants who experienced unexplained arousal should have attributed their symptoms to the emotional characteristics of the situation and adopted the emotional state of euphoria or anger, depending upon which emotion the accomplice acted out.

In fact, these predicted differences in emotional experience failed to emerge as clearly as Schachter and Singer might have hoped. Although participants correctly informed about the effects of the injection consistently reported less emotion than those given incorrect side-effects information, emotion ratings of participants who had been injected with an inert placebo did not consistently differ from those of misinformed aroused participants. In other words, the presence of supposedly unexplained arousal did not make a reliable difference to self-reported emotional experience.

Only after additional reanalysis did some of the crucial predicted effects finally emerge from Schachter and Singer's results. On the basis of responses to a post-experimental questionnaire, the investigators identified a subgroup of 'self-informed' participants who had apparently attributed their internal symptoms to the injection despite misleading side-effects instructions, and excluded these participants' data from the relevant comparisons. After this procedure, differences between placebo and adrenaline-misinformed conditions turned out to be statistically significant after all.

However, there is reason to question the validity of this *post hoc* comparison. The problem is that the tendency to self-inform should not have been treated simply as a methodological artifact because it may well have depended on emotionally relevant factors itself. For example, differences in emotional reactivity to the social situation created by the investigators may have moderated the credibility of the side-effects warning. More specifically, some of the participants in Schachter and Singer's experiment probably did not get emotionally involved in the accomplice's antics at all and therefore would have found it difficult to believe that any of their internal symptoms were actually caused by the current interpersonal situation. For these participants, the recent injection would have provided a plausible alternative explanation for what they were experiencing, making them more likely to self-inform. If this (admittedly speculative) account has any validity, then exclusion of self-informed participants would have resulted in an under-representation of emotionally unreactive participants in the misinformed adrenaline-injected condition, thus providing a direct explanation for the obtained differences between this group and the placebo group (which included low-emotional as well as high-emotional members).

A final problem with Schachter and Singer's results was that participants in the anger condition did not generally report their mood as negative at all: even when injected with adrenaline, misinformed of side-effects, and subjected to a humiliating questionnaire, they still rated themselves as mildly happy (Zimbardo *et al.*, 1977). The investigators explained this fact in terms of participants' supposed unwillingness to offend the experimenter by openly expressing their anger in a questionnaire. Although this explanation is plausible, especially from the point of view of a communicative approach to emotion, it would be difficult to claim that the self-report data provided convincing evidence for the central hypothesis of the study that 'precisely the same state of arousal could be labeled 'joy' or 'fury' or 'jealousy' or any of a great diversity of emotional labels depending on the cognitive aspects of the situation' (Schachter and Singer, 1962, pp. 381-2). In reality, the experimental participants tended to label their emotions in rather similar terms *regardless* of the cognitive aspects of the situation.

Subsequent attempts to replicate Schachter and Singer's study have been similarly inconclusive (e.g. Erdmann and Janke, 1978; Marshall and Zimbardo, 1979; Maslach, 1979; for reviews, see Manstead and Wagner, 1981, and Reisenzein, 1983). One of the main problems with testing Schachter's theory seems to be that it is almost impossible to manipulate arousal and emotional cognitions independently of one another. If arousal is experienced as disproportionate to the perceived emotional implications of the situation, then participants feel that something peculiar is going on. Correspondingly, if a situation contains enough features to make it a convincing cause of emotion, then it is also likely to cause emotion in reality.

Misattribution studies

One of the more conclusive positive results of Schachter and Singer's experiment was the finding that people who attributed their arousal to the injection were less emotional than those who attributed their arousal to the emotional situation. In fact, informed participants in the experiment tended to report weaker emotion than those given a placebo, although their actual level of arousal was greater. This finding arises partly because, as Schachter and Singer themselves admitted, the social situation staged in the experiment was actually emotionally involving for some participants even without the artificial stimulation of an adrenaline injection. However, any of the informed participants who experienced an arousal reaction in response to the emotional aspects of the situation may have misattributed this arousal to the non-emotional cause of the injection, and consequently experienced less emotion.

An experiment by Ross, Rodin, and Zimbardo (1969) similarly attempted to reduce negative emotional reactions by persuading participants that some of their experienced arousal was caused by an alternative nonemotional source, in this case loud noise. Participants were recruited for a study supposedly concerning the effects of noise on performance, and allowed to allocate their available time during the experimental session between working on two alternative puzzles (both of which were actually insoluble). The reward for solving the first of these problems was money, whereas solution of the second problem was said to allow the participant to escape from a threatened electric shock (which was never actually delivered). Therefore the amount of time spent on the shock-avoidance puzzle at the expense of the money-reward puzzle gave an indication of how motivated the participant was to escape shock, which presumably depended on their degree of fear.

During the task, a tape of loud noise was played, consisting of a mixture of the sounds from calculators, mimeograph machines, typewriters, and unintelligible voices. Attribution of arousal symptoms was manipulated by explaining to one group of participants that the noise would probably result in side effects such as palpitations and other symptoms corresponding to the feelings normally associated with arousal (noise-attribution condition). A second group of participants was warned about arousal-irrelevant side effects of the noise, such as ringing in the ears (shock-attribution condition). As predicted, it was found that noise-attribution participants spent less time working on the shock-avoidance puzzle, suggesting that misattribution of arousal to a nonemotional source reduced their emotional reaction of fear.

Findings such as this suggested the possibility of a kind of attributional therapy whereby maladaptive emotional responses might be ameliorated by manipulating attributions for arousal. For example, Storms and Nisbett (1970) succeeded in alleviating insomnia by getting students to misattribute their arousal symptoms to a pill rather than their emotional worries. However, subsequent studies (e.g. Brockner and Swap, 1983) have not always found this *reverse placebo* effect easy to replicate.

Misattribution studies seem to offer evidence that symptoms of arousal and explanations for these symptoms play some causal role in determining the intensity of emotional reaction, in accordance with Schachter's theory. However, the findings have not been universally consistent. Furthermore, alternative explanations for the obtained effects diminish confidence in this conclusion.

One of these alternative explanations was suggested by Calvert-Boyanowsky and Leventhal (1975). These investigators pointed out that the misattribution manipulation in many of the relevant studies was confounded with an inadvertent manipulation of *expectations* about bodily symptoms. Telling experimental participants that the nonemotional decoy stimulus (e.g. pill, injection, or noise) would result in arousal allowed these participants to anticipate how they would feel during the emotional situation, whereas participants in the control group were given no equivalent warning information. Calvert-Boyanowsky and Leventhal reasoned that reductions in emotionality achieved as a consequence of misattribution manipulations may therefore have been due to expectations about symptoms rather than misattribution of arousal.

Calvert-Boyanowsky and Leventhal argued that unexpected events are by their very nature more emotionally upsetting than expected ones (e.g. Johnson and Leventhal, 1974; Leventhal *et al.*, 1979), and that emotional reactions could therefore be reduced simply by providing accurate information about symptoms rather than bothering with the complicated misattributional deception. In their study, they replicated Ross, Rodin, and Zimbardo's study but incorporated an extra condition where participants were simply informed what the experience of shock anticipation would be like. These participants knew what symptoms to expect but were not presented with any alternative neutral cause to which these symptoms could be misattributed. Calvert-Boyanowsky and Leventhal found that there was no difference in shock avoidance between participants who attributed their arousal to the shock and those who attributed it to the noise, suggesting that it was the accurate warning information about symptoms that reduced the emotional response, rather than the misattribution instruction. Thus, it may be that misattribution effects have no general implications about the causal role of arousal in emotion, but instead are based on the simple influence of expectation on appraisal of the emotional situation.

Excitation transfer

Another source of evidence suggesting that autonomic activation can contribute to emotional reactions arises from Zillmann's *excitation transfer* studies (see Zillmann, 1978). Zillmann argued that arousal is usually attributed to a single cause even when it actually derives from a combination of factors. This assumption, coupled with Schachter's proposal about the dependence of emotion on arousal, led Zillmann to the conclusion that arousal due to a primary emotional cause may be supplemented by subsidiary arousal from secondary sources, producing an intensified emotional experience (Dutton and Aron, 1974). Similarly, arousal originating from a *previous* source of stimulation may be carried over to a new source. According to Zillmann, this second effect occurs when participants no longer associate their arousal with the earlier cause. For example, there is evidence that after physical exercise, participants *believe* that their arousal level has returned to normal before actual recovery is complete, and the undetected residual arousal can then be transferred to subsequent emotional reactions.

In one study illustrating this *excitation transfer* effect (Cantor *et al.*, 1975), students viewed sequences from an erotic film after physical exertion on an exercise bicycle. The time interval interposed between cycling and film-viewing was varied between subjects as a way of manipulating the association of residual arousal from the exercise with emotional arousal due to the film. Participants who watched the film six minutes after exercise reported greater sexual arousal than either participants who saw the film immediately after exercise, or participants who waited ten minutes to see the film. The investigators explained this pattern of results in terms of differential awareness of residual arousal. Specifically, they argued that participants in the *no-delay* condition still felt aroused due to the exercise they had just completed but correctly associated this arousal with its actual nonemotional cause rather than the film. The *ten-minute-delay* group in contrast had actually fully recovered from the exercise, so that no residual arousal remained to contribute to their subsequent emotional reaction. The excitation transfer effect was restricted to the *six-minute-delay* condition, because here participants *believed* that they had fully recovered from exercising when in fact their bodies were still aroused. Their unnoticed residual exercise-related arousal combined with the arousal actually due to the film and enhanced erotic reactions.

Zillmann and his research team's results seem to demonstrate that there are certain special circumstances when arousal from other sources can enhance emotional reactions. Thus, arousal may make some small *independent* contribution to the causation of emotion. The exact mechanism underlying excitation transfer effects, however, remains unclear.

False autonomic feedback

Valins (1966) argued that the role of arousal in emotion was not as a direct *energizer* of emotional reactions but rather as a source of *information* to be used in a self-attributional process. According to his account, people infer emotion in themselves when they believe that they have reacted internally to some plausibly emotional object (cf. Bem, 1972). Thus, it is not arousal itself that is important to the experience of emotion, but rather cognitions about arousal. Valins' theory then is a modification of Schachter's position which sees emotion as an attribution of arousal information, rather than arousal *per se*, to a plausibly emotional situation. Where Schachter saw emotion as a product of physiological and cognitive factors, Valins saw it as a combination of two different sets of cognition: one based on bodily information and the other on situational data.

Valins tested his two-cognition theory in an experiment where male students were given bogus information about their own internal reactions. The study was presented as an 'investigation of physiological reactions to sexual stimuli' in which heart beats would be directly recorded using a microphone attached to the participant's chest, while slides of naked females taken from *Playboy* magazine were displayed. Participants were told that, due to the nature of the physiological measurement procedure, they would be able to overhear their heart beat during the procedure. In fact, the presented heart-rate changes were prerecorded so that increases occurred in conjunction with half of the slides and a steady pulse was associated with the other half.

After the experiment, participants were asked to make ratings of the attractiveness of the pictures, and they judged as more attractive those slides to which they had heard their heart rate increase in speed. As a reward for taking part in the study, they were also allowed to choose from a selection of colour prints corresponding to the pictures presented in the study. They tended to pick those that had been associated with bogus heart-rate increase. Preference for these 'reinforced' pictures persisted for up to eight weeks after the experiment.

Despite limitations on the generality of the so-called 'Valins effect' (Parkinson, 1985) and possible alternative interpretations in terms of demand characteristics or considerations concerning the relative salience of the experimental stimuli (e.g. Parkinson and Manstead, 1981; 1986), it still seems as though affective judgements of certain emotionally relevant stimuli can genuinely be modified in some circumstances by manipulating beliefs about internal responses (e.g. Parkinson and Colgan, 1988). In other words, if people think that their bodies have reacted to an object, this may influence their assessment of its emotional power, as well as their subsequent behaviour towards it. Of course, the existence of such an effect does not necessarily imply that arousal information plays a causal role in generating everyday instances of emotion, only that it can alter beliefs about these experiences after the fact. The relevant research evidence only demonstrates that ideas about emotional intensity are related to ideas about specific bodily reactions rather than providing data concerning real-time on-line associations between emotional experience and cognitions of arousal. As demonstrated by research into common-sense ideas about physiological differentiation of emotions, people believe that emotion is associated with bodily change. False autonomic feedback experiments simply make the corresponding point that people believe that bodily change is often an index of emotion (see Box 4.1).

Is autonomic feedback necessary to emotion?

Valins' theory implied that the presence of genuine autonomic feedback may not be necessary for emotion to occur. An experiment by Hohmann (1966), however, suggested that some of the experiential quality of emotion may be lost when no

BOX 4.1: THE INTERIOR DESIGN ANALOGY

What is it like to be subjected to a misattribution experiment like Valins' (1966) study of the effects of false heart-rate feedback? Perhaps by seeing things from the participant's perspective, we can better understand their reactions. In my PhD thesis, I devised the following analogy for the experimental situation faced by the naive volunteer who takes part in this kind of social psychological emotion research, which I still find pertinent:

> My friend warns me that the man she is taking me to visit is involved in the avant garde of interior design, and has a somewhat unorthodox taste in furniture. Having entered what our host informs us is the living area, he invites us to sit down and make ourselves comfortable. I find myself standing by an ovoid object with no arms or legs, and no obvious flat surface for resting on. My friend, meanwhile, has squatted on a nearby rocking horse, and our host is calmly perched on the platform atop a step-ladder. There is nothing else but this rather fluffy egg to sit on. I reach out and test the surface with my hand and it gives way a little under the pressure. Is it a chair? The object certainly does possess at least one central feature that is appropriate by being soft yet supportive in substance. It is also in roughly the right kind of place to be an item of furniture of a relevant variety. To avoid embarrassment, I think the best course of action is to simply sit down on the thing.
>
> (Parkinson, 1983, p. 88)

I subsequently attempted to explain and decode the metaphor, without, I now think, complete success:

> If we are to consider the activity of conducting psychology experiments as little more bizarre a hobby or occupation than interior designing, and if we treat 'emotion' as a category with some similarity to the classes of more mundane entities such as 'chairs', then the example may be instructive for the present purposes.
>
> (pp. 88–9)

Missing from this cursory commentary is any reference to the role relationship between the protagonists of the scenario, the unfamiliarity of the setting, the lack of clear guidelines to follow, the willingness to suspend disbelief, and so on. Experiments are clearly a bit like some other real-life situations, but they are certainly unusual ones. Perhaps this means that people respond to them in unusual ways (cf. Harré and Secord, 1972; Strickland *et al.*, 1976).

arousal is actually felt. In this study, Hohmann interviewed patients with spinal injuries and found that reports of emotionality differed depending on the degree of damage to sensory feedback from the lower body. Those patients most lacking in autonomic awareness as a result of their injuries tended to report that their emotional lives lacked some vital aspect compared with prior to their disability. For example, one participant in this study described his post-injury emotional experience in the following terms: 'it's sort of cold anger . . . it just doesn't have the heat to it that it used to. It's a mental kind of anger' (p. 151). The problem with introspective data collected in this way is that it is very hard to interpret unambiguously. It could be that the quoted patient was simply describing the fact that he no longer experienced bodily symptoms when he felt emotional, but that these bodily symptoms were peripheral rather than intrinsic to his anger.

A second problem of interpretation with Hohmann's findings concerns the fact that those patients with lesions higher in the spinal cord differed not only in the amount of afferent feedback available to them but also in the degree to which their movements were limited by their injury. It seems possible that these patients led less rich lives than the others simply as a result of restrictions on their mobility, and that these changes in their life experiences were the genuine causes of their reduced emotionality. Furthermore, these patients generally had more severe disability than those with lower lesions and therefore may have been more inclined to engage in denial as a way of coping with their negative emotions.

More recent studies have failed to replicate Hohmann's basic findings. For example, Chwalisz, Diener, and Gallagher (1988) found that patients with less remaining autonomic feedback reported lower intensity of negative, but not positive, feelings and concluded that arousal may contribute to certain emotional experiences but is not a necessary condition for emotion in general. In a similar investigation, Bermond and colleagues (1991) found no evidence that emotionality was less after spinal damage; indeed, most of their participants reported *increased* intensity of emotions. Even somatic symptoms of emotion seemed to remain at the same level after injury, possibly due to autonomic imagery or phantom sensations. On the basis of these results, it seems clear that the dependency of emotion on arousal is not as tight as Schachter's (1964) theory implied (Reisenzein, 1983).

Evaluation of two-factor theory

Schachter's theory inspired an impressive array of experimental findings, some of which have been reviewed above. However, many of these findings fail to support the specific predictions of the theory or are open to alternative explanations (Calvert-Boyanowsky and Leventhal, 1975; Parkinson, 1985; Reisenzein, 1983). In the present section, I will re-evaluate the status of Schachter's theory in the light of these negative results.

A central and recurrent criticism of Schachter's theory is that he failed to specify how arousal is usually produced in emotional situations (e.g. Leventhal, 1974). The process of emotion generation begins, according to the model, with a state of supposedly unexplained sympathetic activation. In contrast to this view, theorists such as Lazarus (1991b) would suggest that the causal sequence leading to emotion begins with an appraisal of the situation, which in turn may lead to bodily changes such as arousal. To the extent that appraisal of the situation causes the person to become aroused, the separate impact of arousal in the emotional generation process correspondingly diminishes. Similarly, if activation occurs in support of specific states of action readiness, then it ceases to make an *independent* contribution to the causation of emotion.

Even Schachter admitted that the normal causal sequence leading to emotion did not involve unexplained arousal at all:

> Imagine a man walking down a dark alley when a figure with a gun suddenly appears. The perception-cognition 'figure with a gun' in some fashion initiates a state of physiological arousal; this state of arousal is interpreted in terms of knowledge about dark alleys and guns and the state of arousal is labelled 'fear'.

(Schachter, 1964, p. 51)

In other words, in most emotional episodes, interpretation and appraisal of the situation provide an immediate template for our emotional experience, so that when arousal is experienced, it is felt straight away as emotional arousal of the appropriate variety. According to this account then, arousal does not really contribute to the causation of emotion except in a trivial sense because it is felt as part of an emotional reaction that is already completely specified by situational interpretation.

Of course, it is also possible that arousal might be produced as a function of nonemotional considerations, such as physical exertion (e.g. Zillmann, 1978; see pp. 107–8) or illness, or that variations in the factor occur as a result of biorhythmic variations (e.g. Thayer, 1989). Schachter's analysis suggests that arousal changes caused by any of these variables might conceivably have an impact on emotion as long as they are attributed to an emotional source.

However, the everyday occasions on which a substantial degree of felt arousal is unexplained are likely to be rather rare. Although it is conceivable that people sometimes experience internal reactions that seem disproportionate to the apparent power of the emotional situation, it seems relatively less likely that a salient and powerful activation response would arise *de novo* without *any* obvious precursors. Indeed, if it did, the experience would likely be interpreted negatively as the indication of some kind of physical disorder rather than providing a state that could be interpreted in terms of a wide range of pleasant as well as unpleasant emotions (e.g. Marshall and Zimbardo, 1979). This analysis suggests that two-factor theory may have limited relevance to everyday emotional experience, when the different components of emotion tend to be relatively well integrated with each other.

We are left then with a more limited hypothesis based on Schachter's theory: that emotional interpretations and evaluations of the situation may be partially reassessed as a function of felt internal symptoms of emotion. Because people believe that bodily change is symptomatic of emotion, they may be willing to readjust their interpretation of their own experience or of the emotional power of the situation when internal information is discrepant from expectations. According to this account, the central explanatory factor in emotion remains the situation itself, or appraisal of that situation, with arousal demoted to a more peripheral role feeding into possible reappraisal processes.

Despite my criticisms of two-factor theory and the apparent weakness of its empirical basis, Schachter's general approach signalled a crucial reconceptual-ization of emotional phenomena which made them seem more amenable than previously to cognitive and social psychologists. Before Schachter, social factors were usually thought to play a role only in modifying the *expression* of an unchanged underlying biologically determined state (e.g. Ekman's concept of *display rules*, see Chapter 5), but after Schachter, theorists began to recognize the possibility that cognitive interpretations and social roles could directly shape what it means to be emotional (see Parkinson, 1987a). If emotions were not wholly determined by peripheral physiological variables, then it also seemed more possible to tinker with them using a range of manipulations from the behavioural psychologist's toolbox. Without this insight, the experimental social psychology of emotion could scarcely have got started.

In conclusion, then, Schachter's approach inspired a large body of valuable research by proposing that emotion is far more flexible than straightforward physiological theories seemed to imply, but his specific attributional account of this flexibility cannot be seen as providing a complete explanation of emotion. Rather, attributional factors may have some limited impact on pre-existing emo-tions, or may make some small contribution to emotion generation in certain special cases, which are perhaps best contrived in the experimental laboratory.

Bodily changes as emotional feelings

In the previous section, I argued that bodily changes may play a *cognitive* role in emotion causation to the extent that they provide information that can be inter-preted emotionally by the person undergoing them (Valins, 1966). However, Schachter's (1964) theory does not rule out a second *sensory* or *perceptual* role for internal reactions in the way that emotions are actually felt, as originally proposed by James (1884). James suggested that the essence of emotional experi-ence was the perception of bodily changes, and that without such perceptions, experience could not be emotional. In other words, according to James, the vital ingredients that made emotional experience emotional were feelings arising from inside the body.

Above, I have drawn attention to some of the errors of detail in James's account of emotion. In addition to these specific difficulties, two basic assump-tions of James's general approach to emotion and to the body are problematic from the point of view of current psychological theory. First, James argued that the body provided a 'sounding board' that reverberated in instinctive response to emotional stimuli. This analysis implies that the basic function of internal re-actions is to provide signals to consciousness. In fact, autonomic response serves two more fundamental biological roles: to preserve the body's internal energy economy in the process of homeostasis (Cannon, 1927) and to provide activation for particular (as well as generalized) modes of action readiness. Evolution has not designed the body as a way of telling the animal whether or not it is emotional but as a self-regulating system that is capable of adaptive action. Any conscious signal function of changes is likely to be secondary and derivative to these primary functions.

Of course, this does not mean that humans do not experience their emotions as embodied feelings, or that the removal of these symptoms would not change the feeling of emotion. Instead, I am suggesting that bodily changes do not constitute the essence of emotion but are contingently associated with emotional actions because of the kinds of activation and energy that they require. Indeed, it would seem to be a rather strange design solution to the evolutionary problem of providing conscious feedback about emotional state to incorporate an instinctive mechanism that recognized emotional significance, then registered this significance by activating body systems, which in turn fed back the appropriate signals to awareness. Far more efficient would be the provision of direct feedback of the initial emotional conclusion made by the appraisal mechanism, without time-consuming bodily intervention of any kind.

The second problematic assumption of James's theory concerns his conception of the nature of emotion itself. In accordance with contemporaneous structural and introspectionist approaches to psychology, he was concerned with the issue of how emotional feeling was consciously constituted. From the present point of view, this seems like the wrong question. Emotions as currently conceived are not, or at least not simply, momentary subjective experiences, but rather organized syndromes of appraisal, action readiness, and expression (Averill, 1980; Frijda, 1986). James's starting point for his theory was an unanalysed common-sense idea of emotion as a private experience. But unless such private experiences can be linked up with broader modes of human functioning they remain of only technical interest to present-day psychology.

BODILY CHANGES IN CONTEXT

In this chapter, I have considered evidence that bodily changes are causes and symptoms of emotional experiences. The argument about whether bodily change precedes or follows emotion, is in many senses a futile one (Ellsworth, 1994), because body changes, like appraisals, can serve both these roles: the 'sequence problem' turns out to be a pseudoproblem (Candland, 1976) because our bodies react as a function of emotion, and our bodily reactions, under certain circumstances at least, can provide us with information relating to our current emotional state (Parkinson, 1988). At any rate, in practical terms, empirical resolution of questions relating to the temporal order of events in emotion would require specific time-based criteria for determining the onset of an emotional reaction which are independent of physiological measurement.

A more fruitful approach would be to stop treating body changes as independent or dependent variables and to consider instead how they might relate to other aspects of emotion. As Cannon suggested, the role of physiological change in emotion is more likely to be in service of behavioural response tendencies than as a component of subjective experience. For example, according to Cannon's original theory, emotion served an 'emergency function' that prepared the organism for rapid fight or flight reactions. More recently, appraisal theory has suggested that particular emotional states are evolutionary devices for dealing with rather more specific classes of survival-related situations. In this case, as Smith (1989) has argued, the physiological changes associated with different appraised situations relating to harm or benefit might service more localized behavioural response systems than a general activation reaction. If this analysis is correct, then the distinctive physiological changes associated with emotion may be related to particular kinds of action tendency (Frijda, 1986). Similarly, Smith (1989) suggested that components of facial response were related to appraisals of the situation (see Chapter 6). In short, the alternative views that bodily changes precede or follow the onset of emotions are simplifications of the real dynamic generation of emotional processes. The body is considered as a site where stimuli and responses of certain restricted kinds occur, when in reality bodily changes are typically part of ongoing actions or action tendencies, many of which, as we shall see later, are socially produced and serve specific inter-personal communicational functions.

A second conclusion of the preceding discussion is that it is important to maintain the distinction between personal perceptions of body state from more 'objective' measures. The ways in which we become conscious of veridical or imagined body symptoms are themselves dependent on the way that the unfolding episode directs attention. People do not simply become aware of symptoms, then interpret the situation on the basis of the information that they provide. Rather, body consciousness arises in the context of a situation that already carries certain alternative definitions.

PSYCHOPHYSIOLOGICAL SYMBOLISM

The history of theories of emotion attests to the intimate involvement of physiological processes in its production. Also, common sense supports a connection between these two phenomena. Bodily changes and emotions are both things that are 'felt' in some sense, and both things that are said to be 'internal'. Thus, bodily change seems to be closely tied to the meaning of the term 'emotion'. But is this because the processes involved in producing emotional behaviour are especially closely tied to physiological events in reality or is the connection mainly at the level of ideas of emotion? Averill (1974) has argued for the latter conclusion.

Emotions, in Averill's (1985) view, are 'interpreted as passions rather than actions' (p. 98). They are conceived of as something that comes over a person rather than rationally planned responses. This fact, coupled with the high value placed on rationality and control by Western culture, results in emotion typically being regarded as an inferior mode of functioning (Averill, 1974). Even in pre-evolutionary philosophy, emotions were considered to be animal-like rather than an expression of humanity. Plato, for example, suggested that reincarnation as an animal was the fate of those humans who failed properly to exercise the faculty of reason to control their emotions. According to Averill, this ethical prejudice against emotion has led to an association of the phenomenon with more primitive parts of the nervous system (the 'visceral brain') and with the guts themselves.

One aspect of this prejudice, of course, is the suggestion that physiological arousal is a crucial component of emotion. Averill argued that this relationship is partially based on *psychophysiological symbolism* rather than scientific reasoning. On the one hand, the psychological phenomenon of emotion is devalued because of cultural prejudices, and on the other hand, physiological processes connected with the viscera and phylogenetically older parts of the brain are considered to be animal-like or somehow less than human and so tend to be associated with emotions, together with other apparently distasteful aspects of human function (sweating, digestive processes, defecation, etc.). Thus, irrelevant connotations of the term 'emotion' and of visceral processes have misguided theoretical development towards a connection between the two.

Averill (1974; 1982) explicitly discussed the psychological evidence for an association between activation and emotion, and made the following points. First, not all emotions involve increased arousal. Sadness, depression, and serenity, for example, would not be expected to increase activation. Emotions such as these have in fact rarely been investigated by psychophysiologists perhaps for this very reason. Second, many nonemotional processes are linked strongly with arousal: for example, physical effort and activity, concentration on a demanding mental task and so on. In fact, it can be argued that those emotions that are strongly linked to physiological arousal such as fear, anger, and sexual excitement are exactly those that signal an increase in activity, so that arousal would be expected to occur anyway. Finally, Averill points out that the function of the autonomic system is 'transactional' (Lacey, 1967); it adjusts to situational and behavioural demands, whether or not these requirements are emotional ones. Thus, there is little reason to link autonomic change more closely with emotional than with motivational or cognitive effects.

In Averill's view then, bodily changes belong to people's ideas of emotion rather than to the realities of actual emotional episodes. While I agree that the connection between the body and emotion is often overemphasized in support of a misguided biological reductionism, I still believe that the body really is important in emotion, although not necessarily in the way usually implied by psychological theories. I think that emotion reflects a mode of communication that is at least partly achieved through dynamic gestural and postural changes rather than verbal language (Radley, 1988). Our involvement in emotional encounters and our interpersonal claims that they matter to us are often directly expressed via the body. In short, emotion is embodied communication. Thus, bodily changes may serve not as internal signals but as part of a real-time process whereby emotional messages are transmitted to others.

5   The expressive factor

OVERVIEW

Expression, especially facial expression, provides one of the basic channels whereby emotional information is communicated. Psychologists as well as nonpsychologists have relied on expressive signals to provide diagnostic information concerning people's emotional state, and the diagnoses they make are usually thought to be relatively accurate under normal circumstances. In this chapter, I consider evidence for the common-sense view that particular expressive manifestations are symptomatic of different emotions, and for the argument that facial expressions in particular provide a universal biologically programmed language representing emotional meaning. I argue that the pre-wired aspects of expression are less important in everyday emotional episodes than is usually supposed, and that facial and postural displays find their full meanings only in the context of cultures, subcultures, and ongoing relationships. Furthermore, it may be that expressions serve to communicate information that is not simply or intrinsically emotional in many interpersonal settings. Finally, I move on from consideration of the index function of expressions to a discussion of the more counterintuitive idea, propounded in facial feedback theory, that expressive information can determine as well as reflect a person's emotional state. My intention is to integrate expression into the ongoing interpersonal process, rather than seeing the factor simply as cause or effect of emotion.

COMMON-SENSE IDEAS ABOUT EXPRESSION AND EMOTION

The idea that emotional states are expressed on the face, by gesture, bodily posture, and vocal intonation, is almost universally accepted. Furthermore, it is commonly believed that the connection between emotion and expression is a natural and direct one, with the signifiers of this communicative system having more than just an arbitrary or conventional connection with what they represent. A smile apparently means happiness in a stronger and less controvertible way than saying the words 'I am feeling happy' in any spoken language. The notion that the face in particular expresses emotion naturally and directly dates back at least as far as the Ancient Greeks. As Aristotle wrote: 'Everyone knows that grief involves a gloomy and joy a cheerful countenance' (1913, p. 808).

The basic common-sense model of emotional expression suggests that an internal state having a particular identifiable quality for the person experiencing it typically reveals itself in ways that are relatively easy for someone else to interpret. Knowledge of this process, however, is thought to allow the emotional person to exert at least partial control over the information that gets out. When this control fails, there may still be 'leakage' of the true emotion (Ekman and Friesen, 1974). This intuitive account also forms the basis for many psychological analyses of the relation between emotion and expression. The general assumption seems to be that since it is so widely accepted it must be true. As should become clear in this chapter, however, things are not quite so simple.

The very word 'expression' implies something inside that pushes to show itself externally, thus reinforcing the common-sense theory of how the expressive process operates. For this reason, many writers have preferred the more theoretically neutral terms 'display' or 'signal'. I will stay with the more ordinary usage because although emotional displays and signals may not express an intrapsychic emotion in any simple or direct way, they certainly are expressive of something in the relationship between 'sender' and 'receiver'. My general view of nonverbal expression of emotion is analogous to Vygotsky's (1986) opinion about verbal expression of thoughts, which he stated as follows: 'Experience teaches us that thought does not express itself in words, but rather realizes itself in them' (p. 251). According to Vygotsky, there is not a pre-existent articulated thought or proposition which is then translated into language and expressed, but instead speaking or writing formulates thinking on-line. Similarly, I would argue that emotions are constructed in real-time encounters via the medium of nonverbal (as well as verbal) gestures and actions.

DISTINGUISHING ACTION AND EXPRESSION

In Chapter 3, I suggested that common sense sees emotions as pressing towards action. Similarly, emotions seem to want to find expression. There is no hard and fast line dividing the external aspects of emotion that count as actions and those that count as expressions. Broadly speaking, expressions are manifestations that provide information to other people about your emotional state, whereas actions are oriented to more instrumental goals. Expressions communicate while actions change the world. Of course, the very act of providing information may under certain circumstances serve an explicit purpose, such as when you kick the furniture or smash crockery to show how angry you are or to convince someone of the seriousness of their offence against you. Correspondingly, you might smile at someone in order to persuade them to cooperate with you, or to con them into dropping their guard so that you can attack. These examples suggest that it is not easy to draw up a set of response classes that count simply as either expressions of emotions or actions caused by emotions. Clearly, many of the manifestations of emotion provide information as well as serving other instrumental goals and are therefore actions as well as expressions. However, it is possible to focus on the communicative aspect of these actions in order to examine the role of expression in emotion. Whether such a focus is helpful is a question to which I will return in later chapters.

To offer a working definition then, I will use the term 'emotional expression' to refer to those movements and sounds made by someone that communicate information that has potential emotional relevance (cf. Frijda, 1986). These movements and sounds may not be deliberate or intentional, but will still be expressive to the extent that they have emotional message value to another person. The face is usually considered to be the most important channel of emotional expression, partly because its muscles are capable of making such a wide variety of subtly patterned movements. The present chapter maintains this traditional emphasis on facial expression. However, it is worth remembering that emotion may also be expressed through tone of voice, bodily posture, and gestures.

DARWIN'S IDEAS ABOUT EMOTIONAL EXPRESSION

The psychological theory of emotional expression essentially began with Darwin's (1872) influential book *The Expression of the Emotions in Man and Animals*. Indeed, much of the research that has followed might be described as footnotes to this work. According to Darwin, three principles explained the connection between emotions and expression. All three of these original principles now seem naive in their specific details but their subsequent development by emotion theorists has corrected many of their limitations. The first and most fundamental of Darwin's principles is the *principle of associated serviceable habits* which he explained in the following terms:

> Certain complex actions are of direct or indirect service under certain states of mind, in order to relieve or gratify certain sensations, desires etc.; and whenever the same state of mind is induced, however feebly, there is a tendency through the force of habit and association for the same movements to be performed, though they may not then be of the least use.
>
> (p. 28)

In other words, movements that originally served some purpose during emotional experiences (and perhaps still occasionally do) have become automatic accompaniments of those emotions. For example, when you want to prevent exposure to some visual stimulus you may shut your eyes. Darwin argued that this deliberate behaviour may become so strongly connected with feelings of rejection that it becomes habitual even in situations when closing your eyes may not actually serve any purpose, such as when you disagree with someone during a conversation ('A man . . . who vehemently rejects a proposition, will almost certainly shut his eyes or turn away his face', p. 33).

Similarly, Darwin suggested that certain movements directly relieve the felt symptoms of an intense emotion and the same movements may then generalize to other instances of this emotion ('Another man rubs his eyes when perplexed, or gives a little cough when embarrassed, acting in either case as if he felt a slightly uncomfortable sensation in his eyes or windpipe', p. 32). Darwin further argued that these learnt expressive habits may then come to be inherited from generation to generation: a Lamarckian notion that has, of course, since been discredited.

Although the details of his account now lack credibility, Darwin's insight was that certain expressions of emotions might derive from *functional* behaviour. For example, the facial configuration often associated with disgust where the nose is turned upwards and the face twisted seems to correspond to the way a person might react when exposed to an unpleasant smell. Somehow this same reaction has become metaphorically connected with situations where the bad smell is figurative rather than literal, when someone says something unconscionable, for example.

Darwin's second principle was the *principle of antithesis*:

Certain states of the mind lead to certain habitual actions, which are of service, as under our first principle. Now when a directly opposite state of mind is induced, there is a strong and involuntary tendency to the performance of movements of a directly opposite nature, though they are of no use; and such movements are in some cases highly expressive.

(p. 28)

Darwin's point in this second principle was not that opposite emotions automatically produce opposite expressions, but rather that some emotions are expressed in a way that makes them as distinctive as possible from contrasting states. Probably the clearest example of this is the attitude of submissiveness in animals faced by an apparently unassailable antagonist. Instead of adopting a confrontative attitude 'by erecting its hair, thus increasing the apparent bulk of its body, by showing its teeth, or brandishing its horns' (p. 57) and so on, the animal will cower, make itself appear smaller, and cover its fangs. The point of this display is apparently to communicate to the antagonist that no challenge is intended. To this extent, contrary to Darwin's argument that these antithetically produced expressions are 'of no use', they in fact evidently serve an important communicative function.

The third *principle of action of the nervous system* suggested that 'when the sensorium is strongly excited, nerve force is generated in excess, and is transmitted in certain definite directions . . . Effects are thus produced which we recognize as expressive' (p. 29). In other words, the activation of neural pathways in emotion causes distinctive symptoms which can serve to express the underlying emotion. Many of the expressions that Darwin apparently had in mind when proposing this third principle would nowadays be interpreted as symptoms of high levels of autonomic arousal. For example, there is often restlessness when people are in suspense about some significant outcome. This seems to reflect an urge towards action of some variety for which no appropriate direction is currently available (Frijda, 1986).

Darwin's three principles go some way towards explaining why certain expressions take the particular form that they do, and why they are in some way 'natural' concomitants of particular emotional behaviours. To the extent that Darwin is correct about expressions serving particular instrumental or communicative functions because of their very nature, we might conclude that they are learnt from experience or passed down via culture because of their usefulness, in much the same way that all communities that live in relatively cold climates have learned to make and wear clothing of some kind.

Nothing in Darwin's principles concerning the functional basis of expressive movements necessarily implies that they are transmitted by heredity: indeed, his reliance on ideas of habit and association to explain connections between emotion and expression seems to suggest instead an explanation based on learning. Despite this, Darwin's position, like that of many previous theorists (Russell, 1994), was that expressive behaviour was typically 'natural' and inherited. Indeed, he did not believe that learnt expressions were genuine expressions at all ('we are particularly liable to confound conventional or artificial gestures and expressions with those which are innate or universal, and which alone deserve to rank as true expressions', p. 52). The question of whether emotional expression is genetically pre-programmed or culturally developed is one that has occupied much of the relevant literature since Darwin's time.

Darwin's evidence for innateness depended on reports from informants concerning the apparent consistency of emotional expression among people of different races, even when they had had little contact with Europeans. The fact that these people seemed to have independently developed a similar set of emotion-expression connections suggested that specific expressions were pre-programmed rather than learnt through social convention. Unfortunately, Darwin's evidence was informal and indirect rather than based on controlled observation. More recent studies have adopted a similar but more rigorous approach to this issue, focusing in particular on the face as the site for emotional expression.

The research evidence is usually interpreted as confirming that a limited number of facial expressions corresponding to so-called primary emotions are recognized accurately by people from a variety of cultures including those who have had little contact with Westerners (e.g. Buck, 1988; Ekman, 1989; Frijda, 1986). In fact, this broad conclusion may be an overgeneralization of the available data (Russell, 1994). In the next section, I will review the evidence concerning the emotional information provided by facial displays, before turning to the question of whether expressive communication works equivalently in different cultures.

DO FACIAL EXPRESSIONS CONVEY EMOTIONAL INFORMATION?

Most of us believe that in many circumstances we can tell what someone is feeling simply by looking at their face, but it is hard to say how often we are deceived and how often we actually fail to notice emotions that are experienced by other people. In theatre and cinema, actors use their faces to convey the content of their inner lives, but this fact does not imply that similar relations between expression and emotion hold up in everyday life when there is not necessarily any intention to communicate emotional meaning. This distinction between deliberate facial communication and spontaneous expression of emotion is an important one, as will become clear from the relevant research evidence. Most studies into the emotion-expression relationship have used posed faces and therefore provide data mainly relevant to intentional communication. However, a few studies have looked at how clearly emotional information is transmitted spontaneously by the face.

Readability of spontaneous facial expressions

One of the first experiments to address the issue of whether the face can provide usable information about emotional state recorded spontaneous rather than posed expressions. In this study, Landis (1924) took photographs of twenty-five volunteers (mostly colleagues and friends) as they underwent a series of 17 different emotionally provocative experiences. Some of these situations were apparently relatively mild, such as smelling ammonia, listening to jazz dance records, and viewing 'pornographic pictures'; others were apparently more upsetting, for example feeling around blindly in a bucket of water for a mystery object which turned out to consist of three live frogs – after the frogs had been located, the experimenter proceeded to deliver a strong electric shock through the water for that extra frisson. Finally, in the most disturbing condition of all, participants were told to saw the head off a live rat with a butcher's knife.

To accentuate their expressive movements for the photographs, participants' faces were marked with burnt cork along the muscle lines that were considered most important during emotional display. Landis coded the muscle positions captured in these pictures in order to determine whether particular movements were linked to each of his different emotional situations. He found no consistent relationship between facial expression and situation. Additionally, Landis compared expressive movements with participants' reports of what emotion they had been feeling in each situation. Here again, he found no reliable correspondence between emotion and expression.

In one of his follow-up studies, Landis (1929) used a methodology that was already becoming standard practice in the study of the emotion-expression connection. From his collection of pictures of facial reactions derived from the earlier study, Landis selected those that he believed were most expressive and asked a second group of participants to judge the emotion experienced by the person in the photograph and the situation that might have caused their expression. He found that the observers showed no consistent recognition either of the situation or the emotion as reported by the original participant at the time of the experience.

Of course, there are several problems with Landis's series of studies (for critiques, see for example Arnold, 1960; Ekman *et al.*, 1982; Honkavaara, 1961). The most obvious of these is that the situations arranged by Landis (like those used in research to assess physiological differentiation of emotion; see Chapter 4) did not always seem to have been well chosen to produce consistent emotional reactions in different people, or even in the same person at different times. Viewing erotic material in the context of such a study, for example, might produce embarrassment, excitement, or disgust, depending on the context and on the participant's present state of mind. Additionally, it is possible that many of the situations set up by Landis in fact produced similar emotional reactions. Being asked to go through a series of strange rituals in front of an experimenter holding a camera in itself may have led to general bemusement, embarrassment, or distaste. To the extent that people reacted consistently to different situations, it would be correspondingly more difficult to discriminate their facial responses to these situations. In general, it is likely that many of the situations produced mixtures, blends, or concatenations of different emotions, making the associated expressions harder to read.

A further problem is that the artificiality of the setting is likely to have induced some degree of selfconsciousness which potentially may have inhibited express-iveness. For example, participants had their faces marked with charcoal in an unusual manner and photographs were taken of them at regular intervals during the procedure. Also, no attempt was made to disguise the fact that the study concerned facial expression and this consideration may also have contributed to sensitivity to self-presentational factors. In addition, many of the participants were known to Landis from outside the experimental session, a state of affairs that probably made it difficult for them to express negative emotion to him as experimenter, and which may go some way toward explaining why smiling was found to occur so frequently, even in the negative situations.

Finally, the use of still photographs to record facial expressions removes any dynamic information from the data. It seems likely that it is easier to pick up emotional expressions from a moving face than from one that is frozen at a single point in time (e.g. Bassili, 1978).

Despite these many limitations, however, one thing is clear from Landis's findings: the relationship between emotional experience and facial expression is by no means as direct as common-sense ideas might imply. In situations such as the ones used by Landis, at least, we do not transmit unambiguous evidence about our emotional state by automatically assuming a particular facial position.

Further evidence on the issue of whether spontaneous facial movements can accurately express emotion is provided by more recent research using Buck's (1979a) slide-viewing paradigm (discussed in more detail in Chapter 7). For example, in Buck, Savin, Miller, and Caul's (1972) first study using this pro-cedure, one set of participants ('senders') were shown a series of slides depicting five stimulus categories: nude and semi-nude males or females ('sexual'); land-scapes and street scenes ('scenic'); mothers with young children performing various activities ('maternal'); severe facial injuries or burns ('disgusting'); and camera effects and art objects ('unusual'). While viewing the slides, senders rated the pleasantness and strength of their current emotional reaction and tried to put their feelings about each picture into words by speaking into a microphone. A concealed video camera was used to record covertly each sender's facial expres-sions throughout the procedure.

A second set of participants ('receivers') watched a directly relayed silent video image of senders' facial expressions during the slide-viewing. Their task was to judge which category of slide was being shown, and to rate the pleasantness and strength of the sender's apparent reaction to each picture. Concordance of these judgements with the actual category of slide presented, and with senders' self-ratings of pleasantness reactions, was assessed.

Buck and his colleagues found little evidence of accuracy in identifying picture category on the basis of facial information in male sender–receiver pairs, but five out of ten receivers in female pairs correctly categorized significantly more pictures than would be expected on the basis of chance. Although expression recognition seemed to be based on more than pure guesswork for female participants at least, overall levels of accuracy were far from impressive. For example, using a random strategy based purely on guesswork, receivers should have scored an average of one out of five correct responses in the categorization task. In fact, female receivers scored an average of roughly two out of five correct, and males did even worse. This minimal level of accuracy might be explained by arguing, for example, that receivers assumed that senders looked away when shown disgusting and unpleasant slides, but continued to stare at more pleasant pictures. Simply picking up this single piece of information may well have been sufficient to raise recognition accuracy above chance. Similarly, since receivers also watched senders while they described their response to the slide aloud, it is possible that they were able to draw inferences about reactions by occasional lip-reading of isolated words (Wagner *et al.*, 1986), or from facial and mouth movements indicating emphasis rather than emotion.

Of course, receivers faced the problem in the categorization task of knowing how this particular sender would react emotionally to each category of slide (or indeed to each slide within that category). For example, some of the more prudish senders may have averted their attention from the sexual pictures while other more prurient viewers may have intensified their gaze. In addition, the picture categories do not appear to have been selected because of their ability to produce strong and differentiated emotional response (e.g. Wagner *et al.*, 1986), making the relevance of the categorization task to emotional communication less direct. More useful data on judgement of emotional quality are available from the degree of correspondence between senders' actual pleasantness ratings and receivers' estimates of these ratings. Again, although there was a significant positive correlation between these two sets of scores, it was far from perfect. It seems therefore that the amount of emotional information communicated by the face in this particular setting is not great, even when the dimension of accuracy is based on simple pleasantness ratings.

Wagner, MacDonald, and Manstead (1986) used the same procedure as Buck and his colleagues but selected their slides more carefully so that they produced more consistent emotion ratings in viewers. In addition, receivers were asked to judge the category of emotion experienced by the sender rather than simply rating its pleasantness. Again, although recognition was above chance for some of the emotions, accuracy was generally rather low. For example, the most consistently identified emotion in this study, as in most other studies of this kind, was 'happiness', but less than half of the receivers were correct in their judgements even of this most easily recognizable emotion. These results suggest that receivers do not derive direct evidence concerning the nature of an emotional response from naturally occurring expressions. Instead, as suggested above, they may infer unpleasantness from the fact that eyes are diverted, or interest from scanning patterns.

A general limitation of these two sets of results, however, is that it is not clear that a variety of strong emotional responses can be produced by looking at still pictures. For example, unless the viewer has a specific phobia concerning the object in question, it seems unlikely that a still picture is capable of inducing realistic fear. Similarly, it is hard to get angry about something portrayed in a picture unless some malicious intent directed at the viewer is somehow inferred (the 'anger' slides actually used in Wagner and colleagues' study portrayed scenes such as executions). Although the selected stimuli probably conveyed sufficient *connotations* of the required emotion to be nominated by raters as the dominant affective response, it is unlikely that many participants would have experienced strong and involved emotional responses to the slide material. To the extent that the emotions elicited by the procedure were weak or perfunctory, we would not expect them to be noticeably manifested in facial movement.

A final source of information about the readability of naturally occurring facial expressions is available from experiments concerning judgements of media photographs. Ekman, Friesen, and Ellsworth (1982) reanalysed data from studies of emotional inferences from magazine photographs of news events (e.g. Munn, 1940) and found that judges correctly identified the nature of the emotional situation from the face alone at better than chance levels for eighteen out of twenty-seven selected pictures where the emotional situation was relatively unambiguous. The problem with these results, apart from the disappointing levels of accuracy overall, is that we cannot be certain that the expressions were in fact spontaneous rather than posed for the camera. Even if they were spontaneous, it is unlikely that they were representative of the range of real-life emotional expressions. This is because reportage photographs are often deliberately taken at the specific moment when the subject's emotion is conveyed most powerfully. Editorial selection of submitted photographs also tends to rely on similar criteria of emotional readability, making the pictures that finally appear in magazines even more unrealistically expressive (Hunt, 1941). On top of all this, the investigators conducting the original judgement studies probably made their own selections of stimulus material partly on the basis of apparent expressive legibility as well, with the result that the final set of pictures used in the experiments may have been about as distinctive a set of emotional displays as everyday life ever produces. Yet accuracy of recognition was still far from perfect.

The evidence reviewed in this section suggests that spontaneous facial expressions are far less revealing of emotion than common sense would imply. Direct evidence for this difference between the idea and reality of emotional expression was provided by Wagner (1994), who found that experimental participants shown affectively loaded slides while their facial responses were covertly videotaped rated their own expressions as significantly more readable than subsequent independent judgements in fact revealed them to be.

Readability of posed facial expressions

Landis's (1929) results contrasted with the conclusions of several other early investigators who had demonstrated that judges showed limited consistency in their identification of at least some emotions on the basis of pictures of faces (e.g. Ruckmick, 1921). The basic difference between Landis's procedure and the one used in these other studies was that he had used spontaneous rather than posed facial responses. Landis's own account of the discrepancy in findings was as follows:

> The explanation would seem to lie in the fact that the pictures which these other experimenters have used are not true portraits of the faces of emotion but are rather pictures of the socialized and to a large extent conventionalized reactions which are used as supplementary language mechanisms. There is little or no evidence that such expressions occur in 'emotion' except by chance.
>
> (p. 68)

In other words, Landis argued that people know the cultural meaning of certain symbolic emotional expressions, but these are used explicitly as communicative devices rather than occurring as natural and spontaneous accompaniments of emotional state. If Landis was correct on this point, then it is quite possible that we can decode intentional expressions of emotion without possessing any corresponding ability to recognize naturally occurring emotions on the basis of spontaneous facial position.

Some of Landis's (1924) participants were also asked to pose facial expressions subsequent to his spontaneous elicitation procedure so as to convey the emotional reactions that they had experienced during each of the manipulations. Landis noted: 'With these instructions it was found that subjects did give expressions which could for the most part be readily recognized as the traditional expressions of 'religious feeling', 'disgust', 'fear', and so on' (p. 483). It seemed therefore that deliberately adopted emotional expressions tended to be far more readable than spontaneous ones: a conclusion that has been supported by more recent research (e.g. Motley and Camden, 1988).

Ekman, Friesen, and Ellsworth (1982) reviewed the available studies on accuracy of recognition of posed emotional expression. They found that expressions intended to convey six 'basic' emotions (happiness, surprise, fear, anger, sadness, and disgust) were correctly classified at levels significantly better than chance in most of these experiments. It is important to note, however, that accuracy rarely approached 100 per cent even in a relatively simple task where forced choices were made between the six emotions (see Russell, 1994, for discussion of the limitations of the forced-choice procedure). Generally, judges seemed to be very good at recognizing posed happiness, but rather worse at identifying posed sadness from the face, getting the correct answer less than half the time in many cases. Also, the posed expressions for fear and surprise were often confused with one another. Thus, although the studies apparently confirm that judges can draw some inferences about affect consistently from posed faces, they do not seem to be able to read emotions *directly* from the information they contain.

This conclusion leads to the question of what meaning actually is readable from posed facial expressions. According to Russell (1994), recognizable distinctions between posed facial expressions might be based on common knowledge about smiles and intended pleasantness, coupled with other cues about level of attention which may be discernible from how wide the eyes are opened, or about activation which may be deduced from perceived muscle tension. Such cues might help to distinguish, say, sadness (low attention, low activation) from surprise and fear (high attention, high activation). According to this interpretation, posed faces seem to convey emotionally relevant information but not necessarily emotion itself, otherwise judgements would be expected to be more accurate than they actually turn out to be.

A basic limitation of the positive evidence concerning legibility of posed expressions is that it does not show that emotions can be recognized from the face during everyday life. The photographs used in these studies (and those described below) often show highly exaggerated and stylized facial positions such as would rarely or never occur in our usual dealings with other people. Studies of spontaneous facial expressions show that they are generally less readable. Furthermore, in real-time interactions, dynamic facial displays may incorporate a near-infinite number of nuances attuned to complex evolving situational contexts, making any underlying emotional message even harder to determine from specific facial signals presented in isolation. Finally, in genuinely involving emotional situations, people often have very good reasons to disguise or camouflage their expressions. All these factors militate against faces revealing underlying emotions directly in settings other than the experimental laboratory. In summary, the results of studies of posed expression can be seen as indicating how accurately emotion might be communicated under conditions where readability is optimal, but do not demonstrate that this level of accuracy is ever approached under normal circumstances.

DISPLAY RULES

One way of interpreting the results on judgements of emotion from expression is to assume that posed faces have an agreed shared significance in certain special cases, but no direct or necessary link to the emotion itself (cf. Landis, 1929, quoted on p. 126). For example, a smiling face functions in everyday social life as a welcome or greeting and its secondary symbolic relation to the emotion of happiness may derive from this more primary communicative function. Similarly, the connection between the emotion of disgust and the characteristic wrinkled nose expression may be based on an unconditioned response to bad smells, which has become associated with metaphorically similar situations. If this analysis is correct, the distinctiveness and informativeness of posed faces may have only peripheral relevance to the emotion–expression connection as it occurs in normal circumstances, and spontaneous expressions may not necessarily provide emotional information at all, unless the sender intends them to.

In contrast, several theorists (e.g. Ekman, 1972; Izard, 1971) have defended the relevance of the findings concerning accuracy for posed faces by arguing that the archetypal expressions for basic emotions reflect innately provided neural mechanisms for emotional communication (*facial action programs*). According to this view, the experience of one of the primary emotions automatically evokes a pre-wired muscular pattern for the relevant facial display. If this analysis is correct, the lower recognition accuracy obtained for spontaneous expressions indicates that something must distort the natural display tendency in the everyday run of social life. The set of distorting factors that Ekman has postulated to serve this function are known as *display rules* (Ekman and Friesen, 1969).

Display rules are conceptualized as cultural conventions about withholding, disguising, or exaggerating expressions in general and in specific social settings. For example, it is generally accepted in our culture that one should carry oneself in a sober manner at a funeral, but convey pleasant emotions at a party. Because of these culturally supplied rules of comportment, individuals are thought to suppress visible signs of emotions that conflict with the prescribed expectations, or overlay them with another deliberate display for camouflage. You try to hold back from laughing in church, for example, or pretend that you are actually coughing.

Because display rules are thought to depend upon shared beliefs about appropriateness of expression, then we would expect them to vary from culture to culture. For example, mourning rituals in some societies dictate that grief should be conveyed at funerals with a far greater intensity than it is in Anglo-American settings. Conversely, cultures such as that of the Utku Eskimos have strong prescriptions against the expression of anger (Briggs, 1970). More generally, cultural etiquette requires that members of any society exert a degree of control over the ways in which emotions are expressed, but the manner and degree of this control depends on the specific ideology of the society in question (Douglas, 1971; Radley, 1988).

The idea of a display rule gives a neat explanation for any cultural diversity in emotional expressions while maintaining the underlying notion that expressions are natural and innate. By postulating the impact of cultural display rules, the investigator is able to explain away any difference in expressive display noted between cultures while treating any commonality of response as evidence of the underlying natural connection between emotion and expression.

More direct evidence for the existence of display rules was provided in an experiment by Friesen (see Ekman, 1972) in which Japanese and American students were shown a stress-inducing film. When the film was seen by participants on their own, the expressions of the Japanese and American students were similar, but when it was watched in the presence of a graduate student interviewer with his back to the screen who asked questions while the film was running, the Japanese smiled more and apparently suppressed their negative expressions.

What actually happened in this situation? Ekman suggested that the *under-lying* emotional experience of both groups of participants was their reaction to the stressful film, but that the presence of someone else activated a specific display rule for the Japanese participants, leading them to monitor and modify their natural expressions of this spontaneous reaction. Of course, as ever, there are other ways of interpreting the results. For example, a reverse interpretation still based on the display-rules idea might be that the Americans played up their reactions for the sake of the interviewer who was apparently interested in these responses. Alternatively, the Americans may simply have been temperamentally less reactive than the Japanese to the interviewer's interruptions. Correspond-ingly, the Japanese students, rather than reacting to the film then working on their expression, may actually have been responding directly to the interviewer as well as to the film. Their smiles may have been intended as a display of politeness rather than some putatively 'inscrutable' overlay on their stress reactions, and their stress reactions may simply have not been so compelling under the compet-ing concerns of communicating with the interviewer (Fridlund, 1991a). In other words, differences between the two groups may have been due to their different emotional and social responses to the presence of the interviewer rather than to differences in expressive conventions with respect to their reactions to the film. Putting someone else into an emotional situation does not simply alter expressive conventions but also alters more general aspects of emotional responding. As Fridlund (1991a) argued: 'The display rules concept is inherently problematic, because it is predicated upon the dubious premise that one's emotional state in public could be equivalent to one's state in private' (p. 72).

The idea of a display rule reasserts the common-sense conception of emotion as something that demands expression but whose expression can be controlled or disguised under many circumstances. The point of this notion is that it explains cultural diversity in facial expression of emotion yet maintains the proposition that emotion and expression have a natural and innate connection. If such a connection exists, then we would also expect some cross-cultural consistency in the expression of particular emotions and in the recognition of particular expres-sions. In the next section of the chapter, I review the evidence for the universality of emotion–expression and expression–recognition connections before considering other sources of evidence for a genetic basis for emotional expression.

EVIDENCE FOR A UNIVERSAL EMOTION–EXPRESSION CONNECTION

Even if the evidence for consistency in judgements of facial expression *within* any given culture were stronger, none of it would argue against the interpretation that people have acquired conventions about how to express emotion on their faces as a result of learning. Similarly, if there is some consistency in emotion recognition across cultures this may be a result of cross-cultural contact rather than independent development. There can be few remaining people around the world who have not at some stage been exposed to Hollywood movies or American television programmes, in which the conventional connection between particular facial expressions and emotional situations is repeatedly reinforced. Because of the cultural overlap of most societies to which Westerners have easy access, it is necessary to go further for a demonstration that emotion expression is genetically programmed.

The crucial test of the innateness hypothesis involves comparing the way that emotions are expressed and recognized in societies isolated from Western culture, with the way that they are expressed and recognized within Western society itself. If it turns out that the same expressions are linked with the same emotions in these separate cultural conditions then this supports the notion that the basis of the link is common to all humans, independent of their specific societal learning experiences. Unfortunately, there is no way of perfectly satisfying the criteria for such a controlled experiment in actual practice. As soon as an isolated culture is discovered and contacted by Western investigators, allowing the possibility of the crucial experiment, it ceases to be isolated any more. Despite this obvious limitation, a series of influential studies conducted in the late 1960s and early 1970s approximated the conditions necessary for testing the universality hypothesis: that all humans share certain basic expressions of primary emotions. The results of these studies have convinced many psychologists that much of the facial expression of emotion has a direct genetic basis. In fact, on closer examination, the evidence is less clear-cut than is usually supposed (see Russell, 1994).

It is worth looking at these experiments on emotion expression and recognition in isolated cultures in detail, partly since they are rapidly becoming unrepeatable due to the growth of the global village (Ekman, 1994), and partly because they have been so influential in shaping psychological opinion about the facial expression of emotion.

The most substantial body of research in this area was conducted by Ekman and his colleagues. For example, Ekman, Sorensen, and Friesen (1969) tested judgements of photographs of American facial expressions among preliterate cultures in Borneo and New Guinea. The stimulus pictures were selected carefully from previous judgement studies to be as clear as possible representations of the relevant emotions. The experimental task was a forced-choice procedure where participants attempt to allocate each facial picture to the name of one of the six 'primary' emotions.

As with the within-culture studies described above, the members of the various tribes included in the study were relatively good at recognizing which of the pictures of faces was intended to represent 'happiness' but were rather worse at connecting the other expressions with their respective emotion names. The group of participants who spoke pidgin English (and whose familiarity with Westerners was greatest) were generally better at naming the other expressions as intended, but even they were correct in less than half the cases for the emotions of fear and surprise (the expressions of which are commonly confused in this kind of study) and for disgust, and the majority of participants in other groups misclassified the 'sadness' expression as representing anger. Overall, the highest level of accuracy shown for any emotion apart from happiness was 54 per cent, and even happiness recognition fell short of 100 per cent. These results are disappointing for any theory that assumes a direct and natural connection between emotion and expression, since one might expect near-perfect results from such a procedure, with judges correctly matching genetically programmed expressions to primary emotion categories in a consistent and completely accurate manner. Also, since the tribes investigated had experienced visual contact with Westerners ('many had seen a few movies', Ekman, Sorenson, and Friesen, 1969, p. 88), it seems quite possible that they could have learned any judgement skill that they possessed from their actual observation of the relevant cultural conventions.

Ekman and his colleagues explained the weakness of their results partly in terms of the difficulties of the experimental situation for these participants who were unfamiliar with Western ways. However, the fact that the happiness expression was identified correctly in most cases suggests that the participants at least understood what they were supposed to be doing during the task (Russell, 1994).

One aspect of the investigation that the participants from isolated cultures may have found difficult to understand, however, was the necessity to solve the task using only the specific experimental materials explicitly presented to them. According to our accepted Anglo-American conventions of assessment or experimentation, it seems clear to us that the correct answer should be derived from the information in the pictures rather than from any cues transmitted by the experimenter. However, we cannot expect people from other cultures to share these particular scruples. In fact, experimentally extraneous cues may well have played a role in the reported performance of preliterate participants. Because of language problems, Ekman and his colleagues were forced to use native translators as experimenters in many cases, and these experimenters no doubt quickly became aware of what responses were required. It seems possible therefore that, unwittingly or otherwise, extra cues were passed on to the participants, and that at least some of their apparent accuracy was based on experimenter effects (Rosenthal, 1966). As Sorenson himself later commented, concerning his own independently conducted studies, 'it was likely that at least some responses were influenced by feedback between translator and subject' (Sorenson, 1976, p. 139). Ekman and his associates clearly went to some trouble to avoid similar problems (Ekman, 1994), but it would be hard to remove the possibility of contamination completely. In practice, there is no way of knowing for certain how much this factor may have influenced the obtained results, and inflated estimates of recognition accuracy (Russell, 1994).

Because members of the most isolated tribes were illiterate and thus could not read lists of alternatives for forced-choice procedures, and also seemed unable to remember lists of six emotion words when they were read to them, Ekman and his colleagues used a simpler procedure for assessing these participants' knowledge about emotional expression (Ekman and Friesen, 1971). In this simplified task, participants were read brief stories describing emotional situations and then asked to select from three (sometimes two) contrasting photographs of Western faces which expression corresponded to the one that would be displayed by the protagonist of each story (cf. Dashiell, 1927).

Results using this easier procedure were apparently more encouraging for the universality hypothesis. Again, however, for more isolated cultures, the findings were far from perfect. Heider and Heider's investigation of the Dani tribe, for example, found that only two-thirds of judges correctly allocated the 'anger' face to the appropriate story overall with only two alternatives to choose from, and that the discrimination between the 'anger' and the 'disgust' expression was at no better than chance levels (Ekman, 1972). Given that this procedure allows two obvious ways of reaching the correct answer, either by recognizing that the correct expression matches the situation or by recognizing that the alternative expression does not, the level of accuracy demonstrated was not impressive. Furthermore, the investigators explicitly excluded some of the more difficult comparisons from the procedure, so that the 'fear' face, for example, was never presented as an alternative in the 'surprise' judgement. Finally, the experimental task allowed participants to learn which expressions were supposed to be linked to which stories independently of their knowledge of emotion expressions (Russell, 1994). This possibility arises because each story was presented on more than one occasion to each participant. Since the correct expression always accompanied the presentation of the relevant story, but the distractor item (or items) changed from trial to trial, it was possible for participants to work out which of the faces was always presented when a certain story was told and therefore deduce which was the correct answer by logic rather than insight into emotion expression.

A final problem with the procedure used in this study was that the task does not actually ask for associations between expressions and emotions, but instead for connections between expressions and situations. This means that if the particular situation chosen to represent each emotion had an obvious and natural connection with a facial movement, then this fact could explain a correct response regardless of any knowledge about emotional expression. For example, one of the disgust stories involved smelling something bad. Wrinkling your nose in such a situation may seem a natural response, but this fact in itself does not imply that nose wrinkling is associated with the emotion of disgust, only with malodorous events. Similarly, for happiness, the situation described was greeting a friend. A smile might well be a universal greeting, but this does not necessarily mean that it universally represents happiness.

This final problem was further compounded because of the particular way in which the experimental stories were devised. Instead of using scenarios that had been selected in advance as representing probable occasions for the relevant emotions, the investigators derived many of their situational descriptions from a pilot study where tribe members from the same preliterate culture as the subsequent participants were shown the pictures of facial expressions and asked to recount an episode in which these expressions might occur. Thus, the stories used in the study described situations that were already associated with the relevant expressions within the culture in question. This means that all that the participants had to do in order to give the correct response in the experiment proper was to perform the same task as the pilot judges in reverse, and recognize that the face went with the situation in the same way as the situation had already been judged to go with the face. In effect, the results from such a procedure show us only that there is some agreement within the investigated cultures about what kinds of faces are associated with certain situations. Fortunately, the scenarios used actually did seem to correspond to ones in which Westerners might also feel the prescribed emotions, but this fact in itself still does not mean that the preliterate participants share the same emotion–expression linkages, only that certain specific situations exist in which similar facial expressions might occur. In any case, the failure to achieve perfect accuracy suggests that recognition was not that easy even in a task as simplified as this one.

The final evidence concerning the hypothesized universality of emotion–expression connections concerns recognition by Westerners of expressions posed by members of one of the isolated cultures. Ekman and his colleagues (see Ekman, 1972) recorded videotapes of nine members of the Fore tribe who had been asked to adopt an expression corresponding to each of the stories from the experiment described above. These videotapes were subsequently shown to American students who were asked to select which of the six 'primary' emotions each video clip represented.

Results showed that the Western judges only showed reliable recognition of four basic emotional expressions as posed by the preliterate culture, and even then they were well short of 100 per cent accuracy. The best results were for the 'happy' face which was recognized in slightly less than three-quarters of all cases. The 'sad' face was correctly named in about two-thirds of cases, and about half the judgements were correct for the 'disgusted' and 'angry' faces. 'Surprised' and 'fearful' faces were not reliably recognized. At best these results show that Fore expressions provided limited information about four distinct emotionally relevant situations. We still cannot be sure that the expressions posed were intended to communicate emotion, because they were posed in response to situational rather than affective information. Again, the Fore posers may have wrinkled their nose because something was described as smelling bad rather than because they knew how to express the emotion of disgust with their faces.

Even if the evidence from these judgement studies were taken as confirming that certain emotion–expression linkages are universal across cultures, this in itself would still not prove that the connection was genetically pre-wired. It may be that members of all human societies share common learning experiences, or that different cultural traditions are subject to similar environmental contingencies, resulting in a tendency for particular facial positions to be associated with similar emotional situations. For example, it may be that the expression said to represent surprise is linked to a reflex startle reaction which tends to generalize to other surprising situations. Similarly, the wrinkled nose of disgust may reflect a universal reaction to bad smells that is subsequently associated with other metaphorically similar situations. Finally, it seems likely that smiles are universally and perhaps even genetically linked with greeting other people and this fact may tend also to associate them with happy situations. Derivatively, contrasting expressions may come to be adopted in sad situations across many cultures as a result of learning experience rather than evolution simply because they are as distinctive as possible from smiles (cf. Darwin's principle of antithesis).

In conclusion, if as common sense and some psychological theories claim, the face provides a direct reflection of what is going on inside emotionally, it is hard to understand why the findings concerning the associations between emotions and expressions, and expressions and judgements of emotion, are not stronger than they are. Investigators have gone to great efforts to make the facial expressions used as stimuli as distinctive as possible and the experimental task of matching expression to emotion label as easy as they can. And yet participants still make a substantial number of errors, for all emotions except happiness. It is hard to see why there should be any problem with these simplified experimental tasks if expressions really were tied in a natural way to emotions (see Box 5.1). Thus, although it is absolutely clear that facial expressions are capable of providing some degree of emotionally relevant information, they do not seem to be directly related to any specific emotion with the possible exception of happiness.

BOX 5.1: HOW ACCURATELY SHOULD PEOPLE BE ABLE TO MATCH EXPRESSIONS TO EMOTIONS?

According to common sense, at least within our Western culture, facial expressions are capable of directly reflecting emotional experiences. If this assumption were correct, we would expect that, on being shown selected good and clear examples of basic emotional expressions, people should be able to say definitively what emotion each of these expressions expresses. Of course, when people are asked to perform tasks such as this they often make mistakes even though they actually possess the ability to provide the correct answer under perfect circumstances. Furthermore, it may be that some of the relevant knowledge is tacit rather than explicit and thus not completely implementable in abstract tasks such as naming procedures. Under these circumstances, how well might we expect people to perform in a real-life identification situation assuming that there actually were a familiar and consistent connection between emotion and expression? Russell (1994) reported results of analogous recognition puzzles where participants were asked to allocate category descriptions to familiar non-psychological entities as well as emotional expressions. He found that participants were correct in their assignment of names to vehicles such as motorcycles, trains, boats, and aeroplanes, and animals such as ducks, cows, dogs, elephants, and chickens in more than 90 per cent of cases overall (the lowest score for any of these categories was 80 per cent accuracy for automobiles). In contrast, assignment of emotion terms to facial expressions varied dramatically between categories. Although 91 per cent of participants gave the 'correct' response to the 'happy' face, and 88 per cent to the 'surprised' expression, none of the other 'basic' emotions were recognized at higher than two-thirds accuracy. 'Anger' was identified in only 40 per cent of cases, and 'contempt' was not recognized by anyone at all. The basic conclusion that can be drawn from these results is that whatever connection links most emotion terms to facial expressions is not as tight, or at least not as intrinsic and explicit, as the conventional association that obtains between linguistic names and familiar culturally defined or biologically distinct objects.

DO EXPRESSIONS EXPRESS EMOTIONS?

Emotion investigators have often taken for granted the common-sense assumption that the main point of facial displays is to express internal emotional states. The evidence reviewed in the previous section, however, suggests that although attribution of emotion on the basis of facial expression occurs at levels that are significantly better than chance, the general degree of accuracy is not sufficient to support the notion of a simple and direct link between emotion categories and expressions. Perhaps, therefore, facial expressions are not immediate readouts of intrapsychic emotional experiences at all but, rather, connect up with other factors associated with the emotion process (e.g. Scherer, 1992). In the present section, I consider two related versions of this proposal.

Expressions as part of emotional action tendencies

Developing Darwin's (1872) 'principle of associated serviceable habits' (see pp. 119–20), Frijda (1986; see also Eibl-Eibesfeldt, 1973) has argued that facial expressions often have direct functional significance as part of more general action patterns which include postural changes and integrated movements of the whole body. Some of these action patterns can be seen as belonging to species-specific behavioural repertoires, serving adaptive purposes such as defence ('anger'), rejection of unpleasant substances ('disgust'), and protection from harm ('fear'), while others may depend more on learnt responses. For example, when in a hostile situation, people tend to prepare themselves to overcome resistance by mobilizing muscular energy and by focusing attention on whatever obstacle is impeding their progress. Muscular tension manifests itself on the face in signs such as compressed lips and clenched teeth, and concentrated attention in a steady gaze and narrowed eyes, which can be interpreted as the expression of anger. In other words, the facial expression is not directly related to the emotional *experience* as such but to the mode of action readiness which is adaptive in the emotional situation. As Frijda put this point: 'Expressive behavior has its inherent significance, as relational activity, as the manner in which the subject positions himself with respect to the environment' (p. 24). Of course Frijda's (1986) theory sees changes in action readiness as central and defining characteristics of emotion, so in his view the expression can still be seen as a direct reflection of the emotion itself, but not necessarily of the *feelings* associated with the emotion.

Expressions as communicating intentions

A subset of relational functions identified by Frijda as associated with facial expressions concerns relations with other people. For example, 'angry' faces do not only serve as preparation for certain kinds of action but also as messages sent to other people present about what kinds of action are likely. Indeed, their communicative function may derive partly from their association with the developing behaviour sequence. Specifically, the fact that aggressive behaviour often starts with an increase in muscular tension and directed attention may lead to people recognizing the significance of the facial aspects of this preparatory state as an indication of likely future actions. This is one of the ways whereby particular expressions may come to have an agreed communicative meaning (cf. Mead, 1934). According to this view, staring is not just about fixing attention but also about threat and intimidation, and may have evolved culturally or biologically to serve exactly this purpose. Fridlund (1991a; 1992; see also Andrew, 1963; and Chapter 7) has presented a similar view of the evolutionary function of facial expressions based on the notion of behavioural ecology. According to this account, the primary purpose of expressive displays is communicative: expressions inform (or mislead) other people about what the expresser is about to do. Thus, expressions are always directed towards some actual or imagined audience and are intended to communicate some intention to them. Correspondingly, audiences are biologically attuned to the communicative significance of these expressive messages.

In Fridlund's view, the relationship between expression and emotion is a contingent one. Many emotional situations also happen to be ones where communication of intentions using facial expressions is functionally appropriate, but there is no necessary or direct link between the emotion and the expression as such. When we are angry, for example, it is often useful for us to convey to the person with whom we are angry that we may potentially become aggressive, and this communicative function rather than the emotion itself explains why we tend to adopt certain facial patterns. In other words, Fridlund argued that the emotion can occur independently of expression, and expression can arise independently of emotion, although in practice the two often go together. The expression does not express the emotion, it just signals the associated behavioural tendency to others who are present.

One of the reasons that psychologists have assumed that expressions express emotions rather than communicate intentions is that people apparently engage in facial expression when they are alone and there is no one else around to whom any putative communication might be addressed. Fridlund (1991b), however, explained this phenomenon by suggesting that expressions made in private are in fact usually directed at *imagined* audiences. In support of this idea, Fridlund showed that facial reactions were stronger when experimental participants who were watching an emotion-inducing film on their own, believed that one of their friends was watching the same film in a separate room. In other words, knowledge of a potential audience influences facial expression in private, suggesting that even solitary smiles are sensitive to interpersonal factors and therefore probably serve some implicit communicative function.

Fridlund's claim that expression is distinct from emotion implies that there is a separable internal experience called an emotion which goes on independently of the communicative process. This assumption, however, is not a necessary component of his behavioural ecology thesis. For example, if like Frijda (1986) we conceptualize emotions as constituted by changes in action readiness, then the expression as a device communicating intentions to act becomes a more direct reflection of the emotion itself. Later in this book, I develop an account of emotion as a primarily communicative concept which reconnects Fridlund's view of expression with the psychology of emotion (but not with the psychology of emotion as a private experience).

One of the advantages of seeing expression as tied to action readiness and communication of behavioural intentions is that it helps to explain why particular expressions tend to go with specific emotions. If the relevant connection were between expression and feeling state, it would be hard to explain why gritted teeth, say, should reflect anger rather than happiness. However, if expression is seen as part of a more general mode of action preparedness, then the association seems to be based on intrinsic features of the two related responses. The expression becomes more than just an arbitrary signifier of the signified state (Andrew, 1963).

The present discussion of facial expression has almost imperceptibly shifted the focus of the argument from the realm of individual to interpersonal emotion. Indeed, the very idea of expression implies that something is communicated to someone else. Unless some meaning were conveyed by a facial movement, for example, it could not be seen as an expressive movement. The research into facial expression also implicitly assumes a process of communication, although this usually takes place at least at one remove, with the person transmitting the information being represented in a still photograph or a video clip rather than physically present. In Chapter 7, I will consider more explicitly the paradigms that have been used to investigate emotional communication.

DEVELOPMENTAL EVIDENCE FOR INNATENESS OF EXPRESSIONS

Separate to the question of what facial expressions actually express is the issue of whether the muscular configurations underlying these expressions are pre-programmed genetically. Developmental evidence tends to suggest that facial patterns corresponding to those attributed to a limited number of emotional states appear at a relatively early age, and that some of them occur even in children who are born blind and therefore have little opportunity to learn expressions by imitation.

For example, Eibl-Eibesfeldt (1973) observed the expressive behaviour of five children who had been born both deaf and blind and found that all of them exhibited smiles, frowns, laughter, crying, and raised eyebrows in appropriate emotional situations. It is hard to estimate the exact role of learning in the development of these situation–expression links, but it is likely that genetically programmed reflexes underlay their initial elicitation (Andrew, 1963), leading to subsequent generalization across situations. Furthermore, there seems to be little doubt that the facial patterns themselves were based on inherited factors. Eibl-Eibesfeldt, however, presented no data about expressions corresponding to *fear* or *disgust* which other investigators have considered to be basic emotions, leaving open the possibility that the genetic basis for these expressions may be less rigidly defined.

Turning to the evidence from sighted children, Camras and colleagues (Camras *et al.*, 1992) found that five-month-old Japanese and American children all tended to show similar facial expressions when subjected to nonpainful arm restraint. However, the specific 'angry' expression when it occurred was typically blended with expression of non-specific negative affect or distress. Other investigators too have found that emotional expressions start out as relatively undifferentiated. For example, Oster, Hegley, and Nagel (1992) showed that adults are unable to discriminate between infants' expressions of different kinds of distress, corresponding to primary emotions. Although smiles and distressed faces appear at a very early age, then, there is little conclusive evidence that specific emotional expressions are available in the communicative repertoire of infants. Furthermore, because the children studied in this research were preverbal, we have no way of knowing what their conscious experience was like when they displayed expressions interpreted as emotional by adults. Theorists have disputed about whether distinct facial expressions are accompanied by discrete emotional experiences in young babies (e.g. Camras, 1992; Camras *et al.*, 1991; Sroufe, 1979).

In summary, it seems likely that the particular facial patterns associated with emotionally relevant situations contain some genetic component, that reflex connections lead to their original elicitation, and thus that inherited factors contribute to the development of emotional expression. However, such evidence should not be taken as direct support for the idea that a set of basic emotions are pre-wired and innate feeling states, rather that our emotional lives are constrained to some extent by biological factors, much like any other of our human capacities. From the present point of view however, the biological limits on emotional function are of less interest than the cultural content of emotional communication and how emotions are worked out on-line during the course of ongoing interpersonal interaction (see Chapter 7).

EXPRESSION AS A CAUSE OF EMOTION

The idea that expressions reflect our emotional state is one that is very much part of common sense. In contrast, the notion that the way that our face is positioned influences, rather than is influenced by, the way we feel seems much less plausible. Nevertheless, this idea that facial responses contribute to the experience of emotion is one that has been taken seriously in the psychological literature. Several theorists have argued that we sense changes in the muscular configuration of our faces, and that these sensations can change the way we feel (e.g. Izard, 1972; Laird, 1974; Tomkins, 1962). This proposition is generally known as the *facial feedback hypothesis.*

The attraction of the facial feedback hypothesis is that it seems to provide a way of explaining how different emotional states feel subjectively distinct from one another. Unlike the signals available from the autonomic nervous system, which are often too gross to provide diagnostic information about emotional quality (Cannon, 1929; see Chapter 4), facial expressive patterns show at least some consistent relations with specific emotions. Thus, it is suggested that feedback from facial expression may constitute an important source of emotional feelings.

Fridlund (1991a) attributed the original version of the facial feedback hypothesis to the theory of drama, as proposed for example by the German playwright Lessing who argued that imitation of the manifestations of internal experiences leads to the induction of the corresponding experiences themselves. A more scientific variant of this idea was proposed by Darwin (1872) who suggested that facial responses might affect as well as reflect emotional experience. He argued that: 'The free expression by outward signs of an emotion intensifies it. On the other hand, the repression as far as possible of all outward signs softens our emotions' (p. 365). Darwin's point was that letting oneself go during emotion makes the emotion stronger, not that expression in itself determines emotional experience. Subsequent theorists, however, have seen expressions as exerting a more direct role in the generation of emotion.

Many studies have suggested that facial expressions can have a small but reliable influence on the strength of emotional reactions. For example, in the first experiment of this kind, Laird (1974) positioned participants' facial muscles into a smile or a frown by instructing them to contract or relax individual muscles, ostensibly in order to allow accurate electrode placement for recording of electromyographic activity. Emotional judgements of mildly emotional slides (pictures of Ku Klux Klan members intended to elicit negative emotion, and of children playing intended to produce pleasant affect) were influenced by this procedure, with smiles producing more positive, and frowns more negative, ratings. Although the rating differences under the different expression conditions were significant, they were not large.

A similar experiment by Tourangeau and Ellsworth (1979) failed to produce supportive evidence for the facial feedback hypothesis. These investigators asked participants to maintain their faces in a fixed position to allow accurate physiological recording while they viewed films that were described as containing subliminal stimuli. In fact, participants' faces were positioned in a fearful or sad expression, or in an effortful grimace unrelated to any emotional experience. Three different films were shown: one conveying 'fear' by depicting industrial accidents; the second, intended to produce sadness, showing a small boy forced to stay in an orphanage while his mother was in hospital; and the third being an emotionally 'neutral' film about a flower show.

Tourangeau and Ellsworth reasoned that if facial position affected emotion, then the adoption of an expression that was concordant with the emotional tone of a film should intensify the corresponding emotional reaction, while a contrasting emotional expression should detract from the affective response to the stimulus. In fact, they found that there were no significant differences in emotional reactions to any of the films due to the various expression conditions.

This experiment was strongly criticized by Izard (1981) and Tomkins (1981) whose main argument was that the expressions produced by Tourangeau and Ellsworth's procedure were frozen and unnatural and therefore would not be expected to affect emotional response. According to Tomkins, the only kind of expressive movement that might affect emotion is a spontaneous one. Of course, the practical problem with this reasoning is that if the expression is spontaneous, then according to the terms of the theory, it already reflects an ongoing emotional process and therefore cannot be seen as the independent cause of the same process.

Lanzetta, Cartwright-Smith, and Kleck (1976) tested the effects of expression intensification or inhibition on the experience of pain. Participants' facial responses to varying levels of electric shock were recorded on videotape, and they were told either to disguise their reactions for the camera, or to exaggerate them. Ratings of shock intensity were affected by whether the participant was trying to reveal or hide the facial reaction to the shock, with higher intensity ratings under the exaggeration condition. This result suggested that the extent of an expressive response may moderate the painful effects of shock.

Apart from the fact that Lanzetta and colleagues' experiment concerned pain rather than a more prototypical emotion, its main problem concerns the means by which expressions were manipulated. We cannot be sure what strategies participants used to control their expressive reactions for the camera, but it seems likely that at least some of them achieved this by working on their attentional activity during the pain delivery. For example, in order to reduce their expression of pain, participants may have tried to distract themselves from the stimulus, and succeeded in reducing their actual felt experience of pain rather than simply its overt expression (cf. Spanos and Chaves, 1989).

Laird's and Tourangeau and Ellsworth's studies directly manipulated facial expressions, while Lanzetta and colleagues used an indirect manipulation. Indirect methods are open to the general criticism that any emotional effects may be due to the manipulations themselves rather than the induced changes in facial expression. Direct manipulations, on the other hand, suffer from the problem that it is difficult to modify expression without participants becoming aware that their faces are being positioned into a smile or a frown or whatever. If people are aware of their facial position, this may alert them to the purposes of the experiment, and subtly encourage them to give appropriate responses.

One of the most convincing demonstrations of a facial feedback effect was provided by Strack, Martin, and Stepper (1988) who apparently succeeded in manipulating facial expression directly without participants' awareness. Participants were told that the study was an investigation of how disabled people manage to perform various tasks using parts of the body that are not normally used for these tasks. In the experimental procedure, participants were asked to write using their mouth to hold the pen. One of their assigned tasks was to rate how funny a series of cartoons was. While performing this task, some of the participants were told to grip the pen between their teeth, a position which puts the face in an expression somewhat resembling a smile, while others were told that they were only allowed to use their lips to hold the pen, effectively preventing them from smiling and encouraging more of a frowning face. It was found that subjects who held the pen between their teeth rated their amusement at the cartoons significantly higher than did those who held the pen in their lips. Thus, it seems that our emotional reactions to emotional material can be influenced partially by the expression that we have on our face.

The weight of evidence suggests that small but reliable emotional effects of expressive differences can be obtained under certain circumstances and for certain emotions. Expression can alter the overall pleasantness of an emotion, and exerts possibly specific effects on reactions to painful and humorous stimuli. But how does this influence operate? A range of explanations have been proposed for the facial feedback effect.

Laird's original experiment was based on a self-attributional account of emotion. Like Schachter (1964), he argued that people make inferences about their emotional state on the basis of the perceptual information that is available to them. Some of this information, in Laird's view, might derive from feedback of facial expressions elicited by emotional situations. Thus, whereas Schachter argued that quantitative information about one's emotional state is derived from the body's arousal response, Laird suggested that this information may be supplemented by qualitative data from facial feedback. The self-perception of smiling, for example, might inform us that we are happy in some way. A basic question opened up by Laird's analysis concerns the extent to which the self-attributional process leading to emotion is thought to be conscious or unconscious, and relatedly, whether it is based on sensory, perceptual, or cognitive information.

In Laird's (1974) experiment, one of the participants explained his reaction when his face was in a frown as follows:

> When my jaw was clenched and my brows down I tried not to be angry but it just fit the position . . . I found my thoughts wandering to things that made me angry which is sort of silly I guess. I knew I was in an experiment and knew I had no reason to feel that way, but I just lost control.
>
> (p. 480)

Of course, this participant was perfectly aware that the position of his face was like a frown and this recognition consciously triggered thoughts relating to anger, which in turn made him feel a little more angry. The process connecting expression and emotion was not an explicit weighing up of evidence for this participant but it was clearly an inferential one. This kind of inferential process seems less likely in Strack, Martin, and Stepper's study where participants were apparently not explicitly aware that they were smiling or frowning. In this case, the fact that a smiling face facilitates expression of a humorous reaction may have allowed participants using their teeth to hold the pen to get more involved in the emotional aspects of the situation. In contrast, the fact that participants using their lips to hold the pen were unable to smile may have stopped them engaging in appropriate amusement reactions. Interestingly, both groups of participants rated the cartoons as equally *objectively* amusing: only their subjective reactions to them were different.

Results of an experiment by Leventhal and Mace (1970) suggest that consciousness of expression may interfere with, rather than contribute to, emotional experience. Children were shown slapstick comedy films with or without a canned laughter soundtrack. Canned laughter increased the children's laughter as well as their amusement at the films except in a condition where participants were told to pay attention to their own laughing. In this latter condition, self-attention to laughter reduced ratings of amusement, suggesting that focal awareness of facial responses may interfere with facial feedback effects. It seems that the expressive response needs to be registered to have some effect on emotion, but explicit focused consciousness undermines its influence.

Laird and Bresler (1992) argued that the feeling of emotion is constructed out of perceptual information from various sources of bodily feedback including facial feedback. In their view, no conscious or inferential process mediates the link between facial response and emotion. Rather the emotional experience is simply an integrated pattern of perceived feedback.

Another way in which facial expression might influence emotion was suggested by Zajonc (1985) who argued that part of the function of facial expression is to control the blood supply to the brain, resulting in an increase or decrease in cerebral temperature which in turn might influence the release of emotion-related neurotransmitters. Although this theory might sound rather far-fetched at first blush, Zajonc, Murphy, and Inglehart (1989) have recently provided some evidence for it. For example, they showed that the supposed scent of cool air pumped into the nose was rated as more pleasant than the scent of warm air, and that pronouncing the German vowel 'ü' (roughly equivalent to an abrupt and emphatic 'oo') led to higher forehead temperatures and less pleasant affect ratings than pronouncing the English vowel 'o', presumably because of the different facial positions adopted while making these sounds. It is possible, therefore, that effects of expression on cerebral blood temperature can make small differences to experiences of relative pleasantness. More generally, it seems likely that facial feedback effects are caused by a range of factors whose importance to the general theory of emotion remains to be clarified.

Theorists disagree about whether facial expressions affect emotion directly or via the mediation of attributional or other cognitive or perceptual processes. From the point of view of the present analysis, the limitation of all the alternative accounts is that they tend to focus on a one-way relationship between expression and emotion, rather than looking at the way that expression operates as part of a developing emotional reaction.

EXPRESSION IN CONTEXT

The above discussion treats facial expression either as a symptom of emotion or as its partial cause. In fact, most current approaches to facial expression examine the phenomenon out of context rather than trying to find out how changes in facial position are related to other emotional factors. When studied as a separate phenomenon, facial expression does not seem to link up as closely with the experience of emotion as we imagine it should do: the connection between facial expressions and emotions is neither as direct nor as natural as common-sense ideas as well as classical psychological theories have implied. However, clearly we do read some kinds of emotional information from other people's faces when we are interacting with them. How is this possible if faces do not convey fully articulated emotional information of their own accord?

The answer lies in putting expression back into its proper ecological niche: dynamic facial movements are coordinated with the ongoing flow of a conversation and derive their meaning from the always unfolding context of an episode, within its continually negotiated shared meanings. For example, when someone smiles while making an insulting comment, the expression ironizes the statement rather than expressing happiness about the failings of the insulted party: the dynamic coordination of the presentation is vital in constructing meaning. It is not that we deduce conclusions about someone's inner state on the basis of facial expressions, but rather that we are attuned to changes at certain key points in an encounter. Taken out of context as raw facial information, these same changes might have little direct significance.

In fact there is an entire research literature concerning the issue of whether people make judgements about emotion on the basis of contextual or facial expressive information (see, for example, Nakamura *et al.*, 1990; Walbott, 1988). In the relevant studies, participants are presented with still photographs or film clips showing someone's reaction in the context of a range of situations. Judgements of emotion based on the context alone and of the face alone are compared with judgements based on the whole picture. The almost foregone conclusion of this research is that it depends on the relative informativeness of face or context which is relatively more important in making judgements (although, as we have already seen, faces alone rarely provide unambiguous information about emotion). The problem with these studies is that they imply much too limited a notion of context. In the normal run of events we usually come across facial displays in situations whose definitions we already understand or which we have contributed to defining, so the meaning of any facial gesture takes its part in the unfolding of the significance of the whole integrated encounter.

Traditional research into the relation between facial expression and emotion attempts to find a neutral context which allows the spontaneous and unselfconscious expression of an authentic underlying emotion. Superimposed upon this in normal interaction is thought to be a layer of social dissimulation, of deliberately using expressive means to convey a misleading impression of what is really felt. It is exactly this distorting influence of dissimulation that the neutral context attempts to iron out. In my opinion, no such neutral communicative context for emotion could ever exist (cf. Kappas, 1991). Expression as well as emotion itself achieve their purpose and meaning in the messages that people send to each other (even when the other is internalized or imagined; Fridlund, 1991b).

Putting facial expression back into context also allows a possible causal role for this factor in producing emotion interpersonally. For example, if I read your face as smiling while I talk to you (even if the smile is a side effect of a recent dental procedure of which I am unaware), then my attitude to you will take account of this impression. I may feel warmer to you and this warmness in turn may be read by you and contribute to your good feelings. Alternatively, it seems plausible that we coordinate expressions automatically during social interaction (e.g. Bernieri *et al.*, 1988) and read interpersonal mood directly off the other's display. In this case, the emotional communication does not require any explicit judgement or categorization of what either party is feeling, as long as the display makes some difference to the unfolding encounter. At any rate, the impact of facial expression on one's own feelings in the context of an interaction, though often unpredictable, is virtually guaranteed.

In this chapter, I have considered the role played by facial expression in the causation and development of emotional reactions. In the previous chapters, I discussed the contribution of three other components of emotion. In the next chapter, I consider some of the psychological theories of emotion that have attempted to consider these four factors together, before broadening the discussion by looking at emotion in its everyday interpersonal context.

6   Four-factor theory

OVERVIEW

In the previous chapters, I have considered the contribution of four sets of variables to the constitution of emotional episodes. Each of these factors has been postulated to serve the role of determinant as well as symptom of emotion. I have discussed how different theorists have assigned priority to different factors or combinations of factors but so far have given little attention to the ways in which the different components might fit together. In this chapter, I concentrate specifically on analyses that have attempted to provide an integrative explanation of how emotion works, detailing interrelations between factors during the development of individual emotional episodes. A basic problem with many of these theories is that they assume that a relatively deterministic sequence of cause and effect or input and output shapes the unfolding of ongoing reactions. Instead, I argue that a range of different patterns of dynamic response can characterize emotion. Finally, I suggest that a full account needs to reposition the phenomenon within its everyday social context. In effect, this chapter is an attempt to pull together the theory and research into individual emotion discussed in the previous chapters before moving on to a consideration of emotion as an intrinsically social phenomenon.

THE VARIETY OF EMOTION THEORIES

Emotion as conceived in both common sense and psychology is characterized by situational appraisals, changes in states of action readiness, bodily reactions, and expressive movements. One of the criteria for a successful and complete theory of emotion is that it should specify how these four factors of emotion are related and what particular part each plays in the unfolding of real-life and real-time emotional episodes. In this chapter, I shall consider how different kinds of emotion theories have accounted for the patterning of response across all four factors. Not all of the models that I shall discuss are necessarily mutually exclusive, and I will not be suggesting that there is one true causal path to emotion, but rather that different sequences of event may characterize particular instances of emotional episodes.

There are a number of different possible ways of explaining emotion ranging from the physiological or neurochemical to the historical and political. In this chapter, I will make no attempt to detail all available analyses of how emotion works. Instead, I will be focusing on theories that consider emotion from the perspective of personal experience. Specifically, I am concerned with those accounts that have attempted to explicate the full range of individual factors that apparently operate during emotional episodes. I shall be arguing that, although these theories may provide a relatively comprehensive analysis of *individual* emotion, they are still limited by their inattention to the social dimension which is crucial to many instances of emotion as it occurs during everyday life.

Several alternative classifications of psychological emotion theory are possible (e.g. Averill, 1992), but only some of these are relevant for current purposes. One of the most central distinctions for the present analysis is that between *appraisal theories* and *feedback theories* (Zajonc, 1985). Appraisal theories concentrate on how the external situation is evaluated and processed by the individual, causing it to be perceived in emotional rather than nonemotional terms, and determining what kind of emotion will be produced. For example, Lazarus (1991a; see Chapter 2) argued that individuals weigh up how significant the current encounter is for their personal concerns and how well they can cope with it, and the consequences of these combined evaluations is either an emotional or nonemotional reaction. The main focus of appraisal theories then is on the individual's relation to the external situation. In contrast, feedback theories concentrate on the way that an emotional reaction is perceived 'internally' by the individual, and how the various channels of information are combined in an emotional experience. For instance, the first and simplest feedback theory was James's proposal that emotions are direct perceptions of the bodily changes induced by the emotional situation. In subsequent sections of this chapter, I shall consider the role played by the four factors of emotion according to both appraisal and feedback theories.

Both appraisal theories and feedback theories attempt to present causal accounts detailing the sequence of events that leads to emotion. Another approach to causation looks for underlying generative mechanisms in the general operating characteristics of the cognitive system. In this view, it is best to understand emotion as a function of the explanatory structures that also underlie other kinds of action (e.g. Mandler, 1984). However, such theories typically also try to differentiate emotion from other forms of functioning by explaining the phenomenon in terms of some kind of special process or combination of processes. I call these theories *systems theories* because they try to incorporate emotion within more inclusive systems of behaviour control. In systems theories, the various factors that contribute to emotional experience are understood in relation to the overall constitution of the psychological apparatus.

The final kind of theory I shall be considering shares some of the features of systems theories but tries to understand emotion in terms of the function rather than the structure of the psychological system. The central question addressed by these latter *functional theories* does not concern how emotion fits together or how it fits in with other psychological faculties, but rather what emotion is for. In functional theories, then, the four factors of emotion as well as emotion itself are understood from the point of view of the purposes they serve instead of in terms of their internal or external structural relations. (See Table 6.1 for a summary of these types of emotion theory.)

Note that the fact that a theory belongs in one of the categories I have mentioned does not necessarily exclude it from others. For example, many versions of appraisal theory tend to assume that emotion serves evolutionary purposes, making them in some sense functional theories too. However, assumptions that emotion depends upon appraisal do not in themselves presuppose an evolutionary basis for the relevant phenomena, so the distinction between the two theory categories can still be sustained in principle. By considering examples of these various kinds of theories in the present chapter, I hope to construct a more comprehensive picture of how emotion works, how it relates to other processes, and ultimately why it exists at all.

APPRAISAL THEORIES

In Chapter 2, I reviewed appraisal theory, especially Lazarus's (1991a) version of appraisal theory, in some detail. Now I want to turn to the question of how appraisal theory accounts for the four factors of emotion. The answer to this

Table 6.1 Varieties of emotion theory

Type of theory	Assumptions	Research focus
Sequential theories		
Appraisal theory (e.g., Lazarus, 1991a)	Emotions caused by situational evaluations and interpretations	Processes mediating effects of situation on emotion
Feedback theory (e.g., James, 1898)	Emotions caused by feedback of bodily reaction	Processes whereby emotional experience is constructed: what makes emotion feel emotional?
Systems theories (e.g., Barnard and Teasdale, 1991)	Emotion as a product of general characteristics of the psychological system	How does emotion relate to other modes of function? What distinguishes emotion from other modes of function?
Functional theories		
Evolutionary (e.g., Plutchik, 1980)	Emotions as a result of the adaptational history of the species	What are the universal, biologically given features of emotional function?
Sociocultural (e.g., Averill, 1980)	Emotions as cultural solutions to locally defined societal conflicts	Relation of emotion to cultural roles and norms

question is not a simple one, partly because appraisal theorists have often been unspecific about relations between emotion components, and partly because where they have tried to present definite proposals in this regard, their accounts have not always been consistent with one another. Of course, the main concern of appraisal theory is not to detail how the different factors of an emotional syndrome are interconnected but rather how the emotional syndrome arises from the situation in the first place, so inattention to these issues is perhaps unsurprising. However, two assumptions made by many current versions of appraisal theory lead fairly directly to specific conclusions about how the components of an emotional syndrome must be organized if the approach is a valid one. Both of these assumptions relate to the role of appraisal in the process of adaptation to the environment.

First, appraisal is often considered to be a way of detecting adaptational concerns, implying that the resulting pattern of response will itself be adaptive in some way. Thus, it would be surprising if appraisal did not have direct links to functional states of action readiness (Frijda, 1986) as well as physiological processes supporting these states. Second, appraisal theory usually sees emotions as more flexible than simple reflex connections (e.g. Smith and Ellsworth, 1985), so it seems to follow that the mode of emotional response itself must have some inbuilt flexibility too.

Lazarus's (1991a) account of the organization of emotional syndromes conforms to both of these specifications. First, Lazarus argued that appraisals lead directly to 'action impulses defined by the core relational theme and appraisal pattern' (p. 201). These action impulses in turn require certain modes of physiological support: 'The impulse to attack in anger, for example, provokes a particular motor pattern and psychophysiological response that reflect how the mind and body must be organized to deal with one's plight' (pp. 201–2). In other words, there is a close relationship between appraisal, action readiness, and bodily response, reflecting their common relation to the motivational concern apprehended via the appraisal: 'Each kind of emotion comprises a distinctive cognitive, motor, and physiological response configuration that is defined by the common adaptational (psychological and physiological) requirement of the person–environment relationship, as these are appraised' (p. 202).

As for flexibility of emotional response, Lazarus suggested that this comes from two sources. First and most importantly, appraisal itself is a flexible process whereby different people can appraise the same event differently, and whereby coping can rapidly change the person–environment relation in ways that are open to reappraisal. Second, Lazarus incorporated some flexibility in the pattern of response that follows appraisal. Although, on the one hand, he argued that 'once the appraisal has been made, the emotional response is a foregone conclusion, a consequence of biology' (p. 192), on the other hand, he also suggested that the pattern of emotional response might not be rigidly organized into a fixed program:

> It is possible to imagine an arrangement of the components of the emotion process as relatively independent and responsive to the particular adaptational

requirements connected with an ongoing transaction . . . In this view, which I favor, each component would function in a more flexible way, though still following biological constraints having to do with the demands for energy and homeostatic load in any action sequence.

(p. 196)

In summary, appraisal theory suggests that the appraisal factor determines the onset of emotional response and that the pattern of this response is organized to deal with the adaptational concerns identified by the appraisal. However, there is still thought to be some potential for the different factors constituting the emotional response to vary independently of one another. The partial independence of the four factors of emotion is a theme that will recur later in this chapter.

FEEDBACK THEORIES

Where appraisal theories focus on the link between emotional situation and emotional response, feedback theories concentrate on the issue of how the emotional response itself is constituted. This emphasis means that they tend to conceptualize the four factors as causes rather than contents or effects of emotion. According to James (1898), for example, emotional reactions come before emotional experience and not vice versa.

James provided the prototype for all subsequent versions of feedback theory by suggesting that the essence of emotional experience was the perception of bodily changes. Although most commentators have concentrated on the role that he attributed to autonomic symptoms in the constitution of emotional experience, James did not in fact limit himself to this kind of peripheral response in his explanation of emotion. Rather, he believed that the perception of all kinds of bodily change contributed to the total complex perception:

The immense number of parts modified in each emotion is what makes it so difficult for us to reproduce in cold blood the total and integral expression of any one of them. We may catch the trick with the voluntary muscles, but fail with the skin, glands, heart, and other viscera.

(p. 1066)

Furthermore, James explicitly discussed the role of feedback from expression in determining emotion: 'Refuse to express a passion and it dies . . . On the other hand, sit all day in a moping posture, sigh and reply to everything with a dismal voice and your melancholy lingers' (p. 1077). In order to produce emotional experience, James believed that the whole patterned bodily response had to be present, including facial movements, action tendencies, and internal changes. For example, when explaining why pulling a face does not in itself necessarily bring about emotion even for someone apparently skilled in the specific practice of such expressive manipulation, James argued as follows: 'Probably in him the facial mimicry is an entirely restricted and localized thing, without sympathetic changes of any sort elsewhere' (p. 1080). In other words, James did not prioritize any particular kind of bodily response system in explaining the experience of emotion; rather, he emphasized the importance of the total configuration of the organism.

Not only did James anticipate much of the substance of subsequent feedback theories of emotion, he also gave the first answer to their central problem: that of accounting for the body changes that produce the feedback. James's answer to this question was a straightforward one, perfectly in keeping with psychological ideas at the time. With regard to the various components of the patterned bodily response that he thought caused emotional experience, he argued that 'each . . . is the reflex effect of the exciting object' (p. 1069). In other words, James believed that the external cause of the emotion automatically triggered a complex of reactions which were perceived as an emotion. The basis for these reactions was thought to be instinctive or based on the laws of habit and association.

In Chapter 2, I mentioned that the apparent flexibility of emotional response seems to rule out explanations in terms of simple unconditioned or conditioned stimulus–response connections. This means that James's attempted solution for the problem of the causation of bodily changes seems inadequate to correct the perceived limitation of feedback theories. However, Ellsworth (1994) argued that James did not mean that emotions were simple reflex reactions to stimuli *per se*, but rather to emotional objects as they were appraised by individuals. According to such an interpretation, feedback theory and appraisal theory can be linked together to give a more integrated and complete picture of the overall pattern of emotional response.

COMBINED APPRAISAL/FEEDBACK THEORIES

On the surface, appraisal theories and feedback theories have complementary limitations. Appraisal theories are mainly directed towards identifying the kinds of encounter that might produce emotions of different kinds, but are not usually equipped to analyse the nature of these experiences when they occur. For this reason, these theories tend to treat emotions as if they were intact and irreducible packages of reactions, just as common sense and some deterministic biological theories assume them to be. On the other hand, feedback theories specifically address the issue of what constitutes the experience of emotion, but lack any real analysis of how the various channels of interoceptive and exteroceptive information that combine in the emotion perception process themselves originate. For example, Schachter (1964) argued that emotions are attributions of experienced arousal to plausible emotional situations, but failed to specify how exactly the arousal reaction itself could be produced in everyday circumstances apart from by reference to the general emotional characteristics of the situation.

This discussion suggests that appraisal and feedback theories could be seen as interlocking rather than mutually exclusive. For example, the bodily reactions which constitute the substance of emotional feedback may themselves often be caused by appraisal of the situation, and the effects that these reactions have on emotion may in turn reflect the way that they influence the appraisal process in many cases. More specifically, your heart may start pounding as a consequence of the detection of personally significant considerations characterizing your current transaction, and perception of this symptom may then lead you to look for a plausible emotional cause for this reaction in the situation, which you may then reappraise in more emotional terms. Similar dynamic concatenations of appraisal and feedback processes may also occur in more automatic and less explicit ways. Relatedly, it might be suggested that feedback or 'self- perception' theory explains how the subjective experience of emotion is constructed out of the various available sources of emotional information (Laird and Bresler, 1992), but that appraisal theory extends this account by specifying one possible causal route whereby the syndrome of reactions providing this input for self-perception is originally initiated.

As an example of how appraisal might lead to one of the factors that contribute to the self-perceived emotional syndrome, Smith (1989) has suggested ways in which different bodily responses may be caused by different dimensions of cognitive appraisal. Similarly, as suggested above, appraisals might lead relatively directly to action tendencies which are experienced as part of the emotional reaction (Frijda, 1986). Thus, it is possible to argue that appraisal theory and feedback theory are not alternative but complementary theories, the first explaining the psychological cause of the emotional syndrome, and the second explaining how the various sources of information are combined into an emotional experience with a particular character and quality.

According to this combined model, appraisal is the usual mediator of the set of emotional reactions to the situation. As Lazarus (1991a) argued, apprehension of the adaptational relevance of a person–environment encounter leads to a patterned response across motor and autonomic systems. Furthermore, the emotional state tends to be associated with distinctive patterns of focused attention and biased judgement that are continuous with the original appraisal (e.g. Keltner *et al.*, 1993), as well as facial expressions that communicate the adaptive concerns to other people present. Each of these four factors, however, has some independence, and can arise from considerations other than those relating to appraisal. For example, you might feel aroused because of taking part in physical exercise, or you might smile as a greeting rather than because you appraise the situation in happy terms. However they are initiated, the pattern of the four variables in combination may be perceived by the individual as the subjective experience of an emotion. Finally, the awareness of emotional experience may in turn lead to reappraisal of the situation as a result of emotion-focused coping or simply refocusing of attention (see Figure 6.1, for a diagrammatic representation of this synthesis).

In presenting this model, I do not mean to propose that it represents anything like a definitive theory of emotion. For one thing, the scheme underestimates the degree of interaction between the factors and the extent of their possible interconnections. Furthermore, as I hope to demonstrate, it omits the contribution of social factors in defining and determining the content of emotional experience. Despite these limitations, however, I think that the proposed four-factor approach

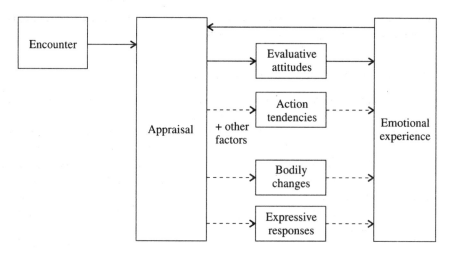

Figure 6.1   A four-factor theory of emotion

Note: Broken lines represent influences that are possible rather than necessary

allows a better appreciation of the many possible causal sequences underlying emotional episodes, than most existing accounts. For example, the model allows consideration of the occasions when emotional response is not entirely dependent on the factor of appraisal (see Chapter 3). If emotional experience is constructed out of our perceptions of multimodal bodily and motor feedback, then any variable that affects any of the channels of relevant information can be seen as contributing to the causation of emotion (Parkinson and Manstead, 1992). For example, arousal levels vary over the course of the day partly as a function of biorhythmic mechanisms (e.g. Thayer, 1989). To the extent that the perception of arousal makes a difference to emotion, time of day may be seen as a causal factor in the production of the experience. More generally, inasmuch as processes other than appraisal lead to bodily response, facial expression, or motivated action, which in turn feed into the experience of the emotion, appraisal is not emotion's exclusive determinant (Parkinson and Manstead, 1992).

It may even be the case that the complete pattern of the four factors is not a necessary condition for emotional experience, and that individuals construct emotional perceptions on the basis of limited information from one or two relevant sources of information supplemented by schema-driven imagery or 'somatovisceral illusions' (Cacioppo *et al.*, 1992). For example, the combination of felt arousal and situational appraisals may in some circumstances be sufficient to result in emotional experience (Schachter and Singer, 1962). Furthermore, to the extent that the various subsystems of emotional response are part of a wider, more integrated system, each factor may in any case tend to recruit other factors so that the presence of one or more factors often leads to the presence of others and the consequent experience of emotion. Such processes might help account for the effects of facial positioning manipulations on autonomic response and emotional experience (e.g. Levenson *et al.*, 1990).

Reflexive and irreflexive emotional experience

Having outlined a potential rapprochement between appraisal and feedback theories (see also Laird and Bresler, 1992), their main remaining disagreement concerns the point in the temporal sequence at which the person should be defined as experiencing the emotion. According to Laird and Bresler and other exponents of feedback principles, emotion emerges from the perception of patterns of bodily response. According to many appraisal theorists, on the other hand, emotion is a direct consequence of the appraisal of a transaction as personally significant, and thus follows immediately from a cognitive-evaluative process, regardless of the state of the body.

This apparent conflict is partially resolvable using Frijda's (1986) useful distinction between reflexive and irreflexive experience (cf. Sartre, 1962). Emotion in the appraisal view does not depend on any recognition that one is emotional, but rather on a certain mode of relating to the situation (*irreflexive* emotional experience). In this kind of emotion, awareness is focused on the emotional object rather than the emotional state itself: our emotional consciousness is not usually consciousness of an emotion but rather a particular way of perceiving the emotional situation, as positive or unpleasant, irritating or heartening. On the other hand, the feedback-theory version of emotion seems to imply some kind of recognition that one is undergoing a certain kind of reaction, and a consciousness of emotion (*reflexive* emotional experience) rather than an emotional consciousness. Of course, such a self-categorization could also lead to a reinterpretation of the situation in emotional terms and a refocusing of attention on the emotional object (irreflexive emotion). For example, people might ask themselves why their heart seems to be beating faster, conclude that something about the emotional situation may be causing this response, and consequently reappraise what is happening (cf. Parkinson, 1985; Valins, 1966).

Thus, appraisal theories and feedback theories seem to be directed at partially distinct sets of phenomena. Although feedback theories seem appropriate to a certain subset of selfconscious emotional experiences, it is also true that recognition of one's own emotion is not a necessary condition for attribution (as opposed to self-attribution) of emotion. As is often argued, a jealous individual is often the last person to realize that he or she is acting out of jealousy, for example (Bedford, 1957).

Some versions of the feedback account, however, may have more direct relevance to irreflexive emotion. For instance, many theorists (e.g. Laird and Bresler, 1992) would argue that the construction of an emotional experience is not necessarily a conscious process whereby individuals decide that they are emotional. Rather, the various sources of information are automatically combined into an emotional perception. Thus, according to this account, what adds emotional colour to our interpretation of a situation is precisely the perception of bodily symptoms, and we do not need to be consciously aware of how the symptoms are contributing, or even that we are emotional. Indeed, data from Cupchik and Leventhal (1974) suggest that explicit consciousness of feedback from expression *removes* any effects it may have on emotional experience.

However, even this analysis presents problems. For example, what is it about the changes that we feel in our bodies that makes a particular emotion pleasant or unpleasant, indeed angry or fearful? Unless it is assumed that bodily changes have direct links to subjective qualities of experience, feedback alone seems incapable of accounting for the complete set of feelings apparently involved in emotion. One possible way in which bodily feedback might directly impact on neural affect centres was suggested by Zajonc's facial efference theory. Zajonc argued that facial movements have direct effects on feelings because of the changes in cerebral blood-flow that they induce. Alternatively, it might be proposed that facial movements are directly linked to affect programs which also incorporate specification of the relevant subjective feelings (e.g. Tomkins, 1962). From the present point of view, however, neither of these contentions allows the flexibility of emotional response that seems readily apparent in everyday life.

SYSTEMS THEORIES

Systems theories attempt to explain emotion by showing how it fits into the broader picture of human function. In practice, this usually means extending or adjusting existing information-processing models to incorporate emotional phenomena. Emotion is seen either as a product of interactions between non-emotional processes or as an emergent property of the operation of the system as a whole. Systems theories often make use of appraisal and feedback principles in their accounts of individual emotion, but these are often complemented by additional, more generally applicable processes.

Leventhal's multimode theory

One of the most comprehensive attempts to integrate emotion into a general approach to psychological functioning was offered by Leventhal (e.g. 1980; 1984). One of the main contributions made by his approach was the recognition that different kinds of cognition are involved in the generation of emotion (Leventhal and Scherer, 1987), not all of which are directly reducible to appraisal or feedback processes. Leventhal's basic assumption was that emotion was controlled by a separate processing system operating in parallel with the system underlying problem-oriented behaviour. Within this emotion-control system, Leventhal argued that three separate sets of processes, and interactions between these processes, produced emotional behaviour and experience.

According to the theory, the first and most fundamental function of the emotion system is provided by *expressive-motor mechanisms* which react directly to stimulus features prior to any extensive cognitive analysis of the situation, automatically producing the relevant facial expression and autonomic response pattern. Leventhal assumed that these bodily reactions and expressions were hard-wired and genetically linked to certain kinds of biologically relevant stimuli (cf. Izard, 1972; Tomkins, 1962).

Leventhal's second kind of emotional processing occurs at the *schematic* level. He argued that emotion schemas consisted of 'integrations of separate perceptual codes of the visual, auditory, somesthetic, expressive, and autonomic reactions that are reliably associated with emotional experience' (Leventhal, 1980, p. 171). In other words, schematic processing involves representations of the actual structure of remembered emotional reactions. These are stored in the form of active procedures, which can be run through in emotional situations, giving the whole set of responses associated with emotion (i.e., the full four-factor syndrome). The set of situations that trigger these schemata depends on generalization from instinctive reactions produced by the more basic expressive-motor processes, so that a schema derived from experience of response to physical pain, for example, may ultimately come to be activated also in situations of psychological pain.

The third and final set of emotion-control processes proposed by Leventhal operate at the *conceptual* level. These processes depend on cultural and individual knowledge and beliefs about how emotions work based on experience, education, and prejudice. In the terminology of the present approach, conceptual processes relate to ideas about emotion. For example, many people believe that emotions manifest themselves in distinctive bodily symptoms and facial expressions, and predispose those experiencing emotion to interpret the situation in particular ways and engage in directed action. The possession of such emotion scripts has implications for how emotional information is processed and how attempts are made to control emotional reactions. Thus, conceptual processes may help to generate a socially appropriate affective reaction, such as the show of sadness and respect at a funeral of a disliked relative. This reaction, however, will not usually be experienced as fully and authentically emotional according to Leventhal's model because of its intentional basis.

One of Leventhal's concerns in developing his theory was to account for the perceived involuntary nature of emotional response. In this regard, he proposed that *feedforward* signals were produced along with emotion-control signals at all three levels of emotional processing. These feedforward signals were thought to arrive at a *comparator* which assessed whether responses were under the voluntary control of conceptual processes or the spontaneous control of the schematic or expressive motor processes. According to Leventhal, it is only when feedforward signals from schematic or expressive-motor processing are stronger than those from the conceptual control system that the resulting expressive or bodily reaction is experienced as a genuinely emotional one. Finally, Leventhal argued that the comparator also receives feed*back* signals from actual expressive and bodily reactions and these too are capable of contributing to the emotional reaction if their actual intensity exceeds that of the intentional feedforward signals. In other words, the emotional processing system in Leventhal's model is constructed in such a way that it automatically recognizes when an apparently emotional reaction is deliberate and when it is spontaneous, and only the latter kind of reaction is experienced as a genuine emotion. According to Leventhal, then, the presence of conceptual analysis is antagonistic to the experience of bona fide emotion which is seen to be heavily dependent upon direct conditioned or unconditioned response.

Leventhal's theory suggests that the four factors of emotion play a variety of different roles in several separate emotion-control processes. At the most basic level, integrated patterns of response are prespecified by sensorimotor processes and run off in direct reaction to instinctual stimulus configurations (much like Tomkins' 1962 *affect programs*). Second, information about the four factors of emotion is encoded into schematic representations of emotional response which are implemented automatically whenever the external situation matches the stimulus specification contained in these schemata. Third, conceptual representations of emotion are likely to refer to the four factors as diagnostic of emotion and thus attempts to control emotion deliberately may well be directed specifically at one or more of these factors.

Different factors also make different kinds of contribution to the causation of emotion, according to Leventhal's theory. Appraisal processes, for example, may occur at all three levels with basic instinctive appraisals directly triggering emotional reactions at the expressive motor level, learnt interpretations and evaluations producing emotion at the schematic level, and considered propositional knowledge about emotion and appraisal moderating reactions at the conceptual level (cf. Leventhal and Scherer, 1987). At any rate, appraisal, broadly conceived, serves as an initiator of emotion, according to Leventhal's model, rather than as part of the reaction. Facial expression, on the other hand, is seen as an effect or symptom of emotion, which may make some contribution to emotional experience on the basis of feedback principles. Depending on whether expression arises spontaneously (from expressive-motor or schematic processing), or deliberately (from conceptual processing) it may either contribute to, or detract from, emotional experience (Leventhal and Mace, 1970). Leventhal argued that, in general, if a conceptual representation of emotion were generated in advance to anticipate the full pattern of emotional reaction, then this reaction would be experienced as deliberate and unemotional, rather than spontaneous and emotional (Johnson and Leventhal, 1974).

In summary, Leventhal's theory provides a rich framework for interpreting potential interactions between the four factors of emotion and details a range of possible causal sequences leading to the experience of emotion. Some of the specific details of the model may seem questionable, such as its reliance on fixed genetic packages of response as the ultimate basis for all emotional experience, and its too rigid distinction between voluntary and involuntary action and emotion, but its overall scope and shape are impressive and represent a valuable attempt to draw together a wide range of experimental and observational data. From the present point of view, its main limitation is that it positions emotion squarely within an intrapsychic architecture, rather than contextualizing the phenomenon in wider social processes.

Interacting cognitive subsystems (ICS)

Although Leventhal's theory was loosely based on existing models of information-processing, its specific structure was purpose-built to accommodate emotion. Other theorists have tried to extend cognitive architectures originally constructed with other uses in mind so that a place can be found in them for emotional phenomena. A notable example of such an extension is provided by Barnard and Teasdale (1991; Teasdale and Barnard, 1993; see also Johnson, 1983).

The basis for Barnard and Teasdale's account of emotion was Barnard's (1985) intricate information-processing theory of *interacting cognitive subsystems* (ICS). In this model, the cognitive system is modularized in several partially independent processors, each of which is specifically designed to handle a particular kind of information. Nine of these subsystems were specified in the revised model adapted to cope with emotional phenomena: three were sensory subsystems dealing with acoustic, visual, and bodily information, respectively; two were effector subsystems controlling speech and movement; and the final four were central subsystems for integrating information and generating plans for action, working on the basis of acoustic and speech data, object specifications, propositions, and implications. Of particular importance for the explanation of emotion are the central implicational subsystem and the bodily state sensory subsystem.

According to Barnard and Teasdale, the implicational subsystem receives inputs from all sensory subsystems as well as the propositional subsystem and integrates the data into a more general sense of being-in-the-world. In other words, implicational processing combines coded sensory information with knowledge about reality. The kind of awareness constructed in this subsystem is therefore holistic and not easily conveyed in words alone. Emotion is thought to arise from implicational processing whenever the pattern of code it generates corresponds to established affective themes, based on earlier experience or genetic inheritance.

For example, relevant data reflecting muscular posture, facial position, and internal bodily feedback may occur in conjunction with a propositional representation of a situation with potential emotional significance, such as a relaxed drink with an attractive companion, and the integration of the whole pattern of sensory and semantic information may match an earlier occasion when you first fell in love. In this case, the implicational subsystem will generate a corresponding emotional code which is not entirely translated into a simple verbal description of what is happening, so that you experience the situation in terms of an emotion (or at least an emotional memory) coming over you. The awareness of the emotion is thought to be a direct function of the encoding of data into an implicational record. Furthermore, the implicational subsystem may then output signals to the effector subsystems resulting in expression and body change which in turn feed back information which contributes to the overall emotional encoding of the situation. One of the distinctive things about emotional implications is that they tend to be associated with feedback from the bodily subsystem of peripheral changes such as heart-rate increase. This bodily feedback is integrated with propositional content to produce the experience of emotion, much in the same way as implied by two-factor theory (Schachter, 1964).

In the ICS model then, the four factors of emotion can serve as both causes and effects of emotion. Appraisal as propositional content integrates with feedback from the body and face to produce the experience of emotion, and the matching of implicational code to pre-established emotional patterns may result in output to bodily and facial effectors as well as reinterpretation of the situation at a propositional level (reappraisal). Each of the factors is seen as partially independent from the overall emotional syndrome.

This abbreviated account of Barnard and Teasdale's model can only give a flavour of the complexity of their analysis, but the general claim of the theory is clear: emotions are products of intrapsychic integration of various kinds of information. Separate channels of data are combined into a meaningful cognitive construction. The main problem with such an approach is that it works on the assumption that significance is something that is added to raw sensory data after the fact. The thinking organism is awash in a rough sea of scattered fragments which need to be fitted together by the mental apparatus before proper navigation is possible. An alternative approach would be to view the world as containing information that is already meaningful and which the instinctively coordinated operation of our senses is attuned to pick up directly (Gibson, 1979). In this view, it is unnecessary to suppose that meaning and emotion are things that are built up piece by piece as a result of intricate interlocking cognitive mechanisms because the real-time co-occurrence of stimulus features prespecifies the actual nature of what is out there in the social world. With regard to emotional situations, the flow of interpersonal coordination may often dictate the appropriate response without the necessity for intervention of complicated internal processing.

The problem with the internal representational account is that it does not even solve the problem it invents for itself: that of explaining how meaning is constructed. Whatever is generated inside the system is not something that is directly usable by human perceivers, who need to make sense of the representation just as much as they need to make sense of the external world. If the implicational subsystem is said to produce an emotional *code*, it seems necessary additionally to specify how and by whom this output is decoded.

Evaluation of systems theories of emotion

Other examples of systems theories of emotion are the models proposed by Carver and Scheier (1990) and Oatley and Johnson-Laird (1987) which were discussed in Chapter 3. These theories share some common assumptions with the two covered in this section, but do not contain such explicit implications about the respective roles of the four factors of emotion. They are also subject to many of the same criticisms, which I shall now summarize.

Systems theories are useful in that they acknowledge the wide range of factors that can enter into the causation and constitution of emotion and attempt to do justice to the complexity of the phenomena involved. However, they have two main weaknesses. First, the availability of such a wide range of explanatory mechanisms make the theories so flexible that they can account for almost any data. Relatedly, it is hard to tease out direct empirical predictions from multimode theories because it is difficult to know which systems are brought into play by any given set of circumstances in the real world.

The second problem, as mentioned above, is that these theories seem to assume that emotional meaning is manufactured as a consequence of the inner workings of an intrapsychic cognitive system rather than unfolding in the course of real-time interpersonal encounters. In the next chapter, I shall try to broaden the provisional individualistic approach to emotion developed in the present chapter by incorporating social factors.

FUNCTIONAL THEORIES

Many of the theories I have discussed in the chapter so far make assumptions about the function of emotion. However, their main focus has been on articulating the processes whereby emotion is generated in real time, rather than the processes that have resulted in the existence of the phenomenon in the first place. Theories that are *intrinsically* functional explain emotion by reference to the purposes that it serves within a broader explanatory framework. This does not mean that these theories ignore the issue of process, rather that they see it as secondary to the question of function. In a sense, then, functional theories are more inclusive than the other kinds of theory that I have considered because they not only detail emotion-generation mechanisms but why these mechanisms are constructed in the way that they are. Instead of simply showing how the internal components of emotion might fit together, they try to locate emotion as a whole, as well as its component factors, within more general systems of causality.

Biological functionalism

The most common variety of functional theory relates emotion to the evolutionary history of the species. Indeed, most of the models discussed so far have made some assumptions about the biological basis of emotion and about how emotional mechanisms might serve purposes that are adaptive for gene survival. Naturally, it seems hard to conceive of emotion or any other aspect of human behaviour as being completely independent of our genetic heritage: people are in some sense animals and as such are partly constrained by the specific constitution of their organismic constitution. However, some writers have gone further than this almost self-evident claim and argued that biology offers the very *raison d'être* for emotion.

Many exponents of the biological viewpoint (e.g. Izard, 1969; Plutchik, 1980; Tomkins, 1962) have claimed that there is a set of basic genetically determined emotions which provide the fundamental essence of all emotional experience. According to Plutchik, these emotions are thought to occur in some form across the whole evolutionary spectrum, from fish and reptiles to mammals including humans. Each of these primary emotions has evolved to deal with a basic kind of existential concern or life problem, and includes a patterned sequential response including communicative as well as adaptive components. Emotions that are not basic biological entities in this way are considered to be blends of primary emotions. In Plutchik's view then, not only are specific components of emotional response pre-wired but also the logical geography of the whole emotional universe is mapped out genetically.

If emotions are inherited packages of response, as biological theories seem to imply, their components are not so tightly wrapped together in everyday experience. Emotions are not intact entities but loosely associated syndromes, so whatever core of emotional experience is built into the structure of the neurological system must either be inherently flexible or subject to differentiation and elaboration over the course of growth and development. What is inherited is potential, subsequently to be fleshed out by experience. Indeed, adaptive pressures on organisms facing complex social environments are likely to favour openness to learning rather than preset solutions to problems (Schwartz, 1974). In practice, then, the genetically programmed part of emotion may not impose strict limits on the adult manifestation of the phenomenon (cf. Averill, 1984).

Rather than assuming that emotions themselves are fundamentally biological entities, I think it is more useful to look separately at the operation of the variables that are implicated in emotional experience and assess the degree to which each is constrained by biology (Ortony and Turner, 1990). In previous chapters, I have shown how each of the four factors of emotion can be seen as serving some adaptive purposes. For example, appraisal may be a way of detecting survival-related concerns in the environment (Smith and Ellsworth, 1985), states of action readiness prepare the individual for flexible reactions (Frijda, 1986), autonomic response mobilizes energy for emergency reactions (e.g. Cannon, 1927), and facial expressions communicate behavioural intentions to others so that action can be coordinated in social groups (e.g. Fridlund, 1991a). However, each of these factors also has some independence from the integrated emotional syndrome, and can be influenced by other nonemotional and nonevolutionary considerations too. The issue that arises, therefore, is whether to place more emphasis on biological determinants or on the other variables that contribute to emotional response. In my view, since it is social factors that make emotion a distinctively human phenomenon, these are more worthy of our attention as psychologists. Of course this does not deny that the biological approach to emotion is also a legitimate enterprise for certain delimited purposes.

Sociocultural functionalism

Some theorists have argued that emotions have evolved in response to societal or cultural needs rather than simply serving goals of species survival. According to this view, emotions should be interpreted by reference to the part that they play in organized social life, not adaptational encounters in the wild. In this section, I consider two theories that attempt to relate emotions to their surrounding cultural context.

Averill (e.g. 1980; 1982) has argued that emotions are transitory social roles supplied by the culture to deal with situations of conflicting norms for action. For example, in Western society conventional rules about assertiveness can contradict accepted principles of nonaggression: on the one hand, people are supposed to uphold justice by demanding retribution for wrongdoing, and on the other hand, they are not supposed to hurt other people deliberately. These two social norms are brought into conflict when someone insults you in some way: other people might consider you weak if you do nothing, but overaggressive if you deliberately strike back in some way. According to Averill, the resolution of this culturally defined conflict is provided by the existence of the short-term social role of getting angry. Anger is something that is conventionally interpreted as an involuntary and partly uncontrollable response, thus enabling the angry person to disown responsibility for any retaliation carried out in the 'heat of the moment'.

In general, emotion roles are available in situations where conflicts of norms commonly arise, allowing the individual to perform the proscribed action without accepting responsibility for doing so. The way that these roles are acted out depends upon cultural conventions, but is likely to include sophisticated signalling channels (e.g. facial expressions) designed to communicate the fact that the individual is not to be sanctioned for his actions. Also, it is likely that these occasions will be sometimes accompanied by arousal or other forms of internal upset since they reflect a disruption of normal functioning, and so on.

At first blush, Averill's analysis seems to apply only to cases of negative emotion, but his discussion of love (which is usually considered to be positive) helps to correct this impression. Averill (1985) argued that love arises as a function of society's simultaneous respect for, and neglect of, the individual. Part of the core of the meaning of love is an idealization of the loved one and reciprocally of oneself, providing a means of preserving self-worth (as demanded by society) within a system that typically has little time or money for the individual's needs. Averill has also offered accounts of hope (Averill *et al.*, 1990), grief (Averill and Nunley, 1988), and fear (Averill, 1987) as culturally constituted roles.

Averill's account presents emotion as a social construction. Although he accepted that the responses that make up an emotional reaction may be genetically programmed, the way that these are organized and interpreted by the individual transcends any physiological analysis. Emotions, in Averill's (1985) view, are 'socially constituted syndromes (transitory social roles) that include a person's appraisal of the situation and that are interpreted as passions rather than actions' (p. 98). They are passions rather than actions because people *interpret* them as things that happen to them rather than as things that they do. However, this experience of passivity is a function of social demands rather than an actual reflection of reality. In fact, emotions are actions for which a person does not take responsibility, because they conflict with social norms of one kind or another.

A related view of emotions as enactments of roles is provided by Sarbin's (1986) analysis which makes more explicit use of the dramaturgical metaphor of life as theatre. Sarbin argued that people intentionally adopt emotional roles for rhetorical purposes to further the development of their self-narratives. In less opaque language, we might say that in getting emotional, people are conforming to a cultural script for making claims about their identity. Emotion roles derive from the myths, legends, and unarticulated common knowledge that are background features of cultural life. People take on these roles when the relevant identity implications fit in with their present life-story. At low levels of involvement, this play-acting is experienced as exactly that, going through the motions of supporting an adopted point of view. However, when the individual has a high stake in the relevant concern, the emotion role will be enacted with total absorption and organismic involvement. For example, when people get angry about something important to them, they emphasize their concern in their posture, their facial expression, and in the intensity of their actions. At such a level of involvement, the emotion is seen as dictated by the situation rather than stemming from the actor's intentions: in effect, the role player is saying 'look how deeply this thing has affected me, how much this matters'. According to Sarbin, once role involvement is deep enough to be expressed with the body, the initiated internal reactions may find their own momentum, shifting control precedence from the head to the heart, and turning the action literally into a passion.

Both Averill's and Sarbin's accounts represent valuable correctives to the conventional idea of emotion as involuntary, genetically programmed, and primarily physiological. However, their emphasis on cultural factors may be slightly overstated. Although culture gives form to many of the roles that we act out when emotional, it seems likely that some concerns are universally shared across the species and constrain the possibilities of socialization. More importantly from the present perspective, many of the occasions for emotion arise from local negotiations in the course of everyday interpersonal interaction and do not directly reflect societally prescribed norms. The conflicts, disagreements, and commitments that lead to emotion may be based on mutually established rights and obligations in relationships which have only a remote connection with culturally imposed rules and roles.

A second and related weakness of the cultural functionalist perspective offered by Averill and Sarbin lies in the explanatory emphasis that both theorists place on individual agency in accounting for the adoption of emotion roles. Again, this claim that emotions are deliberate and intentional (cf. Solomon, 1976) is in specific opposition to the oversimplistic traditional conception of emotion as something to which a person falls victim, and both theorists offer convincing explanations of how this 'myth of the passions' may have arisen (as a result of *post hoc* justification for sanctionable action, according to Averill's account, or depending on the momentum of bodily involvement in emotional concerns, in Sarbin's case). However, their alternative view that people selfconsciously take on emotion roles seems equally restrictive. In many cases, emotion arises not from within an individual's authorial consciousness but emerges in the dialogue of an ongoing interaction as a function of what might be called distributed or socially shared cognition (e.g. Resnick *et al.*, 1991). The acting out of emotion episodes is guided on-line by the affordances offered or denied by other people's ongoing actions, which in turn are mutually coordinated with the actor's own self-presentation.

In conclusion, although there are occasions on which emotion roles supplied by the culture are acted out deliberately, these do not exhaust the full range of possible emotion episodes. Emotions often arise from more local interactional concerns and are shaped from mutually negotiated as well as individually originated intentions. Thus, emotion serves broadly communicative rather than narrowly cultural functions.

Summary

A recurrent trend among emotion theories has been to see the relevant phenomena as serving purposes that are defined by natural selection (see Averill, 1974; 1992). Although certain aspects of emotional response derive fairly directly from our biological heritage, and some particular emotions seem directed towards survival-related goals, I do not believe that it is possible to give a full account of all human emotional states by exclusive reference to evolutionary explanations. What makes emotion most meaningful to us as social animals, I would contend, is its interpersonal functionality.

SYNTHESIS

In this final section of the first part of the book, I shall try to summarize some of my main conclusions derived from the various four-factor approaches to individual emotion, and recommend a less deterministic approach to the question of causal sequences of contributory variables.

From the present perspective, emotion can be seen as a syndrome of partly integrated and partly independent components. Different components may have different roles and priorities at different stages in the real-time development of the syndrome, exerting a variety of informational as well as functional influences. For example, appraisals may serve to initiate emotional episodes, contribute to the content of the experience, as well as shape some of the evaluative consequences of being in the emotional state (Lazarus, 1991a). Similarly, bodily changes can contribute to emotional causation (e.g. Zillmann, 1978), and provide informational and sensory feedback that helps to constitute emotional feelings. Thus, although appraisal may be viewed as the central core of the emotional process, it is certainly not the only factor that determines the way that emotion is played out in real-life encounters.

A related point is that the specific function performed by each factor in the unfolding causal series may vary from one episode of emotion to the next, because there are a range of possible sequences and patterns of components that still count as emotional by conventional criteria. For example, emotion can be activated relatively directly as an integrated response by detection of someone else's emotion, according to principles of primitive emotion contagion (Hatfield *et al.*, 1992), or it may be constructed gradually and in a piecemeal fashion out of various sources of feedback coupled with ongoing interpretations of the real-time situation. Alternatively, emotions may be adopted in a more or less deliberate way as part of the developing drama of an unfolding interpersonal episode, using a number of available evaluative or behavioural strategies. Each of these instances of emotion may show an idiosyncratic time-course and factor content allowing a range of valid explanatory narratives. However, as a general rule, it may be that factors of emotion tend to recruit each other over the course of an emotional episode, leading to a common four-factor structure constituting most examples of individual emotion. Coupled with these recruitment processes, principles of emotional momentum may result in persistence of the patterned response beyond its original occasion for production. For instance, appraisals and their related states of action readiness (backed up by bodily changes and expressed in the body and face) may spill over into subsequent situations unconnected with the original emotional object. Thus, when you are angry, you may snap at somebody who had little or nothing to do with what initially upset you. This generalization of reactivity is partly what makes emotion a more or less intact conceptual entity in its own right, for if emotions were no more than simple evaluative responses bound to particular objects, then there would be little point in developing a specific set of theoretical principles to explain them.

Many of these same conclusions about emotion can also be derived from the communicational account that I have been developing in this book. According to this approach, interpersonal agendas relevant to emotional identity claims may be activated in a range of different ways, depending on the relational nature of the social situation. Furthermore the appraisal content of emotional messages can be transmitted using a wide variety of communicational media and according to many different verbal and nonverbal syntaxes. Emotional momentum also obtains in communicative emotion because adopting an emotion implies taking on a specific social identity with all its associated evaluative and action commitments. The degree of persistence of factors, in this view, depends on the level of involvement with the emotion role and the range of situations to which the relevant identity position applies.

Of course, communicative and appraisal models of emotion are not necessarily competing accounts of the same set of phenomena, but rather may be seen as alternative forms of possible emotional syndrome applicable under different sets of circumstance. However, according to the present perspective, the primary meaning of emotion is as communication, and emotion produced as a consequence of individualized evaluative processes depends on prior experience of expressing identity claims in public. In other words, the communicational sequence may be the original and prototypical form of emotion on which secondary internalized encounters are based. Emotion therefore needs to be understood in terms of its functionality as well as its internal constitution. In the second part of this book, I will discuss some of the strategic and tactical purposes served by emotion within relationships, institutions, and cultures.

Conclusion

Emotion theorists often consider it their task to specify the internal mechanisms that account for emotions. They typically assume that a single and integrated set of processes are responsible for generating the full range of emotional episodes (or at least a subset of those episodes delineated by a revised demarcation of the phenomenon of emotion). However, theories of emotion do not have to conform to this traditional template. Instead of allocating causality to specific mechanisms, emotion can be seen as an emergent product of the operation of the system as a whole (e.g. Barnard and Teasdale, 1991), or, more radically, as being produced by a range of different intrapersonal as well as interpersonal, institutional, and cultural processes. There may not be a single type of emotion episode with a common deep structure, but rather a range of real-life real-time phenomena, which share only family resemblances with each other (e.g. Fehr and Russell, 1984). According to such a view, it misses the point to try to develop one all-purpose explanatory account that is true for every conceivable instance of emotion. Instead, researchers should attempt to catalogue the range of sequences of events that characterize emotions as they are categorized by laypeople and try to work out what the similarities and differences between them really are. Thus, there is not necessarily any single unifying principle underlying emotional phenomena, and there may be no special additive ingredient (e.g. Arnold, 1960; James, 1898; Laird, 1974; Schachter, 1964) that makes emotion emotional rather than simply rational or cognitive. Rather, emotional phenomena may be circumscribed mainly by the functions that they serve in everyday social life.

Part II
Social emotion

7   Interpersonal emotion

OVERVIEW

Having considered emotion as an individual phenomenon in the first part of this book, I move on in this second part to an attempt at contextualizing the relevant processes within social life. In the present chapter, I focus specifically on emotion as an interpersonal phenomenon. First, I consider the prevalent psychological approach to emotion communication and conclude that it depends on a misguided notion of affect as a primarily intrapsychic event waiting to find expression in the social world. I try to articulate an alternative and more radical account of emotion as embedded in episodes that are played out on-line in the interpersonal arena. Given the intricate interlocking of ongoing interactive behaviours, and the dynamic time dependencies of real-time encounters, one of the main problems faced by such a position is to find a workable methodology which allows a principled strategy for data reduction. In the second section of this chapter, I review some of the studies that have attempted to deal with the complexities of real-life and real-time interpersonal emotion in order to suggest potential guidelines for future research. Third, I review research findings relating to interpersonal causes, effects, and functions of emotion. Finally, I recommend adoption of a communicative approach that sees emotion first and foremost as a process of making claims about personal or social identity to particular intended audiences in the context of unfolding social encounters.

INTRODUCTION

In the previous chapter, I discussed both structural and functional theories of emotion. In this chapter, I shall suggest that the issues raised by both these kinds of model can be addressed successfully from a communicative perspective. I shall argue that the on-line temporal *structure* of a developing emotional experience, as well as its internal bodily components, derive mainly from interpersonal considerations. Furthermore, I will suggest that the central *function* of many emotional states is social. We get angry in order to convince someone else to take seriously our moral rights; we get sad or afraid to ask for different kinds of social support; we fall in love so that we may redefine our relationship with someone, and so on. In addition, these interpersonal goals are not always privately formulated in the individual minds of co-interactants but instead often originate in relation to the developing position of the other, either in a mutuality of feeling or a drawing up of antagonistic boundaries. Thus, emotions tend to come in matching or contrasting pairs over the course of an interaction, with anger leading to another's anger or guilt, love begetting love or disdain, and so forth. Our emotional attitudes to one another are part of the continual redefinition of ongoing relationships.

Conventional research sees emotion communication essentially as a two-step process where an emotion is first experienced and then transmitted into the interpersonal world. However, as I have argued in previous chapters, an emotion is not an intact and immediate private experience but something that develops over time and is constructed out of several channels of information and modes of response. In this chapter, I want to extend this analysis of emotions as unfolding episodes by looking at the ways in which social processes enter into the causation and constitution of the sequence of emotional events. The traditional view faces problems when we try to understand what the nature of the private essence of emotion is supposed to be. As psychologists, our only way of accessing this putative entity is via its modes of expression, or in other words, by paying attention to the ways that people present themselves verbally and nonverbally. In this chapter, I will be suggesting that these modes of self-presentation to actual or imagined audiences should be seen as right at the heart of emotion rather than as indirect indices of an underlying state. All that emotion is, in many circumstances, is a particular form of communication.

EMOTION AS AN INTERPERSONAL PHENOMENON

Although most people's idea of emotion is that it is a personal and individual phenomenon, I want to argue that the most important aspects of emotion are social. There are several obvious ways in which social factors affect and reflect emotion. For example, many emotions seem to be about other people, what they say, what they do (e.g. Kemper, 1978); emotions generally seem to have social effects, so that it is hard to ignore the anger, love, hate, guilt, or embarrassment of someone who is close to you (physically as well as psychologically speaking); and emotions characterize our relationships with one another in particular situations, again in terms of contempt, love, sympathy, fear, lust, and so on (e.g. de Rivera, 1984; de Rivera and Grinkis, 1986). My claim in this chapter, however, is not just that social factors influence and are influenced by emotion, but that emotions are socially constituted (cf. Averill, 1980) over the course of our on-line interpersonal encounters. Not only does the idea of emotion emerge from social and cultural discourses and related practices, but also, and more fundamentally, the true nature of emotion is in many cases as a form of communication.

The fact that the interpersonal arena is one of the key venues for the playing out of emotions seems obvious to most people. Cinematic, theatrical, and textual representations of emotional episodes typically rely on character interplay, conversations, and other forms of interaction to exert their dramatic effect: attraction, betrayal, sacrifice, disappointment, redemption – all these are themes worked out as a function of developing relationships and crystallized in actual encounters of protagonists (or of protagonists with antagonists).

However, despite the common-sense acceptance of the importance of relationship and interaction in emotion, the essence of the phenomenon is still supposed to be private (see Chapter 1), and this intrapsychic aspect is also reflected in popular narratives concerning emotion. Many of the most poignant works of fiction start from the premise that a powerful emotion can be hidden or suppressed. Few things are more moving than seeing someone facing impossible problems or irretrievable loss but refusing to give in to, or even openly to acknowledge, their despair (e.g. think of Anthony Hopkins' exemplary enactment of stoicism in the popular 'English heritage' movie *The Remains of the Day*). Furthermore, it is patently true that emotion can be experienced when one is alone, for example, in a darkened cinema, or when one has been deserted by someone for whom one cares deeply. Explaining these evident private and intrapsychic aspects of emotion is one of the main problems facing any interpersonal analysis, and one to which I will return later in this chapter and in the next. First, though, I want to consider some of the research strategies that have been adopted to address interpersonal emotional phenomena.

EMPIRICAL COMPLEXITY OF EMOTIONAL INTERACTION

One of the main problems facing any investigation of interpersonal emotion concerns the difficulty of recording all the relevant variables. Emotional interchanges between people tend to involve intricate patterns of rapidly evolving and coordinated verbal and nonverbal responses and it is near impossible to keep track of everything important. For example, Birdwhistell (1970) argued that it would be necessary to record 10,000 bits of information every second to give an accurate picture of the simple interactive behaviour of two human infants. At the beginning of Birdwhistell's preliminary attempts to construct a notation for recording nonverbal behaviour and its timing at a microlevel from filmed interactions, it took him about 100 hours to transcribe just one second's worth of content. With ten year's practice and experience, this was eventually reduced to one hour per recorded second. Similarly, Peery (1978) found that the true nature of many emotional interactions is only observable using frame-by-frame analysis of a videotape. This technique revealed hidden features of mutual coordination of response, and was thus dubbed the *affective microscope*. Clearly, it is extremely difficult to document everything that is going on moment by moment during real-time interaction.

The solution adopted by most psychological researchers to this problem of complexity is to focus on an artificially simplified version of the phenomenon in question. This approach works fine when the processes uncovered by such a restricted focus turn out to have broader implications, but such a direct assessment of generalizability is rarely conducted except on a conceptual level. We are left, then, with findings whose relevance to the everyday realm of interpersonal interaction remains uncertain.

Despite the obvious complexity of the interface between emotion and the social world, most of the research carried out under the banner of social aspects of emotion concerns the ways in which information about one person's emotion is transmitted to another person. In the following section of the chapter, I consider the limitations of this research, before discussing some of the other ways in which interactions and relationships between people are crucial to our understanding of individual and interpersonal emotion.

EMOTION COMMUNICATION

Communicative phenomena test the limits of available psychological paradigms. Traditional observational and experimental methods, as well as the statistical techniques typically used to analyse the results produced by these methods, are more often than not directed specifically at the responses of individual subjects. In any communicative act, at least two people are involved (implicitly if not in actuality), and focusing on the behaviour of just one of these interactants threatens to unbalance the analysis. Researchers consider the functioning of the person communicating and of the person to whom the communication is addressed separately, hoping that their interactive responses can somehow be correlated into an integrated picture of the communicative process. Unfortunately, it is not so easy to mesh two one-sided accounts to give both sides of the unfolding story. Communication usually operates in two or more directions at once and depends on real-time coordination rather than a turn-taking process of individual action and reaction.

Given these limitations of the traditional psychological approach to communication in general, and emotional communication in particular, it is unrealistic to expect more than a partial account of the relevant phenomena to emerge from the available literature. In this chapter, I hope to locate some of the structural weaknesses and missing sections of the traditional theoretical edifice and offer some tools and materials for filling these conceptual gaps.

One-way nonverbal communication of spontaneous emotion

A good example of the restrictiveness of traditional experimental methodologies for the study of emotion communication is provided by Buck's (1979a) 'slide-viewing paradigm' which was designed to assess the accuracy of nonverbal communication of emotion (see Chapter 5). In this section, I will use this particular paradigm illustratively to draw attention to some of the general limitations of much traditional research into interpersonal emotion. My arguments are not intended to constitute a specific critique of Buck's work, nor do I mean to imply that his series of studies represented a particularly bad instance of empirical practice in this area. In fact, quite the contrary. It is just that Buck's (1984) clear formulation of what he considered to be the important issues surrounding emotion as a social entity highlights many of the significant presuppositions that are implicit in many recent and current research programmes directed at interpersonal affect.

Buck's procedure was based on Miller, Murphey, and Mirsky's (1959) cooperative conditioning experiments. In this procedure, one monkey learned to respond discriminatively on the basis of closed-circuit video images of the face of a second monkey which was presented with the stimulus signalling the availability of reinforcement. The conditioning process was thus apportioned between two animals, one with access to the discriminative stimulus itself, and the other provided with the means of acting in order to receive reinforcement for both of them. Clearly, in order to succeed at this task, the responding animal needed to learn to distinguish facial signals differentially transmitted by the partner animal, and the partner animal needed to learn to display distinctive facial responses in conjunction with the external discriminative stimulus.

In Buck's slide-viewing paradigm, human beings took the place of the monkeys in this procedure. One person (the *sender*) was shown a series of pictures intended to elicit different kinds of emotional responses while their facial reactions to these pictures were covertly recorded by a video camera. A second person (the *receiver*) remotely viewed the silent relayed image of the first person's face while the slides were shown. The experimental task of the receiver was to work out what kind of slide was being presented and to infer the sender's emotional reaction to this slide on the basis of the limited information available from the TV screen. A whole series of studies was conducted using this basic technique or variants of it. In a common modification of the original real-time procedure (Buck *et al.*, 1972), the sender's face may be video-recorded for subsequent presentation to receivers (e.g. Wagner *et al.*, 1986). Of course, it is also possible to replace the slides in the slide-viewing paradigm with other emotional stimuli, such as film-clips (Zuckerman *et al.*, 1976) or experimental tasks (e.g. Miller, 1974).

As reported above (Chapter 5), although accuracy of emotion communication has tended to fall above chance in these studies, its absolute level has usually been far from impressive. Thus, although there is evidence that some information relating to the overall pleasantness of the stimulus is communicated, little of the specific emotional quality of the reaction seems to get across (Wagner *et al.*, 1986; Russell, 1994). These findings tend to lead to the conclusion that if accurate emotional communication actually occurs in everyday ongoing interactions (and studies by Gottman and Levenson, e.g. 1985, suggest that it does), little of it is based on spontaneous facial expressive responses to emotional states or affective stimuli.

A number of alternative interpersonal processes whereby emotional meanings may be communicated suggest themselves. For example, it seems possible that facial actions mainly occur in the context of communication of intentions to someone else, rather than as spontaneous responses to internal states (e.g. Fridlund, 1991a; Kraut and Johnston, 1979; see Chapter 5). By looking more closely at the specifics of Buck's paradigm, it is possible to see what aspects of real-time and real-world emotion communication were specifically excluded in this procedure, and suggest ways of broadening the limited conception of emotion communication implied by this type of methodology. Clearly, the experimental situation is different to what normally happens in everyday emotional communication in a number of ways. The kinds of factor left out of the laboratory situation may be exactly those that are crucial to the actual interpersonal process of concern.

Of course, the features of the experimental design to which I shall draw attention were not accidentally selected by investigators. There is a theoretical rationale for investigating emotional communication in this way, and it is one that conforms fairly closely to the common-sense idea of emotions as spontaneous and intrapsychic events. Many of the assumptions that had been implicit in Buck's slide-viewing paradigm were made explicit by the author in his subsequent book *The Communication of Emotion* (1984). In this book, Buck essentially argued that emotion was transmitted like any other kind of message in accordance with the principles of Shannon and Weaver's (1949) classic model of communication (which is also, of course, one of the cornerstones of cognitive theory). This formulation, then, depends fundamentally on the familiar idea of emotion as an internal experience whose expression is always indirect and prone to misreading. In other words, it is assumed that there is an original message which has to be encoded by a sender, propagated along an available information channel, then decoded by a receiver (see Figure 7.1). Thus, emotion becomes a kind of private meaning which only indirectly impacts on the social world by being transformed into transmittable data.

According to this account, the most important issues surrounding emotional communication relate to the problem of 'accuracy'. It is assumed that the sender has an intrapsychic message to convey which is then transformed accurately or inaccurately into the relevant communication code, transmitted through some medium with a given level of distortion, and ultimately decoded correctly or incorrectly by the receiver. Thus, the experimental assessment of accuracy is a project that derives its agenda from a traditional model of emotion as an internal entity which requires internal processing before being communicated. It is exactly this model that I believe is in need of revision. The points that follow all

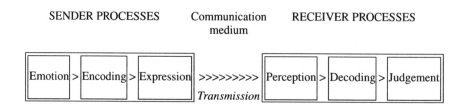

Figure 7.1 Communication of emotion in the slide-viewing paradigm

Source: adapted from Buck (1984)

concern the presuppositions about the nature of private emotion that are implicit in the slide-viewing paradigm and explicit in Buck's translation of information theory into the language of emotion communication.

Spontaneity of reaction

In the slide-viewing paradigm, the sender's facial movements and positions are recorded covertly by the experimenter. The sender is not made aware that there is any receiver present to pick up messages from any nonverbal behaviour that might be given off. Although the studies are intended to be about emotion communication, from the point of view of the sender, no communication is involved in the episode at all. To the extent that facial expressions are normally produced in the context of an actual interaction, where a specific audience is present, and are intended (implicitly or explicitly) to communicate something to somebody else, we would expect less information to be readable when no audience is assumed to be present. In other words, if expressive behaviour is designed (from a cultural, interpersonal, or biological point of view) to be informative to other people, it may well be more appropriate to investigate it in contexts where such communication seems possible.

In this connection, a distinction has often been drawn in the literature between emotional and social uses of nonverbal communication (e.g. Ekman, 1979). In other words, it has been argued that signals can either express internal states or communicate information to someone else (or possibly serve both functions at once). Evidence suggests that in everyday life, the social communicative function accounts for more of the variance in facial behaviour than the emotional expressive function. For example, in a clever study by Kraut and Johnston (1979), bowlers were surreptitiously observed either from the ten-pin end of the lane or from the area where the other players wait to take their turn. The first position allowed observers to record any facial expressions occurring in immediate reaction to the emotional event of scoring a strike or spare, or knocking down a disappointing number of skittles, while the bowlers believed that their faces could not be seen. These responses should therefore have reflected the spontaneous expression of any emotion that happened. The second observational position permitted recording of nonverbal behaviour specifically communicated to the other players. The results of this study clearly showed that there were far more observable facial displays directed to the audience of competitors and supporters than occurred in direct response to the emotional event itself. In other words, faces do not necessarily react in private when something good or bad happens, but rather show (or mislead) other people about the reaction when in public.

Another demonstration of the intrinsically communicative function of facial expression was provided by Bavelas, Black, Lemery, and Mullett (1986) who showed that the timing of a wince of empathic pain depended on the availability of this display to its intended recipient. In a staged incident, the experimenter dropped a colour TV monitor onto his apparently already injured finger in full view of the experimental participant. In the condition where the experimenter was facing the participant when this incident occurred, the participant's facial reaction was attuned to increasing eye contact between the two interactants, whereas when the experimenter turned away after dropping the TV, any initial wincing from the participant soon died away. In other words, this kind of nonverbal communication is specifically directed to an audience and timed so as to be maximally effective and salient to its intended recipient.

Buck, Losow, Murphy, and Costanzo (1992) found that accuracy of emotion judgement in the slide-viewing procedure depended on whether the sender viewed the slides in the presence of another person and on whether this other person was a friend of the sender. Watching with friends increased the degree to which pleasantness information was readable in response to sexual slides, but decreased accuracy of judgements of expressed pleasantness for unpleasant and unusual slides. Buck and his colleagues argued that these results show how spontaneous expressive responses to slide content may be either facilitated or inhibited depending on the nature of the relationship of the sender with co-viewers. However, it is difficult to know to what extent these data arose from indirect effects of the presence of companions on reactions to the slides, or from direct emotional reactions to these companions' perceived reactions, or indeed from interactive emotional communications with companions (cf. Chovil and Fridlund, 1991). From a communicative point of view, expressions seem likely to be most readable in the co-viewing situation when both senders are focused on the slide itself and their reactions find easy accord with those of the potential addressee. In such circumstances, both viewers have a clear emotional message to send and a receptive audience for their communication. Transmitted information is likely to be more variable and ambiguous when attention is directed at the other person as well as at the slide (potentially causing alternating expressive messages), and when there is less certainty about the appropriate response. Arguably, sexual slides are less ambiguous and more attention-demanding than either unpleasant or unusual slides, thus accounting for clearer communication in the former than the latter condition.

Fridlund (1991b) has shown that other people do not have to be actually physically present to serve as implicit audiences for expressive displays. Simply imagining someone else as a receiver of your facial message increases the intensity of the facial reaction. In his study, participants watched a pleasant film privately, but under three different *implicit sociality* conditions. Facial reactions were weakest in the condition where the participant was genuinely alone, stronger when participants arrived for the experiment with another participant with whom they were already acquainted and were told that this other participant would be performing a different task nearby, and stronger still when they were told that this other participant was watching the same film simultaneously in a separate room. In other words, simply imagining someone else going through a similar experience is enough to enhance one's expressive reaction. Similarly, it may be that the clearest responses obtained in Buck's procedure occurred during the slide description phase of the study when senders were addressing their comments to some imagined audience rather than during the simple stimulus presentation period.

The research described in this section implies not only that facial expressions depend more on communicative than expressive functions but also that their supposed expressive function itself may depend on implicit sociality. In other words, private and apparently spontaneous outbursts of emotion may be addressed to imagined audiences, and therefore be developmentally secondary to the primary phenomenon of communicative process. If this argument is correct, Buck's approach was misguided in seeking to understand emotion communication in a situation where this kind of communicative factor is minimized.

Of course, most psychologists and laypeople still believe that emotion expression is based on an internal state which naturally finds expression unless there is any reason to disguise it. If this assumption were correct, one would expect just as powerful (or even more powerful) responses in private as in public. It also seems surprising from this perspective that accuracy in the slide-viewing paradigm tends to be as low as it is.

Buck's (1984) own angle on these issues was that both emotional and communicative functions are served simultaneously in real-life situations, but that the spontaneous expression of motivational–emotional state is biologically the most basic phenomenon, on which the more deliberate and controlled use of expression depends. According to this idea, a neurologically programmed system links primary emotions directly to patterns of facial response. Superimposed upon this fundamental process are culturally modifiable cognitive mechanisms which construct new expressions and adjust existing ones. In Buck's view, emotional expressions of this second kind, which may be responsive to audience effects, deliberate reappraisals, and so on, are always accompanied to some extent by direct and spontaneous expressions of the first kind. In this case, it makes perfect sense to separate out the basic phenomenon of spontaneous emotion expression for controlled study. However, since, according to Buck's model, the primary signal system was evolutionarily designed as a means of informing conspecifics about emotion, it is also necessarily accompanied by an automatic decoding system which allows direct perception of other people's spontaneously expressed emotional state. If such interlocking biological mechanisms exist, then the slide-viewing paradigm evidently fails to activate the appropriate 'natural' form of expression, or else receivers would be able to pick up accurate qualitative information about senders' emotions immediately and without much trouble.

Emotion in direct response to simple stimuli

The slide-viewing paradigm assumed that expressive reactions are elicited naturally and relatively directly in passive observers exposed to simple stimuli. However, appraisal theorists such as Lazarus have argued that emotions depend on the engagement of central life concerns, and it is hard to imagine that looking at a picture for a few seconds in a psychology experiment achieves such a high degree of personal involvement as this. Correspondingly, to the extent that emotional reactions are built up dynamically over time in the person's participative interaction with the environment, the slide-viewing paradigm would not be expected to produce fully developed emotions.

If looking at still pictures does not lead to genuinely emotional experience, how is it that receivers are able to derive any evidence about slide content and reaction to that content by watching senders' faces? One possibility is that conditioned or unconditioned associations cause distinctive movements, for example making a person flinch when presented with gory pictures. This fact, however, does not necessarily imply the presence of any emotional state as such. Similarly, although firing a gun behind someone's head almost universally produces a visible startle response, theorists argue that such a reflex is too inflexible to be considered a bona fide emotional reaction (Ekman *et al.*, 1985; and see Chapter 2). Thus, although Buck assumed that his procedure was assessing emotion communication, it is not clear what kind of information is actually transmitted in the slide-viewing paradigm. The message content might relate to interest, action tendency, or any of a number of attitudinal factors. Wagner, MacDonald, and Manstead (1986) pointed out that receivers may even pick up hints about the sender's opinion by lip-reading occasional words during the stimulus description phase of the study, or by observing informative patterns of gaze direction (see Chapter 5).

Separation of emotion expression and communication

The third limitation of the slide-viewing paradigm is that it divides the emotion communication process into at least two separate stages. Because senders and receivers are physically separated, any emotion communication must depend on expression by one person, and then an independent act of decoding by the other (see Figure 7.1). The sender is involved in one kind of behaviour and the receiver in a different though corresponding one. Of course, this separation makes perfect sense from the point of view of the common-sense idea of emotion as something that is privately experienced and can only be inferred indirectly by someone else. A problem arises only if the possibility is acknowledged that emotion may be experienced in everyday life as part of an ongoing communicative process that intrinsically involves both people together. For example, in a developing argument, emotion may be expressed to emphasize a particular claim. The experiential aspects of this rhetorical process are not distinctive internal feelings (*qualia*) that precede and determine the expressive behaviour but rather are felt concomitants of ongoing interpersonal behaviour. Thus, people do not always react emotionally to something and then express that emotion; rather, their emotional expression and experience emerge in tandem as the interaction develops.

The common-sense view is that any affective information that is transmitted is some kind of readout of a pre-existing emotional experience. In everyday life, as I have argued, emotions do not usually arise as full-blown reactions within an individual consciousness, to be subsequently delivered into the social world.

Rather, emotions *emerge* over the course of an unfolding episode which is typically interpersonal (or at least implicitly so).

In correspondence with the common-sense idea of emotion, the assumption of the slide-viewing paradigm is that an emotion is first experienced as a complete and meaningful intrapsychic event before it ever appears in public. Emotion communication is thus seen as always at least a two-stage process. Research into emotion sending and receiving assumes that communication is a problem because emotion is intrinsically intrapsychic and private, whereas actually people commonly arrive at joint emotional definitions of social situations and share their emotions with one another openly and directly.

Prevention of interaction

A fourth and related restrictive feature of the slide-viewing paradigm is that participants are not only separated from one another physically, but also are prevented from engaging in any kind of interaction with one another. In these studies, emotion communication occurs as a one-way process of information transmission (see Figure 7.1). In short, emotion is sent from one person to another, who is incapable of providing any kind of feedback.

An alternative view of emotional communication would see it as a continually interactive two-way process between participants in the emotional encounter. Person A does not keep on sending out information without any response from Person B. Rather, interchangeable senders and receivers are more likely to be involved in continually adjusting their corresponding emotional positions in relation to each other. If a certain emotional message is clearly not getting across, then adjustments will be made to the communicative process.

Removal of real-time coordination

The procedure of separating the sending from the receiving process not only excludes bidirectional aspects of communication from the slide-viewing paradigm but also undermines any interactional processes that might depend on on-line synchronization between the actions of parties involved in a communicative encounter. Evidence that normal communication depends on a context of ongoing interaction is provided by Murray and Trevarthen's (1985) study of caregiver–infant communication, which directly assessed the importance of two-way coordinated communication using a remote-viewing procedure. In this experiment, six-to twelve-week-old babies interacted with their mothers via two closed-circuit televisions, arranged so that virtual eye contact was possible using life-size screen images. In the second half of the procedure, the live presentation of the mother was replaced on the infant's screen by a video recording, which had been taped earlier in the interaction. The babies showed clear signs of distress as a result of this change. In other words, normal communicative processes crucially depend on real-time coordination of senders' and receivers' signalling. In adults too, the emotional tone of a conversation is typically conveyed by developing interdependencies in mutual nonverbal communication. Eye contact, for example, is something attained between people, rather than as a function of individual intention.

Studies of naturalistic interactions have revealed that communication may break down unless people automatically synchronize various kinds of body movements and nonverbal responses with each other (e.g. Bernieri *et al.*, 1988). During conversations, individuals mutually establish rhythms of interaction which facilitate feelings of togetherness. In addition, we may experience emotion both implicitly as a feeling of being in tune with the flow of the conversation, and more explicitly by registering feedback from our dynamic bodily reactions. If emotion depends on this kind of mutual entrainment of response, then procedures like the slide-viewing paradigm are missing out on crucial aspects of the phenomenon in question.

More research needs to be conducted concerning the ways that emotion arises and is perceived in ongoing social interactions. By physically isolating sender and receiver and removing the real-time element of interpersonal communication, studies using the slide-viewing paradigm have artificially de-emphasized the dynamics of interpersonal emotion episodes. Rather than focusing on the separate and independent subjective experiences of the participants in an interaction, it seems worth investigating the ways in which emotion emerges from developing dialogues.

Closing down communication channels

The slide-viewing paradigm assumes that facial expressions in themselves may be capable of providing diagnostic information about emotional experience. In everyday life, it is extremely rare for a silent face presented out of context to be the only source of emotional information available to the receiver. For example, facial expressions may be used in everyday interaction to consolidate or ironize verbal comments, or to refer to commonly noticed features of the social situation. Thus, a facial expression is normally part of a wider communicative process including also words and body movements, and its meaning often derives partly from this wider context. Moreover, the significance of any particular nonverbal signal also depends on its temporal position in the ongoing flow of interaction, making it unlikely that meaningful semantic content can be registered from isolated pieces of facial information.

Whereas Buck's procedure forced receivers to make sense out of decontextualized information transmitted on a single channel, ordinary processes of affect registration and recognition are often based on direct perception of the dynamic multimodal information provided on-line in the social environment (e.g. Baron and Boudreau, 1987). Signals that could seem meaningless or ambiguous to receivers when presented out of context might make perfect sense when delivered as part of a co-ordinated set of responses to an ongoing situational context.

Communication between strangers

A standard criticism of experimental research in social psychology is that it has tended to focus on interactions between strangers (e.g. Harré and Secord, 1972). In everyday life, such encounters are more the exception than the rule, and an over-reliance on data deriving from this limited approach leads to underestimation of the role of knowledge and skill in our dealings with other people. With respect to emotion communication, there are many ways in which we can become more sensitive to another's emotions as we get to know them better. Indeed, we may develop characteristic modes of relating in different relationships, discussing topics of shared concern, paying attention to mutually agreed channels of information, and so on. By establishing synchrony with one another's nonverbal and verbal behaviours we may also learn with experience to become more 'in tune' emotionally. Against the background of an established and familiar rhythmic structure, key changes and melodic variations are easier to pinpoint.

Pre-existing social relationships not only vary along dimensions of mutual understanding but also in terms of agreed or contested status differentials and interpersonal differences. It may be an accepted feature of a relationship that the co-interactants never pass an established level of intimacy, for example. These negotiated role positions also lend coherence to the specifics of what is transmitted and fed back during an ongoing conversation. In the following chapter, I will consider some ways in which differences in institutional roles between people engaged in emotional encounter may crucially influence the course and content of interaction.

Conclusions

In summary, rather than attempting to find out how people jointly make sense of emotional situations, research using the slide-viewing paradigm (and related procedures) instead tries to answer the question of how (or how well) a person can know what another person (usually a stranger) is feeling based on external cues. No doubt there are situations in everyday social life where people want to know about others' attitudes and emotions but have limited information to go on; however, it seems unrealistic to think of these unusual circumstances as paradigmatic of emotional communication.

Buck's approach to questions of encoding and decoding emotion is a reasonable one as long as it is accepted that spontaneously expressing emotion on the face and reading these expressions are separate processes that can meaningfully be abstracted from the whole emotion communication process. In this regard, Buck explicitly assumed that specific neurological mechanisms are devoted to these functions. My argument, on the other hand, is that emotion communication only makes sense as part of a broader interpersonal process which depends crucially on real-time coordination of responses. The fact that certain people are better able to transmit emotional meaning using their faces, or more skilled at interpreting the signals that are produced in this unrealistic situation, may have little bearing on the way that emotions are formulated, negotiated, and interpreted in the course of an everyday interaction.

These comments about the restrictiveness of the slide-viewing paradigm for understanding emotion communication also apply to a greater or lesser extent to many other methodologies. In the next section of the chapter, I will consider some alternative approaches and suggest ways in which they might be extended to accommodate the complex realities of emotion communication.

Many of the points I have made in this section suggest that the very idea of emotion communication is a simplistic one. Emotions are not private messages that pre-exist their transmission into the social world. Rather, emotions arise in the evolving context of communicative interaction. Furthermore, it is not necessarily emotion *per se* that is communicated when we pick up information from other people's verbal and nonverbal behaviour. Rather we coordinate ourselves to what they do and somewhere along the line emotion occurs between us or is attributed by one of us to the other or to ourself. In the remaining sections of this chapter, I will discuss emotion as an essentially interpersonal phenomenon rather than trying misguidedly to see what happens when individual emotion leaks out into social life.

INTERPERSONAL CAUSES OF EMOTION

Probably the most frequent cause of emotion is other people, so it might seem surprising that most psychological research into emotion has tended to rely on nonsocial manipulations. As Kemper (1978) argued:

> *an extremely large class of human emotions results from real, anticipated, imagined, or recollected outcomes of social relationships*: she says she does not love me; he says I did a good job; I claimed to be honest, but was caught in a lie; he obligated himself to me, but then reneged; and so forth.
>
> (p. 32, emphasis in original)

The problem facing the psychologist who wishes to investigate these interpersonal precursors is that they tend to depend on the existence of established relationships and role differentials: variables that are difficult to manipulate in the laboratory. However, there has been some theoretical as well as empirical work into the ways in which other people can influence emotional reactions. In this section, I review some of these approaches.

Emotion contagion

Buck's research using the slide-viewing paradigm implied that there are a series of intricate subprocesses underlying emotion communication. In his terms, an emotional interaction becomes a complex and protracted interchange of individual mental processes. Emotion is experienced in one person, expressed using the available channels, and transmitted to another person who must then decode the message and ultimately react to its informational content. Any emotional response to the original communication must in turn be encoded then transmitted back, and so on. In everyday life, as I have suggested above, the coordination of emotional signals may be less cognitive and stage-bound. For example, research into mutual entrainment of interactive nonverbal responses suggests that we automatically attain synchronized rhythms in our conversations with others (e.g. Bernieri *et al.*, 1988). To the extent that emotional meanings are contained in the patterns of posture and gesture that unfold in this way, there is little need for any decoding process to feed into the behaviour-control system. Synchrony is established between people automatically and the emotional information may be directly read off the available dynamic perceptual information.

Relatedly, Hatfield, Cacioppo, and Rapson (1992) suggested a way in which emotion might be communicated without decoding of sent signals. They argued that in certain social situations, expressive behaviours are automatically mimicked (cf. Meltzoff and Moore, 1977), and the responses produced by this copying process may feed into the self-perception of emotion (e.g. Laird and Bresler, 1992). If this analysis is correct, there will be a tendency to catch the mood of the person with whom you are interacting via a relatively unconscious and direct process.

Of course, this model is limited in assuming a one-way process of emotion contagion, and it could easily be argued that the real explanation of such effects lies in assuming that interactants jointly negotiate emotional meanings partly via nonverbal communication media.

Hatfield and colleagues' research implied that at least one cause of emotion is another person's emotion. In their view, there is a general tendency for affect to be infectious. However, this is not the only way in which one person's emotional state can lead to another's. If the interaction is antagonistic rather than affiliative, it may be that contrasting or corresponding emotions occur in the two parties not because nonverbal actions are mimicked but because they tend to elicit oppositional kinds of response in the other. For example, if someone is expressing anger at you, the force of their attack may tend to evoke a defensive posture. The process whereby emotion is transmitted and responded to may be analogous to that suggested by Hatfield and her colleagues even in these cases. Nonverbal behaviours may *directly* lead to corresponding nonverbal behaviours and hence emotions. For example, anger tends to involve a forward-leaning attitude along with sharp movements such as finger-pointing directed towards the antagonist. If you are in a weak position with respect to your opponent's stance then you may automatically tend to cower from the attacker and make yourself smaller: a developing posture which mediates the interpersonal emotional attitude of shame or guilt and may be experienced as such (e.g. Stepper and Strack, 1993). Alternatively, given a different set of initial relations, you may resist the advance of your antagonist and counterattack. In this latter case, your own standing of ground is likely to be experienced in terms of reciprocated anger.

Expressive reciprocity

In addition to the possible *direct* effects of nonverbal indices of emotion suggested by the research into emotion contagion, there are also many *indirect* effects of another person's emotional communication on one's own emotional reactions to the interpersonal situation. The way that we believe other people feel about the situation or about us has obvious emotional implications for ourselves. For example, Gottman (1979) showed that marital conversations of dissatisfied couples often contained evidence of affective reciprocity, where communication of negative emotion by one party tended to lead to consequent expression of negative emotion by the other party. The same pattern occurred also with positive affect. In other words, within certain relationships, a tit-for-tat policy applies to emotional interactions, where if one person says something nice then good feelings are reciprocated, but if they say something negative, then the response tends also to express bad feelings. In contrast, Gottman found that successful relationships were characterized by a more complementary pattern of affective exchange, with expressions of negative emotion by one party tending to be followed by reassurance from the other.

Hatfield and colleagues' work suggested that emotion can be transmitted directly from one person to another. Research into emotional reciprocity, on the other hand, suggests that emotional communications may produce corresponding emotional communication from the other party in some kinds of relationship. If we assume that these processes work in both directions, either of them might conceivably lead to a mutual intensification of emotional experience with one person's emotion producing stronger emotion in the other, whose emotional reaction in turn feeds back and strengthens the emotion of the first person, and so on. In other words, the interpersonal feedback loop would tend to lead to escalation in the intensity of emotion over the course of certain kinds of interaction. For example, you might respond to affectionate expressions from your attractive companion with similar displays of liking and your companion might in turn respond to your returned signals. These mutual expressions might lead to emotion directly as a result of facial feedback or indirectly via appraisal of the other's inferred attitude. To the extent that the negotiation of gestures went on at an automatic level, as a function of primitive contagion, for example, your experience might be of an emotional experience coming over you spontaneously rather than as a result of a reasoned evaluation of the other person's behaviour.

Social facilitation of emotion

The research discussed so far in this section suggests that one person's emotion may under certain circumstances produce the same or a different emotion in someone else. Work by Chapman and colleagues on children's humour responses indicated that the presence of other people can have additional facilitative effects on one's own emotional reactions which do not necessarily depend on them displaying emotion as such (e.g. Chapman, 1983; Chapman and Wright, 1976).

The simple presence of another person seems to change the way that the emotional situation is interpreted.

Chapman (1983) reported a host of effects on laughter of subtle interpersonal and relational variables. For example, Foot and Chapman (1976) found that the presence of one experimenter during the presentation of humorous tapes enhanced laughter, whereas the presence of a second experimenter tended to reduce it, suggesting that something about their respective interpersonal styles moderated emotional reactions to the stimuli. The kind of conversation conducted with the children on the way to the laboratory also affected the degree of amusement displayed, with more formalized interaction tending to decrease subsequent amusement (Chapman, 1983).

More relevant from the present point of view were the effects of the presence of other children while the humorous material was presented. In a typical experimental design, Chapman and his colleagues played humorous tapes via headphones or showed cartoon films to groups of children aged between 4 and 11. In some studies, one of the children had been trained as the experimenter's accomplice and engaged in scripted behaviour (e.g. laughter, or looking at the other child) at various predefined points in the procedure, signalled via instructions delivered on the second channel of their headphones.

A general and well-established finding was that children who watched humorous films alone laughed less than those watching in pairs, who in turn laughed less than children in groups of four or more. However, these effects depended on the behaviour of the other children and the relationships that existed between them. For example, children watching humorous material with a friend showed more amusement than those watching with a child they did not know well. Similarly, displayed amusement was greater when the experimental accomplice laughed more or looked at the other child for a greater period of time during the presentation of the stimulus (Chapman and Wright, 1976).

It seems intuitively plausible that our reactions of amusement depend on who else is with us and what they are doing. For example, comedy programmes on television often seem less amusing when watched alone, than with friends. We may *think* that the material is funny, but it is much rarer for us to laugh out loud at the jokes when there is no one there to hear us.

From the broader perspective of a communicative theory of emotion we might expect that certain kinds of affiliative emotion, such as amusement and affection, are directly intensified when other people whom we like are around, but that antagonistic feelings depend more on the presence (imagined or otherwise) of the antagonist, and may be reduced in more friendly social contexts (cf. Buck *et al.*, 1992). An important exception to this latter rule is that discussion of shared antagonisms can crystallize and reinforce existing negative attitudes and indeed can serve to strengthen interpersonal bonds between the people who have these attitudes in common. In the next chapter, I will consider more explicitly the role of ingroup–outgroup relations in the causation of emotion.

Emotional significance defined socially

According to appraisal theory (e.g. Lazarus, 1991b; and see Chapter 2), a neces- sary and sufficient condition for emotion is that the person's current life situation is appraised as impinging significantly on personal concerns. In more pedestrian terms, an event has to *matter* to the person experiencing it to cause emotion: they have to care about what is happening to them. But what is it that makes events personally important in this way? Appraisal theory pushes the necessity for explanation of emotion back one stage but no further. One possible answer to the question it raises is that events often achieve their personal significance in the course of ongoing social encounters and the development of relationships be- tween people. In this case, social variables are crucial to the explanation of many instances of emotion.

To give some simple examples, probably the most important objects in anyone's environment are other people. The things that people do and say are the things that affect us most, especially if we are involved in some kind of estab- lished relationship with them (whether affiliative or antagonistic). If we are abandoned by someone we care about, if someone says things that question our public status, if we are congratulated by someone in authority, if someone to whom we are attracted returns our attentions, then emotion is an obvious response. In all these cases, even if appraisal of some perfunctory kind is a logical necessity for counting the episode as an emotional one, the causes that make the real difference are social.

Research into the precursors of emotional disorder supports the view that other people supply the most important class of emotion-inducing events. For example, Brown and Harris (1978) attempted to understand the specific nature of the stressors that lead to depression. A sample of depressed and nondepressed women were interviewed and it was found that 61 per cent of the depressed women had experienced a major negative life event involving a long-term threat to well-being during the previous nine months, whereas only 25 per cent of the control group had experienced something comparable. These life events mostly involved loss or separation, in particular loss of, or separation from, someone close to them, or loss of a job and its associated role position. For example, some of the women reacted with depression to the death of a parent, to life-threatening illness in someone close, to unpleasant revelations about marital infidelity, to enforced moves to less pleasant housing, to being made redundant, and so on. In other words, many of the stressors found to precipitate emotional disorder may be socially defined, and many others are significant mainly because of their social effects in terms of changed relationships with other people, and decreased social status.

Another set of findings concerning the relationship between interpersonal factors and emotional disorders is covered by the extensive literature on social support. For example, Brown and Harris also found that the effects of negative life events were less for those women who had a close relationship with a confidant such as their spouse or boyfriend. Thirty-seven per cent of women without such an intimate relationship got depressed after their misfortune, as opposed to only 10 per cent of the women who had a confidant. This finding (among others) suggests that the negative impact of life events can be ameliorated, or 'buffered' by the presence of social support. The people around you can soften the blow. There is now a great deal of evidence relating to the role of social support in reactions to stress (e.g. Cohen and Wills, 1985).

Although Brown and Harris and other investigators have seen the effects of social support as a buffer against stress, their data do not necessarily demand exactly this interpretation. Reanalysis of their results by Tennant and Bebbington (1978) suggested that presence of a close confidant had separate and independent effects on well-being irrespective of the presence of stressors, so that it is possible to see social support variables in terms of positive life events rather than as protectors against negative life events. In other words, the loss of social support may provoke depression, and the obtaining of social support may directly lead to recovery. For example, the fact that you are a member of a close group of friends may be a fairly direct cause of your happiness and well-being, whereas the lack of any social contact of reclusive individuals may be a major cause of any depression they experience. Needless to say, from an interactionist perspective, the depression of social isolates may also lead to rejection by others and increased isolation (e.g. Coyne, 1976).

Cohen and Wills (1985) reviewed a wide range of evidence for the effects of social support on reactions to stress, and concluded that different kinds of social support variables have different effects on well-being and responses to stress (see also Barrera, 1986). According to their account, *structural* social support (integration within a social network) has direct effects on well-being but does not in itself ameliorate the effects of stress. On the other hand, *functional* social support (perceived availability of people to help deal with difficult situations) provides a buffer for stress.

Coyne and Downey (1991), however, suggested that much of the apparently beneficial impact of social support can be explained in terms of the lack of negative social factors it implies. People with good social support networks tend not to suffer from discord in close relationships, and it may be this latter factor that makes them less likely to become depressed. In other words, it is not that people who are equipped with social support are more psychologically healthy as such, but rather that those reporting a lack of social support tend to be those who are involved in psychologically unhealthy relationships. Consistent with this analysis, the available evidence confirms that marital discord is a common factor in many depressive episodes. For example, in a survey by Paykel, Myers, Dienelt, Klerman, Lindenthal and Pepper (1969) it was found that the life event that was the best predictor of depression was a recent increase in the number of arguments between husband and wife. A more recent study found that 'being married and being unable to talk to one's spouse' was associated with a massive twenty-fivefold increase in the odds of being depressed (see Coyne and Downey, 1991).

What all these examples show is that many of the things about which people get depressed or, more generally, emotional, relate to other people in some way.

According to appraisal theorists, though, such objects and events will only lead to emotion if they are appraised as being significant for the individual's current concerns. It is usually assumed that this appraisal is a cognitive-evaluative process that goes on in the individual's head. However, it is also possible that appraisal itself may be a social process. For example, negotiations about the affective significance of events may be carried out on-line via the medium of implicit nonverbal signals sent back and forth between people. We might even imagine an explicit interpersonal reasoning process going on in verbal dialogue which leads to a mutual acceptance of the emotional importance of what is happening. Experiences described in terms of 'love at first sight' might happen in one of these two ways, with neither party being conscious of their mutual emotion arising as a result of any individually held intention. More radically, if emotions are communications that derive their meaning only from the context of the surrounding relationship between the people involved, then interpersonal factors are necessarily the substance of the causation of these phenomena.

Other people's emotions change emotional interpretations

As suggested above with reference to emotional contagion, emotional expressions may not always intensify *similar* emotional states in other people, but may also lead to *contrasting* emotions if the interactants do not occupy comparable interpersonal positions. Anger in one person, for example, may lead to fear or shame in another.

A less direct kind of emotional influence leading to different emotional states can occur when one person's emotional reaction helps to establish the nature of the relationship with another person. An example of this second kind of emotional complementarity is provided in an experiment by Zillmann, Weaver, Mundorf, and Aust (1986). In this study, male or female undergraduates watched a scene from the horror movie *Friday the 13th, Part III* in the company of an opposite-sex accomplice of the experimenter, posing as another participant, who displayed distress, indifference, or 'mastery' in response to the film's content. Male participants' enjoyment of the film as well as their attraction to their companion was higher when she exhibited distress, whereas females seemed more attracted to their male companions when they showed mastery, by delivering advice ostensibly addressed to the film's female protagonist about how she should deal with the villain's attacks. In other words, traditionally sex-typed emotional responses to a film-clip depicting a female in distress (fear for females, and mastery for males) encouraged greater enjoyment and interpersonal attraction. Furthermore, adoption of the appropriate sex role by one party in the interaction tended to lead to the corresponding emotional attitude in the other, for example increased mastery by the male led to increased distress in the female. It seems therefore that one person's emotional display can affect the way in which a situation is evaluated and indirectly lead to a different emotional state in the other person. In the next chapter, I will consider further the impact of role and status differences on emotion.

Social comparison of emotion

In the study by Zillmann and colleagues, the emotional display of one person affected another person's interpretation of the role difference between them, and ultimately led the second person to display a different and corresponding emotion. According to the theory of social comparison, on the other hand, if someone is perceived as similar to you, you may rely on their apparent emotional reaction as a guide to interpreting your own feelings, and end up experiencing the *same* emotion as them. For example, Schachter (1959) found that people anticipating a novel and anxiety-provoking test session, where they believed that electric shocks would be delivered, preferred to wait with someone else who was also about to undergo the shocks, as opposed to either waiting alone, or waiting with someone in a different and more pleasant predicament. One of the participants explained this preference in the following terms: 'I wanted to wait with other people to see how they would react while waiting for the experiment' (p. 41). Schachter argued that unfamiliar situations evoke evaluative needs concerning one's own emotional state, and social comparison with others sharing a similar fate helps to clarify the nature of the feelings in question: 'In a novel, emotion-producing situation, . . . the feelings one experiences or 'should' experience may not be easily interpretable, and it may require some degree of social interaction and comparison to appropriately label and identify a feeling' (p. 26).

A similar principle was applied in the procedure of Schachter and Singer's (1962) experiment, where participants experiencing unexplained arousal were expected to interpret their emotional state in accordance with the apparent emotional display of the accomplice, who was playing the role of another participant.

Two basic conclusions about the relation of interpersonal factors to emotion may be drawn from Schachter's research. First, the presence of other people may lead to reinterpretations of the quality of emotional state under certain special circumstances. Second, the presence of ambiguous or threatening emotion may have interpersonal consequences in encouraging the person experiencing it to seek out suitable company to clarify the situation or reassure them about its nature. In the next section of the chapter, I consider this and other interpersonal *effects* of emotion.

INTERPERSONAL EFFECTS OF EMOTION

Above, I suggested that the expression of an emotional state in one person often leads to the experience or expression of a similar or different emotion in another person. So far, I have focused on the first and most obvious implication of this suggestion and argued that other people influence the causation of emotion. However, this conclusion also leads to the secondary implication that emotions have interpersonal *effects* as well as causes, for example in that they may influence other people's emotions. Evidence relating to this second aspect of the interpersonal emotion dialogue has already been discussed indirectly, for example in the sections on emotional contagion and reciprocity. Therefore, I will focus in this section on interpersonal effects of emotion which are not based solely on reflected, reciprocated, or retaliatory affect.

The first point to make is that the emotional reactions of other people around you are usually difficult to ignore, and often seem to demand some kind of interpersonal response. One possible reason for this, based on appraisal theory, is that emotional reactions imply personal significance, and if something is significant to someone else then there is a chance that it will also be significant for us. At the very least, it seems sensible to take other people's feelings about the emotional value of situations seriously. Indeed, one of the ways in which the importance of an event can be judged is by considering other people's reactions to it (e.g. social referencing; Campos and Stenberg, 1981). If someone in a similar situation to us expresses fear, we feel that there may be something to be afraid of. Likewise, if everyone around us seems to be pleased about something, we often end up feeling pleased ourselves. Analogously, when you come across a group of people who are all looking at something or pointing, it is very hard to resist looking in that same direction.

However, it is not always the case that our emotional evaluations of the social situation easily find accord with those of others, otherwise social life would run completely smoothly and with a boring predictability. Sometimes someone else's emotion demands a reaction precisely because it implies an interpretation of your relationship or of something else going on that you cannot let pass without protest or rejoinder. For example, you can get angry about someone else's anger, depression, fear, embarrassment, happiness, love, or hate. Moreover, it is possible to return love with hate, or even hate with love. In all of these cases, the fact that the other person expresses a particular emotion endorses a particular appraisal of what is happening that you feel compelled to contest.

Thus, it is not simply the fact that emotional reactions tend to be related to important things that leads us to be attentive to other people's emotions. More accurately, emotions have particular social meanings which contain evaluative attitudes towards the situation, and these evaluative attitudes may be accepted or rejected by the other people involved. In either case, if the target of evaluation is a topic of mutual concern, then it will be difficult simply to let pass any emotion that is expressed about it. Furthermore, the expression of the emotion by someone with whom you are currently in contact itself attaches significance to the evaluative object, even if it previously had none for you.

The implication of this analysis is that one of the direct interpersonal effects of emotion depends on the fact that emotions contain appraisals of the situation, so that expression of the emotion becomes a public presentation of the evaluation and interpretation implied by that appraisal. For example, getting overtly angry involves making a claim that someone is responsible for violating your personal rights (Averill, 1982; Sarbin, 1986). The person at whom the anger is directed will therefore be obliged to submit to your claim or else to invoke a counterclaim, which itself may be expressed as anger.

According to this account (see also Chapter 2), the relationship between appraisal and emotion is not the direct causal one implied by Lazarus (1991b).

Emotions certainly contain appraisals in the sense that they are part of their accepted social meaning. However, the expression of emotion in any real-life context does not necessarily follow a process of appraisal, rather it makes a claim about how the situation should be appraised. When I get angry, I want someone else to accept that my rights have been infringed in some way. When I say I am in love, I want a particular person to accept my definition of our mutual relationship.

If this analysis of the interpersonal functions and effects of emotion has any validity, then emotion is something that only makes complete sense when looked at in the context of the encounter within which it arose. Thus, in order to understand the phenomenon it is necessary to consider the nature of the relationships that surround it.

INTERPERSONAL FUNCTIONS OF EMOTION

It takes only a short step from saying that emotions make claims about the definition of the social situation to the argument that the *purpose* of expressing emotion is often to make these claims, or to achieve the indirect social effects that making these claims produces. Certainly, it is true that political speakers and others involved in attempts at persuasion often deliberately express emotion in order to invoke a particular kind of reaction in their audience. Since the time of the ancient Greeks, the value of emotional appeals in rhetorical argument has been well known (e.g. Aristotle, 1909). For example, partisan references to political injustices are traditionally associated with at least a perfunctory level of indignation. Similarly, sports coaches try to work up a sense of team spirit and determination in their charges by conveying the appropriate emotions relating to solidarity with co-members of the team, and enmity towards opponents. (Emotion in intergroup situations such as this will be a specific focus of the following chapter.) Of course, no one would want to argue that these examples of deliberate or at least partially contrived emotion are representative of the full range of emotion episodes. The standard idea is that emotion usually comes over us and grips us in ways beyond our conscious control. Nevertheless, it is possible that the functions served when emotions are used intentionally correspond in some respects to the interpersonal dynamics of apparently more spontaneous passions. (I shall return to this issue of intentionality later in the book.)

Evidence relating to the interpersonal functionality of emotional displays in more everyday contexts is provided in research by Biglan and colleagues (Biglan *et al.*, 1985). These investigators observed problem-solving interactions of couples including a depressed wife, and compared these with similar interactions between members of nondepressed couples. As might be expected, depressive wives tended to express complaints more than nondepressed wives. More pertinently, the level of aggressive behaviour of husbands and wives was highly correlated, a finding that is consistent with the idea that in arguments anger tends to lead to anger from the person with whom you are angry. Furthermore, in couples who reported general marital distress, the conditional probability of aggressive behaviour in the husband was reduced following depressive behaviour in the wife, supporting the idea that depressive complaints serve the function of reducing aggression from interactants. Correspondingly, depressive communications from the wives tended to be reduced following aggressive comments from the husband, suggesting that aggression may have been motivated by an attempt to reduce complaining.

The underlying basis of the evaluative dialogue in these dysfunctional encounters seems to concern claims and counterclaims about the nature of the relationship and its inequities. The wife's depressive complaints served as one side of an argument which emphasized the pressures and burdens being placed on her. On the other hand, the husband's aggressive comments implied that the wife was to blame for the state she was working herself into, and that things were really not as bad as she made out. Faced with such a rebuff, the wife could only intensify her display of distress to reinforce her position as a victim, not only of the previous pressures and burdens, but also of a husband who attacked her when she was already down. It easy to see how the two parties in such an exchange might get locked into an intensifying spiral of escalating negative emotion.

To summarize the implications of this research, displays of aggressive and depressive emotions may have specific consequences on the ensuing emotions of the other party in a conversation. Furthermore, at some level the display of depression may be specifically directed at ameliorating the other person's attack.

The dynamic functionality of emotional displays during ongoing interactions featured also in Coyne's (1976) interactional description of the development of depression. The main advantage of Coyne's reasoning from the present point of view is that it considered both sides of the interpersonal equation rather than seeing emotion as an intact response of a single individual confronted by an independent social situation. Not only is emotion seen as a response to social factors but also as a communicative act designed to serve specific interpersonal functions, even if its actual social effects are not always those that were intended.

Coyne suggested that depressive symptoms are best interpreted as part of a system of social relationships rather than expressions of the intrapsychic conflicts of a single individual (see also Gotlib and Colby, 1987). He argued that the kind of social feedback elicited by depressives confirms and exacerbates the negative view that they develop of themselves and their social effectiveness. In other words, depressives behave in a manner which tends to produce interpersonal reactions which sustain and intensify their depression. The basic assumption of the analysis is that depressive symptoms are messages sent out to other people, asking for reassurance about the person's continuing importance to these people. Unfortunately, the fact that any reassurance given is produced on demand rather than spontaneously undermines its value to the person who has requested it.

According to Coyne's account, the starting point for depression is typically some kind of threat to the person's social standing, such as the breakdown of an important relationship or the loss of a job. The victim at first responds to this threat with withdrawal and expressions of helplessness, both of which serve as communicative acts intended to get other people to take control of any interaction with the depressed person. In other words, the depressed person calls for help and often receives it from significant others.

The sufferer is now faced with two conflicting ways of characterizing the support offered by other people. Their sympathy might reflect continuing concern for the depressive, or alternatively, it could simply be a direct response to the received request for help. Given that a threat to identity is what precipitated depression in the first place, and reassurance is exactly what is required, it is important for the depressive to determine which of these alternative interpretations is more viable. Unfortunately, the only way of obtaining clarification of the apparent messages of support involves renewing the call for help by producing more depressive symptoms.

For family members and friends close to the depressive who have been offering comfort, this continued exhibiting of symptoms is hard to understand. Eventually, they begin to suffer a kind of compassion fatigue, and although they may continue to respond with sympathy out of a sense of duty, their expressions of concern will be given with increasing reluctance. This reluctance will be partially detectable in nonverbal concomitants of their overt verbal reassurance. In other words, messages of support arrive mixed with other qualifying messages. Of course, this means that the communications received by the depressive are now even more ambiguous than before. Again the depressive seeks to clarify the status of the relationship with those around with additional appeals for reassurance.

These calls for help are responded to with increasing reluctance, producing even more mixed messages. Also, by this stage those close to the depressive are beginning to avoid contact with the sufferer. Now any attempts by the depressive to ask other people around about their true feelings will only be interpreted by them as further unpleasant symptoms of depression. Because the other people have come to view questions of their relationship with the depressive as touching on a sensitive issue and bringing up feelings of guilt and so on, it is likely that these enquiries will only produce denial and anger, which add further fuel to the development of the depression. Any attempt by these others to reassure the depressive that they still really do care will be indistinguishable from the previous untrustworthy reassurances and therefore cannot be taken at face value. Thus, an exacerbating spiral of rejection and loss of support leading to more complaints and more rejection is set up.

In Coyne's view, the interactive social behaviour of depressives leads to increasing rejection from others which those others will themselves explicitly deny. If this is true, the supposedly distorted thought processes focused on by cognitive therapists (e.g. Abramson *et al.*, 1978; Beck *et al.*, 1979) may actually reflect relatively realistic doubts about relationships with others. These other people may say that they care about the depressive, but the way that they express this care is bound to arouse legitimate suspicions.

If Coyne's analysis is correct, individualistic accounts of depression can never give a complete picture of how the emotional syndrome is caused, nor how best to deal with it (Coyne, 1982). Many of the crucial variables only become apparent when looking at the interactions between people in the developing social situation. It may be that part of the impact of these interactions on the depressive's emotional reaction depends on the way that they are *appraised*, but this is only a small part of the story, and not one that necessarily makes an important difference to how emotional sense is created in this situation.

The advantage of Coyne's model of depression from the present point of view is that it allows us to examine emotions (and appraisals) as part of a *dialogue* between the individual and relevant others, rather than as private, internal states which may or may not be expressed by the person experiencing them.

SOCIAL SHARING OF EMOTION

A basic social effect of emotions is that they often make us seek out company. For example, as mentioned above, Schachter (1959) argued that the experience of ambiguous emotional states in unfamiliar social settings can evoke evaluative needs which are best resolved by social comparison with someone else who faces a similar situation. However, the need to evaluate the appropriateness of our emotions does not necessarily depend on their ambiguity. It may be that we know very well what we are feeling but want to know whether we are experiencing it to a reasonable degree. More generally, it may be that instances of many kinds of relatively intense emotion are accompanied by a desire to be with other people. This is certainly so in the popular conception of love, but also seems to apply to other kinds of joy and happiness, as well as negative emotions such as fear and general distress. The specific motivation for seeking social contact may be different for different emotions, however. (Possible exceptions to the rule that emotions are associated with wanting to be with other people are grief and sadness which often seem to be connected with a need for solitude rather than company.)

Research by Rimé, Mesquita, Philippot, and Boca (1991) has shown that when people have recently been through an emotional episode, they almost always talk about it to someone else (usually someone close) afterwards. In over half of the reported cases this *social sharing* of emotion took place within a day of experiencing the emotional incident.

Why do we share our emotional experiences with other people? Rimé and his colleagues suggested that the process may depend on the disruptiveness of emotional events, and the need to work through unresolved issues. A more obvious explanation, based on appraisal theory, is that emotions are about things that are important to us (at least at the time) and our feelings about what is important often influence our selection of conversation topics. From the point of view of the present analysis, talking about an emotion afterwards restates the evaluative claim it contains and assesses consensus for it. We want to feel justified in our emotional attitudes, and the only possible authorization is an interpersonal one.

EMOTION AS INTERPERSONAL COMMUNICATION

In the foregoing sections I have attempted to show that the phenomenon of emotion is surrounded on all sides by interpersonal variables. Other people or imagined other people crucially influence the causation of emotion and its inter-personal expression; emotion has direct and indirect interpersonal effects; and the expression of emotion serves specific social functions in an interaction. In this section, I want to take this analysis a stage further and argue that this cluster of interpersonal factors constitute the essence of emotional processes. My claim is that emotion is constructed on-line as part of the developing relationship emerg-ing from a real-time encounter between people. Any internal experiential aspects of this process do not provide a central essence or driving force for emotional episodes, but are epiphenomenal and of only secondary interest to the inter-personal analysis. Our common-sense emphasis on such personal and private aspects reflects the individualistic ethos of Western civilization (e.g. Sampson, 1977) which is designed to support an ideology where a single person can be brought to account for his or her own actions. I will have more to say about the ideological functions of emotion theory in a later chapter. For now, I want to indicate the possibility of analysing emotion as being at its very heart a form of communication addressed to a real or potential audience.

My basic point is that emotions are ways of communicating evaluations and appraisals. Research by Fridlund (1992), Kraut and Johnston (1979), and Bavelas and colleagues (1986) reviewed in Chapter 5 suggests that our emotional expres-sions are often intended as communicative acts addressed to another person rather than being direct reflections of an underlying mental state. The usual interpret-ation of these findings is that emotion is experienced privately by people and sometimes spontaneously expressed but that much of the variance in real-life nonverbal behaviour is accounted for by interpersonal functionality (e.g. Jones and Raag, 1989). I want to go one stage further and say that emotions themselves are syndromes of action that are intrinsically directed towards an audience. There is not a mysterious internal part of emotion that remains insulated from its modes of expression; rather, getting emotional involves presenting oneself in a certain way to a particular audience (even if that audience is internalized and imagined). Emotions, in my view, make identity claims in the context of a relationship. This account will be developed in more detail in the subsequent chapter when I discuss emotion and role involvement. To anticipate the course of my argument, I will be suggesting that emotion is invoked as a wholehearted bodily representation of a person's claim about changed status in an encounter. We get emotional in order to notify some audience that they should treat us differently, either in the long term or in the short term.

Of course, I do not want to be read as saying that emotions are adopted deliberately or intentionally to convey evaluations in all cases. Rather, when the concern expressed by the emotion is strong and central to a person's role identifi-cation, the reaction will tend to be experienced as completely compelled by the situation (Sarbin, 1986). It is not the intensity of an internal feeling that seems to overpower us but the fact that something so important to us is involved. Even in these cases of unpremeditated passion, the point of the emotion is to display the evaluation to some intended audience.

RESEARCH STRATEGIES

In this chapter, I have tried to argue that the interpersonal arena is the place where the emotional action is. Much of what I have said has been speculative because psychologists have only made tentative forays into the area of real-life and real-time social interactions. There are two main reasons for this lack of exploration. First, many investigators believe that because the discipline of psychology is specifically devoted to understanding how individual human beings function, it is best to analyse them at the individual level. The problem with this approach, however, is that personhood is a function of participation in social life and not a natural possession of a single human animal (Gergen and Davis, 1985). The surrounding culture shapes the course of our development and, once socialized, our actions often only derive meaning from their impact on others. Most of the things we have to deal with in the real world (which itself is at least partly socially manufactured), as well as the ways that we have of dealing with them, derive from other people, who are around us now, or who have lived before us. What we do as individuals makes little sense when abstracted from its embodiment in the ongoing physical and social world.

The second and more banal reason for neglecting social interaction in psychology is that studying it is extremely difficult. Again, this is partly because there has been little development of usable methodologies as a consequence of psychology's single-minded focus on the individual. However, inattention to interpersonal factors is also a result of the very complexity of interaction. Although we apparently possess substantial implicit skills for dealing with encounters with others, the knowledge that we deploy is difficult to articulate, and even harder to extend so that it encompasses interaction from a wider angle than that of our own subjective point of view.

A great deal more observational work needs to be done before a workable theory of interpersonal emotion becomes available. However, there is a danger of getting bogged down in the minutiae of interactive coordination of tiny movements. A more profitable approach than subjecting social life to the 'affective microscope' (Peery, 1978) may be to make use of participants' own tacit knowledge about encounters, in particular those encounters in which they themselves are, or have been, involved.

For example, the work of Gottman and his colleagues (e.g. Gottman and Levenson, 1985; Levenson and Gottman, 1983) provides a promising research paradigm. In these experiments, marital interactions were videotaped and subsequently reviewed by the involved parties, who were asked to code what happened at junctures that they themselves defined as important. This procedure has several advantages. First, it allows attention to the dynamic time-based aspects of an interaction without the need for intrusive interruptions while it runs its course.

Second, the methodology allows identification of meaningful interchanges in a principled way without having to sift through a mass of irrelevant recorded data. Finally, the research addresses an ecologically valid phenomenon in which the participants are already involved and can display their real-life interpersonal skills, personal talents, and inadequacies. This is surely a better strategy than studying people who do not know each other in artificial settings. I believe that this kind of research is capable of addressing some of the most important issues about what emotion is, and how it works, and the results obtained so far are already highly promising in some cases.

INTEGRATING ASPECTS OF INTERPERSONAL EMOTION

The central argument of this chapter has been that emotion is not just a private meaning that indirectly surfaces in the social world but rather something that emerges directly through the medium of interaction. Interpersonal factors are typically the main causes of emotion, and emotions lead people to engage in certain kinds of social encounter or withdraw from such interpersonal contact. Emotions have relational rather than personal meanings (e.g. de Rivera, 1984) and the expression of these meanings in an emotional interaction serves specific interpersonal functions, depending on the nature of the emotion. To summarize, emotion is social through and through. Its fundamental basis is as a form of communication.

The usual objection to such a radical and superficially counterintuitive claim is that emotion is demonstrably experienced and expressed in private, for example when watching TV alone or when a lover abandons us. A number of points can be made in defence of the interpersonal viewpoint. First, as Fridlund (1991b) has demonstrated, many instances of private expression can be explained in terms of implicit sociality. Often there are clear proxies present in the situation to stand in for our intended audience. When rejected and left alone by someone, our emotion may be addressed to the person who has deserted us. When watching an emotional drama, we identify with characters and direct our emotions to the other characters who may seem real to us at the time. The fact that we sometimes talk to ourselves does not lead people to believe that the primary function of verbal language is to support a private process of naming, so why should we feel any different about our nonverbal communications?

Having said all this, it is undeniable that certain reactions which contribute to emotional expression and experience are automatic and unresponsive to social variables, and occur demonstrably even when alone without any potential audience. For example, surprising and sudden events usually cause us to jump. However, the startle reflex, even though it shows clearly on the face, is not *itself* an emotion (Ekman *et al.*, 1985) and so these phenomena should not deceive us into believing that conditions such as anger, embarrassment, love or hate sometimes burst spontaneously into a nonsocial consciousness.

Emotions do occur in private, although their expression often seems weaker than during a corresponding public episode (e.g. Chapman and Wright, 1976).

Furthermore, even implicit sociality enhances private reactions. My conclusion from all this is that private emotion is a derivative phenomenon which depends on prior experience of interpersonal emotion. As many developmental psychologists have argued, emotional meanings are learned in the context of the primary intersubjectivity between caregiver and infant (e.g. de Rivera, 1984; Trevarthen, 1984).

However, another angle to the argument about the privacy of emotion remains to be addressed. This concerns the suspicion that the emotions that we 'feel inside' sometimes do not correspond in intensity or quality to what is expressed to the public world. We act as if we really like someone, believing that no one but us can tell that we actually do not like them at all. We pretend to be annoyed at a child when they are careless and hurt themselves, in order to teach them a lesson, but inside we are upset rather than angry. What, then, is the nature of the obvious difference between feeling an emotion and simply going through the motions of expressing it? Surely here we have direct and incontrovertible evidence that the true essence of emotion is individual feeling. In the next chapter, I try to develop a nonessentialist interpersonal and intergroup explanation of these phenomena.

8 Institutional and cultural emotion

OVERVIEW

In the previous chapter, I offered an interpersonal perspective on emotion that broadened the traditional focus on individual experience by incorporating dynamic interactional variables into the analysis. I suggested that getting emotional often involves making claims about one's identity or the definition of the social situation in the course of ongoing relationships with other people. This chapter takes an even wider view of emotion by contextualizing these dynamic interactional factors within institutional settings in the cultural world. Issues relating to interpretation and evaluation of social situations and actors' relative positions within them are not worked out solely through the medium of interpersonal negotiation but are also shaped by the constraints of the surrounding organizationally structured reality as well as the broader societal backdrop. In effect, the identity claims involved in getting emotional are based on *role commitments* and derive at least partly from the individual's position in pre-existing interpersonal social networks. Transactions with others are often shaped by predefined communication channels that are provided by the social institutions and groups to which we belong or to which we lend our services. In formal situations, the relationships between participants and the rules of action and emotion they follow may be prescribed relatively exhaustively, leaving little scope for negotiation or private reinterpretation. In less formal settings, such influences may be less restrictive but are rarely completely absent. In this chapter then, I try to integrate factors relating to role and social identity into my account of interpersonal emotion. I review the growing research literature concerning emotion at work, and suggest that in many circumstances we express and experience emotion partly because the rules pertaining to our institutional position and cultural identity implicitly or explicitly encourage us to do so.

A WIDER CONTEXT FOR EMOTION

From a psychological and common-sense perspective, the usual idea of emotions represents them as things that happen to individuals faced by external events that have personal significance for them. In contrast, I have suggested that getting emotional is in reality something that people often do actively in order to influence others in support of particular self-presentational goals. Emotions, in other words, may be identity claims addressed to specific audiences. Such an analysis implies that people are motivated to create and sustain certain public impressions during the course of everyday social life. But what is the source of the identities that are claimed? In the present chapter, I suggest that our relative social positions within institutions define many of the presentational requirements that are satisfied by emotional performance. In addition, these institutional positions are themselves located within a wider cultural context which both partly determines institutional structure and also provides independent prescriptions about emotional conduct in the interpersonal world. The existing social arrangement of the interpersonal world guides our emotional encounters within it and fuels the concerns that are defended when we are angry, afraid, jubilant, and so on. Thus, emotion is not only an interpersonal, but also necessarily an institutional and cultural affair.

EMOTION RULES AND EMOTIONAL REALITY

The impact of institutions on emotion is typically explored within the province of sociology (e.g. Kemper, 1991) rather than psychology, and the influence of culture is most centrally an anthropological area (e.g. Shweder and LeVine, 1984). Research in both these fields has provided evidence that emotional performance is influenced by commonly held norms and beliefs. In this chapter, I want to consider some of the specifically psychological issues raised by this research in related disciplines (see also Averill, 1982; 1992; Harré, 1986).

Most studies in the sociology of emotion have addressed the impact of social structures of various kinds on the conduct of emotions. The relevant findings are mainly descriptive, showing how organizational and cultural settings often contain inbuilt expectations or requirements about what kind of emotional expression is appropriate. For example, investigators have detailed the explicit and implicit rules about emotion contained in American popular media (e.g. Cancian and Gordon, 1988), the training in emotional conduct provided by certain service industries (e.g. Hochschild, 1983), and interview studies have explored shared expectations about emotion within particular organizational contexts (e.g. Rafaeli and Sutton, 1987). Similarly, anthropological investigation has revealed cultural differences in representations of emotions (e.g. Lutz, 1988; Rosaldo, 1984). Thus, the existence of institutional and cultural emotion injunctions seems beyond question. Clearly organizational and societal reality shape people's ideas of emotional propriety, of what ought to be felt in predefined social settings, but to what extent do these prescriptions and guidelines about what to express and what to feel actually influence emotional conduct?

According to the traditional view, the existence of norms and rules about emotional conduct has an impact on the expression and sometimes even the experience of emotion, but there are biological limits on the degree of influence of social systems. For example, we may know that it is appropriate to express serious concern about our company's fortunes, or about the death of a distant family member, but may still be unable to manipulate our posture and facial display in accordance with these explicit requirements (e.g. DePaulo, 1992). Our true private feelings may leak out (e.g. Ekman and Friesen, 1974). Furthermore, it is argued that many emotions are based on pre-wired neurological and physiological systems whose operation underlies basic emotional experience and upon which cultural and institutional socialization can only ever be an overlay (e.g. Ekman's notion of a *display rule* 1972; see Chapter 5). Of course, no one would want to deny that there are material constraints on human action based on the structural constitution of the body. However, it is an open question whether these biological factors themselves represent any intrinsic feature of emotion.

Above, I have suggested that emotions can be defined in terms of identity claims which are explained largely in terms of changing social positions. In this view, the manner in which these claims are expressed is necessarily dependent on the body's available media of communication (together with any technological prostheses which either amplify the signals, or provide alternative channels of information). However, these considerations are largely irrelevant to the *message content* of the emotional communication itself. The identity to be claimed when getting emotional, as well as the conventional languages (verbal and nonverbal) in which the claim is expressed, are institutionally defined and constituted.

This position is in accord with the social constructionist idea that emotional action only achieves meaning in relation to a system of social conventions and heuristics (e.g. Averill, 1982; Harré, 1986). Getting emotional would have no point, in this view, unless there were shared and negotiable understandings about the implications of such a relational position. According to such an approach, emotion is interpersonal, institutional, and cultural right down to the heart.

The conceptual distinction traditionally drawn between cultural norms and beliefs about emotion on the one hand, and actual emotional experience on the other, implies that institutional and societal factors (like interpersonal variables) exert only indirect effects on the underlying phenomenon of bona fide private emotion. However, this gap between ideas and realities of institutional and cultural emotion is one that can be narrowed in at least three ways.

First, as Hochschild (1983) has shown, people are explicitly trained to appraise emotionally relevant situations in institutionally appropriate ways. The way that organizations define emotional reality may *directly* shape emotional responses to it. Similarly, socialization may lead to conventional appraisals of culturally defined emotional situations.

Second, ideas about how emotion ought to be expressed do not exist in some Platonic realm divorced from everyday conduct. Rather they are discourses that are put into practice in evaluating action, as well as intersubjective schemata for interpretation (see Chapter 9). To the extent that spoken or written, implicit or explicit rules are implemented by the powers that be, their effect on emotion is bound to be more than a notional distortion of the way that it is expressed. Institutional and cultural rules about appropriate conduct guide the behaviour of the people around us and directly constrain or facilitate certain forms of emotion.

Finally, and least controvertibly, ideas about emotion permeate the very fabric of the institutions and the societies that surround us. It is not just that certain emotions are encouraged or forbidden with respect to certain people, but the physical organization of our institutional and cultural world places concrete boundaries on what we can or cannot do emotionally. A simple example of this is the way that people in authority often erect various social as well as structural barriers against uncontrolled contact with underlings. Emotion can only be communicated directly to someone who is present, so the physical positioning of functionaries controls their affective exchanges in quite tangible ways.

In short, there are a number of direct as well as indirect ways in which rules and norms about emotion can influence the conduct of emotional performance. Many of these possible relations between ideas and realities of emotion can be clarified by reference to theatrical metaphors which imply that enactment of institutional and cultural scripts about emotion depends crucially on the allocation and renegotiation of roles, and on the stage-setting that has been done behind the scenes before the acting ever takes place.

EMOTIONS AND ROLES

A common idea in discussions of the effects of organizational and social structures on actions is that people occupy particular institutional niches in their communal lives, and that their conduct is guided by more or less organized collections of rules and norms, which may be likened to theatrical *roles* specifying the position of the protagonist in the drama of everyday interpersonal reality, and providing guidance about the script that should be followed (e.g. Goffman, 1959). In other words, our location within any organizational or cultural arrangement pre-specifies possible movements and channels of communication. Where we are positioned in a given social network partly determines our vantage point and perspective on the world, just as our particular status in the hierarchy equips us with the interpersonal resources to perform relevant functions and activities (to mix some other relevant metaphors). For example, as a psychiatrist you are permitted to ask personal questions; as a patient you should submit to the authority of your beneficent interrogator and try to give answers. Correspondingly, guards are able to exert a certain authority, but for prisoners more restrictive rules are embedded in the interpersonal, physical, and textual structures that surround them on all sides. Most people operate for most of the time somewhere between these possible extremes of coercion, but none of us can completely escape our roles.

The role concept has been incorporated into psychological theories of emotion in two basic ways. First, various institutional roles and cultural scripts contain prescriptions about what emotions should be expressed in particular circumstances (Goffman, 1967), and even about what emotions ought to be felt (Hochschild, 1983). Second, some theorists have argued that the playing out of any particular emotional episode is itself based on short-term roles corresponding to the cultural content of the relevant emotional meaning (e.g. Averill, 1980;

Sarbin, 1986; see Chapter 6). The first point about organizational and societal roles and their emotional impact is the main topic of the present chapter.

INSTITUTIONALLY AND CULTURALLY PRESCRIBED EMOTIONS

Although the Western idea of individual responsibility implies that our everyday conduct follows personal decisions and choices (e.g. Sampson, 1977), in fact our social environment not only places practical limits on the kinds of action that are open to us, but also supplies more or less explicit guidelines concerning behaviour and comportment. In order to have their intended social effects, our actions must be meaningful to other people and must therefore conform to shared conventions of significance. We cannot start from scratch and invent completely new ways of communicating or influencing one another. We operate always from within an existing and more or less articulated social framework, and our degrees of freedom for bending conventions depend on how our deviance will be received by others. So too with emotional communication. It is simply not the case that people routinely choose from an unconstrained range of emotion options. Rather, certain emotional actions are appropriate to any given social setting, others are deviant but understandable, while others are so socially unintelligible that their display may be treated minimally as a joke or even, in more extreme cases, as grounds for psychiatric referral.

For example, it is unorthodox to break down and cry in an official meeting, although this might be considered acceptable if a large-scale lay-off of employees were being discussed and the target of these redundancies included people close to you. (Even here some retrospective accounting would be necessary for letting yourself go in this official setting; in fact, you would probably make your excuses and leave the situation before 'giving in' to your feelings.) Overt expressions of extreme jubilation in this context would usually be considered highly suspect however, even if the news meant that some long-standing enemies might suffer as a consequence of the decision.

Similarly, at a cultural level, different societies have different conventions about the appropriateness of different emotions. For Utku Eskimos, for instance, displays of anger are considered childish and have no place in adult interaction (Briggs, 1970), whereas North Americans tend to believe that specific kinds of anger are necessary and even admirable under certain circumstances (e.g. Averill, 1982; Stearns and Stearns, 1986). Similarly, to take a more familiar anthropological example, there are wide disparities between the conventions about duration and intensity of mourning in different cultures (e.g. Goody, 1962).

It is worth noting that in many of these examples, wholehearted conformance to cultural and institutional prescriptions implies that people should actually *experience* the specified emotion to the appropriate degree, and not simply go through the motions of expressing it. Thus, our emotional performance may be shaped by *feeling rules* (Hochschild, 1983) in addition to display rules.

In short, norms about emotion expression and experience are implied or specified in almost any social situation (the more formal the setting, the more explicit the rules). Sometimes these conventions even become crystallized in the physical organization of the interpersonal environment (e.g. Foucault, 1977). For example, Western society is currently more or less articulated around family units, and relatively permanent homes are constructed to provide intact and partially isolated spaces for the playing out of their specific interpersonal concerns, and as a means of guarding their privacy against outsiders. The constraints and potentialities put on emotional function by such an arrangement are obvious.

On a more mundane institutional level, the spatial arrangement and compartmentalization of offices determines the possibilities of emotional contact at work. For example, it is impossible to follow an angry impulse and have a face-to-face confrontation with your boss if you cannot get to her without dealing with the secretary who controls the door. Similarly, it is not easy to express one's disgust directly at representatives of government, who are protected by a series of abstract as well as concrete barriers. Most of social life (as well as the architectural arrangements that support it) is set up so that you are in contact only with people that it is necessary or appropriate (from the point of view of the surrounding organization or culture) to communicate with, and this places obvious limits on the range of emotions and emotional objects that are available.

The institutional environment does not only serve a constrictive role on emotional life, however. In many cases, explicit or implicit prescriptions about the quality and degree of emotion in organizationally defined settings may encourage exaggeration rather than attenuation of emotion. If no emotion is forthcoming, the rules suggest that it be conjured up, whereas if a pre-existent emotion exceeds the bounds of convention, it ought to be controlled. For example, medical doctors are expected to show concerned sympathy to their patients and their relatives, but not to get so emotionally involved that they are profoundly upset by the loss of life or serious illness. Similarly, psychiatrists whose professional concern slips into passionate intimacy run the risk of being officially sanctioned for their misconduct. Shop assistants and other service workers who are surly towards customers may be encouraged to be more affable. More generally, anyone whose institutional role defines their relationship with others (clients as well as colleagues) is subject to emotional control of some sort by the organization that surrounds them, which typically places lower as well as upper limits on the intensity of emotion expression and experience, as well as outlawing or encouraging specific kinds of emotion (see Table 8.1). And that includes everyone, even the people in charge of things.

EMOTIONS IN ORGANIZATIONAL LIFE

Having considered the impact of cultural and institutional roles on emotion in general terms, I now want to focus on more specific organizational contexts in order to give more substance to the abstract analysis offered so far. In this section, then, I will consider existing theory and research directed at the way that emotions are played out in particular institutional settings.

Our everyday ideas about emotions in institutions, like our ideas about emotion

Table 8.1 Some possible institutional and cultural prescriptions about emotion

		Restrictive prescriptions	*Expansive prescriptions*
Degree of emotion	Display rules	Express less emotion (e.g., courtly love, comportment conventions)	Express more emotion (e.g., passionate love, abandonment conventions)
	Feeling rules	Feel less emotion (e.g., the sin of pride, don't get too involved with your patients)	Feel more emotion (e.g., love the one you're with, care more for clients)
Kind of emotion	Display rules	Do not express specified emotion (e.g., laughter in church, anger in service encounters)	Express specified emotion (e.g., respect for the dead, affability towards customers in service encounters)
	Feeling rules	Do not feel specified emotion (e.g., 'don't get mad, get even!', restrain sexual feelings towards patients)	Feel specified emotion (e.g., love thy neighbour, care for your clients)

in general, tend to underestimate the degree to which they are public communicative events rather than intrapsychic disturbances. Because emotion is traditionally considered to be a personal affair, its relation to institutional life seems peripheral at best. Feelings are either thought to be irrelevant to the way that one conducts one's official business, or to constitute a distracting or interfering influence on organizational efficiency. People are given time off, or time out, from official business to sort out personal problems. Correspondingly, employees may be accused of letting their emotions get in the way of their bureaucratic function. Thus, an almost impermeable conceptual as well as practical barrier is constructed between personal and professional life, with emotions consigned largely to the former.

In psychology, too, the main discussion of emotions at work or emotions experienced as part of institutional life has often concentrated on how emotions can get in the way of efficient function. For example, there is a large literature concerning the role of 'stress' as a factor to be avoided or alleviated (e.g. Cooper and Payne, 1988). In many ways, emotions seem to be things that organizational psychologists want to get rid of.

Of course, this characterization of the role of emotion in organizations is a caricature of the real situation (cf. Fineman, 1993). In fact, we are often far from detached from the emotional implications of what we do when operating as part of any social institution. We are committed or disenchanted functionaries, pit against the demands of those with whom our organization must deal and whose emotions we have to heed; we care or pointedly do not care about what happens to us in the organization and about what may happen, or has already happened to the organization itself (e.g. Gabriel, 1993); in some cases, we are even given specific guidelines about what emotions we should express or feel in the conduct of our institutional roles, and what emotions we should avoid expressing or feeling (e.g. Hochschild, 1983).

In the following sections, I will consider some of the ways in which organizational involvements may shape emotional episodes. My general point will be that our everyday interpersonal encounters often take place against an institutional backdrop which sets the stage for the adoption of different role positions. Even in our most informal interactions we work from preformulated relative identities and statuses which make a real difference to any emotional negotiation that is subsequently conducted. Indeed, many of our roles carry direct emotional implications or prescriptions which partially determine our expressive performance towards other people. These considerations become even more obvious and explicit in formal organizational settings, and it is therefore on these that much of the subsequent discussion will be focused.

Role distance and role proximity

Although we often follow role prescriptions while conducting ourselves in public life, it is extremely rare for these prescriptions to specify completely and precisely what we must do and how we must do it. The parts we play in our institutional encounters are not necessarily rigid structures that determine our every movement. There is usually some psychological room for manoeuvre. In fact, skilled performers may be able to convey some detachment from the parts they play. For example, Goffman's (1961) idea of *role distance* suggests that social role-players may be able to go through the motions of their required performance while selectively communicating their lack of personal investment in its implied identity. 'Nonchalance' is an emotional attitude that tends to produce exactly this effect.

On the other hand, social identities can also be embraced wholeheartedly. Some people may identify so closely with their organizational role that its performance becomes 'second nature' with the consequence that almost everything they do comes to be seen as an expression of their institutional identity. In the following sections, I will talk about the factors that might determine the level of identification with an institutionally defined emotional role, and some of the possible consequences of emotional role distance and role proximity.

Organizational commitment and emotion

Within the occupational psychology literature, two of the most commonly discussed affective variables are job satisfaction and stress. Unfortunately, both of these factors tend to be treated at an empirical and conceptual level as simple reactions rather than as indices of ongoing institutional and interpersonal processes. For example, various job characteristics are thought to be predictive of the amount of stress or the level of satisfaction experienced at work (e.g. Rizzo *et al.*, 1970).

One of the few exceptions to this general trend of viewing affective variables as purely outcomes is work into the impact of satisfaction on job performance relating to *organizational citizenship* (Bateman and Organ, 1983; Organ, 1988; Organ and Konovsky, 1989). Citizenship behaviours are work-related activities that are not explicitly part of the job but which oil the wheels of company functioning. For example, it is possible to be either obstructive or facilitative with respect to colleagues at work without stepping outside the official parameters of the task at hand. You can respond to all circulars promptly, restock the photocopier when the paper runs out, leave equipment in a condition fit for others to use, and so on, or you can ignore all demands on your time unless you are specifically required to respond. More crucially for the present discussion, you may be polite, helpful, and friendly to co-workers, or you may engage with others only when it is absolutely necessary for you to do so. You may help to maintain a positively toned *emotional climate* (e.g. de Rivera, 1992) in your work group or you may undermine any mutual strivings. Organ and his colleagues suggested that all of these kinds of action are affected by evaluations of the job and satisfaction with it. In short, more contented workers are more likely to engage in organizational citizenship behaviour. Of course, to the extent that engaging in these behaviours makes the workplace a better place to be, organizational citizenship behaviour also tends to foster employee well-being, leading to further citizenship behaviour, so that its effects may ultimately be self-sustaining.

To translate this analysis into role terms, it might be assumed that closer identification with the work role is the crucial factor in shaping citizenship. To the extent that workers take on the company's values as their own, they will tend to behave in accordance with these values even when there is no explicit surveillance of their actions.

If the work role contains implicit or explicit guidance about how to feel and what to express, a person's level of identification with the role may determine the extent to which these prescriptions are followed. As I have suggested above, any emotion implies identification with some social role (cf. Thoits, 1991). Rather than assuming that appraisals of motivational relevance and congruence (Lazarus, 1991a) are always straightforward judgements based on purely individual considerations, it is possible that the definition of the concerns that are relevant to the supposedly private calculation arise from the role structure of the situation. So emotional involvement may depend on role identification, and correspondingly, ambivalence or half-heartedness of emotion may be a function of the availability of alternative role identities. Thus, if employees accept their work roles as defined by the institution (either because no other usable identities are available or because the work roles as specified are easily assimilable to pre-existent personal identities), then they will tend to act out their citizenship in ongoing affective and instrumental conduct at work.

To take this analysis a stage further and integrate it with the communicative approach to emotion developed in this book, it may be that the activation of alternative identity positions depends specifically on the presence of particular real or imagined audiences. According to this account, one of the crucial factors determining role distance is the extent to which the intended audience for the performance matches up with the institutionally defined and sanctioned one. For example, when presenting a conference paper in front of a mixed group of personal friends and other colleagues, there is often a tension between maintaining a professional demeanour and not making yourself look too pompous and self-important. More generally, you may be performing a work role that is partly incompatible with your identity with respect to an important reference group from outside work, and the communicational agenda relevant to this alternative group may be activated by one of its members entering the scene, either in actuality or imagination. Thus, the phenomenon of role distance may, in some cases at least, be a direct function of conflicts between the communicative requirements of different available audiences.

In the next section, I focus on institutional roles that imply identity positions with respect to more than one audience. Specifically, I shall consider service occupations where employees have to address their emotional communications to clients as well as co-workers, with the result that the potential conflicts between social and personal identities become correspondingly more obvious and pronounced. (Similar considerations apply also to other 'boundary-spanning' positions in institutions or cultures; cf. Wharton and Erickson, 1993.)

Institutional factors affecting emotional performance in service industries

The possibility of an organizational influence on emotion arises in connection with any institutional role that involves dealing with other people in any way. For example, a person's relative position within any organization establishes access to certain channels of information transfer and closes off others. It sets up a matrix of possible interpersonal contacts which determines the kind and level of intimacy that can be expressed with respect to each of these contacts. Thus, as a member of middle management in manufacturing industry, you are shielded from direct contact with production-line workers on the one hand, and only permitted occasional and pre-arranged interchanges with directors and senior management, on the other. Even if rules about the kinds of permissible interaction are not set down in any official set of guidelines, the way that the offices are arranged and the routinized time structure of the work-day set an implicit template on what can happen between people.

This situation becomes even more intricate and interesting when the institution is one that is not only oriented towards a particular customer group, but also the manufactured product itself involves a form of interpersonal interaction. Lawyers, doctors, nurses, masseurs and masseuses, prostitutes, police, teachers, actors, therapists, waiters and waitresses, hairdressers, and many others are all in the business of including some kind of self-presentation to the client in the work for which they are paid.

All institutions prescribe appropriate interpersonal emotional conduct, but rarely are the rules so obvious and explicit as in service industries. In the face-to-face (or voice-to-voice) interaction between employee and client, the industry has an immediate point of contact with its market. What happens in this encounter has implications for customer satisfaction and corporate image and quite often directly affects sales. If the company's representative presents a personalized, positive, and efficient facade, then this is likely to have wider implications for how the business is perceived and performs (e.g. Peters and Austin, 1985; Surprenant and Solomon, 1987). In the context of a competitive economic system, a company that succeeds in distinguishing itself from its rivals even marginally in these apparently superficial concerns can yield significant net gains. No surprise, then, that so much attention is paid in training and appraisal to impression management during the service encounter.

Different organizations offer different levels of control over emotional performance, and different injunctions on what kind of emotional demeanour should be presented. A number of factors contribute to the degree and nature of emotional guidance that is provided:

1 *Economic relationship of employee and client* Different occupations require different modes of interaction with their clients, simply because of the economic and interpersonal relations that exist between the participants in the service encounter. For example, some companies have a relatively pure service function and try to accommodate themselves as much as possible to clients' perceived requirements. At the other end of the scale are companies that have a more coercive role with respect to their clients. Thus, Hochschild (1983, p.16) contrasted flight attendants with debt collectors as the 'toe and heel of capitalism', respectively. Anyone who has bought from, as well as sold to, assistants in shops dealing in second-hand goods will have noted the dramatic change in the manner of the staff to customers in these different positions: the buyer is always right, but the seller is often in a position of weakness in such an exchange. This analysis also implies that different kinds of demeanour may be presented to different kinds of clients from the same organizational role position.

2 *Medium of service encounter* Some companies are engaged mainly in face-to-face interactions with clients but others conduct their business via telephone, letter, fax, electronic mail, video link-ups, and so on. Obviously in each of these different situations, different kinds and degrees of emotional control are required. In general, it seems likely that the fewer channels of information are available for emotional contact between the employee and customer, the easier it will be to manufacture an appropriate emotional impression. For example, it may be relatively straightforward for operatives to convey a specified kind of emotion using just their voice on the telephone, but a more comprehensive and involved performance may be required if they actually have to deal with customers in person. Of course, here again, employees in a single occupational group may have to present themselves across a range of media, and make suitable adjustments to their performance in response to the relevant constraints. These abilities may require particular varieties of social skills and emotional intelligence (e.g. Salovey, Hsee, and Mayer, 1993).

Looking at the service encounter as a two-way rather than one-way presentation, it becomes clear that the characteristics of the communication medium can also lead to differential availability of feedback from clients. For example, although telephone contact may bring the advantage to the employee of not needing to exert such rigorous control over expressive output, it also carries the corresponding drawback that it becomes harder to gauge the customer's affective reactions to the communication. In fact, some situations of expressive presentation have a built-in imbalance in the information available to the two sides of the interaction, for example in the case of television or radio newscasters who must control their display without any direct feedback from their target audience whatsoever.

Conversely, manipulative institutions may try to stack the data deck in their own favour by actively restricting the amount of information they give out, and opening up as many incoming channels of communication as possible. For example, customs officers, interrogators, and social psychological investigators often observe their target populations from behind one-way glass, or listen in on apparently private conversations. Clearly, whoever is in control of the setting where the service encounter takes place can arrange the mode of information transfer to optimize personal benefit.

3 *Duration of service encounter* There are also differences between service occupations in how long the interaction with the customer typically lasts. In a fast-food establishment the staff–customer interchange is often over in a few seconds, whereas a psychiatric consultation or a visit to the hairdresser can take an hour or more. Shorter-duration service encounters are likely to require less emotional control and involvement from employees. In addition, during such brief interchanges, customers may be more concerned with efficiency than affability, so any expressions of bonhomie can be relatively perfunctory. For example, Sutton and Rafaeli (1988) found that when the checkout queue was long in convenience stores, sales assistants were less likely to express positive emotion. Relatedly, they observed that customers in these situations tended to become irritated by sales assistants who apparently wasted time by being courteous. As one store manager remarked: 'Customers who are in a long line don't care if we smile or not. They just want us to run like hell' (p. 475).

4 *Repeatability of service encounter* Many service encounters are relatively anonymous affairs where there is little probability that the interactants will meet again, or will remember each other even if they do. For example, you are unlikely to know employees of roadside fast-food restaurants by name, except by reading the relevant information from their badges. However, other employee–client interactions occur repeatedly over a period of time, when the client is a regular customer of the service provider, for example. Of course, this dimension does not depend only on the structure or purpose of the organization because many service industries deal with regular and occasional as well as one-time customers. Nevertheless, there are certain kinds of occupation where the relationship with the client is something that is more likely to develop from one meeting to the next. For example, many people develop friendly relation-

ships with their doctors, analysts, manicurists, and hairdressers. Indeed, if they did not, they might well consider taking their business elsewhere. Part of the emotional job in these cases involves memory work designed to demonstrate that the operative individuates each of a range of more or less interchangeable customers. For the client, the provider of the service is clearly distinctive as the only person occupying this particular role with respect to them, but not so for the employee. Thus, there is often a fundamental intimacy imbalance in the service relationship, but one that it is usually considered impolite for the service provider to acknowledge.

5 *Emotional culture* Different businesses and organizations try to develop distinct identities in the marketplace to encourage general customer loyalty, or the patronage of a particular kind of client. For example, higher-class emporia tend to set different standards of intimacy than those that are cheaper and more cheerful. Indeed, some service employees may attune their emotional display to specified subsets of potential customers, such as when assistants in expensive shops are attentive to well-dressed browsers, but more shirty with the obviously down-at-heel. Similarly, bouncers at night-club entrances often implement explicit or implicit dress requirements, so that those conforming to the code are treated pleasantly and ushered inside, whereas punters who are too smart, too casual, or simply not fashionable enough, are excluded, often with some insistence. In general, the manner of employee emotional conduct conveys subtle as well as not-so-subtle messages about the character of the surrounding organization, and therefore employers will likely seek to control these displays in conformance with the desired image, especially in interactions with targeted client groups.

What this provisional taxonomy of characteristics of service encounters should make clear is that the task of emotion communication is crucially affected by the specific institutional context in which it takes place. Investigation of interpersonal emotion therefore needs to take account of organizational and structural factors which may in many circumstances directly impact on the implementation of strategies of expressive control.

The dimensions considered obviously do not exhaust the range of possible variables that might determine the degree and kind of emotion regulation practised by service employees, but they make a start at indicating potential research directions in this relatively underexplored field. Clearly, a wide variety of constraints are placed by organizations on employees' emotional performance and it seems worth considering what difference these different modes of control make on the course of actual emotional encounters. Furthermore, it is important to consider whether different kinds of emotional goal as prescribed by different kinds of organizations have different success rates and different effects on employees and customers. Some provisional evidence relating to these issues is available from existing research. In the next section, I review and extend one of the most influential approaches to institutional emotion.

Emotional alienation in high-contact service work

The following quotation is from a textbook on marketing in the restaurant industry but may equally apply to management's perspective on workers' emotions in any service occupation:

> When employees come in contact with guests, they represent the operation. They cannot make this representation a good one unless their attitudes are positive. They must be trained to project the spirit of hospitality.
>
> (Reid, 1983, p. 273)

Employees provide the public face of the business and employers attempt to control what is shown on this face. But what goes on behind the scenes and below the surface while this process of image management is taking place? What are the effects on the individual's emotions when the rules of expression are imposed from above? How do workers in this position know what they really feel? These are some of the intuitively important questions addressed in groundbreaking exploratory work by Hochschild (1983).

In an intensive qualitative investigation of flight attendants working for an American airline company, Hochschild showed how, during formal and informal training, these service employees were instructed in explicit as well as implicit ways about what emotions they should express in different situations. For example, attendants were told that they should be polite and courteous to passengers even when provoked, and should refrain from expressing anger despite the crudest insults. Thus: 'In the flight attendant's work, smiling is separated from its usual function which is to express a personal feeling, and attached to another one – expressing a company feeling' (p. 127).

There are two basic ways of fulfilling this institutional demand for emotional control, according to Hochschild. In the first, the flight attendant monitors and modifies emotional *expression* in order to convey the appropriate comforting affective messages to passengers (cf. DePaulo, 1991). In other words, the worker's emotional display is regulated by forcing smiles and disguising frowns. Unfortunately, this kind of *surface acting* often comes across as obvious dissimulation because it is common knowledge that service employees are paid to be nice. Customers discount superficial displays of friendliness as simply being part of the job, and the currency of expressive exchange becomes consequently devalued. In order to stay a step ahead of the competition therefore, employers often attempt to encourage more spontaneous and 'authentic' emotional attitudes in their workers. Instead of simply working on emotional image, they try to manipulate flight attendants' actual underlying emotions.

The way that this is achieved is by suggesting various strategies of *deep acting* during initial and recurrent training, so that attendants learn to change the way that they think and feel about their service interactions rather than simply controlling the expression of their emotions. For example, in a technique analogous to Stanislavski's (1965) method school of acting, flight attendants are instructed to view the passenger cabin as if it were their living room at home, and the passengers as their guests. Within this rather literal extension of the idea of an air 'hostess', troublesome passengers ('irates') can be treated as if they were misbehaving children, or as people trying ineffectually to cope with problems of their own, rather than creating new ones for the flight attendant. This new perspective on the situation can lead to a whole different set of emotional attitudes and reactions. As one of Hochschild's interviewees explained:

> I try to remember if he's drinking too much, he's probably scared of flying. I think to myself, 'he's like a little child.' Really, that's what he is. And when I see him that way, I don't get mad that he's yelling at me. He's like a child yelling at me then.

(p. 55)

According to Hochschild, the downside of this kind of deep acting is that the worker becomes over-involved with the emotional needs of the job and may eventually suffer a kind of affective burnout.

The importance of Hochschild's examples is that they demonstrate ways in which emotional *experiences* as well as expressions can be imposed by the organizational structure that surrounds them. Even in cases of surface acting, if the audience takes the institutionally prescribed display at face value, it may consequently feed into the worker's underlying emotional attitudes. For example, one attendant commented: 'If I pretend I'm feeling really up, sometimes I actually cheer up and feel friendly. The passenger responds to me as though I were friendly and then more of me responds back' (p. 56). In other words, to the extent that a dissimulated display is taken to be valid by its recipients, it may lead to genuine emotional consequences.

Hochschild's work suggests that there is a relatively hard and fast distinction between surface acting and deep acting, in that one is directed at expression and the other at the underlying emotion itself, which she took to be a 'biologically given sense' (p. 219) 'that tells us about the self-relevance of reality' (p. 85). In other words, there is a private and natural essence to emotion that is untouched by the social context that surrounds it (see Parkinson, 1993). However, it is also possible to view the emotion that is worked upon during deep acting as equally socially constructed, although probably in different ways (Averill, 1992). For example, flight attendants' anger at unruly passengers may reflect socialized cultural norms about their moral rights as individuals rather than innately programmed reactions to frustration.

From the perspective of the present communicative approach, any underlying and supposedly spontaneous emotion is in fact addressed at some kind of imagined audience, however vestigially this audience is represented in consciousness. For example, it seems possible that flight attendants experience emotional conflict because the way that they are presenting themselves to passengers does not accord with the way that they would like to be seen as presenting themselves, either by colleagues who are actually on the scene, or by friends to whom they might have to account for their behaviour afterwards. Indeed, one potential audience is the self, and many instances of detached emotional performance may be designed as means of communicating reflexively that what one is doing is not actually what it seems, and that one does not really mean it. Relatedly, emotional role distance may be intended to avert uncomfortable future memories of identity-inconsistent interactions. For similar reasons, children sometimes cross their fingers while telling a lie (Fleming, 1994). In effect, people do not want to have to think of themselves as acting out of character, especially when that character is positively evaluated by a relevant reference group.

Socializing emotional styles

In the previous chapter, I argued that emotions communicate identity claims. Now I want to show how such identity claims may arise directly from social identifications that are activated by the specific interpersonal processes in institutional settings. Hochschild's account of how institutional roles shape emotional experience and expression provides a good starting point for such an analysis. As she argued: 'A role establishes a baseline for what feelings seem appropriate to a certain series of events' (p. 74).

Central to Hochschild's account is the notion that people can become alienated from their true feelings when they have to work on them as institutional rather than personal reactions and attitudes. But where do the putative underlying 'true' feelings and 'personal' reactions come from? From the point of view of the present approach, emotions reflect identity claims anyway, whether these claims come from interpersonal relations or intergroup comparisons. The apparent conflict experienced between 'natural' and manufactured feeling may thus be translated into a mismatch between two kinds of socially constructed feeling, one of which happens to be more central to the actor's currently salient social identity (e.g. Turner, 1982; see also Ashforth and Humphrey, 1993, for a similar analysis). In other words, it may be that Hochschild's flight attendants were not losing touch with their biological *humanity* by transforming their feelings, but rather changing on-line their level of identification with an alternative reference group, such as that of their family, friends outside work, or previous occupational role, any of which would normally contribute to their personal collection of available role positions.

A related way of describing this same phenomenon is to say that the person experiencing emotional conflict is caught between the conflicting communicational agendas of different potential audiences. According to this second account, emotion work is conducted by changing the addressee for an intended self-presentation, so that a different mode and content of communication becomes appropriate. For example, some of the flight attendants in Hochschild's study addressed themselves to imagined misbehaving children in place of the irritating adult passengers with whom they were actually obliged to deal.

This perspective suggests that the experience of working on emotions can be seen as depending either on two (or more) conflicting identifications, or on the contrasting self-presentational demands exerted by two (or more) potential audiences, when one of these identifications or communicative agendas has come to seem more spontaneous or 'natural'. The imposition of role distance thus implies access to an alternative interpersonal position in relation to the audience. A consequence of this is that the experience of emotional conflict is likely to be most prevalent in situations when the individual is not fully integrated into the group, has not completely identified with the role, or has not learned to attune communications automatically to the prescribed addressees. As Hochschild argued:

> we are most likely to sense a feeling rule *as* a feeling rule, and deep acting *as* deep acting, not when we are strongly attached to a culture or a role, but when we are moving from one culture or one role to another. It is when we are *between* jobs, between marriages, or between cultures that we are prone to feel at odds with past feeling rules.
>
> (p. 75)

In these situations of role transition, the previous frame of reference and set of standards implied by prior identifications is vividly juxtaposed with the outlook encouraged by the newly adopted role.

For this reason, it seems useful to look at the experiences of people who have recently taken on an unfamiliar role, or are experiencing disillusionment with an existing role, when investigating institutional influences on emotion. In a study inspired by Hochschild's work, I tried to get at some of these issues by talking to trainee hairdressers about their experiences of managing emotions at work and asking them to fill out a series of standardized questionnaires concerning interpersonal functioning (Parkinson, 1991). Some of these trainees had chosen hairdressing as their first choice of career while others took on the course simply because participation in the government training scheme was at the time compulsory in this country for teenagers with no other job or educational commitment. Moreover, some of the trainees found it easy to adapt their interpersonal and expressive style to the task of communicating with clients on the job, while others were confronted with what seemed like a completely new way of dealing with other people.

My idea was that trainees who were least committed to the interpersonal role implied by the job would be aware of the greatest distance between the emotions that they were expressing and the feelings that they were experiencing on the job. However, I also thought it possible that emotional performance would come to seem less artificial and more natural as trainees picked up relevant interpersonal strategies and found out how well these strategies worked in practice during encounters with clients as well as with people outside the salons. Thus, it seemed likely that for adolescent trainees the role of hairdresser might spill out from the work context and become part of personal identity in everyday situations. In this case, these trainees would learn how to be natural in interpersonal situations by coming to identify wholeheartedly with their role-prescribed emotional performance. Emotional spontaneity, in this view, might be something that can be manufactured over time.

Because the data from this study were cross-sectional, it is hard to draw firm conclusions about such hypothesized developmental processes, and clearly more intensive longitudinal follow-up work would be useful. However, some of the results of this exploratory study were suggestive of the processes that might be at work during emotional socialization in service occupations.

The findings indicated that specific strategies of expressive control and emotional management were related both to employee well-being and to client satisfaction with job performance. Two factors emerged from the analysis of questionnaire items which seemed to reflect different interpersonal styles used by trainees in their interactions with clients. The first of these was indexed by items from *self-monitoring* (Snyder, 1974) and *social anxiety* (Fenigstein *et al.*, 1975) scales and was connected with the theme of *openness* in dealing with other people. Items loading highly on this interpersonal openness index apparently reflected estimates of social ease and self-expressiveness. For example, the two highest loading items were: 'I don't find it hard to talk to strangers' and 'I can make impromptu speeches even on topics about which I have almost no information'. Both these statements have obvious relevance to hairdressers' work roles and self-presentations with respect to their clients.

Participants' comments during the semi-structured interviews helped to clarify the meaning of the openness factor. For example, an experienced second-year trainee gave the following advice about being a good hairdresser: 'You just have to open yourself up to everybody's problems. You have to open yourself up and just be yourself.' Another respondent suggested that openness was more difficult with clients than with friends:

> You can really be yourself with your mates, you can't really open up to customers . . . I mean you can tell them things to a certain extent but you couldn't, like, swear to them or anything, like you do to your mates, you know, tell them who you fancied or anything like that, or what things were like before, when you got drunk and that – they might not want to hear that.

According to a third trainee, it was more difficult to be open with some customers than others:

> There's some really nice ones, you can feel really relaxed with and just talk about how you can with your friends and your family, but some you talk to like when you went for your interview, right uptight and right polite and agreeing with what they say, things like that. It depends what kind of person it is.

As can be seen from these quotations, the discourse of openness was drawn upon extensively by interviewees when talking about their jobs, with some trainees being more willing than others to attribute this interaction style to themselves.

Scores on openness showed a reliable positive correlation with length of training experience and were significantly higher in second-year trainees, suggesting that this strategy may develop as a result of experience of face-to-face interaction with clients. Openness was also positively correlated with the reported level of received tips, suggesting that customers prefer their hairdressers to be friendly in a way that appears unforced. This seems to confirm that trainee hairdressers can *learn* how to be natural, and how to *manufacture* a sense of spontaneity.

The results concerning openness are also interpretable according to the communicative approach to emotion. From this perspective, the development of interpersonal skills relating to this factor depend on a process of attunement to the informational agenda of the target client group, with more open trainees being those that have learned to be responsive to the appropriate verbal and nonverbal signals given out by customers.

The second interactional style suggested by factor analysis of the questionnaire items (specifically, items taken from Snyder's self-monitoring scale, 1974) involved a deceptive strategy of impression management when dealing with clients. The items showing the highest loadings on this factor were: 'I may deceive people by being friendly when I really dislike them' and 'I'm not always the person I appear to be'. This index was statistically unrelated to the openness index. Respondents who rated their interaction style as high in deceptive impression management also tended to show worse self-reported psychological adjustment (according to the General Health Questionnaire; Goldberg, 1972) and reported feeling less satisfied with their jobs. Connections between well-being and some of the other measured personality variables helped to clarify this relationship between the deceptive impression-management strategy and psychological adjustment.

Greater well-being was found to be associated with lower levels of private self-consciousness (Fenigstein *et al.*, 1975) and with higher levels of perspective-taking on a self-report empathy measure (Davis, 1983). In other words, it seems that better-adjusted trainees were more able to see things from the other person's (e.g. the client's) point of view, and to pay less attention to their own personal feelings.

In summary, those trainees who identified less with their work role and found it harder to see things from the client's point of view tended also to consider their job as requiring putting on an act, and felt generally unhappier with it. The conflict that they felt between the experience and overt expression of emotion reflected, in my view, their superficial identification with their occupational as opposed to personal identity, or their failure to align to the communicational demands of the service encounter, rather than the force of social pressure set against their supposed deep natural sense of individual emotion. Such experiences of role or audience conflict, I would argue, partly underlie our misguided intuitions about the priority of private emotion experience.

As with the openness factor, deceptive expression management was alluded to commonly in interviewees' answers to the open-ended questions. Trainees varied in the extent to which they described their jobs as necessarily involving 'putting on an act'. This kind of strategy was said to be most common when dealing with awkward customers. Describing her attitude to clients, for example, one trainee commented: 'Some will tell you all sorts of rubbish, and you just don't want to know. You just agree with them or be nice to them.' Another respondent found dealing with children difficult: 'It's worse when you're doing kids' hair, you just want to scream at them, and you've just got to say 'will you just keep your head still' and you feel like slapping them around the face.' A third trainee summed the situation up as follows:

> If you don't like people, you can't tell them that, can you? You've got to be nice to them, instead of telling them what you really feel like, like kicking them or drowning them, you've got to be nice to them. If you don't like them, you've got to put a brave face on.

In other words, many trainees felt that the work role often demanded that you 'plaster a false smile on your face, grin and bear it.' Clearly, these interviewees were all reporting conflicts between a real and ideal audience for their self-presentations.

The results of my study provided little support for Hochschild's (1983) argument that emotional identification with the work role leads to psychological maladjustment, and that continuous deep acting can cause burnout. Trainees in my study who assimilated their expressive performance to their own identity and rated their interaction as undeceptive showed lower levels of psychological symptoms and higher job satisfaction. Furthermore, those respondents who rated themselves as higher in empathic concern were also more likely to rate their jobs as better than they had expected, suggesting that emotional involvement in other people's (e.g. clients') problems reduced rather than increased disappointment with the job.

Two factors may help to explain this set of findings. First, the work role of a hairdresser is far more flexible and open to personalization than that of the flight attendants studied by Hochschild, so the respondents in my study may not have needed to make such drastic emotional readjustments in order to identify with their performance, or to attune their self-presentations to clients' needs. Second, adolescents just beginning their work career such as those interviewed in the present research may be at a relatively malleable stage of development with respect to their social identities. Rather than having to use deep acting to get inside their work roles, many of the hairdressing trainees may simply have assimilated the required codes of emotional management and expressive control into their growing repertoire of social skills. For example, one respondent explicitly claimed that adjustment to the role of a hairdresser helped her to develop a general sense of social ease:

> My boss said 'you've got to learn to talk to people or else you won't be a good hairdresser'. Then, I just decided to do it and I'm all right now. I can just go up to anybody, like, at a night-club, and just talk to them. It doesn't bother me. Before, I were right shy and that . . . now I've come out of my shell, I'm all right – a different person completely.

A compatible account of why emotion work may not always lead to ill effects on psychological well-being was suggested by Rafaeli and Sutton (1989):

> If employees believe that offering false emotions should not be part of the job, then they are *faking in bad faith*. But if employees offer false emotions and believe that offering them should be part of the job, then they are faking in good faith. We contend that emotional dissonance will be most strongly related to strain among people who fake in bad faith since their level of

psychological discomfort will be much higher than people who *fake in good faith.*

(p. 37)

Of course, higher ratings of satisfaction and well-being do not necessarily rule out long-term negative consequences of identification with the hairdresser's work role. Even in the short term, it might be argued that trainees who were more involved in their work roles had a larger stake in presenting themselves as happier in their jobs and that their ratings may have been distorted as a function of strategies of impression management actually implemented in the face-to-face interview situation. There is always a problem in trying to study emotion and impression management in a research context where the very strategies that are the focus of the investigation may be used by participants on the researcher to conceal that these strategies are being used at all. In other words, it is quite possible that some sophisticated interviewees gave answers that would indicate interpersonal 'naturalness' specifically to deny that their image was manufactured and put on, because this allowed them to take more personal credit for their apparent social skills.

The implication of these findings seems to be that hairdressers whose emotional expression is 'spontaneous' and 'natural' will be more successful in their jobs. It is important to remember, however, that the emotions and attitudes expressed by these apparently well-adjusted trainees still arise from within the context of an institutionally defined encounter. There are express limits on the kinds of things that hairdressers are allowed to do or say to clients without losing their jobs. Successful adjustment seems to require taking the customer's point of view (perspective-taking) and ignoring one's own personal feelings (low private self-consciousness). Socialization to the work role of hairdresser probably involves learning to pay attention to specific social cues at the expense of others. In other words, 'natural' emotions may be socially *manufactured* as a function of identification with one's occupationally defined role, as someone friendly and understanding whose purpose is to serve the client.

In this research, I used self-report personality measures and interview techniques as a shortcut to the assessment of strategies of emotional management and styles of social interaction. The study was intended as an exploration of a relatively uncharted research area, and before any definitive conclusions can be drawn, it clearly needs to be followed up with more detailed investigations of real-time interpersonal interactions with clients, as well as longitudinal research into the process of development of strategies of emotion management and their relationship with role identification and audience attunement.

CONFLICT BETWEEN EXPERIENCED AND EXPRESSED EMOTION

Much of the research reviewed in previous sections relates to experienced conflicts between personally felt and institutionally demanded emotion. Of course, during everyday life outside the work context, we also manipulate our emotional expression and experience. For example, we may feel either that we are in danger of getting carried away by the dangerous intensity of our passionate infatuation with someone, or alternatively that we do not care deeply enough about a person with whom we are involved. In each of these cases, we may engage in various strategies to bring our feelings in line with what we think they ought to be (Hochschild, 1983). As a consequence what we actually experience as emotional is felt to be something separate from the values that we personally want to endorse or are otherwise encouraged to support.

All these work and nonwork examples have an intuitive validity and seem to support the common-sense idea that emotion is something spontaneous, personal, and independent of our controlled conscious processing. Where, then, does this experience of conflict come from? According to Hochschild and the common-sense perspective, there is an internal essence to emotion that remains private and untouched by the contingent interpersonal world. Similarly, Ekman's (1972) concept of *display rule* (see Chapter 5) implied that social factors are overlaid on a basic biological affective system.

The alternative perspective that I have tried to present in this chapter is that the underlying emotion as well as the more deliberately constructed one set against it arises from role positions of one kind or another with respect to specific audiences. The fact that one of these identifications is experienced as having subjective priority, and as giving more spontaneous and natural guidance for emotional performance, does not mean that it reflects a biologically programmed sense, only that it is more central to our socially derived personal identity, or more in tune with the currently salient communicative agenda. All of us occupy a range of interpersonal roles which are brought on-line as the situation demands. On occasion, more than one available role is relevant to the present audience, and each of these alternative identities may imply different values which might be expressed in different emotional reactions. As a hairdresser, for example, you are there to serve and be courteous to your clients, but as a committed atheist you may also feel dutybound to argue about the existence of God if they should start espousing Christian beliefs, even if their faith is so deeply held that they treat any scepticism on your part as a personal insult. How such conflicts are resolved, and how their emotional implications are worked out, depends on which of your social identities are more strongly activated by the communicative demands of the interaction, which in turn may depend on audience characteristics and on relative levels of identification with the available role positions (e.g. as a compulsively honest person, or as a 'natural' compromiser). If one of the relevant identities is so familiar and well practised that it surfaces spontaneously and automatically, then this is likely to provide the basis for what is experienced as the underlying emotion, which subsequently may be disguised, expressed, or otherwise worked on.

The experience of privacy of emotion, then, is not necessarily evidence for a biological or basic-process model. Rather it just confirms that different levels of social identification are perceived as more or less controllable, and more or less as figure rather than ground. Of course, these sets of role priorities can change from one social setting to the next as different actual and imagined audiences enter the scene, as well as in response to general developmental (or regressive) processes. For example, one's role as a supporter of a particular football team may become salient in interactions with fans of other teams, but remains irrelevant to formal encounters in a work context. Furthermore, football may come to seem less important to you as you develop alternative interests over the years. Correspondingly, socialization into new groups and role arrangements can lead to increased appropriateness of certain previously underdeveloped identities (Averill, 1984).

One of the sources of roles that we experience as relatively central to our personal identity is the culture or subculture into which we have been socialized. Culturally important moral values are instilled in us at an early age and may come to affect our emotional appraisals automatically, leading us to believe that they reflect a natural core of our very being. In the next section, I consider the general impact of cultural factors on emotion.

EMOTION AND CULTURAL ROLES

Much of the above discussion has focused on institutional rather than cultural roles because their impact on emotion is more obvious and more familiar to most of us. In this section, I turn briefly to societal prescriptions about emotion. By separating the topics in this way, I do not mean to imply a rigid distinction between cultural and institutional reality. On the contrary, I want to claim that, in some sense at least, cultures can be seen as constituted by structured or unstructured arrangements of formal and informal social organizations. Thus, many of the effects of culture on emotion are specifically mediated by institutions. However, I do think that there are some differences in the ways that cultures and institutions operate on emotional conduct which are worth emphasizing.

In much the same way as institutions implicitly and explicitly predefine emotional roles, societal structures also shape the ways in which emotion is experienced and expressed. Like institutions, cultures can be seen as collections of partially related possible role positions, except that the articulation of these roles may be more diffuse and less explicit when considered at a cultural rather than organizational level. The practical difference between discussions of institutional and cultural influences on emotion concerns the fact that the former tend to be easier to detect and formalize whereas the latter tend to operate in the background and are thus harder to isolate and pin down.

Culture surrounds us more completely than any particular institution because we move quite easily between different institutions and their different formulations of reality (specifically emotional reality), whereas it is harder to escape from our given culture. Indeed, we start to pick up cultural presuppositions directly from our earliest encounters with the social world, with the result that they come to provide us with a bedrock of apparently common-sense knowledge. We learn what the world is like and what reality contains, working from accepted cultural premises which directly contribute to our experience of things. This is what is usually meant by the process of *enculturation*. Thus, culture is everywhere yet typically outside or beyond focal awareness: we are caught inside but scarcely aware of the fact, much as fish are said to be insensitive to the concept of water. It is only with the shock of contact with a radically different cultural outlook that we are made conscious of the contingency of our accepted social reality, and with the globalization of communication networks, this shock comes ever more rarely, leading us to believe that culture is just the way that things are done everywhere. Thus, we become tempted to mistake the culturally manufactured for the biologically natural. This is a danger that I am trying to avert in the present discussion.

Unlike institutional roles, then, cultural roles usually make up a more or less intact and integrated package. We may occupy several conflicting institutionally defined role positions, but we normally only belong to a single society, however loosely it may be defined. This means that there is less chance for discrepancy of cultural prescriptions for emotion. What we are socialized to feel as a function of our cultural identity tends for this reason to be felt as spontaneous and natural.

Having implied that society is something relatively stable and pervasive, I should also point out that there is no monolithic and permanent crystallized set of rules and assumptions that characterize any given culture. There are local as well as historical variations in the applicability of different prescriptions. Furthermore, within any given culture, there often exist a number of unexamined contradictions between the implications of different cultural rules. For example, the cultural rules that we should stand up for our rights, and that we should not deliberately hurt another person, come into conflict when we are faced with a situation where retribution seems appropriate. According to Averill (1982), culture provides the short-term social role of getting angry to allow people to pass through such problematic situations while disowning responsibility for their rule-breaking. Another implication of these cultural contradictions is that there is tension in the system which may ultimately lead to ideological change (cf. Kuhn, 1962).

Cultural assumptions do not always remain unquestioned and disputes can arise when members of discrepant subcultures come into contact and must negotiate the definition of a shared situation. Political and religious disputes often arise in just this way and represent obvious occasions for various kinds of emotion. In general, cultural rules are continually reformulated in ongoing dialogues and adjusted to the changing constraints of the always evolving society that regenerates them. Although culture may thus be seen as a continually renegotiated accomplishment, it is still something that has an existence that is partly independent of any individual or group contained within it. As Bhaskar (1989) argued: 'People do not create society. For it always pre-exists them. Rather, it is an ensemble of structures, practices and conventions that individuals reproduce and transform. But which would not exist unless they did so' (p. 76; see also Berger and Luckman, 1967).

By subscribing to the values of our culture and getting emotional in the ways that society prescribes on the occasions when emotion is considered appropriate, we also reproduce the values and emotional roles that guide our actions. However, by questioning values and developing new ways of expressing and experiencing emotions, culture may be transformed, leading to new forms of emotional life (e.g. Averill and Nunley, 1992). Thus, not only does culture shape emotions but also emotions may lead to changes in culture.

IMPACT MODES OF INSTITUTIONS ON EMOTION

In the above discussion, I have suggested that cultural and institutional roles carry implicit and explicit prescriptions about what emotions should be expressed and experienced in particular situations, and to what degree these emotions should be displayed. But what kind of leverage is exerted by roles on people's actions? What factors determine whether these emotional injunctions are actually followed? In this section, I will consider some of the possible points of access to emotional reality for the role prescriptions contained in the cultural and institutional worlds. Institutional and cultural reality also imposes more direct constraints on emotional performance, due to the layout of the manufactured physical and social environment and the kinds and degrees of emotional movement that it can accommodate. These other influences on emotion will be discussed in the present section as well. More generally, I will be looking at the range of possible ways that institutions and cultures might exert an impact on emotional performance.

Deliberate emotion regulation

The most obvious way in which cultural and institutional factors can influence emotion depends on implementation of explicit regulation techniques (e.g. Parrott, 1993). We are all familiar with situations in which we try to disguise or modify spontaneous emotional reactions using conscious control strategies, such as self-distraction, posing or camouflaging expressions, and so on. For example, if we feel the urge to laugh during a formal religious service, we may try to think of something else, preferably something suitably sombre, or we may affect a cough to disguise our outburst. Clearly, one of the reasons that we perform such manoeuvres is that the surrounding institution or culture carries implicit and explicit rules of propriety about what emotions are suitable in particular settings.

Different societies and organizations put different values on different kinds of emotional experience, encouraging some forms and discouraging others, so the degree and target of emotional control probably varies from one setting to the next. Furthermore, cultures may explicitly supply control techniques when a particular emotion is to be discouraged. For example, American and English children are often taught to count to ten when they are angry (cf. Tavris, 1984).

According to the conventional account, strategies of deliberate emotion regulation usually leave the underlying emotion itself untouched, and only modify one or more of its modes of expression. However, even superficial changes in emotional display can lead to deeper emotional consequences over the course of an interaction. For example, if you succeed in dissimulating a convincing smile of greeting towards someone concerning whom you have no particular feelings, they may in turn respond with a smile of their own. To the extent that you take this returned smile as a genuine expression of affection, you may come to feel more favourably disposed to the other person. Thus, over time, controlled display can lead to more spontaneous emotional consequences.

A second way in which conscious emotion control may influence the basic essence of emotion is suggested by Hochschild's (1983) analysis of emotional labour. According to her account, service employees may learn to reconstrue emotional situations in such a way that they elicit different qualitative reactions. For example, by trying to think of passengers as like children, flight attendants may actually be able to change the way that they feel about those who misbehave. This description of the implementation of feeling rules suggests that one of the ways that emotion regulation might work is by changing *appraisals* of the emotional situation. This topic is considered next.

Role-based appraisal

A second way in which roles might influence emotion is via appraisal. We interpret and evaluate the world in accordance with cultural and institutional presuppositions and this fact has obvious emotional consequences. For example, if emotion presupposes interpreting an event as impeding or facilitating personal projects, then the nature of the emotion experienced will depend on what these personal projects are. Obviously many of the goals that human beings pursue are common to all members of the species (e.g. food, shelter, sex) and any emotions that implicate these goals are likely to have some biological basis (cf. Mesquita and Frijda, 1992). However, as we have seen above, many of the things about which we get emotional depend on our relative position in social relationships, and thus the nature of these relationships, along with our conventional understandings of mutual rights and obligations, will impact on the kind of emotional response that is appropriate or available.

Of course, the social situations that are available for interpretation and appraisal themselves also depend upon cultural and institutional organization. It would be hard, for example, to get angry about one's lack of status in a society where status was not an existent concept, just as it would be unusual to suffer claustrophobia in an environment without enclosures of any kind.

Identity processes

The appraisal account of emotion implies that social roles influence emotional conduct indirectly by defining personal values and priorities. In contrast, the communicative model of emotion presented in this book suggests that the very substance of emotional performance comes from identity presentations. Emotion directly reflects role-playing. Indeed, theorists such as Averill (e.g. 1982) and Sarbin (1986) have argued that getting emotional involves *deliberately* adopting a particular culturally supplied role position with respect to others. In my view, conformance to institutional and cultural roles is a less selfconscious process than this, typically arising as a function of interpersonal negotiation rather than individual calculation. Further, I believe that it is not emotion roles *per se* that are taken on by members of a culture or subculture, but more general social identities which secondarily carry implications about emotional performance in particular situations. These implications become salient only when relevant interpersonal conditions arise. For example, in one's role as a teacher, one may get angry when a student fails to display the required degree of respect. The emotional presentation that ensues may be partly shaped by shared representations of what anger involves (see the next section) but the more important causal factors concern the identity role itself and the values that it implies with respect to this particular audience. In my view, the performance of getting emotional is often shaped dynamically by the unfolding structure of the interpersonal situation rather than run off in accordance with a prespecified internal script.

Manners of getting emotional

Cultural influences on appraisal and identity determine the range of emotions that are available within a given societal context. However, culture can also influence the ways in which particular emotional responses are expressed through or with the body (e.g. Douglas, 1973). In other words, culture not only influences why but also how people get emotional. Role prescriptions shape the media of emotional conduct as well as the quality and degree of the emotion that is expressed.

Different societies have different norms about bodily conduct. In some cases, members of a culture may even be taught explicitly to comport themselves in certain ways. For example, a popular image of the English 'finishing school' depicts pupils promenading with books balanced on top of their heads in order to attain the appropriate upright posture. Rules of comportment are also picked up more implicitly by imitation, and by the possible bodily positions allowed by the manufactured world around us. For example, differences in typical room size, chair shape, general population density, and so on exert relatively direct effects on how we position ourselves and the way we move about, all of which may impact on our manner of emotional expression. These environmental arrangements themselves may in turn derive from cultural assumptions about proper behaviour. Argyle and Dean's (1965) finding that people intensify their expressive displays to compensate for increased interpersonal distance provides one example of how simple spatial factors such as these might influence emotional presentation.

One set of cultural comportment norms concerns the extent of control that is imposed on bodily expression. The traditional British reserve, for example, is often thought to be reflected in a tightness of posture and an avoidance of unnecessary physical movement. At the other extreme, some tribal cultures actively seem to encourage bodily expression, and lay on specific rituals where people are expected to loosen bodily control and let go, leading ultimately to emotional states such as trance or religious ecstasy (e.g. Radley, 1988). Even within Western societies, developments such as the emergence of 'rave culture' in the late 1980s seem to legitimize similar experiences in specific social contexts such as night-clubs, warehouse parties, and festivals.

In general, it seems that cultural norms set constraints and possibilities for the ways in which emotions are expressed in everyday social life. The kinds of things that we feel the urge to do when emotional depend on the cultural repertoire of available actions. These potential modes of expression, however, are not simply limited to bodily conduct as such. In certain subcultures, for example, one way of expressing anger is to drive very fast. Clearly the specifics of this action tendency depend on the cultural availability of cars and roads (and probably also on shared rules about the ways that cars should be used on roads).

INTEGRATING INTERPERSONAL AND INSTITUTIONAL FACTORS

In this chapter, I have considered emotion within its social structural context and switched focus from the on-line interpersonal interactions discussed in the previous chapter. In fact, these two sets of social factors can be seen as intimately interrelated, even to some extent mutually constitutive. Institutions are not simple sets of fixed roles into which people fit, and act out the parts that are predefined for them. Rather they contain overlapping sets of more or less negotiable prescriptions about how to behave and what values to endorse. People do not just follow preset guidelines, but are continually engaged in negotiation of their rights and obligations with respect to other people. They reformulate their identities over time, and contest unwanted attributions. In general, interpersonal life is played out against a shifting backdrop of structural constraints, some of which are concretized in the manufactured physical reality that surrounds us, while others are reproduced in our conformity to shared assumptions about how things should be done. In some institutional and cultural settings there are relatively clear and formal guidelines about how to behave, but other situations are more open and anarchic. In short, the ways in which the flexible role prescriptions contained in institutional and cultural reality map onto real-time interpersonal encounters in the everyday social world are many and varied and well worthy of further research attention from psychologists, who have too long overemphasized self-contained individualism (Sampson, 1977) and legitimized ethnocentrism (Bond, 1988).

9   Emotion representations

OVERVIEW

While previous chapters have looked at emotional conduct as it might be influenced by representations of emotion, the present chapter turns the focus onto emotion representations themselves. In the first sections, I summarize research that has directly investigated people's interpretations of emotion terms either by examining relations and oppositions between different emotional meanings, or by exploring the internal structure of emotional categories. In later sections, I re-evaluate the status of these data concerning representations with respect to their relevance for general theories of emotion. My review considers various possible relations between ideas and realities of emotion (descriptive, interpretational, and constitutive) and examines the relative validity of these postulated connections. I conclude by drawing attention to three limiting assumptions characterizing most previous explorations of the logical geography of emotion terms: that such studies give access to a 'deep structure' of emotion; that emotional language is purely descriptive; and that the descriptions it offers can be seen as more or less 'accurate' in some absolute sense. In contrast, I shall suggest that there are a variety of grammars of emotion which are differentially implemented in different contexts; that emotional talk should be studied from a pragmatic as well as semantic perspective (i.e. that it serves linguistic functions in addition to simple description); and that the interrelations between emotional talk and emotional conduct are far more complex and intricate than implied by a simple one-way accuracy mapping. Studies of emotional meaning may help to clarify how emotions are dealt with by individuals, couples, groups, institutions, and societies, but the information that they provide allows no quick shortcut to a psychological theory of emotion. Research attention should be redirected towards the ways that emotional talk is deployed in its everyday conversational contexts, and to the effects that this deployment may have on the construction, reconstruction, and deconstruction of emotional episodes.

EMOTIONAL MEANINGS

Since 'emotion' is a term that is used in everyday language, common sense seems an obvious place to look when trying to understand what it means. Unfortunately, attention to shared ideas about emotions has not so far succeeded in revealing too many hidden truths about emotional reality. The reasons for this failure are many. First, there are difficulties associated with the intractability of common sense. It changes, even over the course of a simple conversation between people; it varies from culture to culture and subculture to subculture; it is inconsistent; it is not phrased in terms of propositional assertions; and it is atheoretical. More generally, common sense as it happens does not really contain a monolithic and timeless set of propositions about the world (including the psychological part of this world). In this chapter, I will be considering some of the characteristics of the common sense of emotion in order to determine their implications for other kinds of emotional conduct. My argument will be that studies have tended to adopt oversimplified assumptions about the relationship between representations of emotion and individual emotional experience, or in other words, about the possible mappings between ideas and realities of emotion.

By drawing the idea–reality distinction again in this way, I do not, of course, mean to imply that these two topics are completely independent of one another. For one thing, talking emotionally or about emotion is not simply an ideational activity but also feeds into the social reality that is constructed during conversation. Moreover, the ways in which emotion and emotions are described influence the explicit strategies that are used for dealing with them. Finally, the performance roles for emotion supplied by a culture may also tend to be codified in its categorical distinctions. So I am not talking about separate realms corresponding to ideas and realities of emotion but about the many ways in which culture predefines what passes for emotion and how emotions are acted out.

Whatever else emotion might be, it is certainly a term that can be found in people's formal and informal discourse. People talk about emotion, and the way that they talk about it partly influences the way that they enact and respond to it. In this chapter, I will talk about talk about emotion in at least two ways. First, I will consider specific emotion terms as descriptive categories of psychological functioning. In other words, I will be discussing the ways that people characterize their own and other people's emotional states, when trying to define them and explain what they are like. My specific focus will be on psychometric studies of emotional meanings. This descriptive use of emotion language, however, tells far less than the whole story. Another important part of the common-sense use of emotion terms concerns pragmatic rather than semantic meaning. Unfortunately, there has been far less research into the ways that emotion talk serves specific institutional and interpersonal ends, but I will consider some potential research directions which might exploit an analysis of emotion talk as directed towards self-presentational and rhetorical purposes.

DEFINING REPRESENTATION

When I talk about representations in this chapter, I am referring to the use of some medium of communication to make claims relating to phenomena that are at least partly separate from this medium of communication itself. For example, when people talk about emotions, they are representing something that is considered to have a degree of independence from their representation of it. There is the language on the one hand, and the emotion on the other, and although the language may be used emotionally and the emotion may be expressed partly through language, there is still a workable distinction between the representational and the emotional processes. In other words, representation implies some mode of correspondence between two partly distinct sectors of reality, one of which is used to represent the other. However, this does not necessarily mean that representation can be treated as something that goes on in an entirely separate realm from the emotional phenomena themselves. Rather, there are always modes of contact and interpenetration of the representational and emotional functions.

There is also an alternative cognitive sense to the term 'representation'. According to this usage, representations are structures contained inside people's heads that guide interpretation of incoming data and may also shape behavioural output. It is often assumed that the constitution of these conceptual entities can be inferred on the basis of evidence from the way that people communicate with each other or respond to relevant stimuli. Indeed, much of the research that has been conducted on emotion representations implicitly adopts this second idea, that when people use emotion words or describe emotional experiences, they are accessing internal concepts and category systems rather than performing communicative acts. In this chapter, my theoretical focus will fall on the communicative phenomena themselves rather than the operation of the information-processing machinery that supposedly goes on behind the scenes, although much of what I say will also have implications for how such machinery must be constructed, if it is really to account for what goes on when people make emotional representations to one another. My main aim, however, is to show how emotional representation, like the overlapping phenomenon of emotion itself, is a primarily social activity.

MAPPING THE LOGICAL GEOGRAPHY OF EMOTION

In this section, I will review studies that have investigated emotion representations and summarize their general conclusions. The general assumption of this research is that people possess some kind of internal category system whose function is to represent emotion, and which can be accessed indirectly using various experimental tasks, many of which depend on people's use of emotional language. In later sections of this chapter, I will question the wisdom of buying into this assumption, but for now I try to understand the implications of the data on their own terms. At the very least, the results of these studies provide evidence concerning people's criteria for using emotional terms, and thus give some leverage on weighty definitional issues such as what people mean when they talk about 'emotions', how they characterize distinct emotional experiences, and how they compare and contrast different emotion words.

There are two basic approaches to the study of emotional meaning. The first of these depends on the idea that people's representations of emotions locate them along simple dimensions of semantic meaning. This *dimensional approach* focuses on judged similarities and distinctions between sets of emotion words or emotional facial expressions. The alternative *categorical approach* pays more attention to the distinctive representation of each particular emotion when considered individually, rather than on its relations with representations of other emotions. Of course, these approaches are not entirely mutually incompatible and most investigators assume that emotion representations can both be arranged by reference to dimensional mappings and also contain some specific semantic content that is not wholly exhausted by reference to these relational continua. In the sections that follow, I will consider some of the empirical results arising from studies conducted in both dimensional and categorical traditions.

Dimensional representations

The first approach to emotional representation takes literally the spatial metaphor for differences in emotional meaning. The relevant semantic universe is charted by triangulating distances between conceptual coordinates of various emotion names in an attempt to map out the logical geography of the domain.

The dimensional approach to emotional meaning exploits the fact that some emotion terms can be directly contrasted with one another, while others seem to have more similar referents. For example, in some sense at least, people consider *happiness* as well as *joy* to mean roughly the opposite of *sadness*, and likewise *love* to mean the opposite of *hate*. It therefore seems feasible to chart a structural arrangement of the relations and oppositions between representations of different emotion names. One way of achieving this is by comparing ratings of semantic similarity of mood adjectives in order to determine which are closest and which most distant from one another in meaning.

For example, Russell (1980) analysed similarity ratings of twenty-eight different affect adjectives to derive a consensual representation of their interrelations. He found that these affect terms can be reliably arranged in a circular representation (called a *circumplex*) with axes labelled 'pleasantness' and 'arousal' (or 'activation'). The pleasantness (or evaluation, or valence) dimension reflects the fact that affective states are thought to range in quality from highly unpleasant to highly pleasant. Activation refers to the contrast between states such as tranquillity which are associated with low levels of activity or arousal, and conditions like astonishment or anger which are thought to involve high degrees of arousal. In Russell's circumplex, a state such as fear is characterized by high activation and low pleasantness and is thus the direct opposite of calmness or relaxation which are judged to be highly pleasant states associated with a low degree of activation (see Figure 9.1). In general, terms that imply similar levels of pleasantness and activation are near to one another on the edge of the circle, and terms that have opposite meanings are separated by the circle's full diameter.

According to Russell, all words describing affective states can be arranged at some point around the edge of the circumplex, or, to put this another way, all

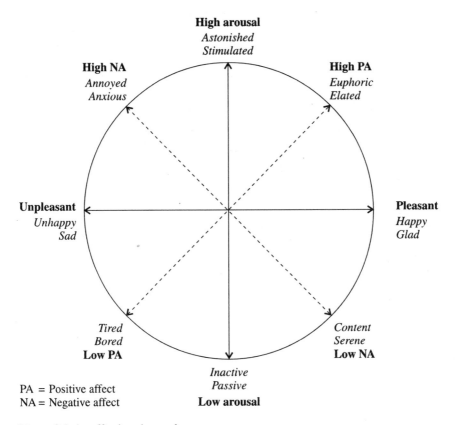

High arousal
Astonished
Stimulated

High NA
Annoyed
Anxious

High PA
Euphoric
Elated

Unpleasant
Unhappy
Sad

Pleasant
Happy
Glad

Tired
Bored
Low PA

Content
Serene
Low NA

Inactive
Passive
Low arousal

PA = Positive affect
NA = Negative affect

Figure 9.1 An affective circumplex

Source: from Larson and Diener (1992)

affective meanings can be precisely located and characterized according to their supposed level of activation and pleasantness.

Previous models of affective meaning were also broadly consistent with Russell's dimensional system. For example, one of the earliest psychological accounts of the structure of affect was provided by Wundt (1897), who based his model on introspections about the feelings that accompanied simple perceptual experiences such as listening to auditory rhythms produced by a metronome. Wundt claimed that regular rhythmic patterns produced more agreeable feelings than irregular ones, and so concluded that affect could vary along a dimension of pleasure–displeasure. He also noted that between clicks the expectation of the arrival of the next click produced a feeling of tension, then there was a sense of relief after it had come. This subjective distinction led to the postulation of a dimension of feeling corresponding to strain–relaxation. Finally, Wundt observed that faster rhythms tended to cause excitement whereas slower rhythms had a more calming effect, leading to a third affective dimension. According to Wundt, these three dimensions exhausted the kinds of conscious distinctions between feelings that were possible, and all affective experiences were thought to be completely definable by their location along these three specified continua. Although Wundt's representation of emotion space differed from Russell's circumplex in containing an extra dimension, the general structure of the model still maps fairly well onto the two-dimensional scheme.

Support for the circumplex model of emotion representation does not only come from self-report or introspective data. Schlosberg (1952) devised the precursor of the contemporary two-dimensional model of affect. In his research, participants were asked to categorize facial expressions of emotion and their differential errors allowed Schlosberg to judge the relative proximity of the various categories of affect that they used. He concluded that the expressions differed according to their judged pleasantness, and according to whether they were seen as indicating attention or rejection. Similarly, Abelson and Sermat (1962) asked respondents to rate the similarity of pairs of facial expressions directly, and used a multidimensional scaling procedure to determine the structure underlying these judgements. Again, these authors found evidence for a pleasantness–unpleasantness dimension, as well as a second dimension relating to sleep–tension combined with attention–rejection.

The pleasantness–activation circumplex model also appears to apply in different cultural groups. Essentially comparable dimensionality has been obtained for bilingual Chinese, Croatian, Gujarati, and Japanese speakers living in an English-speaking area of Canada, confirming that the circumplex applies in different linguistic contexts (Russell, 1983). Furthermore, Russell, Lewicka, and Niit (1989) found similar results when native Estonian, Greek, and Polish speakers judged the similarity of the same basic set of translated affect adjectives. Finally, judgements based on standard photographs of emotional facial expressions by these same national groups yielded similarity ratings that conformed to the original circumplex, confirming that it has a reasonable level of cross-cultural generality. Other studies have obtained compatible results (e.g. Sjoberg, Svensson, and Persson, 1979; Watson *et al.*, 1988).

It should be noted that these findings do not mean that people in different cultures necessarily experience or conceptualize mood in exactly the same way as Anglo-Americans do. In fact, anthropological studies suggest that emotional concepts may be used very differently in different cultures, especially those that have had little contact with Western civilization (e.g. Lutz, 1988; Rosaldo, 1984). However, the data do imply that a basic set of emotional adjectives can be translated successfully into different languages, and that people from different cultures have similar ideas about how these particular terms and associated facial expressions relate to, and contrast with, each other.

A second alternative circumplex mapping of affect words has been suggested by Watson and Tellegen (1985), among others (e.g. Meyer and Shack, 1989), who argued that it is more useful to see Russell's arrangement from a different angle, and draw the axes at 45 degrees from the vertical. Watson and Tellegen suggested that moods and emotions are judged to differ along the two separate dimensions of *positive affect* (PA) and *negative affect* (NA). In their view, high PA reflects pleasurable engagement with the environment and is characterized by words such as *euphoric, peppy,* and *elated,* which imply a combination of pleasantness and activation, whereas low positive affect is marked by depression and lethargy and described in terms such as *drowsy* and *dull* which indicate a lack of pleasantness and activation. Correspondingly, high NA includes distressing and unpleasant affective states such as anxiety and anger, suggesting high activation and high unpleasantness, while low NA implies calm and relaxation (see Figure 9.1). Basically, PA and NA tend to emerge from factor analysis when dimensions are rotated, whereas pleasantness and arousal are often the simple unrotated dimensions that are obtained (Watson and Tellegen, 1985).

Essentially, Russell's and Watson and Tellegen's schemes are intertranslatable, with high PA combining high levels of pleasantness and arousal, and high NA, low pleasantness with high arousal. Correspondingly, high pleasantness can be viewed as a combination of high PA and low NA. To the extent that the two schemes of classification both map onto an identical circumplex, the choice of dimensions may be seen as an arbitrary decision based on preferred procedures for factor analysis (Larsen and Diener, 1992).

However, there do seem to be logical as opposed to methodological reasons for favouring the pleasure–arousal mapping suggested by Russell over the PA/NA scheme proposed by Watson and Tellegen. The first problem with the latter model concerns the fact that the labels 'positive affect' and 'negative affect' are confusing because low values of positive affect are in fact experienced as negative and unpleasant states, and similarly low values of negative affect are pleasant rather than neutral (cf. Larsen and Diener, 1992).

A second and more serious problem concerns the supposedly basic nature of the representational dimensions of positive and negative affect. Intuitively, it seems possible to translate the meanings of these constructed concepts into pleasure and arousal terms, whereas it is not easy to conceive of pleasure as being reducible to a combination of high PA and low NA. Similarly, Reisenzein (1994) argued that pleasure and arousal seem to be phenomenologically more fundamental than PA and NA, supporting Russell's model.

Although both circumplex mappings have obvious relevance to emotional meaning, it is worth mentioning that their intended purpose was as general representations of *affect,* rather than of *emotion* in particular. According to the distinctions proposed in Chapter 1, emotion is a specific form of affective experience characterized mainly by its intentional relation to some aspect of the current psychological situation. Anger, for example, is not thought to be just a feeling, but rather a feeling *about something,* and what it is about is considered to make a crucial difference to the experience of the emotion. Similarly, emotions can be represented in terms of a narrative temporal structure: they are considered to have beginnings (instigations), middles (feelings, appraisals), and endings (action tendencies, consequences). The implication of the circumplex models is that representations of affective states can be contrasted simply with each other in terms of momentary feelings rather than articulated internal structure. Clearly this tells rather less than the whole story about how emotions are understood to unfold over time and how they are thought to relate to specific situational evaluations.

Emotional meaning, because of its intentionality and temporal articulation, tends to be richer and more multifarious than any two-dimensional model seems to imply. For example, on closer attention, it becomes difficult to see many emotional terms as simple opposites of one another. Even happiness is only the opposite of sadness when considered simply in terms of pleasantness; in other ways the two emotional meanings are not opposites at all. Similarly, love may contrast with hate in that it is considered a positive rather than negative feeling towards someone else, but it is usually agreed that both emotions share the common characteristic of being directed at other people. Furthermore, although the subjective feelings associated with love and hate are certainly different, they are not necessarily interpretable as opposites as such. In fact, it is hard to think of many examples of emotional names that really do represent direct and pure contrasts with one another.

A related problem with the two-dimensional representation of affective meaning is that it puts emotions which seem to have quite distinct meanings close to each other in the hypothetical semantic space (for example, fear and anger are located in the same quadrant of the circumplex, see Figure 9.1). Both of these points suggest that the postulated affect dimensions do not wholly exhaust the representational content of emotional terms (although they may conceivably account for most of the perceived quality of the *momentary feelings* associated with emotions; cf. Reisenzein, 1994).

The common assumption of the circumplex models is that affective representational space can be adequately mapped out using only two dimensions. Clearly, this assumption reflects something of an oversimplification. Nobody would want to argue that *all* the judged differences between affective conditions can be specified using just two variables. For example, there is clearly more to our representation of the experience of embarrassment than a particular mixture of pleasantness and activation, or positive and negative affect. Some researchers have reacted to this problem by rejecting dimensional approaches and looking at representations of different affective states independently (e.g. Davitz, 1969; Shaver *et al.*, 1987; see next section). Another solution is to consider additional dimensions of affective meaning.

A study by Parkinson and Lea (1991) attempted to give a richer picture of the range of possible distinctions between emotions by using Kelly's (1955) repertory grid technique. Respondents were asked to compare sets of three emotional terms and to think of a feature that characterized two of the terms but did not characterize the other. They then made ratings of a wider set of emotion terms using the dimension or distinction implied by the attribute generated in the earlier comparison procedure. For example, if a respondent were comparing anger, grief, and love, they might say that anger and grief both involve unpleasant feelings, whereas love usually makes you feel good, or that love and grief were both considered humane emotions whereas anger was more antisocial, or that love and anger were both directed outward towards other people, but that grief was more of an inner-directed emotion, and so on.

One of the advantages of this procedure was that it encouraged respondents to think fairly deeply about emotional distinctions and forced them to generate a fairly exhaustive set of dimensions. Ratings made according to respondents' self-generated constructs allowed the use of factor analytic procedures to calculate commonality of the representational continua. Although some elicited constructs were truly personal and idiosyncratic, there was also a degree of consensus. One of the main conclusions of the study, however, was that even apparently simple dimensions of emotional meaning such as pleasantness can be used in a variety of ways and need to be reconceptualized before fine-grained distinctions can be made.

For example, although a positive–negative dimension emerged as a clear factor in a principal components analysis and explained the greatest amount of variance in ratings, people often used more than one variant of this dimension and different people characterized it differently. When deciding whether an emotion is pleasant or unpleasant, good or bad, positive or negative, people may consider a number of related criteria, not all of which always lead to the same conclusion. For example, they may think about whether the emotion involves pleasant or unpleasant feelings, whether it leads to positive or negative consequences, whether it is a healthy or unhealthy thing to feel, or whether it is considered a good or bad thing from a moral perspective to experience the emotion (e.g. the 'sin' of pride). Similar subtleties and distinctions are hidden in many other of the traditionally conceived dimensions. The semantic structure of affective space is not as cut and dried as usually implied.

Several other investigators (e.g. Averill, 1975; Daly *et al.*, 1983) have also provided evidence that extra dimensions may be present in the implicit semantic space of affect. Additional representational dimensions that have been proposed include control, depth of experience, intensity, and locus of causation.

A sceptical view of research into the dimensions of affective meaning might point out that respondents usually rely on simple and relatively general classification criteria when instructed to compare large sets of words, whether these words relate to emotions or other concepts (Clore *et al.*, 1987). Indeed, the emotional dimensions of pleasantness and activation are very close in meaning to the 'evaluation' and 'activity' dimensions that factor out in semantic differential studies of non-emotional verbal categories (Osgood *et al.*, 1957). The problem is that the significance of this result is not entirely clear. We cannot really say whether the comparison procedure is yielding dimensions that are truly meaningful and relevant to respondents or whether the simple fact of forcing comparisons where they would not normally be made results in the construction of artificial but still relatively consistent representational continua. It is important to ask what criteria people are actually using when judging similarity of word meaning. When respondents are asked to articulate the basis for their distinctions and comparisons as in Parkinson and Lea's (1991) study, it turns out that their meaning is far from simple or univalent. The *categorical* approach to affective meaning (considered below) assumes that emotion representations do not relate to each other in simple or direct ways. Each emotion may be seen as lying opposite to some others on some dimensions of meaning but none are judged as directly contrasting pairs.

Dimensional representations of emotional appraisals

The assumption of much of the research considered so far is that meanings of different emotion names relate to and contrast with one another according to the quality of the associated feelings. An alternative possibility is that the implicit organization of the emotion category reflects other components of emotional function. For example, Smith and Ellsworth (1985; see Chapter 2) suggested that the *appraisals* characterizing different emotions can be aligned along six orthogonal dimensions. Although their study was presented as an exploration of the structure of emotional experience, I have suggested above that its findings may be more relevant to emotion representations.

In the experiment, respondents were asked to remember specific examples of pure emotional experiences, rather than thinking about each emotion name in the abstract. This procedure clearly encourages respondents to interpret emotions in their everyday situational context rather than as putative self-standing internal states. The strategy of asking for real-life emotional exemplars does not, however, ensure that the results of the study are relevant to dimensions of experience rather than dimensions of representation. This is because respondents select the specific instance of each emotional term by reference to their ideas about when and how such an emotion occurs, rather than sampling randomly from emotional episodes that are somehow independently classified as examples of the particular emotional category. In other words, when respondents perform the task of remembering an emotional episode they can only try to generate a narrative that fits in with what they believe to be the characteristic features of the emotion called for. For example, if I am asked to think of a good example of when I have been angry, I will think back to occasions when I categorized myself as angry, or when someone else told me I was angry. Either way, my memory search depends on definitions of anger, not some independent intrinsic feature of what it means to feel angry. Even if we were to assume that past emotional episodes are appropriately pre-allocated to some internal memory store, the basis of the initial categorization would still depend on the respondent's own conception of what originally defined the particular emotional state as such. Of course, it may be that all that 'anger' signifies is being sufficiently involved in a relationship when someone else insults you, but in that case, the related appraisals are not contingent features of the emotion, but constitutive facts about the accepted nature of the emotion in question (see Chapter 2).

What I am suggesting here is that dimensions of appraisal studies such as Smith and Ellsworth's are actually convoluted procedures for getting at the meaning of different emotional terms. What their results demonstrate, therefore, is that use of an emotion vocabulary presupposes some kind of representation of the domain of emotion words, that can be described in terms of appraisal dimensions. By focusing specifically on emotional states in real-life settings, Smith and Ellsworth were able to uncover a previously untapped richness in how emotions are represented in terms of appraisal.

One disadvantage of Smith and Ellsworth's approach, however, is that respondents may be constrained by the limited range of dimensions included in the scales. Because the variety of available common-sense distinctions between emotions has never been systematically investigated, there must remain doubts about the comprehensiveness of any presupplied rating battery.

A study by Reisenzein and Hofmann (1990) attempted to catalogue the full range of available appraisal-based distinctions between emotions, using a simplified version of repertory grid methodology (Kelly, 1955; and see pp. 234–5). Typical scenarios for twenty-three different emotions were described by one set of participants, then another set of respondents were asked to compare pairs of these scenarios and to generate an attribute or dimension that distinguished them from one another. For example, a scenario for guilt might refer to an occasion on which a relative dies after the respondent has failed to stay in contact with them, and a scenario for anger might refer to a car accident when the other driver was at fault. In comparing these two scenarios, the respondent might say that in the first case, the person experiencing the emotion was to blame whereas in the second someone else was to blame. By contrasting a series of pairs of situations, it is possible to generate a wide range of representational distinctions between the situational interpretations and evaluations implied by different emotions.

Reisenzein and Hofmann found that participants made use of many of the dimensions of appraisal reported by Smith and Ellsworth (1985) as well as additional dimensions relating to the quality of the social relationship implied by the emotion, other-involvement, and so on. Of course, the nature of the task used in this study means that some of the distinctions made by participants may not have reflected *dimensions* of appraisal as such, but rather supposed present or absent features of the situation in which the emotion typically occurs. The importance of Reisenzein and Hofmann's (1990) findings lies in their demonstration that direct investigation of representation of emotional appraisals uncovers a more complicated picture than implied by the dimensional scheme produced when using predefined scales. People may use idiosyncratic appraisal distinctions, and the subtlety of many of their comparisons is not easily captured in closed-ended rating scales.

Reisenzein (1994) suggested that Russell's pleasantness–activation theory needs to be complemented by appraisal theory to give an adequate mapping of emotional meaning, and that emotional terms should be conceived as referring to feeling states which are necessarily and intrinsically caused by different kinds of appraisal (see also Reisenzein and Schönpflug, 1992). One of the problems with this approach, however, is that appraisals can be viewed as *part* of the emotional feeling, and as determining the specific quality of pleasure or displeasure, activation or deactivation that is experienced (e.g. Frijda, 1986; Lazarus, 1991b), rather than as a separable process that yields a particular pleasure–arousal combination.

In an unpublished study, I have also attempted to use a different knowledge-elicitation technique to get at the full range of appraisal-based distinctions between emotions. In this study, respondents took part in a guessing game analogous to 'twenty questions' where their task was to find out what emotion had been selected from a list by asking a series of yes/no questions relating to the situation in which the emotion might occur or to the way that situation was evaluated or interpreted by the person experiencing the emotion. In other words, respondents were supposed to ask appraisal related questions in order to calculate what emotion was being imagined by another person (see Parkinson, 1990, and pp. 241–2, for a fuller description of a related procedure).

Although this study succeeded in uncovering some of the previously postulated appraisal dimensions such as *responsibility* and *expectedness*, respondents usually performed the task by referring to specific situations rather than abstract dimensions. Since asking specific questions was a slower and less efficient procedure than using appraisal dimensions for completing the experimental task, my conclusion was that respondents found it hard to think about appraisal-based emotional distinctions in general terms: indeed, many participants found the experimental task rather demanding. This fact suggests that people do not spontaneously make use of explicit representations of appraisal dimensions, but are more comfortable working with more concrete script-based representations of what different emotional states typically involve. More sophisticated techniques are required to get them to generate abstract representations. For example, Reisenzein and Hofmann (1990) elicited appraisal dimensions by having respondents compare specific emotional *situations*, rather than general emotion terms.

Categorical representations

The second general approach to emotion representations is based on the idea that each emotion term is represented as a distinctive set of states or events that may be related to other emotional meanings but not in simple and purely dimensional ways. For example, concepts may be specified by lists of present or absent features rather than, or in addition to, their positions on continua (e.g. Rosch, 1978). Alternatively, it is possible that people view each different emotion term as corresponding to a temporally structured narrative episode, with different kinds of features and events occurring at different stages in the development of the emotion (e.g. Fischer, 1991; Parkinson, 1990; Shaver *et al.*, 1987). According to any of these categorical approaches, the best way to get at emotion representations is to ask people to characterize particular emotions singly and in detail rather than comparing pairs or sets of emotions to explore their interrelations.

It is worth noting that few theorists would adopt a pure categorical approach to emotion representation. Instead of assuming that each emotion is represented as completely distinctive and unrelated to any other, most researchers suggest that it is natural for people to compare at least some emotions with some others along at least some dimensions. For example, although the judged time-course and feature-structure of hate and love do not present completely contrasting sets, they are at least considered opposites along the dimension of evaluation of the other person who is the object of the emotion. The only group of researchers who might be seen as viewing the meaning of each emotional term as quite distinct from each other are those who believe in primary emotions, as structures devised for their own particular adaptive purposes (e.g. Oatley and Johnson-Laird, 1990; Panksepp, 1992).

A number of knowledge-elicitation procedures are possible within the categorical approach, but the most common ones use straightforward open-ended or closed-ended questions about each emotion, in the context of interview or questionnaire studies. In this section, I will make no attempt to provide a comprehensive review of the range of research employing these procedures. Rather, I will discuss a few representative experiments, and summarize the general conclusions available from the findings.

One of the most obvious ways of finding out what people mean by emotional terms is to ask them directly for their own definitions. For example, Davitz (1969) produced a dictionary of emotional meaning by systematically eliciting such free verbal descriptions. On a much smaller scale I conducted an exploratory survey of representations of six supposedly 'basic' emotions (e.g. Ekman, 1992) as part of my postgraduate research (Parkinson, 1983). In this study, university students were asked to write down a description of the typical situation in which each of the target emotions might be experienced, based on their own experience, a dream, or a fictional episode from a book, film, or their own imagination. This stage of the procedure allowed some preliminary assessment of the consistency of cultural narratives of emotional episodes, and also put the respondents in a situation where it was relatively easy for them to imagine the emotional experience itself. In the second stage of the procedure, respondents were asked to list the characteristic features of the emotional state in rough order of importance.

Some illustrative results from this exploratory study may help to give a flavour of how participants responded to this procedure. Here are three versions of one of the most typical narratives recounted in the fear condition:

(a) Walking alone at night and hearing footsteps following. Even when you turn a corner the footsteps still follow. The pace is similar to yours and yours is the only house on the road and the footsteps are still following.
(b) Walking down a dark street at night then noticing you're being followed. The quicker you walk, the quicker they walk. Then they catch up and it's obvious they're going to mug you. That moment of uncertainty just before the action occurs is probably the most frightening.
(c) Knowing that something unpleasant is about to happen or believing that it might. For example, walking at night, alone, and heavy footsteps behind you
. . .

Fifteen out of the forty participants describing a typical fear episode wrote about being followed by someone in the dark. Part of this consistency may depend on common experiences of student life of being out late and walking home alone. It seems clear from the accounts offered, however, that people have a fairly well-articulated and shared idea of what situations cause fear. Note also, that in narrative (c), the participant even succeeds in describing the abstract structure of the fear episode, in terms not entirely dissimilar from those used by Lazarus (1991a) in specifying the *core relational theme* for this emotion. Similarly, in (b), the respondent places particular emphasis on the characteristic of *uncertainty*, which Smith and Ellsworth (1985) and others have suggested is a key appraisal component for fear. Given that this study was conducted in 1981 on second-year psychology students with no specific training in emotion research, it would be hard to see these intuitive ideas as deriving from the subsequent more formal theories. It seems more likely that appraisal theory is a formalization of our common-sense ideas of what different emotions involve. Another apparently insightful characterization of the abstract structure of the fear episode was the following: 'A prediction of what might happen in the future which will cause some kind of suffering, e.g. will I fall off this cliff I am climbing?'

In the second part of the procedure, participants listed characteristics of the emotion. Again, there was a great deal of consistency in the answers given. Over 90 per cent of the participants characterizing fear mentioned bodily reactions as a defining characteristic, most commonly referring in particular to increases in heart rate (see Chapter 4). The proportion of participants listing bodily changes as a key characteristic varied from emotion to emotion, however, with only 30 per cent of sadness definitions specifying this factor. Across all six emotions studied, about two-thirds of the definitions included reference to bodily reactions, and approximately the same number referred to situational or appraisal factors. This emphasis on appraisal, however, may have been partly a consequence of the procedure of generating a situational context for the emotion before listing its characteristics.

To summarize the results of this study, respondents had no difficulty in describing situations in which different emotions might occur and the characteristics associated with these emotions. Furthermore, their answers were very consistent for each emotion, suggesting that they were drawing on shared representations of each emotion. Finally, the descriptions of emotion episodes suggested that respondents had an intuitive understanding of what psychologists have recently formulated as appraisal theory.

In this exploratory study, I investigated two aspects of emotion representation from a categorical perspective: ideas about the structure of the emotional situation, and judged characteristics of the emotional experience itself. Both these topics have also been covered in more recent and more rigorous studies, which I will now briefly review.

Shaver and colleagues (1987) asked respondents a series of questions about typical or remembered experiences of fear, sadness, anger, joy, and love, and used six coders to categorize and give a temporal structure to the characteristics generated by this procedure. Prototypical scripts for the different emotions were derived from analysis of these results, suggesting that emotions are conceived as being caused by appraisals (*antecedents*), characterized by experiential, expressive, and behavioural *responses*, and finally, in the case of negative emotions, subjected to *self-control procedures*. Thus, there are considered to be at least three stages in the temporal articulation of most emotion episodes.

With respect to previous approaches to emotional meanings, Shaver argued that the circumplex dimensions often derived from similarity scaling methods are not pure abstract continua used by respondents but are emergent generalizations produced when comparisons based on several different sets of characteristics are made:

> When subjects in an emotion-sorting or similarity-rating study compare two emotions, or two mental representations of emotions, they may think about antecedents, responses, self-control efforts, or all three. It may be a mistake, therefore, to think of the abstract dimensions of emotion . . . as properties of . . . any single aspect of emotion.
>
> (p. 1080)

In another of my own studies of emotion representation (Parkinson, 1990), I looked specifically at the criteria that people use to distinguish different emotions from each other. The procedure was based on the parlour game 'twenty questions' and respondents took part in pairs. The experimental task involved one player thinking of a particular emotional state and the other asking questions designed to determine what the state was. The questions generated from a series of these games were then categorised separately by another group of participants, and their classifications were subjected to cluster analysis on the basis of how many times each question was put into the same category as each of the others. Questions broke down into three main categories, corresponding roughly to a temporally based representation of the course of emotional reaction. First, there were questions about the *causes* of the target emotion, then about *characteristics* of the experience itself, and finally *consequences* and symptoms of the emotional state (see Table 9.1). Like Shaver and his colleagues (1987), I concluded that the representation of emotion has a temporally articulated narrative structure.

A study by Conway and Bekerian (1987) employed cognitive tasks to assess the role of situational knowledge in emotional representations. These investigators found that lexical decisions about emotion words as well as an emotion-naming task were facilitated when relevant situational information was primed. For example, respondents who were primed with the sentence 'It was the third anniversary of the death of his wife' were subsequently quicker to recognize 'sadness' as a word rather than a nonword, than they were to make a similar lexical decision for 'happiness'.

The exact mechanism for such effects is unclear, but the results certainly suggest that there are implicit and specific connections between representations of situations and representations of emotions. If *sadness* had no semantic connection with remembering the loss of loved ones, it would be hard to explain any differential cognitive effect. Also supporting the implicit connection of situational and emotion representations, the investigators found that respondents were faster at generating images of emotion-related situations when they had

Table 9.1 Questions asked to determine imagined emotions

Causes	Characteristics	Consequences
Was the emotion caused by someone else?	Is it a self-centred feeling?	Would you show this emotion?
Do you feel it when in contact with other people?	Does it build up inside you?	Would it make you act out of the ordinary?
Is the emotion directed towards another person?	Is it a strong feeling?	Does it lead to other emotions?
Would you like to be with people?	Do you feel good?	Does it lead to disturbed thought processes?
Is the emotion caused by an external object?	Would you tell anyone about this emotion?	Would tranquillizers remove the state?
Is the emotion related to an event?	Would being happy counteract the feeling?	Does it make you feel all soppy?
Is the emotion triggered by something you see?	Does it last a long time?	Would it stop you sleeping?

Source: adapted from Parkinson (1990)

been primed using the name of a relevant emotion. For example, when the word 'sadness' was presented on the computer screen immediately before respondents were supposed to imagine 'two lovers' final parting after a long and friendly relationship', respondents reported producing an appropriate image more quickly than if the image-cue sentence appeared after the word 'terror'. In this task, respondents reported that their images often came from particular remembered personal experiences, or from scenes from books and films.

To summarize this research, people seem to draw on a well-articulated and shared representation of what particular emotions involve, which is structured as a narrative sequence and includes specification of features which are typically present when the emotion is experienced. Emotions are implicitly represented as having a developing structure over time rather than simply as momentary reactions to delimited stimulus events.

Variety in emotional representation

On the basis of their experimental results using a variety of procedures for assessing situational representations of emotion, Conway and Bekerian (1987) speculated that emotions were represented in memory at a number of different, hierarchically organized levels. At the most general level, they postulated the existence of semantic emotion representations in terms of *context-free knowledge*. This kind of knowledge is thought to allow respondents to contrast and relate different emotional states to each other in terms of the characteristic intrinsic features of the experience (body changes, behavioural impulses, expressions, etc.). For example, people generally believe that happiness is related to smiling and that it has a high value on the dimension of pleasantness: both these attributes are therefore specified as part of our semantic knowledge about this particular emotion.

Conway and Bekerian's suppositions about emotion representation at the semantic level are compatible with Bower's (1981) model of the organization of emotion knowledge in memory. According to Bower, representations of particular emotions are located as nodes within an *associative network* (Anderson and Bower, 1973; Collins and Quillian, 1969). Each emotion node is linked to other nodes representing situational, evaluative, behavioural and other information relevant to the emotion. For example, positive emotion nodes are connected to memories that have been encoded with pleasant associations. The strength of association of connected nodes depends on the frequency of their simultaneous activation as a result of external information or internal rehearsal. When an emotion node is activated by presentation of the emotion word or other relevant input, activation spreads also to adjacent nodes, making the specified information more accessible to consciousness. Such processes provide one possible explanation of mood-congruency effects on judgement and behaviour (see Chapters 2 and 3). Additionally, Bower proposed that inhibitory as well as excitatory connections exist, such that information contrary to a particular kind of emotional association will raise rather than lower the threshold for activation of the relevant nodes.

The specific mechanics of Bower's model are not the central topic of concern here. More interesting from the present perspective is Bower's notion that emotional representations are definable in terms of their changing connections with related or contrasting information. The cognitive architecture suggested by this proposal reifies the idea of an internal structural mapping of emotion concepts organized as sets of associative links. My own view, in contrast, draws more attention to the working out of emotional meanings in real-time encounters between people than to the internal workings of some putative cognitive machinery.

Conway and Bekerian's proposed second level of representation encodes emotions in terms of the general categories of setting in which they might occur, analogous to what Schank (1982) has termed *scenes*. According to this idea, sets of basic emotions are thought to be alike in that they tend to occur in broadly similar classes of setting which people are able to picture readily in imagination. For example, happiness, joy, and pride might be connoted by the scene of inspecting an examination results board.

Postulation of a scene-based level of emotion representation is probably the most original and most controversial of Conway and Bekerian's proposals. Unfortunately, however, the evidence offered for this kind of representation apparently depended on asking respondents certain idiosyncratic questions that may have forced them to think in unusual ways about emotion. As with semantic knowledge, there remains some doubt whether people would ever represent emotions in this way *spontaneously*. Furthermore, it is not clear how consistently scene representations would be associated with particular sets of emotions even if they were commonly deployed in everyday life outside the laboratory. Emotional distinctions seem to be based on personal meanings of situations rather than situations themselves (e.g. Lazarus, 1991a). Static settings in themselves do not usually carry any fixed emotional meaning. Even an obviously emotionally relevant place like a church where a wedding ceremony might take place only has the appropriate emotional impact when the particular occasion is a wedding rather than, say, a funeral or a regular religious service. Thus, it is not the setting itself but how actions are organized and how events unfold over time within that setting that is usually judged to make the important emotional difference. Of course, if dynamic narrative factors are incorporated into a scene-based representation then its emotional connotations become more definite and obvious, for example, if the scene is a superior's office in which you are told off, or a football match immediately after a goal is scored. However, this kind of emotion knowledge then begins to seem more script-based than scene-based, and Conway and Bekerian explicitly attempted to distinguish between these two kinds of representation.

At the level of situational knowledge, Conway and Bekerian (1987) argued that specific knowledge about particular emotions is represented in terms of scripts and autobiographical memories. For example, people might interpret anger in terms of episodes in which someone else says or does something to offend them, and they might also possess a relatively general script specifying how such episodes typically unfold. It also seems likely that people can bring to mind specific occasions conforming to this script from their own remembered experience (e.g. Russell and Fehr, 1994). The script may be based on generalized autobiographical memories, and the representation of these specific memories in turn may accommodate to the structure of the general script. Although these two kinds of emotion representation are clearly related to each other (cf. Reiser *et al.*, 1985), it still seems important to maintain a conceptual distinction between them.

Conway and Bekerian's (1987) approach is valuable because it calls into question the assumption that there is one basic and definitive set of organizing principles for emotion representations. Different kinds of emotion representation may be deployed, depending on the nature of the task and the pragmatic aims of the person involved. The specific mechanisms underlying these representations, however, must remain in question.

A major problem with many studies in this area is that they fail to rule out the possibility that the kinds of representation apparently used by participants were not at least partially determined by the specific experimental procedures used. For example, in their everyday lives people are not accustomed to grouping together sets of emotional states and thinking about what features they have in common. The results of being asked to perform such an activity may tell us more about how people respond to unfamiliar cognitive tasks than how they would normally represent emotions. Similarly with regard to research into dimensional representations of emotion, it is not clear whether pleasantness and activation are genuine and spontaneous dimensions of emotional meaning or simply constructed consistencies in response forced by an artificial experimental procedure. It seems likely that people are capable of applying a wide variety of possible constructions to emotional experience, given amenable circumstances, but this does not mean that it is necessary for researchers to review exhaustively all these conceivable ways of representing the semantic domain. Rather, it seems more sensible to focus specifically on distinctions and categories that are employed regularly in everyday emotional situations.

Although my 'twenty questions' study (Parkinson, 1991; see p. 241) did not entirely solve the problems associated with imposing artificial comparison tasks on people, it did at least allow participants to develop their own questions about emotion. The results of this study offered partial support for Conway and Bekerian's suppositions about the availability of different kinds of emotion representations in a less constrained and artificial setting than the one set up by these investigators.

For example, many of the participants asked questions relating to bodily reactions, expressive displays, and behavioural impulses during their attempts to work out what emotion was being imagined by the other player. The fact that players used these questions spontaneously, and apparently expected the other player to be able to answer them in an informative way, suggests that people generally have access to shared ideas about how different emotions are connected with different feelings and symptoms at a semantic level.

The utilization of script-based representations was similarly supported by respondents' use of questions about both causes and consequences of the emotion, implying that respondents were in some agreement about the temporal structure of different varieties of emotional episode (Shaver *et al.*, 1987). However, there was no evidence for representations relating to emotional *scenes*, since none of the respondents asked questions relating to the general classes of setting or the specific situation in which different emotions might occur. If, as Conway and Bekerian argued, subsets of emotions tend to go together with broad groupings of situations, and people know about these connections, then it seems surprising that they did not utilize this knowledge in ruling out sets of possible correct answers when performing the experimental task.

Conclusions

To summarize the evidence reviewed in this chapter so far, many studies have been conducted on the ways that emotions are represented by people, and evidence has been found for a number of different kinds of representation. When comparing a wide range of emotions with one another, two or three dimensions of meaning are typically derived which correspond roughly to the dimensions that are obtained when large sets of any kind of word are compared (Osgood *et al.*, 1957). In some sense, particular emotions can be defined according to their level of pleasantness and activation, but these dimensions certainly do not exhaust common-sense emotional meaning. Incorporating extra dimensions relating to appraisal into the spatial mapping provides a representational scheme capable of accounting for a wide range of emotional distinctions (e.g. Smith and Ellsworth,

1985). However, it is not clear that appraisal-based representations are part of the spontaneous common understanding of emotion. Rather they seem to be distillations of more situational and relational characteristics of emotional representations. Research into categorical representations suggests that emotion representations may be structured like a temporal narrative or script (e.g. Shaver *et al.*, 1987), and that people are quite able to describe in detail the kinds of situation in which different emotions occur (Russell and Fehr, 1994). Thus, it is possible that appraisal representations may be inferred from script-based knowledge rather than vice versa.

The danger of discussing emotional representations in abstract terms is that it tends to imply that people possess relatively fixed intrapsychic models of how emotions work, which in turn guide their interpretation of actual instances of emotion. There seems to be a common idea that we can get at the basic deep structure of emotion knowledge by asking questions about what happens *in general* when people get angry, afraid, and so on. In contrast, I believe that there are a range of available repertoires for accounting for emotions that are used in different social circumstances (cf. Potter and Wetherell, 1987).

In my view, common sense does not contain a single unitary set of interrelated propositions about emotions, but a variety of sometimes incompatible formulations which are used as and when appropriate (cf. Billig, 1987). For this reason, it is important to look at the way that emotions are represented in different social contexts. For example, the representation of emotion drawn upon to excuse action in the courtroom (crimes of passion) is different to that invoked when expressing commitment to an interpersonal project (team solidarity). On the one hand, emotion is seen as an uncontrollable factor interfering with rational action; on the other, a motivating principle for actions adopted in good faith.

A related point is that emotion representations should be examined in the context where they are deployed, as conversational moves, rather than in supposedly neutral and abstract settings. Emotion representations may be seen as representations made to someone else, rather than as lying somewhere inside the psyche waiting to find expression. There is no need to reify some putative private aspect of what emotion means to people in their everyday lives. Of course, such a communicative view of emotion representation echoes some of my earlier claims about the interpersonal basis of emotional experience itself. In the next section of this chapter, I consider the relevance of research into emotion representations for general emotion theory, as a further step towards an integrated account of ideas as well as realities of emotion.

IMPLICATIONS OF RESEARCH INTO EMOTION REPRESENTATIONS

Although all the studies discussed so far in this chapter were specifically directed at ideas about emotions, the conclusions that have been drawn from them by investigators tend to concern emotional experience itself. For example, it is usually assumed that the fact that people represent different emotional experiences in terms of distinctive patterns of cognitive appraisal suggests that these appraisal patterns determine the quality of emotional experience on-line during a real-time encounter (Smith and Lazarus, 1993). Similarly, the model of emotion contained in people's script-like accounts is typically supposed to be an objectively accurate one (e.g. Shaver *et al.*, 1987). Finally, investigators sometimes assume that emotional experiences really are constituted by pleasure and arousal (e.g. Reisenzein, 1994). In short, investigation of emotion representations is often taken as a shortcut for getting to the essence of individual emotion itself (whatever that might turn out to be).

It would be pointless to deny that there is at least a grain of truth in many of the ways that people conceive of emotion. Likewise, it seems just as naive to refuse to admit that many aspects of our commonsense understanding of emotion may be limited or mistaken (otherwise emotions would never surprise us). The main difficulty facing researchers in this area is usually thought to lie in sorting out which aspects of our representations correspond with real aspects of emotion, and which do not. The problem with such an approach is that without independent criteria for what counts as emotion, there remain nothing but different sets of representations to match against one another. The correspondence question may, for this very reason, turn out to be empirically undecidable, given current conceptions. In the discussion that follows, I shall briefly consider the general issue of the relative accuracy or inaccuracy of emotion representations, before moving on to discussing the limitations of the assumption that ideas and realities are the kinds of things that can be directly and simply matched against one another.

Why study ideas of emotion?

Psychologists have been interested in the ways that people talk and think about emotion for a number of different reasons, although rarely has the full range of possible connections between emotional ideas and emotional reality been spelled out. Investigators tend to work on the assumption that the connection between emotional representation and emotional conduct or experience is simple and mainly unidirectional, with the former providing an after-the-fact mapping of the latter (see Chapter 1). In this section, I hope to demonstrate that the fabric of emotional life is shot through with emotional talk, and that ideas and realities of emotion are interwoven in a variety of fashions. In order to make a start on this analysis, I will outline the ways that previous commentators have conceived of the link between emotion and how it is represented by people. My intention is to suggest an integrative model which is capable of contextualizing the process of emotion representation, and of emotion itself, within the broader function of making identity claims to particular audiences.

Relations between conceptions of psychological function and psychological function itself are traditionally the province of social cognition, particularly attribution theory, and most introductory texts in this area (e.g. Fiske and Taylor, 1991) suggest possible reasons that psychologists might be interested in people's ideas about psychological functioning. These same points also help to formulate a conceptual rationale for an implicit psychology of emotion.

The first and probably most trivial reason for investigating people's ideas about emotion is that they can be seen as phenomena that are interesting in their own right (e.g. Fiske and Taylor, 1991, p. 1). Talking and thinking about emotions are things that people do in their everyday lives and as such are apparently worthy of our psychological attention. Few committed researchers would be ready to draw a line under their analysis at this stage, however. Rather, most would want to know what significance talking and thinking about emotion in particular ways has for emotional phenomena in general. The question then becomes: how does emotion representation fit in with the rest of emotional reality?

The two traditional answers to this question were provided by the originator of attribution theory, Heider (1958), who argued as follows:

> the study of common-sense psychology is of value for the scientific under-
> standing of interpersonal relations in two ways. First, since common-sense
> psychology guides our behaviour toward other people, it is an essential part of
> the phenomena in which we are interested . . . If a person believes that the lines
> on his palm foretell his future, this belief must be taken into account in
> explaining certain of his expectations and actions. Second, the study of
> common-sense psychology may be of value because of the truths it contains.
>
> (p. 5)

According to Heider then, common-sense psychology contains a working *knowledge* of scientific psychological principles, and also helps to shape perceived meanings of actions and events, ultimately leading to changed behaviour. In the first *descriptive* relationship, ideas about psychological functioning are directly informative about psychological principles, and in the second *interpretational* relationship reactions to events are mediated by the way in which the events are understood. It is worth considering these two possible relationships, between what people say or think and what people do, in some detail with specific reference to the topic of emotion.

Descriptive relations

According to common sense, individuals are the best authorities about the content of their own personal experience. Similarly, many psychological researchers (e.g. Davitz, 1970; Shaver *et al.*, 1987) have assumed that people's ideas about emotion reflect emotional reality more or less accurately, and that by studying emotion conceptions we can get indirect but still valuable information about the structure of emotion itself. This postulated accuracy-mapping link between emotion representation and emotion experience has also been concretely realized in the research practice of measuring emotion in terms of self-ratings (representations of emotion), then defining the phenomenon operationally using these same measurements, as if they somehow indexed the essence of the emotional experience itself. If people represent emotional reality accurately, then it makes sense to make use of their representations when trying to get at the underlying phenomenon, but if their representations are distorted in any way, then psychologists relying on self-reports are in danger of developing theories based on emotional ideology instead of emotional reality.

Belief in the general descriptive accuracy of emotion representations has been defended in a number of ways, which I shall now consider in turn:

1 *Knowledge based on individual experience* A common justification for the argument that emotion descriptions are accurate depends on the idea that people's everyday experience with their own and other people's emotions has provided them with a useful working understanding of how and why the relevant phenomena actually occur (e.g. Kelley, 1992). According to this account, we learn about emotions by observing our own and other people's reactions, and by drawing generalized inferences from the information that we pick up over the course of development. Assuming that our sample of evidence is representative, and our reasoning processes are unbiased, emotion representations should be self-correcting in this view, so that most people would ultimately attain substantially valid knowledge about emotion.

Despite its apparent defence of the general accuracy of descriptions and explanations, the main focus of much social cognition research has been on detailing the ways that reasoning processes can go wrong as a consequence of faulty sampling of data or misapplication of inferential rules (e.g. Nisbett and Ross, 1980; Nisbett and Wilson, 1977), and the evidence produced by this approach clearly casts general doubt on any claim that *all* emotion knowledge is valid. However, most theorists in this area contend that errors and biases in social reasoning are the product of using heuristics and sampling procedures that produce correct conclusions in normal circumstances (e.g. Nisbett and Ross, 1980), so it would be equally misguided to argue that all emotion knowledge was false. In short, social cognition research tends to work on the assumption that people usually make relatively accurate social inferences but can be led astray on certain predictable occasions, such as when cognitive processing capacity limitations are exceeded (e.g. Fiske and Taylor, 1991; Hamilton and Trolier, 1986) or when salient objects or events draw attention away from the true causes of social phenomena (e.g. Taylor and Fiske, 1978).

One of the primary tasks faced by social perceivers, according to the social cognition approach, is to reduce the overabundance of available data input to manageable proportions. In this view, it is necessary to filter out irrelevant and distracting information in order to respond adaptively to what is genuinely important. With experience, people learn to what they should pay attention and what they ought to ignore. Thus, the schemas that develop to structure incoming data may become accommodated to the real co-occurrences of features in the psychological and social environment (Rosch, 1978). For example, the everyday use of the emotion term 'anger' may reflect the fact that certain predictable features of the psychological episode picked out by the word tend to go together in everyday social life, and the relevant concept has become attuned to these reality constraints (e.g. Shaver *et al.*, 1987).

The general problem with this perspective on the accuracy issue is its assumption that the categories that people use in everyday life have developed for purely descriptive purposes. In reality, categorization can serve a variety of functions apart from neutral sense-making (e.g. Billig, 1987; Potter and Wetherell, 1987). For example, people may deploy categories to defend a valued social identity (e.g. Tajfel and Wilkes, 1963), to demean someone else's actions, to excuse behaviour, or for many other socially motivated reasons. With respect to emotional categorization, we may take on emotion roles in order to disown responsibility for our actions (Averill, 1980), or may attribute emotion to others in order to imply that their conclusions are irrational and not worthy of serious consideration (e.g. Shields and MacDowell, 1987). To the extent that our systems of accounting are attuned to ends other than objective description, there is little reason to suppose that they have developed solely to reflect psychological reality in any direct or simple way.

The argument that the terms of our psychological discourse are not necessarily intended to render objectively the scientific facts about social reality becomes even clearer when considering the attributional approach to social cognition (e.g. Kelley, 1967). One of the most basic presuppositions made by subscribers to attribution theory is that common sense on one hand, and psychology on the other, are enterprises which essentially share the same topic area and purpose. The task of laypeople in their everyday lives, according to this view, is to make rational sense of the objective psychological facts presented to them. In order to do this they make observations and conduct experiments so as to develop viable models of the way that the social world works.

Of course, this caricature oversimplifies the actual content and function of common sense (as well as those of psychology). The first problem is that laypeople are not usually concerned with supposed scientific ideals of accuracy and the development of general theories of behaviour in their everyday dealings with the social world. Instead, the typical goal of reasoning is to solve a specific practical problem. Because of this, the 'naive' social perceiver tends to focus on concrete information that relates directly to the problem at hand (e.g. Read, 1983). The success of such reasoning can only be assessed by reference to the particular circumstances at the time in the context of the problem-solver's concerns and interests. Application of statistical canons of validity to such a process (e.g. Nisbett and Ross, 1980) seems therefore to miss the point in an essential way. The layperson is a pragmatist, not a realist (White, 1984). Thus, the traditionally conceived scientific goals of prediction and control do not wholly determine social cognitive activity. (A case might also be made for a pragmatist view of science itself, in which prediction and control as such rarely concern the psychologist either, but that is not the current issue at stake: the attributional view of common sense, at any rate, is based on a simple representational view of how science operates.)

More crucially from the present point of view, explanations and categorizations are manufactured for *conversational* ends (e.g. Hilton, 1990) and are addressed to specific audiences rather than simply reading off the facts about a supposedly independent psychological reality (Edwards and Potter, 1993). When we account for our own behaviour or someone else's in terms of emotion, for example, we are often making a specific kind of claim about the social situation in specific response to, or anticipation of, someone else's counterclaim. We are *formulating* social reality rather than engaging in a detached intrapsychic process of making sense of what is happening. Saying that someone is emotional, then, can be part of undermining or excusing, praising or blaming, instead of simply describing. If categorizing phenomena or accounting for them in terms of emotion is responsive to nonobjective demands such as these, then the knowledge distilled in these terms cannot be assumed to represent an accurate model of the phenomenon itself (whatever that might turn out to be). Indeed, criteria relating simply to accuracy are not the only criteria relevant to our evaluation of common-sense representation.

Having made the case against the general accuracy of emotion represent-ations, it is worth noting that there must be some *referential* grounding of the representational function for the pragmatics of language to work. Repre-senting emotions in particular ways could have no social effects unless the currency of the transaction were authorized against the gold standard of an accepted independent reality. For example, when I represent someone else as angry in order to undermine the rational basis of their argument, this under-mining would be unsuccessful without the agreement of participants in the encounter that anger really is something that might interfere with reason. In other words, this pragmatic use of language depends on anger being an accepted social object with certain specific characteristics. Otherwise my representation would not perform its intended undermining effect at all.

In conclusion, a general problem with the social cognition approach is that it focuses on the near-intractable issue of accuracy of representation without addressing the nature of the actual concepts used by 'naive psychologists'. It is assumed that there is an objective set of dispositions and internal entities that serve as the causes of behaviour, to which the professional psychologist has access (with the aid of statistics and experimental techniques), but not the person on the street. According to this view, laypeople talk in the right kind of terms but do not always apply them correctly to social reality. It is also worth reconsidering the basis for the terms themselves.

2 *Knowledge based on cultural experience* Instead of implying that our personal interactions with social and physical reality yield valid and accurate knowl-edge about the psychological world, many theorists have argued from a more historical point of view that cultural rather than individual experience leads to general descriptive accuracy (cf. Harré and Secord, 1972). According to this account, ordinary language provides a refined and sophisticated represent-ational system which has evolved in order to provide exactly the kinds of categories that are of service to human beings in their everyday task of explaining and interpreting the social world. Thus, when people employ the emotion representations contained in the common language, they are buying into a valuable currency of descriptive distinctions.

It is certainly true that people do not develop their own personalized theories of behaviour *de novo*, as the social cognition approach sometimes seems to imply. Rather, they must necessarily subscribe to a pre-existing set of cultural repertoires for representing action. However, cultural representations, like personal representations, have not evolved in response to purely adaptive forces that ensure an optimization of descriptive power. Instead, ideological considerations impact on the development of psychological category systems.

For example, many systems of representation have developed in order to support existing power relations (e.g. Foucault, 1977), and indeed may be used explicitly as mystificatory rather than clarifying devices. For example, strong and controversial statements of opinion by women may be dismissed by men in authority as mere expressions of emotionality, and as such not worthy of serious consideration (cf. Shields and MacDowell, 1987). Similarly, increasing demands made on workers may result in a series of negative reactions including illness, emotion, and rebellion, but attention is diverted from these real problems of exploitation by the cultural construction of the quasi-medical category of 'stress', which is conceived as something that can be dealt with at a personal rather than organizational level (cf. Pollock, 1988). Clearly, these kinds of ideological representations have not evolved neutrally to reflect what is going on, but have been developed specifically to defend certain vested interests. Unfortunately, we often mistake cultural prejudices for empirical facts in our unselfconscious dealings with the world and assume that we are working from objective premises even when we are not. Trapped as we are within the thought paradigm of the culture that surrounds us, the history of linguistic practices gets obscured and the lattice of interpretations contained in the common language tends to become rationally invisible (cf. Garfinkel, 1967; Shotter, 1993). The world of cultural emotion representations comes to be second nature for us.

3 *Knowledge based on evolutionary experience* A final defence of the accuracy of emotion representations is based on evolutionary arguments about the adaptive structure of the mind, and its attunement to the content of the environment. According to this position, over the history of the human species our mental apparatus has developed an internal representational system that already provides all the meaningful categories for interpreting emotional experience, and language simply reads off these presupplied internal connections.

This account contains a number of implicit assumptions about the constitution of emotional representation and emotional reality which are worth unpicking. First, in order for any pre-wired category system to be adaptive, it must correspond to a species-wide and relatively permanent set of phenomena. In other words, emotions themselves must be universal or else there would be little evolutionary advantage in representing them in a fixed way. In fact, although psychologists have tended to focus on a small range of emotions that do seem to be similar across different cultures, there are also many emotions that are experienced in certain cultures and at certain historical periods but not others (e.g. Harré, 1986; Lutz, 1988). Furthermore, even the so-called primary emotions (e.g. Ekman, 1994) are manifested differently in different societal contexts. Under these circumstances, it appears unlikely that a completely programmed representational system would be flexible enough to cope with the vicissitudes of all emotional life across all relevant adaptational situations.

The second assumption of the biological determinist view is that people *represent* emotions in the same ways universally. However, anthropological evidence suggests to the contrary that there are wide differences in the use of emotion words across cultures, with some cultures not even possessing a category that corresponds to emotion at all (e.g. Lutz, 1982; Rosaldo, 1984). Of course, this evidence does not necessarily bear directly on underlying mental structures but does at least show that if these representations exist, language does not reflect them in any simple way.

In offering these arguments against a rigid evolutionary account of emotion description, I do not wish to be read as claiming that nothing about emotional experience or its representation is shaped by biological factors. Naturally it is. However, I feel that emotion has too often been seen in overdeterministic terms, and it is worth redressing this emphasis. At any rate, biology does not constrain emotional phenomena to a sufficient extent that it is legitimate to use evolutionary theory as a comprehensive justification for the accuracy of emotion descriptions.

In this section, I have tried to show that the idea that emotion descriptions accurately represent emotional reality is oversimplistic. One of the most serious problems with the accuracy position is that it is difficult to separate out a pure descriptive function from all the other possible uses of emotion terms within language (e.g. Austin, 1962), so that we cannot say to what extent the cultural or individual evolution of emotional category systems has been shaped by realistic, ideological, or rhetorical forces. Emotional language serves to praise, blame, appeal for help, and so on. For this reason, trying to distil the descriptive essence of emotion representations seems to miss the point in an important way. Saying that I am angry, for example, is not always intended to provide the listener with accurate information about my internal symptoms, nor even about my likely future actions, but rather is often meant to stake a claim for personal justice (Bedford, 1957).

Of course, none of this should be taken to imply that what people have to say concerning emotions has nothing to do with what emotion is actually about. It is just that when people formulate emotional representations even in a supposedly neutral laboratory context, they are always addressing a specific intended audience and tailoring their representations to suit the real or imagined communicative context. There are a variety of ways of conceptualizing emotion available to most competent users of the language and not all of them can be seen as appropriate to all circumstances. Rather, each is a partial account that is workable within specified settings. Although it is possible that there is a common core to the range of representational repertoires potentially applicable to emotion, it is well worth examining their diversity and flexible functionality as it operates in everyday situations, rather than trying to divide through by any differences in order to get to the lowest common denominator of some putative abstract emotional grammar.

Previous research into descriptive relations between emotion representations and emotional reality often works from the common-sense assumption that emotions are simple internal objects which may be denoted simply by focusing attention in the correct direction. In fact, as argued above, emotions are complicated communicative acts with flexible internal structure, and as such they cannot be so easily pinned down and defined by individual perceivers. Furthermore, to the extent that the communicative content of emotions can be conveyed using emotional language, it may turn out that the relevant representations are in some circumstances better seen as part of the phenomenon itself, rather than as an entirely separable retrospective commentary on emotional experience.

Interpretational relations

Even if we accept that people's everyday representations of emotion are not necessarily accurate in the scientific sense, it is still possible to argue that the fact that they represent emotion in a certain way has other consequences for the way that they act. According to this *belief assumption*, talk about emotion is worth investigating because it reflects implicit theories about emotion, which, regardless of their correspondence with reality, may be of relevance to the extent that they are put into practice in interpreting and dealing with the individual's own or other people's emotions.

For example, people depend on an implicit theory of emotion when constructing excuses designed to allay someone else's anger at their misconduct. If you explain your failure to meet an obligation in terms of external, uncontrollable, and unintentional factors then you are considered less culpable than otherwise (Weiner *et al.*, 1987). In other words, people try to control other people's anger by presenting the causes of their actions in accordance with their beliefs about how this emotion works. Whether or not their implicit theories are correct is a separate question to that of how these theories influence action (and emotion).

Similarly, people might depend on their theories about emotion in their deliberate attempts to control their own feelings (e.g. Parrott, 1993). For example, the idea that emotional problems at work may be due to 'stress' is likely to lead to distinctive ways of dealing with these problems, such as taking a holiday, or going to a stress-management clinic. To give another illustration, Maori warriors apparently believe that the fear-like emotion experienced before a battle is actually caused by the anger of ancestral spirits, and consequently they ritually seek recourse to the supernatural power supposedly possessed by the genitalia of high-born women in order to dissipate such feelings (Smith, 1981). Thus, cultural as well as individual beliefs about emotions clearly have implications for the way that people deal with them. If someone believes that emotions are caused by spirit possession, say, their regulation strategies are likely to be different to those that they would use if they believed that emotions arose from concrete situational conflicts or pressures.

The connection between emotion representations and emotion management strategies may turn out to be even closer than implied by these examples. Indeed some studies have suggested that self-regulatory aspects are part of the meaning of many emotion terms (e.g. Mayer and Gaschke, 1988; Mayer *et al.*, 1991; Shaver *et al.*, 1987) rather than indirect consequences of holding certain beliefs about emotion.

If the representational account of idea–reality relations is correct then investigating representations of emotions might help to explain how emotions are interpreted and managed in ourselves and in others. However, assuming that a range of interpretative options are available, there still remains the practical problem of determining which particular form of representation will be applied in any given case. For example, the representations used by participants when asked to categorize, define, or compare emotional meanings in experiments do not necessarily correspond to those that they might use spontaneously in actual ongoing social situations. The former representations might be specifically constructed for the purpose of performing abstract tasks rather than ready-made solutions to everyday problems of emotional interpretation. If this conclusion is correct, then the results from the studies of emotional meanings reviewed earlier in this chapter may be practically irrelevant to questions concerning how emotional reality is normally understood by people. On the other hand, it is certainly possible that there is some degree of commonality between the ways that emotions are represented in experimental studies and the ways that they are interpreted in everyday life.

A potential though tentative resolution of these interpretative alternatives is to draw a distinction between selfconscious explicit uses of emotion representations and spontaneous and implicit representational phenomena (cf. Fazio, 1990). The former cases are more likely to be clarified by studying the articulated emotion representations contained in verbal accounts than the latter. For example, in certain special circumstances, it is possible that people make reference to verbalizable theories of how emotion works in order to draw reasoned conclusions about what to do or how to interpret what is going on. The purest case of such a scenario may be found in the laboratory when people are confronted with ambiguous situations and have to improvise an appropriate response. For example, hearing your supposed heart rate increase while a slide of a more or less attractive semi-clothed person is displayed may cause you explicitly to rethink your characterization of how you feel about this picture (Valins, 1966), based on the common accessible belief about emotion that it is typically characterized by bodily change of this kind. Deciding in this way that a particular state of affairs has had emotional effects may in turn bring into play certain distinctive and deliberate strategies of information search and may result to some extent in the acting out of the relevant emotional script. Clearly, there are also occasions in everyday life outside the laboratory when an event is categorized as emotion, either in ourselves or in other people, after a protracted and verbalizable attempt to make sense of a problematic or ambiguous situation (e.g. Schachter and Singer, 1962), and this categorization in turn has implications for behaviour. If it is assumed that the representations used in such categorization processes have a consistent structure for different people and in different situations, then investigation of this structure may be revealing about the interpretational process. In this book, I have argued that people tend to characterize emotions in terms of four factors, and it may be that this explicit structure has a relatively wide degree of generality at least within our culture (e.g. Parkinson, 1983; Roseman *et al.*, 1994). Thus, information relating to any of these factors may lead to emotional interpretation when deliberative processing is in operation (cf. Petty and Cacioppo, 1986).

Of course, not all of our behavioural reactions to emotion in ourselves or in others are mediated by consciously realized representational processes of this kind. In many circumstances our negotiations through the terrain of emotional reality depend on *tacit* rather than explicit representational processes (cf. Polanyi, 1958): we know *how* to deal with certain emotional situations without also knowing *that* we should use a particular strategy or interpretation, and would find it hard to articulate this implicit understanding in words or along rating scales. Thus, it also seems possible that there are emotion representations that influence action in spontaneous, automatic, and unselfconscious ways.

Another example of how emotion representations might influence judgement and behaviour without the mediation of explicit deliberation is suggested by Bower's (1981) semantic network theory. According to this model, emotionally relevant information may activate emotion nodes in memory and this activation may then spread to associated nodes leading to specific affect-congruence effects on judgement and behaviour. Clearly, much of this process must be assumed to go on below the level of awareness.

Both these cases present problems for traditional studies of emotion representation because the particular representational processes specified seem inaccessible to conventional knowledge-elicitation procedures that rely on explicit judgement tasks. The kind of unconscious emotion representation that automatically influences emotional interpretation and action seems unlikely to surface in our verbal descriptive attempts, and thus requires other techniques of investigation (e.g. Conway and Bekerian, 1987).

I have argued above that emotion representations of various kinds exist at different levels. For example, emotional accounts presented in talk, or emotional comparisons performed in the laboratory, have no necessary relation to any putative silently operating cognitive systems of emotional information registration. It is an open question how important for the theory of emotion each of these kinds of representation is, but my own prejudices lead me to focus on emotion as it is represented in ordinary conversation and explore the impact of such representations on emotional life as it is actually conducted interpersonally.

Investigators endorsing an interpretational rather than a descriptive relation between ideas and realities of emotion treat emotion representations as a *topic* instead of simply a *resource* for psychological theory. This move seems like a step in the right direction as long as the diversity and flexibility of available representational resources is acknowledged. Representing experience emotionally clearly makes some kind of difference, and this difference becomes even more important when it is acknowledged that other people respond to one's formulation of emotional reality. In other words, what people say about emotion contributes directly to the evolving interpersonal representation of the social situation.

Of course, when people deploy emotion representations in everyday life, they do not do so only in order to make sense of what is going on, but also to achieve other pragmatic communicational ends. Thus, the impact of emotion representations on actual interactions is not simply an interpretational one but also depends on more direct effects of these speech acts (cf. Austin, 1962). For example, if I tell someone that I am in love with them, then their response will not simply depend on an inference about my current state of mind, but also on the implied intent of making such a representation to this person at that moment, and the obligations and duties such a declaration inevitably brings about (cf. Averill, 1985). Indeed, the act of making such a declaration with a certain level of sincerity and at the appropriate stage of an ongoing relationship, accompanied by the relevant nonverbal signals and a suitable degree of bodily involvement would, according to the present perspective, count as an example of emotion in itself. Added complexities of the representation–reality connection implied by examples such as this are discussed further in the next section.

Constitutive relations

A third way in which emotion representation might be related to psychological reality, specifically emotional reality, is constitutively. A constitutive relation obtains between emotion representation and reality when application of the representation contributes to the causation of the emotion itself. A completely constitutive relation would imply that emotions are nothing but emotion representations, and that emotions would not exist if we did not believe in them or have words for them (e.g. Gergen, 1987). Few theorists would want to endorse such an extreme claim as this. However, it does seem plausible that representations of emotion go some way towards shaping the course of emotional episodes.

Impact of real-time representation on emotion

One way in which representations might help to constitute emotions becomes apparent when the individualistic interpretational model discussed in the previous section is extended to incorporate dynamic interpersonal factors. If we assume that someone, for whatever reason, comes to characterize themselves or someone else in emotional terms, this fact is likely to make certain differences to the way that this person interprets the social situation which in turn may influence their action in particular, potentially emotional ways. More importantly, however, if the representation has overt consequences either on nonverbal expression or on the person's verbal self-characterizations, these will tend to influence other people's interpretations of the encounter, to the extent that they pick up the relevant emotional signals. In short, interactants often react to each other's verbal or nonverbal representations of emotional state, whether these representations are reflexively or interpersonally directed.

One of the possible consequences of such an interactive process is that public emotional representations may lead to a corresponding emotional reality. For example, if I represent myself as being attracted to the person with whom I am conversing, their response to my emotional representation, to the extent that it is encouraging, may itself actually be emotionally attractive to me. This analysis assumes a simple back-and-forth, turn-taking form of conversation. If the representation is conveyed nonverbally rather than verbally, then the other person's reaction may be more direct and immediate, because our nonverbal communications are more likely to be coordinated on-line continuously during interaction (e.g. Bernieri *et al.*, 1988). Under these circumstances, the real-time development of mutually interlocking emotion representations may become practically synchronous and identical with the generation of the emotions themselves. Indeed, to the extent that emotions can be seen as communicative entities addressed to specific audiences anyway, the distinction between the process of emotion representation and the emotional process itself becomes increasingly harder to draw in unfolding real-life situations.

According to this interactional account, presenting oneself as emotional to someone else may in certain circumstances be practically equivalent to getting emotional. However, this does not imply that the *only* way that emotion arises during interpersonal encounter is as a consequence of the activation of emotional representations, even if the emotion process is always a self-presentational phenomenon. To clarify this point, it is worth drawing a distinction between various possible sequences of interpersonal interaction which might conceivably result in emotion.

First, the primary and prototypical form of emotional episode occurs when ongoing interpersonal dynamics require a realignment of an interactant's relative identity position. For example, a person may not be getting a fair share of attention in a developing group conversation and may send out nonverbal signals to this effect. The causes of the emotional self-presentation in such a situation reflect the emerging communicative agenda of the interaction and do not correspond to any particular conscious intention on the part of any of the actors caught up in it. This is exactly why the emotion is often seen as coming over the person rather than being deliberately initiated. Furthermore, reflexive awareness of being emotional is not a necessary feature of such scenarios although it may arise at some point during the interaction, for example, when the other person draws attention to one's apparent expressive behaviour. If reflexive awareness of emotion occurs, the emotional self-characterization may have effects on the control of the self-presentation in some way (e.g. deliberate suppression or intensification of the emotion; Parrott, 1993). In some cases, however, it is possible to perform the complete act of emotional self-presentation without any knowledge that one is acting emotionally.

In specific contrast to this kind of 'bottom-up' emotion process, a second possible case of emotion causation occurs when a person deliberately adopts an emotional position in order to achieve the associated identity realignment. For example, you may get angry in order to get your own way in situations of conflict. In such a performance, the actor is using cultural knowledge about the effects that emotion has on other people to develop a manipulative strategy of interpersonal influence. The emotion is imposed on the encounter explicitly and in a 'top-down' manner. Rather than acting out the emotional syndrome of response, similar though possibly weaker effects may be obtained simply by overtly characterizing oneself in emotional terms. The power of such an explicit delivery of an emotional representation probably depends on how sincere the avowal is taken to be, which in turn may relate to the presence of relevant nonverbal accompaniments. Clearly, in this last case, the deployment of an emotion representation may contribute towards the causation of a selfconscious emotion. Furthermore, to the extent that the actor gets involved in the self-presentation, the action may come to seem reflexively more like a passion as it develops over time (e.g. Sarbin, 1986).

Somewhere in between these two extreme formulations are a range of situations in which interactants consider the possibility that they are getting emotional and test out this interpretation in their actions and expressions (cf. Barefoot and Straub, 1971). Trying out emotional positions for size in this way may also result in emotional consequences to the extent that they fit into the real-time development of the relationship with the other person in the encounter. For example, you may wonder whether you are emotionally attracted to the person with whom you are conversing and may tentatively attempt to attain eye contact. If the interpersonal sequence unfolds in accordance with your original hypothesis then corresponding emotional consequences may ultimately ensue.

In real-life interactions, emotions probably arise from a mixture of these processes (and others). For example, there are fringe cases between deliberate adoption of an emotion role and spontaneously asserting an identity, and reflexive awareness of emotion may come and go over the development of an encounter. The line between taking on an emotion representation and presenting one's identity in a particular emotional way is a difficult one to draw in everyday social interaction.

The difference between the standard emotional process and the representationally constituted one, then, is that the latter involves representations of emotion rather than representations of relative identity positions, but in many actual cases both representational processes may occur in tandem or in sequence. There may be points during an interaction when we realize that we are emotional and do nothing to control it, just as there may be moments when we are completely unaware that we are acting emotionally, or when we deliberately try to make ourselves more emotional. Each of these moments may lead quite directly to any of the others.

Pragmatic effects of emotional language

When we look at psychological reality in the interpersonal sphere, rather than considering the individual functioning of a single person, the separation between words and other relevant phenomena also breaks down. People interact with each other through the medium of language (among other things) and the psychological phenomena that they display are interpenetrated with words. People characterize their performances to themselves and to others in talk, but also talk is more than this, and people do things apart from describing by using words. For example, they accuse, praise, blame, congratulate, insult, taunt, offer sympathy, welcome, criticize, approve, apologize, express attitudes, and so on. When people make these representations, they are not simply reporting on their own or other people's state of mind, but are performing actions (Austin, 1962; Bedford, 1957), as well as formulating and reformulating how the encounter is to be defined. Some of the actions performed by emotion words are emotional actions, just as some of the reformulations of reality that they achieve define the situation in an emotional way.

For example, the statement 'I love you' is rarely a simple description of a state of mind. Instead it implies a commitment to the other person and a kind of promise about your future treatment of the loved person (Averill, 1985). Of course, none of this negates the experiences that sometimes accompany such an expression of love. It is just that in our Western society such feelings are overvalued and emphasized. Furthermore, if a romantic partner were to ask you whether you loved them, then your answer would probably not depend on how you were feeling at that second. Your mind might, for example, be totally preoccupied by a toothache, or the warmth of the bathwater, and no definite internal symptoms of love available to your awareness. In this case, you would still be unlikely to say 'No, I need to see the dentist', or 'Yes, but it might be just the temperature of the water'.

When we use emotion words reflexively in ongoing interactions, this is not simply a process of self-description but also a social act with intended effects on its recipient. Sincerity of the avowal is not the same thing as accuracy of a report. Rather, to say 'I am angry with you', for example, means claiming the right to respond with force to something judged as an insult. Thus, the use of emotion words may in certain circumstances be seen as part of what it means to be emotional, rather than simply the application of detachable labels to underlying experiential states.

Effects of emotion representations on social and cultural reality

A final indirect way in which emotion representations may contribute to the causation of emotions depends on the impact of accepted ideas about emotion on the construction of the social environment. In general, the way that we organize our relationships with others (formally and informally) is influenced by emotional representations, and this organization can in turn bring emotional realities into line with these representations. Conventional rules about appropriate emotional conduct lead us to call ourselves and others to account should these rules be broken, suggesting that in normal circumstances we unselfconsciously go with the grain and texture of shared definitions of emotional situations. Emotional representations are not abstract structures but devices that are implemented in manufacturing a common formulation of what goes on in our dealings with others.

Shared ideas about how emotion works help to constitute explicit practices that regulate emotions in institutional settings. For example, service industries often prescribe guidelines for emotional conduct based on the accepted common sense of emotion. To the extent that such guidelines are wholeheartedly internalized by employees, they may come to shape the articulation of actual emotional performances.

Representations of emotion also help to shape emotional reality in a related but more concrete way. The architectural, temporal, and social arrangement of the institutional environment is often a reification of ideas about how people normally do, or normally should, interact with each other, including how emotions ought to be expressed, by whom, and to whom. For example, appropriate awe is invoked in subjects facing their monarch by constructing palaces on an epic scale, and ensuring that any contact takes place in a setting that physically reinforces status differentials. The queen sits high on her throne in all her finery while her inferiors must look up at her from a distance. Similar environmental arrangements and stage-setting encourage appropriate respect for deities and so on.

Summary

The usual presupposition of research into emotion representations is that the emotion word is a detachable label for an individual experience or an organized syndrome of sequenced reactions. But emotion representations can also enter directly into the constitution of an episode as an emotional one, and it is not always possible simply to prise apart the idea and the reality. What we say about our emotions can help to *produce* emotions in ourselves and in others, and, more crucially, can define the situation as an emotional one in the first place. Getting angry, for example, is about finding insult in another's actions, and to impose such a narrative structure on an interaction (with the appropriate level of involved identification with the roles that the narrative prescribes) can be seen in some circumstances as exactly the same thing as getting angry. However, there are also other ways of getting angry which do not depend on such explicit use of emotion representations.

A fundamental problem with the idea that representations *reflect* emotional experience is that representations do not simply function as ontologically neutral descriptions but are also ways of reformulating social reality, and of making emotional identity claims. Representation and reality are not in a pure correspondence relationship, because representations do things apart from depicting. For example, emotion representations do not merely map an independent psychological reality but also help to construct that reality. Furthermore, when people represent emotions in real-life situations, they are not simply attempting to give a descriptive rendering of what has happened or is happening, but making representations to someone else with particular purposes and intentions. The abstract task of characterizing emotional meaning is alien to the realm of every-day social life, and it is not clear that the results of such a decontextualized representational process have any necessary relevance to such a world.

To summarize the conclusions of this section, emotion representations can be seen as descriptive, interpretative, as well as constitutive of emotion itself, and each of these possible functions overlaps to some extent with the others, and none operates in an uncontaminated way in any conceivable real-life circumstance. Emotion representations describe but never only describe, and do not always describe accurately. Emotion representations interpret but always for some prag-matic purpose in addition to simple characterization of the world. Furthermore, there is not just one all-purpose set of emotion representations available to individuals but a variety of flexible and interlocking repertoires for making sense of, or imposing meaning on, emotional situations of different kinds. Finally, emotion representations can in some circumstances contribute to the constitution of emotion episodes, but that does not mean that all emotions are nothing but emotion representations (Greenwood, 1994), simply that their deployment is sometimes part of the establishment of a particular identity position with respect to an intended audience.

LIMITATIONS OF RESEARCH INTO EMOTION REPRESENTATIONS

To close this chapter, I want to draw together some of its basic themes into four basic criticisms about the assumptions of research into emotion representations. My aim is to suggest some ways to move on rather than to close off a potentially fruitful field of enquiry.

1 *Simplicity of representation* Studies of emotion representation tend to adopt an assumption that people's ideas about emotion locate them along simply speci-fiable dimensions, or categorize them as collections of basic attributes. For example, Russell's influential view of affect has been taken to imply that emotional meaning is exhausted by consideration of two basic dimensions of pleasantness and activation. I believe that people's emotional representations are considerably more intricate and involved (as well as more flexible) than such an analysis seems to imply, and future investigations should employ methods that attempt to do more justice to the sophistication of people's implicit theories of emotion, as they are employed in everyday social inter-action (e.g. Parkinson, 1990; 1991; Parkinson and Lea, 1991).

2 *Representation for its own sake* Although studies in this area are specifically directed at ideas about emotions, the conclusions drawn from them tend to concern individual emotional experience. It is assumed, for example, that the fact that people rate different emotional experiences in terms of distinctive

patterns of cognitive appraisal suggests that these appraisal patterns determine the quality of emotional experience on-line during a real-time encounter. In short, the representations of emotion that people provide in these experiments are taken to be accurate, and investigation of these representations is used as a shortcut for looking at individual emotional experience.

In my view, representations of emotion are not only important because they might be true, but also because they help us to understand how emotional phenomena are conceptualized and dealt with at an institutional and cultural level. For example, ideas about appropriate emotional display and experience are explicitly formulated in the training programmes for certain service occupations (Hochschild, 1983).

Furthermore, to the extent that emotions may be partially constituted by representational processes, investigating emotion representations is already in some sense investigating emotional reality and there is correspondingly less need to look beyond for any underlying or transcendent phenomenon.

3 *Emotional grammar* An additional and related point concerns the traditional supposition that there is a single and integrated mental system for representing emotion in all possible circumstances. In contrast, I believe that a variety of representational repertoires are provided in the currency of the surrounding culture, to be deployed as and when appropriate. According to this view, there is no deep structure to the grammar of emotion, just an untidy arrangement of available formulations (cf. Potter and Wetherell, 1987).

4 *Purity of the descriptive function* As Austin (1962) has pointed out, words always do things in addition to describing reality. Emotional talk in real-world contexts is never only a characterization of state of mind, but is often also an explicit move in an ongoing dialogue, in defence of a certain identity claim. Unless we pay attention to the plurality of uses of emotion representations in everyday interpersonal situations, we can never hope to get to the heart of ideas or realities of emotion.

In conclusion, rather than trying to examine relationships between emotion representations on the one hand and emotions themselves on the other, investigators should refocus on the issue of how emotion representations fit in with the rest of emotional reality. Only then will it be possible to start building a realistic theory of the intricacy and flexibility of emotional life at large. In this chapter, I have suggested that the theoretical separation of ideas and realities of emotion often becomes unworkable in practice, and that emotions, in some sense at least, are always in fact representations made by someone to someone else. This conclusion implies a reformulation of both emotion and representation which treats both as communications made in real-time real-life situations rather than abstract and static intrapsychic entities. In the final chapter, I will try to develop this reformulation, and make suggestions about an integrative approach to emotional conduct and communication.

10 Reconceptualizing emotion

OVERVIEW

In this final chapter, I attempt to weave together the strands of the argument teased out in the book so far, and illustrate how the patterned individual responses of emotion might mesh with the interpersonal, institutional, and cultural worlds. More specifically, I want to summarize and develop the theory that getting emotional involves making identity claims that are physically communicated via the various channels of individual emotional expression with the socially appropriate level of bodily involvement. Because emotions are typically addressed to an intended audience, their true home is within the functional context of an ongoing interpersonal encounter. Such a setting in turn partly derives its structure and content from institutional and cultural forces, but its formulation always remains open to some degree of on-line renegotiation by interactants. Seeing emotions as dynamic interpersonal episodes rather than private momentary reactions opens up a wider view of the topic area and facilitates a refreshed perspective on some familiar issues in the field.

The structure of the present chapter is as follows: first, in order to clear the way for an interpersonal analysis, I will call into question many of the reasons that psychologists as well as people in general tend to conceive of emotion as an essentially private phenomenon. Second, I shall explicitly present the basic principles of the general communicative approach to which I have alluded elsewhere in this book. Third, I will show how an interpersonal reconceptualization of emotion helps to deal with some of the perennial issues that continue to occupy current psychological research into emotion. Finally, I will consider some of the potential limitations of my approach before summarizing the main conclusions of the book. In short, this chapter reviews the general theoretical implications of a communicative approach to emotion by contrast with the traditional intrapsychic account, and tries to present an overarching framework for understanding the relevant phenomena in their social and societal context.

OLD AND NEW IDEAS OF EMOTION

A recurrent theme of this book has been that common-sense as well as psychological understanding of emotion and emotions has been constrained by the intuitively convincing idea that we are dealing with something that is essentially a subjective and private mental state, and which can only be coaxed out into the light of the consensual world with the utmost care and attention. There are many philosophical as well as practical arguments against this basic position (e.g. Wittgenstein, 1953), but rarely has a workable alternative view been articulated. The task of this book in general, and this chapter in particular, is to push understanding a little further in the direction of such an analysis.

The problem with arguing against the individualist account is that it is so deeply entrenched in our spontaneous and familiar ways of speaking, and in our conventional cultural practices, that any alternative can seem inexpressible, nonsensical even (Shotter, 1993). In much of everyday conversation as well as more formal discourse, we take for granted the assumptions that we have 'minds' which provide an arena for private events such as emotions, and that our language serves to represent in a descriptive way what goes on inside and outside. Although it is hard for us to imagine how things could be otherwise, it is worth remembering that these presuppositions are in fact historically as well as culturally specific (e.g. Foucault, 1977; Geertz, 1984). Like any other set of principles they are adequate for certain local purposes but fail to capture the full range of possible realities that might otherwise be available to us.

In the present chapter, I want to do two things: first, to account for the tenacity of the popular intrapsychic view of emotion; and second, to show how an interpersonal and communicative reconceptualization helps to deal with some of the philosophical and practical problems presented by the more traditional approach.

CONSTRUCTION AND DECONSTRUCTION OF THE PRIVACY ASSUMPTION

Our metaphorical understanding of emotion often works from the basic idea that bodies and minds are receptacles for the relevant phenomena, which are conceived as objects, events, or forces occurring within either or both of these kinds of container (cf. Kövecses, 1990). Such a model underlies many common-sense and psychological claims about emotional reality, pushing interpretation implicitly in certain predefined directions, and providing a background of accepted knowledge against which 'findings' are evaluated for their apparent plausibility. These findings in turn reinforce the foundations of our belief in the validity of the original metaphor, thus reproducing its ideological content, and sustaining the cultural practices on which the metaphor depends. In this section, I want to make explicit some of our foundational ideas of emotion in order to see how well they can survive closer examination in full light of day.

Although many of the accepted assumptions about emotion are more or less interrelated in a loosely structured narrative, it is instructive to consider the different aspects of this account separately:

1 *Emotions are experienced internally* Often when we get emotional we also

experience symptoms that are felt as coming from inside the body. People say that they experience a rush of excitement, butterflies in their stomach, a sinking feeling, restlessness or non-specific pressure, and all kinds of other internal sensations in emotional situations. On the other hand, when people claim that they are not emotional (and not suffering from any illness), they less often mention pangs, thrills, or twinges that arise from within.

The common-sense association between internal events and emotions was partly what led James (1898) to the conclusion that bodily reactions constituted the very substance of emotional experience, and that without such changes, no emotion was possible. Others have suggested that although there are specific kinds of private feeling connected with emotion, they are not necessarily manifested in simple physical terms. At any rate, the idea that emotions are essentially *internal* events is a popular one in psychology as well as everyday conversation.

The main problem with seeing emotions as private objects is that there would be no way of consistently recognizing, knowing, or categorizing them if that is all that they really were. Publicly verifiable criteria are needed for establishing definitions of any kind of concept, even if its explicit referent is an internal one. Any introspectively directed naming ceremony designed to attach a label to something that is only ever experienced from within is incapable of yielding a reliable association between the word and whatever it signifies, so that we cannot know what we are really experiencing purely on the basis of private acquaintance (Wittgenstein, 1953; and see Chapter 1). This means that our use of emotional concepts must be based at least partly on external and consensually accessible considerations.

A second issue about emotion's supposedly close association with private events is that in fact, nonemotional states are also clearly correlated with certain internal feelings, such as the proprioceptive feedback that we pick up while walking, or the muscular experiences associated with physical exertion. Just about any kind of psychological activity has concomitant sensations and intrapsychic qualities, so why is it that emotion is usually seen as more entirely internal and private than, say, talking to oneself or tensing an unseen muscle? One of the answers seems to be that the symptoms experienced when intentionally performing any action arise as part of the consciously realized plan and thus are perfectly predictable and tend to pass unnoticed (cf. Leventhal, 1980; 1984). In contrast, sometimes when we get emotional the feelings seem to come over us out of the blue in a partly unexpected way, and therefore the experience is seen as having an internal origin and essence. Thus, the apparent passivity of emotion also contributes to the privacy doctrine.

2 *Emotions are experienced as happening to us* Coupled with the idea that emotions are experienced inside the body is the notion that the internal experiences arise almost of their own accord. If emotions are not only internal but also outside our direct control, then they must emanate from a very private place to which even our own consciousness does not always have access (e.g.

Freud, 1900). We often feel ourselves to be victims rather than originators of our emotion, suggesting that something vital must be going on in the darkest recesses of our internal machinery to produce such a compelling set of signals.

In specific opposition to the common-sense account, many authors have argued against the so-called 'myth of the passions' (Solomon, 1976), suggesting, for example, that we only *present* our emotional actions as unchosen in order to deny responsibility for them (Averill, 1980), or that we express emotional attitudes at different levels of bodily involvement and that the associated physical processes attain their own momentum in the course of this deliberately initiated process (Sarbin, 1986). In support of such arguments, it seems clear that emotions are sometimes consciously selected as intentional acts, such as when we want to convey the urgency of our concern to children in order to teach them that what they are doing is dangerous or otherwise wrong. However, there are also occasions when the original causes of emotion are really not personal decisions, but emergent social formulations of a shared situation. For instance, mutual attraction or antagonism may emerge spontaneously in the course of an interpersonal encounter. In these and similar cases, emotions can be passions but still not actually private and occult events. Emotions can feel uncontrolled because the developing situation demands an emotional stance towards it, rather than because the urges and desires underlying the phenomenon come from somewhere deep inside.

3 *Emotions are things that are felt* Another part of the privacy doctrine is the common idea that emotions are a kind of feeling. Since feelings are considered to be things that are clearly located in the body, emotions too must be internal events. The trouble here is that the verb 'to feel' is used in a number of different senses which tend to get conflated in discussion of emotion. Feeling happy is not necessarily analogous to feeling warm or feeling pain, feeling your way around, or having a feeling that something might be wrong, but it is often assumed that because we feel emotions, emotions are also feelings of a more specific kind. For example, the ambiguity of the common polite enquiry 'How are you feeling?' allows responses that relate to mood, emotion, illness, external temperature, general discomfort, and so on, thus confusing the boundaries around these conceptually separable kinds of phenomenon. Instead of assuming that emotions can be considered in similar terms to sensations, it is perhaps worth emphasizing a different common usage of the verb 'to feel', as a way of hedging the evidential basis for what one is saying. For example, if there are personal reasons rather than reasoned arguments for a suggestion that I want to offer in a social setting, I am more likely to say that 'I *feel* it would be better to do such and such' instead of claiming to *think*, or *believe* the same. Similar considerations apply to situations in which people say they *feel* rather than *are* emotional. You may feel angry about the way your friend found so little time to talk to you at a social gathering, say, but you are more likely to state your position as *being* angry about a situation when someone insults you in an unambiguous and public way. Thus, emotions might not always be seen

as feelings but sometimes as specific interpersonal stances that are taken rather than given. In these cases, at least, it seems difficult to see emotion as purely an internal entity.

4 *Emotions are about things that matter to us 'deeply'* A related set of metaphors about emotional reactions is that they cut us to the quick, touch us in a profound way, or affect us deeply. Such language reinforces the container metaphor and the idea that emotions occur in a private and well-hidden place. Here again, however, there are other ways of reading the fathomlessness of emotion. First, the 'depth' of a passion often refers simply to its intensity or vigour, neither of which make direct reference to the location of the phenomenon. A second related use of this metaphor relates to the depth of involvement, the *extent* to which what is happening matters to you, how much your position is a *heartfelt* one. Similarly, appraisal theory sees emotions as reactions to personally significant events. In contrast to the privacy view, then, it seems that if the thing that one is deeply involved in is an interpersonal role defined by the social structure of the situation then greater intensity of emotional involvement puts one further *outside* oneself rather than being something that comes from a place that is deeper down inside.

5 *Emotions are felt directly* Knowledge of our own emotions seems to be direct and unmediated. We are intimately acquainted with our own feelings, and know them as personally as it is possible to know anything, so it seems. As Descartes claimed (1649): 'They are so close to, and so entirely within our soul, that it is impossible for it to feel them without their being actually such as it feels them to be' (p. 343). Our apparent proximity to emotions makes it seem more likely that they might be found right at the core of our being, deep down in our hearts. Of course, there are other kinds of knowledge apart from emotional knowledge that we feel are apprehended directly. For example, we put ourselves in direct contact with objects that we are touching, and similarly pick up sights, sounds, and smells, often without feeling that there is any need for interpretation. It is only when put in an unfamiliar situation, or where the signals are weak, that there is any real doubt about what is out there. So too with emotion. Sometimes, our feelings are clear and well defined, at others they seem difficult to pin down. Even when we know what we are feeling with perfect clarity, however, this does not mean that we have direct internal access to the signals. Instead we might read off the emotional quality of an action or interaction from information that is specified in the dynamic aspects of the external situation (cf. Schachter, 1959), or from our own emerging movements within it (Stepper and Strack, 1993).

Although we assume that emotions are felt directly, much like localized pains and sensations, in fact it seems unlikely that we can apprehend emotional state directly on the basis of momentary feelings. This is because emotional concepts contain more than just affective information, and their application depends on complex unfolding relationships with other people or the wider social environment. If a certain kind of feeling suddenly appeared in the absence of any obvious situational context, then it would be unlikely that we would recognize this feeling as an example of embarrassment, envy, pride, or contempt immediately and on the spot. We need to place ourselves in a system of relationships in order for any of these self-definitions to make any sense (cf., Becker, 1953). Similarly, Wittgenstein (1953) contrasted the case of a complex emotion like grief to that of a simpler internal sensation like pain as follows:

> 'Grief' describes a pattern which recurs, with different variations, in the weave of our life. If a man's bodily expression of sorrow and joy alternated, say, with the ticking of a clock, here we should not have the characteristic formation of the pattern of sorrow or of the pattern of joy.
>
> 'For a second he felt violent pain.' – Why does it sound queer to say: 'For a second he felt deep grief'? Only because it so seldom happens?
>
> (p. 174)

In more general terms, Wittgenstein's examples seem to suggest that the meaningful content of many human emotions derives not from internal signals that are directly perceived, but from what is going on outside in the social world.

6 *Other people may be mistaken about our emotions* In contrast to our apparent intimate acquaintance with our own emotions, other people's recognition of our feelings often seems misguided and imperfect. We believe that no one else can ever know how a person really feels, deep down. Thus, once again, there seems to be something about emotion that is kept in a secret place inside the person experiencing it. Indeed, we have all been in situations where we have deliberately restrained the expression of a personal emotion so that others do not see it. These separations of experience from expression are perhaps the most compelling considerations supporting the privacy doctrine.

Of course, few people would claim that expression of emotion is *always* discrepant from its experience. In fact, some of the best examples of emotion seem to relate to expressing emotion with complete involvement. For instance, imagine pouring your heart out about a failed relationship or recent bereavement, or shouting out loud at someone who has offended you.

According to the communicative approach, occasions on which emotions are held back are derivative phenomena based on basic experience of unselfconscious and direct emotional expressions. The paradigm cases of emotion are those in which the intended identity claim finds its appropriate audience without the interference of any alternative interpersonal agendas. However, our relative social positions are rarely so simply specified that there is only one thing that we want or need to communicate to a single and easily defined addressee. Rather, we simultaneously occupy several sometimes competing role positions which are differentially relevant to our many relationships with others. Conflict between emotional experience and expression arises when the communicative agenda emerging from the current interaction is in some way incompatible with, or discrepant from, another simultaneously activated identification. In these situations, much as we might say one thing yet think another, we can also express one emotion and experience a different or less intense one. In either case, the private expression is simply an internalized version of what we might otherwise let out: a communication addressed to an imaginary or internalized audience. Thus, although some emotions can be seen as private, their privacy is not part of their essential nature, but a contingent fact depending on prior social experience. The ability to express an emotion internally rather than externally is a learnt skill analogous to reading silently instead of out loud.

7   *Authentic emotions differ from dissimulated emotions* Not only do we feel that we are able to refrain from expressing an experienced emotion, but also we think that we can make people believe that we are either more emotional, or experiencing a different kind of emotion than we really are. Some of our emotional presentations seem to be more authentic than others (Hochschild, 1983), suggesting that some vital internal component is missing in the case of the less heartfelt displays.

The common experience of conscious faking of emotion (done for the sake of politeness or more machiavellian purposes) is a major consideration supporting the idea of underlying private emotion as something distinct from superficial displayed emotion. Because in many situations the way that we act does not correspond to what we feel, we consider what we feel to be at a deeper, more personal level. But what we feel is just what we show to ourselves, or what we would like audiences with whom we identify more closely to receive from our emotional communications.

In my view, the apparent authenticity and spontaneity of emotion does not depend on the deeper internal origin of the feelings, but on lack of conflict about current social goals, as well as the urgency and compellingness of the interpersonal concerns to be communicated. The main difference between emotion expressed deliberately to promote some social effect (e.g. anger used tactically to persuade someone to do something) and emotion that is felt as involuntary and uncontrollable is that in the latter case the actor identifies more completely with the interpersonal role implied in the rhetorical content of the emotion. When the communicative intention of the emotion relates to highly valued personal concerns, the emotional individual is less likely to draw a distinction between what is felt and what is shown. To restate, this is not because of the existence of powerful internal feelings (which in any case may be brought on in more deliberate episodes; Sarbin, 1986) but because there are fewer potential audiences in front of whom you feel it prudent to disown your angry intent.

Of course, I do not want to deny that there exists some kind of interior conflict in situations where people are consciously dissimulating their expressions. My point is simply that this conflict is not between an underlying emotional experience and the emotion required by the situation, but between conflicting communicative demands inherent in the same situation as socially defined by separate reference groups. Consider, for example, how you might feel watching a football match with two good friends, both of whom support the opposing teams, especially if you started out with an equally positive allegiance to either side.

8 *Emotions that are held in eventually find a way out* A final related justification for the privacy doctrine comes from supposed deleterious effects of 'bottling up' negative emotions like grief and anger. Common sense as well as thera-peutic dogma tells us that if feelings are repressed they eat away at us from inside and often eventually come pouring out, or burst through the dam-like defences that have been set up (Tavris, 1984). Such hydraulic metaphors also concord with common phrases referring to 'letting off steam' and 'blowing one's top' (e.g. Lakoff and Kövecses, 1987).

The analysis offered above of the dynamics associated with restraining emotional expression partly accounts for these apparent effervescences too. During therapy, analysts may specifically encourage clients to express the kinds of emotion that are directed towards people who are psychologically significant to them ('What would you really like to say to your father?'). In this case, it is not simply that something that has been held back is unleashed, but rather that an appropriate context for the kind of emotional communication that ordinarily finds no place in the everyday social world is provided. Obviously, there are unresolved issues in many of our most important relationships with other people and things that we would like to say and do given the chance, but this does not mean that the associated emotions stay inside waiting for their chance to get out, but rather that they appear when an appropriate context activates the relevant set of interpersonal concerns.

If you refrain from communicating an important identity claim to its in-tended addressee, then your emotional attachment to that identity does not necessarily build up, but you will have failed to resolve the current inter-personal agenda, and unless there is a spontaneous change of heart in the intended recipient of your emotional message, it is possible that at some future moment you will come into a similar situation where the same claim is again relevant. If you do nothing about an interpersonal situation such as this it may improve anyway, get worse, or stay the same. In the first case, the bottled-up emotion just seems to dissipate; in the second, it may feel as if it bursts forth; and in the third, it simply recurs with a similar force to before. In fact, explanation for any of these possible effects does not depend on the release or restraint of internal energy but on the developing history of our relationships with others in the external world.

Conclusion

In this section, I have argued that many of the common-sense assumptions contributing to the privacy assumption are based on phenomena that are open to a different pattern of interpretation using interpersonal rather than intrapsychic principles. The pieces of the jigsaw can be fitted together in an alternative and potentially more satisfying way. Another way of critiquing the idea that emotions are private would be to show how it is part of a broader ideological framework of individualized explanation (e.g. Sampson, 1977), which in fact is culturally as well as historically relative (e.g. Markus and Kitayama, 1991). This book is not the place for such an analysis. Instead, I want to proceed by sketching out the shape of an interpersonal and communicative approach to emotion, and show how this reconceptualization can deal with many of the central theoretical and empirical problems faced by the traditional intrapsychic and individualist account.

RECONSTRUCTION OF EMOTION AS INTERPERSONAL

If emotions are not simply internal events, what else are they? Scattered in the previous chapters of this book are fragments of an account of emotions as communicative acts addressed to specific audiences. In this section, I want to put these pieces together and present a more systematic analysis of this interpersonal approach in order to demonstrate what I believe to be its advantages over more traditional ideas.

In the first chapter of this book, I summarized three kinds of phenomena that have been investigated by previous research, relating to experience, communication, and representation of emotion. One of the aims of the current approach was to work towards a theory capable of providing an integrated treatment of these three levels of analysis. Rather than seeing emotions as essentially internal experiences which only indirectly manifest themselves in communication and representations, I want to suggest that emotions are at heart communicative phenomena and that the messages that they transmit are partly defined according to conventional cultural representations. The internal and experiential aspects of emotion, in this view, are derivative of its original communicative function, rather than communication being overlaid on a pre-existent internal phenomenon.

In this section, I will contrast the basic principles of the communicative approach to emotion at each of the three levels, with the common-sense assumptions made by traditional accounts of emotion (a summary of these new and old ideas is given in Table 10.1).

Emotional experience

Focusing on the experiential aspects of emotion, it seems that emotional feelings can vary according to their quality and their intensity (Reisenzein, 1994), and that people can be aware of their emotions in different ways (Frijda, 1986). According to many intrapsychic approaches, these experiential dimensions exhaust the semantic content of emotion and the task of the theorist is to determine how the different aspects of the experience are affected by external forces and how they in turn influence action on the environment. From an interpersonal perspective, on the other hand, the experiential aspects of emotion can be seen as arising from a broader communicative process. In this section, I will contrast the communicative with the intrapsychic view of each of the three experiential aspects of emotion.

Table 10.1 Intrapsychic and interpersonal accounts of emotional experience, communication, and representation

	Intrapsychic account	*Interpersonal account*
Emotion experience	Basic level of analysis: variables determining emotional quality, quantity, and consciousness operate inside the mind or body.	Secondary level of analysis: experiential quality and quantity of emotion derive from interpersonal identity positions; internal symptoms reflect bodily involvement with these positions.
Emotion communication	Emotion is a private meaning that must be encoded before entering the interpersonal world.	Emotion is always already a mode of interpersonal communication so no translation is necessary.
Emotion representation	Emotions are represented internally according to a unitary system of descriptive distinctions.	A variety of emotion representations are culturally available to communicators and their semantic and syntactic content depends on the pragmatic purposes to which they are to be put.

Principles of emotional differentiation

A key question in the psychology of emotion has been how the particular varieties of emotion, such as love, hate, anger, and embarrassment, are differentiated from one another. Two kinds of answer have been offered. The first is that emotional quality is determined by the pattern of internal information perceived by the individual, suggesting that each distinct variety of emotion is associated with a specific matrix of symptoms which are fed back to consciousness and thus constitute the particular emotional experience (James, 1898; Laird and Bresler, 1992). In contrast to this *feedback* account, *appraisal* theorists (e.g. Arnold, 1960; Lazarus, 1991a) have argued that the differences between emotions are a result of perceptions, evaluations, and interpretations of the psychological situation rather than the internal environment.

The communicative approach argues that both of these kinds of process play some role in the constitution of distinctive emotional experiences, but that neither the feedback nor the appraisal view does full justice to the functional significance of emotion in social life. Each focuses on a delimited aspect of the emotion process under specific circumstances rather than giving a complete account of how emotion is played out in the real world.

Taking the appraisal notion first, it is certainly true that different kinds of emotion are characterized by different appraisals of the social environment. It is also true that in some situations appraising the situation in a certain way can lead directly to emotion of the corresponding kind, for example when we piece together the evidence that a lover is deceiving us and consequently feel jealous. However, although appraisals always *characterize* emotions and are *sometimes* the cause of emotions, their role is not *always* a simple causal one. Rather than starting with a situation that impacts on the individual, the true beginning of many emotional episodes lies somewhere in the developing interaction of two or more people. The dynamics of an interpersonal encounter can lead to someone making an identity claim that carries an appraisal implication and is therefore emotional, but which is not based on a prior intrapsychic process that produces this appraisal. In more concrete terms, you can get angry at someone in a conversation not because you have interpreted one of their comments as offensive, but because in order to defend your reputation in this evolving context it becomes necessary for you to take exception at what is being said. Although your anger will convey the appraisal of *other-blame* (Lazarus, 1991a), it is not logically necessary for any specific intrapsychic appraisal process to precede the emotion.

Rather than assuming that emotions are caused by different kinds of appraisals of personal significance, the communicative approach sees them as motivated by different identity goals. Furthermore, instead of viewing the emotion as a detachable internal experience that somehow follows (however directly) the appraisal process, the current perspective works on the assumption that the evaluative position implied by an emotional stance actually constitutes a large part of the distinctive experience of the emotion. Our feeling of anger as a *quality* of experience, for example, is often little more than the subjective aspect of taking offence at something (cf. Solomon, 1976).

Feedback theories offer an even more problematic notion of a decontextualized emotional experience. Here, the emotion is constructed out of various channels of internal information, but little attention is paid to the ways that these channels modulate over time in attunement with the developing external situation. According to the present approach, bodily and facial feedback can make some contribution to the experience of emotional quality in two basic ways. First, the detection of an internal signal in an ambiguous or unfamiliar social situation can push the emotional interpretation of this situation in a particular direction. For example, feeling gastric symptoms when waiting for an unexpected or undeserved award to be presented may lead one to interpret one's experience in terms of anxiety or embarrassment rather than excitement. Second, there are possible indirect interpersonal feedback effects on emotional experience such as when someone else's reaction to your expression and posture leads ultimately to a change in your own emotional state. For example, someone may take your frown as a sign of disapproval and reply with expressions of nervousness which in turn are interpreted by you as having emotional implications for your own position, and so on. In short, bodily reactions can contribute to the evolution of an interpersonal emotional episode leading to secondary experiential consequences, but they are not usually a primary determinant of emotional quality. However, to the extent that bodily reactions, action impulses, and facial displays are part of the process of conveying an appraisal, they are also implicated in the differentiation of emotion, not because of their signal value, but rather because these modes of communication are involved in the ongoing delivery of the emotional message.

The communicative approach also suggests a way of remapping the logical geography of emotion concepts. Rather than assuming that emotions differ on the basis of their pleasantness and activation, it is possible to redefine emotional quality in terms of relational variables (e.g. de Rivera, 1984). For example, one important dimension of emotional meaning relates to whether an emotion is intended to put another person in a *closer* or *more distant* relationship to you. Other dimensions might relate to the particular form of the pre-existing relationship between interactants, the extent of realignment required by the emotional person, the permanence of the relational adjustment intended, its restriction to specific aspects of the relationship, and so on.

Principles of emotional amplification

Appraisal theory and feedback theory offer explanations of emotion intensity that correspond to their accounts of emotional quality. According to appraisal theory, the main determinant of the strength of an emotional experience is the level of appraised personal significance, whereas from the feedback point of view, the vigour of bodily reactions is the crucial variable underlying intensity. Again, my position is that both of these sets of factor may co-vary with felt emotional intensity but neither necessarily represents its cause in all circumstances. The power of an emotional communication may be conveyed by increased bodily involvement (Sarbin, 1986), and by presenting the claim as more personally significant; but these are contingent rather than necessary aspects of the emotional process itself.

The communicative approach does not see emotional intensity as a simple dimension of emotional experience (cf. Frijda *et al.*, 1992), but rather as relating to a range of aspects of the communicative process broadly concerned with *emphasis*. Intense emotion occurs when the identity claim underlying the appraisal message needs to be conveyed with some force in order to achieve its interpersonal effect. Thus, emotional strength is not always a direct function of appraised personal significance as such (Lazarus, 1991a). Instead, it reflects the extent to which the relevant concern is *presented* as mattering to the emotional individual.

A number of variables may contribute to the intensity of an emotional presentation, according to the present perspective. First and most centrally, since emotion is seen as an interpersonal strategy for realigning relative identity positions, the fervour of the communication is likely to depend on the extent of realignment that is required. For example, if people are treating you like a complete idiot, and you want to stake a claim for possessing a high degree of intelligence, then the salience and compellingness of your expressive demeanour should be correspondingly pronounced.

Second, level of emotional involvement depends on how closely the person identifies with the role position supporting the emotional appraisal. For example, if an insult questions one's status as a competent human being, this is likely to be a more intense emotional experience than if the same person questions one's right to be standing in a particular place at a particular moment. The former identity is one that extends over many areas of a person's life and thus requires more spirited defence, whereas the latter is obviously more localized and as such can be easily discarded. Sarbin (1986) argued that in situations where a person takes on a social role wholeheartedly, their performance is likely to be reflected in more intense bodily involvement (their acting is more physical and less intellectual; cf. Stanislavski, 1965), so depth of identification might also be contingently connected with vigour of bodily symptoms.

A third variable underlying felt emotional intensity concerns the urgency of the communicative requirement of the emotion. In certain circumstances, there are limited and unrepeatable opportunities to defend a threatened identity (e.g. legal interrogations, marriage vows, and divorce decrees) and it is necessary to make a fervent self-presentation in order to get the point across quickly. Of course, this factor only contributes to intensity if the relevant communicative agenda is also important, because if the concern is trivial, even the utmost urgency will not make the associated emotion a powerful one.

Finally, and most problematically from the point of view of appraisal theory, emotional intensity also often depends on the resistance of the intended audience to the specific identity claim being made. Sometimes when defending a position in an argument, claims and counterclaims become increasingly emphatic and involved. Thus, it seems that emotion does not simply reflect an evaluation of the situation but the communicative purpose of an interpersonally defined position in a dialogue.

In summary, the communicative approach assumes that the intensity of an emotion relates mainly to how discrepant one's assigned role position is with the intended alternative status, and how emphatically one needs to embrace this identity with respect to the current addressee or addressees. When the claimed identity is one that need not be concealed from any of the audiences (internal and external) present, then the emotion is likely to be *wholehearted* as well as intense. As with experiential quality of emotion, felt emotional strength is not a separable effect of identification or emphasis, but rather reflects the subjective aspect of engaging in this kind of interpersonal process over time.

Principles of consciousness

A final set of variables differentiating emotional experiences is the mode of awareness that the individual has of the emotion itself. In this regard, Frijda (1986), following Sartre (1962), distinguished between *reflexive* and *irreflexive* experience of emotion. Reflexive experience implies that the agent is aware of the emotion taking place, and that the emotion itself is the focus of consciousness. On the other hand, irreflexive emotional experience is consciousness of the emotional situation as it is coloured by the fact of being emotional. Of course, these two categories can merge into one another in situations when we have a background awareness that we are emotional but are mentally occupied with the emotionally provoking task at hand. Furthermore, over the course of an emotional episode, the characterization of ourselves as emotional may slip in and out of our awareness.

Most of the points that I have made so far about emotional experience being constituted by appraisals and relations to the interpersonal situation apply best to irreflexive emotional awareness. The emotional experience is our particular mode of consciousness with respect to the communicative activity that we are performing by getting emotional. The feedback approach, on the other hand, seems to give a better account of reflexive emotional awareness, explaining how people can come to characterize themselves in emotional terms rather than how they come to feel emotional about something. Reflexive consciousness of emotion is not necessarily a central problem for emotion theory because it can be seen as something that does not always reflect or affect the emotion process itself. Furthermore, people often only explicitly characterize themselves in emotional terms after the fact, and might even deny their emotional status at the time, for example when someone shouts 'I'm not getting angry' during the course of an escalating argument.

According to the present approach, consciousness of emotion (as opposed to emotional consciousness) depends on common-sense cultural representations of what being emotional involves which are not necessarily directly related to the real-time interpersonal processes underlying emotional communication. However, deciding that you are emotional in a reflexive way may also lead to irreflexive emotional consciousness of the situation in some circumstances, so again the distinction becomes increasingly blurred. Furthermore, having decided that you are emotional, presentation of yourself to others in emotional terms can serve almost indistinguishable functions to getting emotional in the usual irreflexive way (see Chapter 9). Thus, feedback processes can initiate genuinely interpersonal emotional processes under special circumstances but they do not lead *directly* to irreflexive emotional experience, which arises only from the process of making an identity claim.

Emotion communication

Whereas most traditional approaches assume, at least implicitly, that emotions are essentially individual things, the communicative model works from the supposition that getting emotional is primarily an interpersonal activity. By saying that emotion's interpersonal function is primary, I mean that it is developmentally prior as well as more fundamental from a theoretical point of view. Emotions first arise as part of infant–caregiver intersubjectivity (e.g. Trevarthen, 1992), and subsequently remain basically communicative phenomena and only derivatively private events. Arguing that emotion is primarily interpersonal implies that many of the traditional problems of emotion communication concerning how a private meaning gets encoded, then decoded (e.g. Buck, 1984), either simply disappear or take on a more tractable form (see Chapter 7).

Principles of emotion expression

According to traditional analyses of emotional communication as a process of information transfer, a private meaning needs to be translated into a mode of expression before it can be transmitted to anyone else. This model has led to a research focus on individual differences in *encoding* ability (e.g. Manstead, 1991), and to investigations of factors interfering with the connection between the internal emotion and the external expression (e.g. Buck, 1984; Ekman, 1972). The present point of view sees emotion fundamentally as a mode of conveying appraisals using nonverbal as well as verbal language and from this perspective there is no experience–display translation problem as such. Nothing is specifically *encoded* because expressive behaviours are the medium through which emotional meaning is conveyed in the first place. In other words, getting emotional typically involves *expressing* emotion in some way from the very start.

However, a real problem faced by the interpersonal reconceptualization is how to account for the apparent fact that people not only differ in expressiveness, both dispositionally and from one situation to the next, but also that these differences do not seem to be directly related to differences in emotionality as such. For example, some people characteristically seem to suppress their emotional expressions but still feel the private symptoms perhaps even more strongly (*internalizers*), while others seem to be able to reduce their emotionality by expressing what they feel (*externalizers*; Buck, 1979b; Jones, 1960). Correspondingly, there are some situations where we all do our best to hold back from revealing our feelings, but this does not necessarily dampen the underlying emotional tendency (e.g. laughter in church). Both these sets of phenomena imply that there is not a simple identity relation between emotion and expression, at least as long as we want to incorporate personal experience in our definition of what emotion involves. In other words, expressing emotion is not the same thing as being or feeling emotional.

The present approach deals with disjunctions between expressive and experiential aspects of emotion by considering the surrounding interpersonal dynamics. Such discrepancies are typically caused by presentational dilemmas in which the costs of making the emotional identity claim seem outweighed by alternative role requirements or by more general considerations relating to social propriety. For example, to get angry when other academics unwittingly insult me by ridiculing a theoretical position to which I happen to subscribe risks opening myself to accusations of oversensitivity or inability to defend my position using more 'rational' modes of argumentation. Similarly, people who seem characteristically inexpressive often may be motivated by a desire not to give away too much of their identity by getting emotional in front of unfamiliar audiences whose judgements they are not yet in a position accurately to gauge. Because expressing emotion makes an identity commitment public, it gives people clear personal information that they may be able to use against you when claiming the same or another identity in the future.

Any felt emotion that remains, despite your failure to express it, relates in this view to the internal rehearsal of what you might say or express in such a situation.

It may correspond, for example, to the anticipatory stage of a communicative act that is never articulated fully (Mead, 1934). Its content resides in the words spoken under one's breath, the tightening of one's bite, or indeed just some vestigial activation of an internalized plan for the relevant social act. The key difference between this account and the traditional intrapsychic one is that here the experiential aspects are derivative of prior social experience, rather than the primary phenomenon itself. One needs to know how to get emotional properly by expressing it in public before one ever gets to the stage of experiencing a private emotion and holding it back. Similarly, it is clear that people only learn how to talk to themselves on the basis of their experience of actual interpersonal conversation (cf. Vygotsky, 1986).

Principles of emotion reception

Expression in the communicative view is the social performance of emotional meaning, but what impact does this performance have on its intended audience? The main difference between the communicative and intrapsychic approaches concern what is actually received when someone gets emotional in your presence. The traditional view assumes that expression simply provides *information* concerning an internal state which is decoded by the receiver, whereas the communicative view suggests that emotion reception also involves reacting directly or indirectly to someone else's rhetorical stance. In the latter view, then, the metaphor of *decoding* only covers one aspect of what happens when someone else's emotion intrudes into your life space. For example, in situations where anger is directed at us, our response does not always or only involve registering the other person's frown and clenched fists, inferring that they are experiencing the corresponding emotion, and then making consequent adjustments to our behaviour. Rather, we often respond directly and on-line to the course of their nonverbal responses by cowering in supplication, or by matching their posture in mutual antagonism, in addition to any cognitive interpretation of what is going on. Inferences about emotional state have no *necessary* role in this basic interpersonal process.

Some of the social impact of emotion on others relates to an implicit coordination of interpersonal expressions whereby a rhythm of synchronized nonverbal behaviour is mutually established (e.g. Bernieri *et al.*, 1988). Moment-by-moment reactions to another person's displays are not mediated by any conscious emotional conclusions about what these expressions signify but rather are part of one's skilled and automatized engagement in interpersonal life, and one's ecological attunement to the unfolding dynamic aspects of the situation (e.g. Gibson, 1979; Neisser, 1988). Some aspects of this coordination process are probably based partly on pre-wired reflex responses, for example, where a sudden leaning forward movement tends in certain circumstances to lead instinctively to withdrawal by the other person.

A second mode of impact of one's emotional expressions on others relates to cultural conventions about the appropriate responses to them and their accepted social meaning. For example, we are socialized to comfort someone who is crying and appease or retaliate against someone who is angry (e.g. Saarni, 1989). The traditional interpretation of such interpersonal sequences is that the receiver infers an emotion in the sender which then leads to an appropriate response. However, there is another way of reading these situations. If emotions are communicative acts designed to produce specific effects on their intended audiences, then shared ideas about what responses are appropriate may also contribute to the sender's original adoption of an emotional position. Anticipation of the response to the adopted emotion by the sender and agreement to engage in this response by the receiver are not two stages in a one-way process but rather simultaneously developing aspects of the same continuous transaction. There is no point in the sender producing an emotion intended to elicit a particular response until the receiver has reached the moment of being willing to offer such a response. Thus, the expression emerges from the course of a coordinated interpersonal behaviour sequence at the stage where sympathy, for example, seems available and displays of sadness therefore seem useful. Because the two (or more) participants in any emotional episode occupy a shared situation that is mutually formulated, any action–reaction sequence cannot be seen as the product of parallel single origins of action, but instead should be recognized as arising from a joint project (e.g. Shotter, 1984) that is always already under way.

Principles of audience attunement

A crucial set of variables affecting the emotion communication process concerns the specific constitution of the audience for the display, and this audience's relationship with the person expressing the emotion. The traditional approach suggests that emotional expressions are often spontaneous but may be modified using display rules depending on the characteristics of other people who are present. The current approach, on the other hand, suggests that emotions are typically directed at specific audiences in the first place and therefore the nature of the communication is often determined by the effects that the sender anticipates having on the receiver. For example, the reason that most of us refrain from expressing joy to other people present at a funeral is simply that there would be no advantage and much potential disadvantage in engaging in an outward communicative process to such an unreceptive audience. Joy is a tactic for making a certain kind of identity claim to addressees who are in some way prepared to receive such a claim (who seem ready to join in the fun, for example). Being joyful in determinedly sombre company serves little purpose for any participant. Of course, this does not mean that partial failures of control cannot occur whereby one's desire to express joy to someone not there (or there but suffering similar social constraints) threatens to overcome the emotional demands of the current situation, but in these cases the underlying effervescent emotion is not a private experience trying to escape as such but rather a communicative act addressed to an imagined other.

Fleming (1994) has drawn attention to some of the communicative problems faced by individuals who have to deal with multiple simultaneous audiences. In many social situations what we say or express is received by other people in addition to its intended target, and we may have different and conflicting interpersonal agendas with respect to these others. These agendas may reflect institutional or cultural role requirements as well as less formally negotiated relationship norms. For example, among any group of acquaintances, there are likely to exist allegiances and antipathies that do not perfectly match up with each other (balance theory notwithstanding; Heider, 1946). Jake is great pals with both Jacqui and Jill but Jill cannot stand Jacqui; Joe hates all three of them but gets on well with you, and so on. When these people are together in a social situation, there are likely to be embarrassing moments when it seems appropriate to express one's sympathy or support to someone present. However, in doing so, you risk alienating this person's enemies who are also on the scene.

In circumstances such as these, an interpersonal dilemma needs to be resolved. Fleming suggested that one way of dealing with these situations is to embrace publicly the required role position but at the same time to convey surreptitiously your distance from this identity to the secondary audience. You might, for instance, wink at the secondary audience while the primary audience was not looking, or make your actions ambiguous to both audiences by using faint sarcasm. Note that on such occasions, the conflict experienced as lying behind the emotional expression does not reflect a hidden private experience but an alternative set of communicative demands. However, imagine that you faced a similar communicative dilemma but it happened that you had a closer relationship with the secondary audience than the primary one. Here, assuming that you went along with the less important friend's request for sympathy, you might feel that your expression was inauthentic and lacking the heat of true involved emotion. Again, however, the distance from your display actually reflects identification with an alternative social identity position. As a final example based on this simple interpersonal situation, consider what might happen if you had a close positive relationship with both of the other parties involved. In this case, you would be required to display and simultaneously not display wholehearted sympathy. The only way through such a conflict might be to get emotional about one's position in this difficult and unbalanced network of people. Clearly, taking simple interpersonal relations through simple permutations relating to different identity configurations produces a wide range of fascinating emotional phenomena, which are typically ignored by the traditional individualistic approach.

The situation becomes even more complicated and interesting when internalized audiences are added to the picture. For example, when talking with friends who do not share our political views, there may be a strong social pressure to conform to the consensus of the present audience, but the fact that we identify with an alternative reference group often causes us to enter into debate with them and risk ridicule. The social motivation for such anticonformity behaviour may be any of the following, singly or in combination: that we know that we will be called to account for our conduct later by someone (possibly ourselves) who will not be prepared to accept the excuse that we were just going along with the flow of conversation rather than making our position publicly known; that we may be in a situation in future when the present company is joined by others who share our allegiances making it necessary for a consistent position to be maintained; or that we have internalized certain group norms about attitude expression that encourage us to present a distinctive position in such situations. Of course, most of us have flexible representational repertoires at our disposal which enable us to endorse mutually contradictory attitudes under different circumstances (e.g. Billig, 1987; Potter and Wetherell, 1987) so these questions of interpersonal consistency, ethics, and etiquette may only arise when the attitude in question reflects our identification with a role that is relatively pivotal to personal identity.

One of the central claims of the communicative account of emotion is that all of the conflicts that people experience between what they feel and what they express (e.g. Hochschild, 1983) derive from multiple-audience situations such as the ones discussed above (see also Fleming, 1994). The putative pure and private emotional essences that supposedly lurk behind the scenes of our public performances actually reflect our intimate identifications with specific roles taken with respect to particular audiences, although these audiences may often be imaginary and internalized rather than physically present (cf. Averill, 1992).

Principle of communicative function

The present approach is a functional rather than structural account of emotion. It assumes that emotions primarily serve the purpose of conveying identity claims in real interpersonal situations. Of course, having learnt how to get emotional publicly in social life we may also come to engage in similar processes when we are on our own, although even here the relevant responses often remain sensitive to implicit interpersonal variables such as the presence of internalized and imaginary audiences (cf. Fridlund, 1991b; Mead, 1934; Vygotsky, 1986). For example, our private angers, jealousies, joys, and embarrassments are often contextualized in silent arguments and declamations that we hold with ourselves but with someone else continually in mind (cf. Billig, 1987).

Clearly not all of our communications to other people are purely emotional (although it is possible that most of them involve emotion at some level), so it becomes necessary to delimit the communicative phenomena that should be included in the terms of the theory, and distinguish them from those that fall outside its range of convenience. Another way of looking at this definitional requirement is to say that the existence of emotion as a real category of psychological phenomena implies that it serves specific functions not served by other processes. What, then, makes getting emotional different from other forms of communication?

Most analyses of interpersonal interaction assume that its main purpose is to convey information which is usually conceived in factual declarative terms. What people do when they communicate, in this view, is to transmit items of data for the use of another person. Although it is arguable whether such an account can accommodate even the simplest of real-world interchanges between people, the idea of communication as exchanging facts nevertheless remains a compelling and popular one. Indeed, within many of our day-to-day dealings with other people, we can maintain the illusion that all we are doing is shuttling bits of information back and forth between us. We may correct someone else's false statement by telling them about something that they did not know and they will readily accept our correction, working on the assumption that we share a common view of the constitution of the relevant portion of reality (cf. Grice, 1975).

However, if things were always as simple as this, communication would rarely break down and there would be little scope for lasting disagreements, or sudden conversions. Communication, even within the information-transfer model, may be disrupted when people convey false information due to misremembering, present a limited perspective of the facts, over- or under-interpret, or simply tell lies. This injects an element of scepticism and suspicion into our reception of supposedly neutral data, and allows some of the grounds for emotion.

More generally, emotional communication is brought into play when more than one viable formulation of a shared concern is available, and when accepted reason-based criteria for defining the mutual situation are incapable in themselves of resolving matters. In other words, emotion occurs whenever communication does not simply accord with the traditional fact-exchange paradigm, so that relevant claims need to be made from specific identity positions rather than from the supposedly neutral and interchangeable standpoint of any competent member of society. Emotional communications in this view are inherently contestable self-presentations.

It seems worthwhile to catalogue a series of examples of these identity-based rather than reality-based communications. First, as already suggested, when data presented in a conversation are dubious or otherwise questionable, we may step outside the bounds of simple information sharing and call attention to alternative motivations for what is being said. Think, for example, of Mandy Rice-Davies undermining the quality of evidence contradictory to her own claim simply by remarking 'Well, he would say that, wouldn't he?' (cf. Edwards and Potter, 1992). Clearly, comments such as these call attention to the original speaker's value as an honest reporter of facts and imply that self-interest distorted their version of events. In order to reassert the legitimacy of one's testimony in such situations and defend one's public reputation, it may be necessary to engage in rhetorical devices such as righteous indignation, aggressive counterattack, or defensive backtracking. These communicative tactics are exactly the kinds of thing that are regarded as emotional.

Second, some topics of disagreement that arise during conversation are simply not resolvable by reference to any consensually acceptable factual state of affairs. However, rather than surrendering our rights to make definite claims in these circumstances and agreeing to differ, we often defend our position even more vehemently. This may be because the opinions and attitudes that we express reflect something that is often seen as the essence of distinctive personality and as defining group allegiances and antagonisms (e.g. Turner *et al.*, 1987). When we get into an argument about whether Oasis are a better rock group than Suede, whether Martin Amis is a misogynistic writer, or whether Tarantino's films are gratuitously violent, the statements and expressions that we make are not simply factual but matters of value and taste, but we are often willing to defend them to the hilt.

The examples that I have given so far represent communicative occasions for negative conflict-based emotions, but it is also the case that rhetorical, non-descriptive functions are served by positive emotional stances in an encounter. An obvious illustration is love (although it is by no means clear that this *positive* emotion always corresponds to a *pleasant* experience as such). Love is not a private reaction to an appraised object but a position in an ongoing relationship with someone else. It is a move made when an interactant intends to realign his or her interpersonal position with respect to someone else. A declaration of love, for example, may be partly a request for reciprocation, and partly a promise to maintain certain sets of duties and obligations with respect to the target (e.g. Averill, 1985; Shotter, 1993).

Emotions are also brought into play when some of the separate areas of our lives overlap or collide. We are all of us involved in several interlocking systems of interpersonal relationships, each of which may have differential relevance for the current situation. I speak to my friend as colleague, as senior colleague, and as enemy of other of my friends, antagonist of my boss with whom I must also maintain courtesy, affiliate of other tormentors, and so on (Fleming, 1994). At any given moment, any one of these potentially conflicting role relations may become salient. As our conversation proceeds, what I say or otherwise commit myself to may have consequences that I would not want for other of my relationships even if the momentary advantage within the present context is obvious. Here again, the need for tactical deployment of emotion may arise.

When people argue that emotion signals some natural sense of the situation (e.g. Hochschild, 1983), all that this actually means is that it emerges from considerations that are at least partly separate from current accepted concerns. When people say that emotion is intrusive and irrational (cf. Oatley, 1990), that is from the point of view of one ongoing set of relations which happen to be discordant with the values communicated by the emotion. Certainly, emotion is always at odds with at least one possible formulation of the situation: even when we get upset predictably, the reaction is an emotional one by virtue of the fact that we cannot carry on with the everyday business of our lives without acknowledging the thing that predictably has happened. In a hypothetical world where we were involved only in simple and consistent roles that never overlapped and never competed with other people's situational definitions, perhaps there would be no need for emotional communication at all, but this world is not like that and, as it happens, never could be.

In summary, emotion provides signals to others (and derivatively to ourselves) that the role relationship as apparently accepted in the assumed mutual definition of the situation needs realignment. For example, by being hurt about the behaviour of a romantic partner, a person may be implying that the demands that she is making would be unproblematic if the relationship were as she wants to claim it is. The common factor in all emotional episodes is an attempt to reconfigure role relationships. Emotional communication can thus be defined as communication directed towards interpersonal positioning, rather than reason-based reporting or factual description.

Communicative content of different emotions

Appraisal theory (e.g. Lazarus, 1991a) has provided a useful characterization of the core relational themes associated with different emotions. The present approach takes these themes to represent the consensually accepted communicative content of adopting culturally specified emotional positions in interaction. Rather than defining how a situation must be conceptualized before someone reacts by getting emotional, my argument is that these themes characterize what the person getting emotional is communicating to the target of the emotional action, or rather what effect the emotional display is intended to have on its specified audience. Inspection of the questionnaire items used to index core relational themes reveals that they actually express this kind of interpersonal message very clearly in many cases.

For example, Smith and Lazarus (1993) argued that anger is defined by the core relational theme of other-blame which is assessed using the following self-reports: 'I've been cheated or wronged'; 'Someone else is to blame for this bad situation I am in'; 'I've been dealt with shabbily', and so on. In my view, the content of anger is better conveyed by the corresponding second-person accusations: 'You've cheated me'; 'You are to blame for this bad situation'; 'You've dealt with me shabbily', etc., as they might be addressed to the intended target of the emotion. Indeed, these are some of the things that someone might actually say (in the appropriate tone of voice and with the corresponding posture and gestures) when angry and confronted by the person with whom they are angry. Of course, this person need not be physically present or available for the angry display, but playing out internally one side of an imagined dialogue can only happen after a person has had direct experience of being angry with someone who is actually there.

I would argue that anger does not depend on concluding that someone else is to blame, as appraisal theory has implied, but rather is an interpersonal tactic for blaming someone else. Indeed, in many cases of anger, we do not really believe that the other person is to blame at all; it just suits our present and immediately compelling purposes to blame them (cf. Frijda, 1993).

Table 10.2 presents a preliminary translation of core relational themes for different emotions into the terms of the communicative model. Instead of assuming that separate emotions are dependent on specific interpretations and evaluations, I characterize them in this table as conveying particular interpersonal meanings roughly translated into a linguistic imperative, or a performative utterance which has the illocutionary force of an order or request (cf. Austin, 1962). For example, being sad or depressed is a way of communicating a socially compelling request for comfort and reassurance (cf. Coyne, 1976).

Table 10.2 Appraisal themes and corresponding communicative agendas characterizing different emotions

Emotion	Core relational theme	Communicative agenda
Anger	Other-blame	Take me seriously, and give me the respect I deserve!
Fear	Danger	Help/protect me!
Guilt	Self-blame	Forgive me!
Happiness	Success	Let's celebrate the moment!
Hope	Potential for success	Let's not give up!
Love	Desiring or participating in affection	Be/stay my special ally! Let's be intimate friends!
Pride	Enhancement of ego identity by taking credit for an achievement	Adjust your opinion of me upwards in accordance with my achievement!
Sadness	Irrevocable loss	Comfort/reassure me!

Source: core relational themes adapted from Lazarus (1991a) and Smith *et al.* (1993)

Emotion representation

The intrapsychic account of emotion assumes that we have the closest possible experiential contact with the entities in question. The traditional view of emotion representation assumes correspondingly that people possess internal category systems that map onto an abstract descriptive grammar of emotion, however imperfectly. Taken together, these two implicit presuppositions suggest that our minds contain more or less accurate knowledge about emotions which can be conveyed (albeit imperfectly) by language. Thus self-reports are the key empirical measure of emotion, and studies of the meanings of emotion words and concepts remain the most popular way of understanding how real emotions are different from, or similar to, one another (e.g. Shaver *et al.*, 1987).

The traditional approach to emotion representation, then, assumes that what people say about emotion in neutral contexts, when they have no need to distort or lie, gives as good information as it is possible to get about the deep structure of emotion experience itself. According to this view, there is a simple and unidirectional descriptive connection between emotional reality and emotion representation.

The present approach sees language as more than a merely descriptive device and argues against the idea that there is a unified grammar of abstract emotion knowledge somewhere inside our heads. In my view, emotion representations develop as a function of their usage in real-life communicative contexts and serve other pragmatic functions in addition to simple characterization.

Relations of representation to reality

According to the present approach, emotional representations relate to emotional reality in a variety of ways in addition to simple description (see Chapter 9). First, formulation of an interpersonal episode in explicitly emotional terms can help to constitute the episode as an emotional one. For example, two people may discuss whether what they are feeling is love and act on the basis of their conclusions. Second and relatedly, shared cultural representations about the course of emotional episodes including their associated appraisals, action impulses, bodily changes, and expressive displays may guide our interpretation of ongoing actions in other people and in ourselves, leading to a conclusion that emotion is going on and a tendency to act in accordance with this conclusion (e.g. Strack *et al.*, 1988). Third, tactical deployment of emotion representations can provide one way of explicitly making similar identity claims to those made using nonverbal emotion displays. For example, rather than bursting into tears, one can say 'this is making me very upset'. The latter strategy is weaker in most circumstances because it does not activate the coordinated interpersonal processes implicated in nonverbal expression quite so directly. Fourth, some kinds of emotion representations provide a moral commentary on the appropriateness of emotion and lead to attempts at emotion control. Fifth, people engage in emotion regulation using strategies that are based on their implicit representations of how emotion works. By representing our own or other people's emotions in certain terms, we lock into a system of cultural knowledge which instructs us in ways to proceed and provides guidance for dealing with what is happening to us.

Having outlined these several possible relations between different kinds of emotion representations and emotional conduct, it is also worth pointing out that many varieties of emotion representation need have little to do with the way that real emotions are worked out in many interpersonal situations. What we think and say about emotions may often function as an independent commentary after the fact, to excuse or defend emotions or to construct purely speculative theories of how emotion might work.

To understand the nature and purpose of emotion representations, it is necessary to examine how they are used in different real-life contexts rather than trying to access some putative natural grammar which is rigidly specified by the inherent structure of the human mind.

Principle of pragmatic function

I have argued that the psychology of emotion and emotion representation has been constrained by the assumption that language just describes, and works in a simple correspondence relationship with reality. A related assumption is that mental concepts corresponding to emotion words contain knowledge about the logical structure of real-life emotions. These internal representations are also thought to map onto reality in a simple descriptive way.

The present argument is that emotion words do things other than describe. What we say when we talk in emotional terms is never intended simply to characterize something that is happening inside us, although such a characterization may be one of the effects achieved. Emotion representations are deployed in particular contexts to serve specific social functions. The nature of the function determines the content of the representation that is deployed. For example, saying that someone is angry may in certain situations be a way of undermining the rationality of what they are doing or saying. Similarly, characterizing *oneself* as having been angry may be an apology or excuse for having acted without due consideration. However, saying that you are angry may also serve to support an identity claim and assert one's rights in a situation. Anger may be represented as controllable and justified, or uncontrollable and unjustified depending on the context of representation. Of course, neither of these social effects would work unless the word 'anger' also carried some agreed content relating to how such a condition might affect behaviour and so on. However, the point is that this content is not rigidly defined and does not reflect purely descriptive knowledge.

The basic argument of the present approach to emotion representations is that there is no conceivable context in which these representations may be deployed simply to describe or give a name to independently existing states of mind. The use of emotion representations always involves some other interpersonal agenda, even when this agenda is to make it look like one is merely describing what is happening. This fact also has implications for how emotions are represented internally. Rather than supposing that there is an integrated deep structure of emotion knowledge residing in the mind, the present approach assumes that we have internalized guidelines for when to use appropriate formulations, based on social experience of presenting and representing emotions. Any internal representational system derives from actual usage of emotion concepts rather than pre-existing and determining their usage.

Principle of discursive flexibility

According to the present approach, emotions are open to a variety of representations which are deployed as appropriate to the interpersonal pragmatic context. This means that people have available to them a range of culturally supplied discursive repertoires for representing their emotions. There may be common aspects to these repertoires corresponding to a shared cultural set of representations, and some parts of some of the representations may be more deeply internalized, but none necessarily provides a straightforward mapping of how emotions really work. Indeed, one common assumption of current emotion concepts is that they are individualized and private reactions, whereas according to the communicative approach, they are in fact primarily interpersonal phenomena.

General principles

In addition to the theoretical principles operating at the separate levels of emotional reality, the communicative model may also be characterized according to its more general principles which either apply to more than one level or explain how levels are interrelated.

Principles of social causation

The basic claim of the communicative approach that getting emotional serves rhetorical purposes in communication addresses the issue of emotional function but does not directly answer questions about the working of the actual processes that generate emotion. Most traditional psychological analyses seem determined singlemindedly to uncover an underlying set of mechanisms that pull the strings of emotional action from behind the scenes. Attention to such issues has diverted the research focus away from the place where the emotional action really takes place, in actual ongoing interpersonal interactions. Instead of looking inside the psyche for emotional processes, it seems worth attempting to construct at least a preliminary account solely by reference to what is going on in the public social world, and what we understand about this world as competent users of conversational tactics.

Many of the things that are typically said to be the consequence of internal processes turn out to be less problematic when examined in their everyday context as part of an interpersonal process. The usual assumption of theories based on cognitive principles is that individuals make sense of the social world by deploying internal representational mechanisms. Of course, no one would want to deny that representing of some form must take place in order for actions and expressions to be meaningful, but it is possible that at least some of the work imputed to cognitive processing is actually done on-line during the course of negotiations between interactants (e.g. Hutchins, 1991), or ongoing transactions with the physical world (cf. Gibson, 1979). Further, in most familiar situations what is happening follows accepted conventions and already makes sense without the need for cognitive interpretation. People having a conversation follow preset but always negotiable paths defined by the physical structure of the situation, organizational and cultural rules about how to behave, and local agreements constructed in the specific relationship in question. Again, it may be that automatized cognitive structures can be seen as carrying out the implicit interpretational work in these situations, but in fact much of what is happening is clarified by the ongoing dynamics of the interaction and by the flow of already meaningful information that it provides, and not by mental work on momentary meaningless data.

According to the communicative view, the causation of emotional episodes is social in at least two ways. First, our relative role positions in any encounter are to some extent predefined by social and cultural factors. Second, interactants reformulate the nature of their relationship in the course of their dialogue using verbal as well as nonverbal resources. Their negotiations of relative positions in the relationship and statuses defended from outside the relationship are the basis for getting emotional. For example, if I am in a romantic relationship with someone and they express their desire to have a liaison with someone else, I will quite properly get angry or jealous in order to reassert my position as the person with principal rights over their affections. The grounds for this assertiveness arise from our common formulation of the relationship, and the specific stimulus for my getting emotional is the other party's interpersonal act of stating an intention. My partner may attempt to redefine our relative role positions in response to my anger and question my rights over her attachments by getting angry in return. It is clear that such claims and counterclaims are largely determined by the pre-existing social structure of the relationship and the specific locally formulated intentions negotiated over the course of the interaction.

In more formal settings, where official rules of conduct are explicitly laid down, similar kinds of process can occur. In these cases, however, the room for manoeuvre from established role positions is more limited, so that people only have a restricted range of emotion options with respect to the others with whom they interact. In these cases, emotions are more likely to feel scripted rather than spontaneous.

Developmental principles

From a developmental perspective, we can see the precursors of relative emotional positions in early caregiver–infant interactions. For example, de Rivera (1984) defined basic emotions in terms of physical movements between the two participants in this primary intersubjective context: the infant's withdrawal from the caregiver represents an early version of a primitive fear reaction; pushing the other away is the basis of anger; clinging tight to the caregiver is a form of longing; and close interpersonal contact with the other in an ongoing interactive dialogue constitutes the basic template for love. Thus, many of the varieties of adult emotional response may derive directly from interpersonal communication in early life.

De Rivera also delineated a series of emotional reactions that arise from the child's relationship with the physical world, but argued that exploration of the environment required a stable interpersonal 'base camp' from which excursions could be made. Further, the affective meaning of physical objects derives from the uses to which they are put in interaction as well as action, and infants learn about the emotional significance of things as a result of social referencing processes, where they check the caregiver's nonverbal signals to see whether unexplored areas and objects are safe (e.g. Campos and Stenberg, 1981). Here, the communicative significance of displaying emotion is perfectly clear and in the open.

Other theories of early development also support the idea that emotions emerge from the primary intersubjective relationship between infant and caregiver (e.g. Hobson, 1993; Trevarthen, 1992). This is not the place for a comprehensive review of this literature, but the central message is clear: emotions originally start out by being interpersonal and communicative.

In later development, more complex modes of emotional function also derive from initial interpersonal learning. For example, Harter and Whitesell (1989) showed how children's first ideas of pride and shame depended on other people being proud or ashamed of them, and only later were they able to apply the emotional concepts to themselves. Furthermore, it seemed as if the earlier experiences of pride and shame were linked to the presence of an audience, which only later became internalized. In this connection, one nine-year-old child was asked whether it was possible to feel shame when no one else was watching and replied as follows: 'Well I might be able to be ashamed of myself if my parents didn't know, but it sure would help me to be ashamed if they were there' (p. 96).

Principle of internalized audiences

I have argued that the primary site for emotion is an interpersonal situation in which someone makes an identity claim in order to influence a specific target person. Thus, emotions are essentially attuned to their intended audience. However, it is also true that emotions can occur when people are alone. The present approach sees these instances of emotion as derivative of primary inter-personal experiences, and as such still in some way attuned to an internalized audience (Fridlund, 1991b), even if this audience only takes the form of a generalized other (Mead, 1934). In other words, often the form taken by an emotion experienced in private is the internal rehearsal of things that one would like to say in a certain tone of voice and with the associated actions and gestures to someone in particular or the world at large. Some of our internal audiences are important figures in our life whose standards we respect or reject, such as parents or schoolteachers, or celebrities we admire.

Internalized or imaginary audiences also impact on our emotional life in situations when we are not alone and underlie some of our familiar experiences of disjunctions between expression and experience. For example, in occupational settings, our unwillingness to indulge in enthusiasm for work tasks may reflect that we would not want to be seen taking seriously such trivial routines in front of an ingroup audience who might treat such activities with the contempt that we also feel that they deserve.

Principle of opposition

The existence of the psychological category of 'emotion' implies that emotional phenomena can be contrasted from phenomena that are not emotional. Emotion seems to have an agreed meaning that sets it in specific opposition to other categories such as reason, logic, and control. Do these oppositions reflect facts about emotion or about emotion representations? Predictably, the answer is a bit of both.

The original reason for the existence of emotional modes of communication may depend upon cultural contradictions such as those pointed out by Averill (1980). The accepted rules of society often make conflicting demands on action, such as when we are simultaneously expected to stand up for our rights in an assertive way, yet not perform any action that might intentionally upset or harm someone else. In such circumstances, Averill argued that we signal our lack of responsibility for an inevitably unacceptable action or inaction by getting emotional. Similarly, but on a more local level, we are often confronted with situations where whatever we do or say is inappropriate for at least one of the audiences that is present (Fleming, 1994), or for an internal imagined audience. Again, the tactical use of emotional communication can get us through our discomfort in these settings. More generally, emotion functions to deal with situations whose rule structure is indeterminate or uncertain, where the only way forward requires the adjustment of relative role positions, or the realignment of relationships.

This general analysis helps us to understand the traditional conception of emotion as something that contrasts with reason and control. When there are no clear rules to follow, then it is hard to account for action in reasonable terms, and control seems lacking. Of course, familiarity with social situations in which these kinds of role conflict and ambiguities concerning underlying rules arise leads to the cultural and personal development of specific conventionalized strategies for getting through them, and emotions themselves develop their own role structure. Indeed, skilled social performers learn about how emotional deployment can change the formulation of a social situation to their own advantage, and become capable of getting angry in order to win an argument, or upset to avert someone else's attack (cf. Biglan *et al.*, 1985).

In short, I am suggesting that emotion occurs in those places and at those times where the local or general moral or rational order breaks down or simply loses relevance and events become unaccountable in terms of what is taken for granted. The result of emotion is often a realignment of expectations and role relationships between the people involved. For example, falling in love occurs when people feel that they can no longer carry on in the standard pattern of relating as acquaintances, and declaring this love results in each person treating the other in different ways, expecting different things of them, as well as being defined differently by other people around. Similarly, anger occurs when one's rights are not respected within an everyday encounter, so you need to assert them using other than 'rational' means. The result of such a strategy is often that people now pay attention to the thing that was disturbing you. You make an identity claim and people either listen or ignore it. By making the emotional claim that something matters, you draw other people's attention to your concern.

Our cultural need to support, defend, and reproduce the taken-for-granted moral orders of everyday life together with the fact that we are compelled to work from within certain locally defined sets of assumptions which cannot be sustained under all possible contingencies results in us taking emotion for something other than it really is. We see emotions as temporary disruptions which can be repaired, rather than as indictments of the entire basis of our restricted world view. We see them as disturbing order rather than revealing part of a deeper, wider, and never fully recognizable structure of realities unsensed. There might come a time when we readjust our institutional and personal conceptions of how people relate to each other, what the world contains, and how it operates, in order to encompass emotional phenomena more readily. However, even after such a shifting of ground, the reformulation of accepted reality would still necessarily remain a partial and contingent one, and something would continue to seep out through its cracks, to be dismissed as merely emotional and thus as somehow beside the rational point.

PROBLEMS SOLVED BY A SOCIAL APPROACH TO EMOTION

Although the position outlined in the previous sections may seem a relatively radical one, I hope that it makes some contact with the basic issues that have concerned emotion theorists over recent years. In the present section, I want to examine some of the implications of adopting a communicative theory for dealing with some of the perennial concerns of traditional research into emotion.

Emotion and cognition

One of the consequences of seeing emotions as entities whose primary existence is intrapsychic is that they must operate partly independently of what goes on in the environment, so that it becomes necessary to articulate modes of interaction between the internal and external realms. The simplest mechanistic way of dealing with these questions is to assume that something that happens outside unidirectionally produces something inside, often after the mediation of some explanatory mechanism. Many of the problems of emotion theory relate to the question of how the original stimulus for emotion is processed before the personal response takes place.

The affective primacy debate is a direct consequence of this way of thinking. Zajonc (1980) provocatively argued that affective responses may arise in direct response to emotionally relevant aspects of the situation independently of and prior to any articulated cognitive processing of the relevant stimuli. Lazarus (1982; 1984), on the other hand, defended the appraisal position that in order for a reaction to be genuinely emotional it must be preceded by an appraisal of the situation, however primitive this cognitive-evaluative process might be. The dispute, then, concerns whether an emotion can occur without prior cognitive processing. As many commentators (e.g. Leventhal and Scherer, 1987; Parkinson and Manstead, 1992; and see Chapter 2) have pointed out, the problem is not so much a substantive as a definitional one. According to Lazarus's formulations of emotion and cognition, no emotion is possible without prior appraisal (which in his terms always counts as cognition) by definition. In Zajonc's terms, however, there are phenomena that he is willing to say are 'affective' that do not require any protracted cognitive processing before they are activated. Lazarus would not call these latter phenomena emotional, but might call any of the processes that led to them cognitive. In other words, whether cognition necessarily precedes emotion depends what you want to call 'cognition' and what you want to call 'emotion'.

However, this definitional resolution of the affective primacy debate is limiting because it implicitly takes on some of the misguided assumptions of the original formulation of the problem. Specifically, both positions take for granted the idea that emotion is a personal reaction to something that has happened in the environment. According to the present approach, emotion is not fundamentally a private occurrence in the first place, and is thus not necessarily the second stage in a deterministic and unidirectional causal sequence leading from external stimulus to internal response.

Getting emotional in any real-life social situation is certainly preceded by some kinds of cognitive as well as emotional work but neither of these are necessarily direct or complete causes of the interpersonal stance taken. Emotion, in my view, depends on the existence of a set of communicative demands which may be contained in the personal or interpersonal definition of the situation, in the direct implications of something that happens, or as part of an ongoing pattern of coordinated response to someone else's presentation. Emotion is not a simple momentary reaction but a mode of social action and it usually develops over time rather than being triggered by an intact piece of information or a delimited interpretation. Instead of focusing on simple precursors of emotion at single moments and in supposedly neutral laboratory settings, researchers should pay attention to how the overall pattern of social response develops in its everyday interpersonal context.

A step in the right theoretical direction is the realization that cognitions influence emotion and emotions influence cognition. Furthermore, different processing styles seem to constitute different emotional modes (Oatley and Johnson-Laird, 1987; Parrott and Sabini, 1989; Schwarz and Bless, 1991). Thus, in real-life situations cognitions and emotions may not be separate stages in a causal sequence but rather interlocking aspects of the same dynamic process. The supposed stimuli and responses apparently operating in emotional episodes do not inhabit separate worlds but are both part of the same complex syndrome of developing interpersonal action.

What makes emotion emotional?

A prevalent assumption of emotion theory is that something must be added to everyday experience to make it emotional experience. For example, James (1898) argued that 'without the bodily changes following on the perception, the latter would be purely cognitive in form, pale, colorless, destitute of emotional warmth' (p. 1066) and Arnold (1960) suggested that

> to perceive or apprehend something means that I know what it is like as a thing, apart from any effect on me. To like or dislike it means that I know it not only objectively, as it is apart from me, but also that I estimate its relation to me, that I appraise it as desirable or undesirable, valuable or harmful for me, so that I am drawn toward it or repelled by it.
>
> (p. 171)

These two very different views of emotion, the first the original version of feedback theory, and the second the prototype for the appraisal approach, share a key assumption, that there is an extra element in emotional consciousness compared with everyday consciousness of the objective world, and that by incorporating this element into experience, experience is made emotional.

This presupposition also persists in recent emotion theories. For example, Schachter (1964), Laird (1974), Mandler (1984) and Zajonc and McIntosh (1992) in different ways have all followed James in arguing that bodily changes of some kind add the emotional ingredient to experience. From the appraisal angle, Lazarus (1991a) has continued to claim, following Arnold, that what makes emotion emotional is the basic apprehension of personal significance. Other related accounts include Frijda's (1986) position that felt control precedence of action tendencies is the vital additive that transforms rational function into emotional function.

The common weakness of all these accounts is their theoretical starting point which assumes that emotion is distinctive because it contains something special, or, in other words, that emotion is like normal behaviour with something else tacked on (Parkinson, 1987b). Furthermore, in accordance with the idea that emotion is essentially an individual experience, the special thing that is added is typically assumed to be something personal and private (e.g. an internal symptom, quality of consciousness, or idiosyncratic evaluation). If emotion is basically interpersonal rather than intrapsychic, then attention to such factors seems misplaced.

According to the communicative model, emotion is not what happens to experience when an emotional factor is incorporated, but rather a specific mode of interpersonal communication with rules of its own. In other words, emotion contains nothing distinctive in itself, but is emotional because of the social functions that it serves. Above, I have implied that emotion is a way of making claims about issues that are not resolvable using simple presentation of accepted evidence. Because rational considerations seem to slip away on these occasions, we experience our communication as uncontrolled and unreasoned: in short, as emotional. For example, when we are aiming to form a romantic alliance with someone, it would be hard to defend our desire using evidence of our objective suitability, so our declaration of love seems underdetermined by the usual justifications for action. Similarly, if our position in a relationship is defined in an unspoken way, and our feelings of connection are based on uncoded nonverbal synchronies and sympathies, then there is nothing that can easily be put into words that explains how we feel. Emotion, therefore, seems to reside in our inability to account for our actions in conventional reason-based or cognitive terms. Nothing special is added: it is just that the accepted accounts of action cannot easily cope with these situations.

What makes emotion emotional is the use of certain nonverbal strategies of identity realignment and relationship reconfiguration which do not easily translate into the official idea of reasoned argumentation and information exchange. In practice this means that there may be no single identifiable factor that in itself serves to add emotional quality to experience, but rather a range of interpersonal considerations that make anger angry, embarrassment embarrassing, happiness happy, and so on.

Heart and head

The distinction between emotional experience and ordinary experience is captured in common sense by a metaphorical dichotomy of heart versus head (cf. Sappington and Russell, 1979). Much of what we do in our everyday lives can be explained by reference to intentions and plans, and the head seems to stay in control. However, another set of more mysterious internal processes sometimes seems to overwhelm the functioning of the head from a location deeper down in the body. Sometimes, it is said that your head tells you one thing but your heart says something else, and the heart is often thought to be the organ that paradoxically comes out on top in these disputes. Indeed, the standard popular advice in such circumstances is often to trust your instincts and follow your heart.

Some of our common head–heart conflict experiences cause particular problems for cognitive accounts that assume that emotions depend on interpretations and evaluations of situations. On occasion we feel guilty or angry, happy or sad, but cannot explain why, indeed would deny that we are appraising the situation in the appropriate terms to experience such emotions (Frijda, 1993). For example, Kroon (1988) found that when telling the story of their guilt experiences in the context of a psychological study, people often did not report themselves to be actually responsible for the event that supposedly engendered the emotion, and many of them refuted the idea that they had actually done anything wrong, but they still could not get over their feelings of guilt. They knew that there was no logical reason for feeling this way but that knowledge did not stop the emotional experience. Many of these experiences were based on actions or omissions with respect to important figures in participants' lives with whom they had an ambivalent relationship. One participant reported feeling guilty after hearing that the boyfriend that she had recently abandoned had suffered a serious accident. The accident had nothing to do with her leaving and she felt she had been right to go, but she nevertheless experienced guilt about the episode.

From the appraisal perspective, it requires considerable ingenuity to make a case for these emotions being dependent on interpretations and evaluations of the situations because the expressed interpretations and evaluations contradict the actual emotional conclusion. Either a deeper unconscious appraisal process activated the experience, or the participants were actually feeling guilty about something other than the reported event itself. However, nothing in Kroon's data supports either of these conclusions.

From the communicative point of view, on the other hand, these examples present few problems. Rather than seeing the guilt as dependent on a prior judgement of self-blame, the present approach takes the emotion to be a communicative act directed to the person who has suffered harm, asking for forgiveness from them. In other words, within the context of the relationship with the individual about whom the guilt is felt, an appeal for absolution makes perfect sense, even though in presentation of the rational structure of the episode during a psychological interview or confession, no personal responsibility is accepted for what happened. From the imagined perspective of the victim, the guilty person is seen as someone who ought to have been able to help with what went wrong or avert it, and so in internalized encounters with this person, the perpetrator feels a communicative need for apology in order to avert the inferred reflected blame. Thus, emotion's apparent illogicality, its government by heart rather than head, arises from implicitly interpersonal situations in which people try to explain their position to an audience that does not share the same relationship-contingent assumptions about proper action, rights, and obligations.

Basic emotions

If, as traditional accounts imply, emotions are special modes of processing that seize control away from rationality, it might also be concluded that their origins depend not on learnt experience but on more deeply rooted and natural forces. Many theorists have argued that a small set of emotions is biologically pre-programmed in the brain and that other emotional experiences depend on blends, concatenations, or elaborations of these basic emotions (e.g. Ekman, 1992; Izard, 1977; Oatley and Johnson-Laird, 1987; Plutchik, 1980). Other researchers have argued against any simple notion of basicness at either the biological or psychological level (Ortony and Turner, 1990; Turner and Ortony, 1992).

There is at least one issue on which both camps agree in this debate: that many of the emotions experienced by human adults incorporate certain biologically determined processes. However, there remains the issue of whether any of these incorporated processes or combinations of these processes should themselves be seen as basic emotions or simply as fundamental components of emotions. Proponents of the basic-emotions view argue that the central nervous system is pre-wired to produce organized patterns of response which correspond to basic emotions, and which combine to form more complex emotions, whereas critics of the view suggest that it is better to look at emotional structure as constituted from components that are not in themselves emotional (Ortony and Turner, 1990).

Take the case of embarrassment, for example. Basic-emotions theorists would say that this 'complex' emotion is made up either of more than one more basic emotion (fear together with disgust directed at the self, perhaps) or of one basic emotion plus some cognitive components. The problem with this account is that it is very hard to think of how anyone might demonstrate that a given instance of embarrassment might actually contain a different and more fundamental emotion. Even if it were the case that a consistent neural or physiological substrate had been found for basic emotions, the presence of a similar set of responses in the case of embarrassment could not show that the basic emotion itself were embedded within the supposedly new complex, only that similar components were activated. Indeed, it is hard to get a precise sense of what it would mean for one emotion to include another. Of course, if theorists wish to define emotions in terms of subsets of their associated responses, then the claim could be given some meaning, but this move would reflect a reconstitution of the topic area that took us away from the reality of lived emotional experience as something flexible and multicomponential. A more supportable claim in these circumstances would seem to be that emotions sometimes share biologically determined components in common with one another (Ortony and Turner, 1990).

From the present point of view, emotions attain their social power and significance from the communicative role that they play in an interaction. If this analysis is correct, then the criteria for an emotion counting as an emotion are socially rather than biologically defined, and there is no sense in the suggestion that a real emotion can be basic through and through in a biological sense. However, I do believe that human brains are pre-wired in such a way that our active senses are attuned to certain aspects of displays from other humans. For example, infants are more interested in human faces than other equally complex stimuli (Fantz, 1965). Relatedly, there seems to be a pre-programmed tendency for newborns to mimic the facial expressions of others with whom they are interacting (e.g. Meltzoff and Moore, 1977). Vocal expressions also seem to elicit consistent responses from a very early age (e.g. DeCasper and Fifer, 1980; Simner, 1971; Wolff, 1969). Furthermore, babies are able to detect directly whether their expressive behaviour is coordinated moment-by-moment with that of their caregiver (Murray and Trevarthen, 1985). Finally, there seem to be certain patterns of physical interaction between caregivers and infants that recur with sufficient frequency to suggest that they are in some sense biologically prepared (e.g. de Rivera, 1984).

My interpretation of this evidence is that precursors of emotion which are closely dependent on innate structures arise in the course of a child's primary relationship with its caregiver. These basic pre-settings for interaction allow the baby to develop a socialized understanding of the interpersonal and physical world. However, their functional value is not directly survival-related but rather arises from the fact that they establish the necessary conditions for meaningful interpersonal communication and the transmission of cultural values. One of the most distinctive characteristics of the human animal is its flexibility which allows it to deal with rapidly changing environments and to solve problems culturally instead of instinctively. A large proportion of our lives is spent growing, learning, and developing rather than running off biologically pre-programmed responses. Infants are 'environment open' so that they can learn what matters as a result of enculturation. Little of contemporary human experience is motivated directly by a need to stay alive, and correspondingly little of our emotional lives derives from purely evolutionary concerns.

Emotional differences

The basic-emotions thesis not only maintains that some emotions are made up from other more simple ones, but also that these more fundamental emotions are real intact entities that are physically manifested in the operation of neural mechanisms. Other theorists would argue instead that emotions are cultural constructions rather than genuine psychological referents (e.g. Gergen, 1987; Harré, 1986). So the question arises: are differences between emotions based on ideas or realities?

In fact it is unnecessary to adopt such an extreme case formulation of this issue. Instead of seeing emotions as either coherent objects located entirely in the psychological world, or purely as categories imposed on experience, the present account suggests that emotions are constituted out of real interpersonal processes as well as representations. Specifically, the communicative perspective suggests that emotions *really* differ because of their respective functional roles in interactions, but that their constitution in terms of psychological components may vary from one instance of a particular emotion to the next, so that cultural representations may be required to provide structural coherence to each emotion concept, as well as to shape the real-time regulation of ongoing emotional episodes.

Of course, the claim that emotions have a genuine existence in the realm of interaction does not imply that this existence is culture-independent because the identity and role positions that people occupy in everyday social life as well as their conventions of relating to one another arise mainly from society-specific paradigms. However, these paradigms do not operate only via mental representational processes but also because of the way that the institutional and architectural world is structured. Our identity projects derive at least partly from our position in a pre-established system of relationships which is to some extent also concretized in the physical arrangement of the manufactured world.

It is also possible that some aspects of some of the communicative functions of emotions recur relatively consistently from one culture to the next, making emotion a partly universal phenomenon. For example, it is hard to conceive of any society at the present historical moment that is completely immune from concerns relating to the relative status position of its members. Thus, power struggles with their related emotional identity claims are likely to be fairly pervasive throughout the contemporary world, and possibly also over much of the course of human history so far.

My middle position in the idea-reality debate concerning the nature of emotion combines the classical (e.g. Clore and Ortony, 1991) with the prototype (e.g. Russell, 1991; Russell and Fehr, 1994) views of emotional definition. On the one hand, the communicative agendas underlying each particular kind of emotion may be specified according to necessary and sufficient conditions, so that the *functions* of different emotions may be seen as having an underlying classical structure. On the other hand, however, the specific nature of the emotional communication itself may vary across instances of the same kind of emotion, with different modes of message delivery, different sets of component, and different sequences of events characterizing different cases. Thus, the common *structure* of exemplars of any given emotion may only be specifiable by reference to their family resemblance to a defining prototype.

An added complication for this analysis arises from the fact that the language of emotion does not necessarily match up in any simple way with the real functional differences that exist. There are at least two reasons for this. First, emotion categorizations develop from ideological as well as realistic considerations. Second, emotional language serves pragmatic functions in addition to direct description. The consequence of these conclusions is that our cultural ideas about emotion do not map directly onto psychological reality.

This slippage between emotional language and the functional basis of emotion also confuses the definitional issue, because the imposition of emotion represent- ations can itself make a difference to the way that the psychological process unfolds. For example, the cultural belief that anger is a certain kind of entity constrains our interpretation of anger-like episodes in certain circumstances and may shape the way that people respond to them (e.g. Stearns and Stearns, 1986), so that they turn out to be more like the representation specifies than they might otherwise have been. In other words, shared beliefs about different emotions can in some cases themselves make emotions different. For example, we may have access to scripts that specify the way that a particular kind of emotional episode should unfold, and in ambiguous situations this script may provide guidance for our actual conduct. Thus, part of the integrity of emotion categories may derive from the real-time application of these same categories to real-life emotional episodes.

A last point about the idea–reality connection in this regard is that the set of emotion terms that we currently employ does not correspond perfectly to the actual range of emotional communications that are deployed in social life. For one thing, people may negotiate completely original ways of relating to one another in the course of their encounters for which no language is yet available. Additionally, cultural priorities about roles and statuses change over time and emotions change in a parallel way. As new identity projects emerge as a result of cultural and interpersonal development, new modes of emotional response may emerge and old words as well as the emotional syndromes associated with them may begin to disappear (e.g. Harré and Finlay-Jones, 1986). Finally, we may formulate new kinds of emotional communication between us and ultimately invent new words to go with them (cf. Averill and Nunley, 1992).

WHAT THE COMMUNICATIVE APPROACH FAILS TO DO

The approach that I have presented in this book will not satisfy everyone. Many readers will accept the relevance of some of my examples but disagree with the conclusions that I have drawn from them. In this section, I address some of the potential problems and weaknesses of the communicative model as presented in this book.

Failure to specify cognitive mechanisms

The main criticism that I anticipate from my imagined audience is that my explanation is incomplete, and that even if all the interpersonal and cultural processes that I have proposed actually do operate in the ways that I have suggested, this fact still leaves the traditional intrapsychic account of emotion untouched. Critics taking this position might argue that the impact of roles, relationships, ongoing interactions, and audiences on emotions is always ulti- mately mediated by some kind of internal process which somehow translates what is out there in social reality into an individual experiential response.

I have two countermanoeuvres to make against this anticipated attack. The first is simply to accept the internal processing metaphor as an alternative and equally viable paradigm. In one sense, cognitivism simply represents either a different way of formulating the problem, or a way of formulating different problems. Indeed, I am quite happy to agree that the specification of processing mechanisms would be a proper aim of certain kinds of theories constructed for particular purposes. However, even from this cognitive perspective, I would argue that what needs to be explained may be different and more tractable once dynamic interpersonal factors are incorporated into the analysis. Correspondingly, I believe that the information-processing perspective is not well suited to the job of dealing with data that are not simply momentary (cf. Gibson, 1979), or processes that transcend the boundaries of an individual psyche (e.g. Coyne, 1976; 1982; cf. Resnick *et al.*, 1991). In my view, emotional phenomena tend to carry both of these cognitively problematic characteristics.

My second more straightforward defence is that the supposed requirement for internal mechanisms to generate emotion depends on the idea that emotions are fundamentally individual, whereas in fact, as I have argued, they are not individual things at all. Emotions exist centrally in relationships, in the movements and messages that pass between people, and so it is best to look for their causation there, rather than in some separate mythical realm of intrapsychic machinery.

Problems of functional explanation

Although I am not too troubled by the anticipated cognitivist critique, there are some potential concerns with the communicative approach which need addressing more urgently. Perhaps the most significant structural weakness of the framework is its apparent dependence on functional explanation. The problem here is that it is not usually considered sufficient explanation for a phenomenon to refer to the purposes that it serves (e.g. Hempel, 1965). The ready-made solution to this problem is to allude to an agent's active intentions as causative mechanisms and leave it there. In this way, it is easy to gloss over whatever links goals to actions because common sense fills in the missing details by taking a purposive view of action control for granted, so that behaviour seems to be fully accountable in terms of the actor's plans and projects. In short, people are thought to do what they do because of their beliefs and desires: end of story. Let me be clear, however. Saying that emotion serves communicative goals does not in itself provide a complete account of emotion, because it leaves hanging questions relating to the constitution of goals and the mediation of their effects on behaviour. For example, if emotion is goal-directed, where do the goals come from, what do they consist of, and how do they influence what we do? These are exactly the explanatory gaps that cognitive theories attempt to close up (while at the same time opening up other ones that, in my opinion, are even more intractable).

I can perhaps clarify my own position best by rejecting a possible misinterpretation. I do *not* mean to imply that all emotions are controlled by conscious intentions. At any rate, even if I did want to say that emotions are always *misconstrued* as passions rather than actions (cf. Averill, 1980), I would still need to provide an account of how actions are controlled. However, I do not think that people always or even usually get emotional in a deliberate way, though certainly there are occasions when this can happen. My claim is a more modest one: that emotions serve communicative functions in interactions. One possibility is that people have learnt implicitly that emotions have tactical value but still use them in an unselfconscious way. However, I do not want to restrict emotion to these instances either. Instead, I want to say that emotions are necessary to the process of relating to others in a complex society made up of interlocking but not always congruent relationships. What sustains these local tactics is not always individual intention or implicit reward value but the need to deal with contradictions at a cultural and institutional level.

Often the specific structure of an emotional episode is not determined by individual decisions, whether conscious or unconscious, or even by personal habit, but by emergent properties of the relationship as a unit that is formulated within the framework of a wider cultural context. Our communicative actions are partly shaped by the verbal and nonverbal texts that we play out rather than vice versa. All this may come across as rather abstract and metaphysical, but essentially all that I am saying is that it is necessary to consider the communicator, addressee, and the surrounding sociocultural context in order to understand the emotion process completely. The exact form of the theory that such investigation might ultimately produce, however, unfortunately remains beyond the scope of the present undertaking.

Lack of generality

A final concern with the present approach concerns my sweeping claim that all emotions are essentially communicative. This proposal inevitably draws out counterarguments concerning the universal applicability of the analysis. 'Do all existing and possible emotions actually serve communicative goals?', a critic would be entitled to ask. In other words, an issue that requires addressing is whether my approach is sufficiently general to cover every case of emotion.

The glib, but no less pertinent, answer would be that this depends what is meant by the term 'emotion'. In the absence of a definite set of criteria for identifying proper instances of the category, my argument at best can only be that it is possible to draw up defensible boundaries around a set of phenomena conforming to the principles outlined here, and that these boundaries will stake out a similar territory to that currently occupied by the common-sense view of what emotions are. However, it is also true that some popularly defined emotions do not fit in with the approach that I have sketched out as easily as others. For example, the emotion of fear as commonly conceived depends on exposure to life-threatening situations which are not necessarily social in origin or constitution. It may be that fears of this kind are simply not amenable to a communicative theory. However, it is also true that everyday anxieties often do relate to social situations: we are often frightened of making a fool of ourselves in front of others or being otherwise hurt by them, for example. Furthermore, the expression of fear certainly serves the communicative function of eliciting protection from others in a wide range of situations.

There seem to be two possible ways of dealing with the apparent inapplicability of the present perspective to certain examples of emotion such as fear: either some instances of the category fit the model and others do not, or else the apparently nonsocial kinds of emotion are secondary varieties based on basic developmental experience with interpersonal emotions, and still remain responsive to communicative variables (e.g. Fridlund, 1991b). In either case, the exceptions do little damage to the central claim of the communicative theory. A weaker way of making this claim is to admit that the theory may not necessarily cover all the things that everybody would want to call emotional, but at least offers a tenable analysis of the cases to which it does apply. It is always possible that the currently accepted idea of emotion might adjust over time to fit in with a theoretical approach such as the one offered anyway (cf. Farr and Moscovici, 1984).

In history-of-science terms, it might be argued that competing research programmes do not necessarily address identical problem areas, but rather that new approaches deal with some of the issues thrown up by previous paradigms while leaving others untouched. Indeed, these latter topics may ultimately come to seem irrelevant from the point of view of the revised perspective. Another way of looking at this phenomenon is to say that theoretical principles partly *define* what merits attention, rather than being applied to topics that are already of inherent scientific significance (cf. Kuhn, 1962; Lakatos, 1970). From the admittedly partial perspective of the present approach, social factors are the most important aspects of emotion, and I believe that such a focus is useful during this particular conversational turn in the ongoing dialogue of psychological emotion theory.

What I have offered in this book can be seen more as an *approach* to investigating emotion than a comprehensive theory of how emotional phenomena are caused. The main reason for this is that although I believe that emotion can be fenced off as an appropriate arena for psychological investigation, emotions do not represent a set of delimited phenomena that are subject to a single set of basic deterministic mechanisms. The usual mistake of emotion theories is to suppose that an emotion is a simple momentary event that represents a break from 'normal' psychological functioning. As long as such a view is held, mainstream psychologists can ignore emotions, and emotion theorists can explain it away in elementary special process terms.

In summary, whether my arguments are ultimately correct does not concern me so much as whether I have provided a helpful reconceptualization of the relevant phenomena at the present stage of the discipline. The most I could hope for is that some of the ideas conveyed in this book may contribute to a continuing debate about the nature and function of emotion.

CONCLUSIONS

Behind the scenes of the psychological approach to emotion hangs an often unnoticed backdrop of common-sense assumptions which sets the stage for contemporary research practice. Many of our theoretical and empirical claims only make sense when their blindspots and omissions are filled in with this unquestioned common knowledge. One of the aims of this book is to reconfigure our position in the emotional landscape by taking a perspective right at the heart of the action and in the thick of the improvised drama that goes on in our everyday interactions with other people, instead of from some detached and abstracted vantage point backstage.

Emotion, according to the common-sense account, is private, reactive, and partly uncontrollable (e.g. Lutz, 1988). In contrast, I have tried to make a case for taking at least some aspects of emotions to be public, active, and tactical. Instead of seeing common-sense ideas about emotion as simply a resource for theorizing, I treat emotion representation as a topic in its own right, which partly overlaps with the general theory of emotion. The fact that people talk and think about emotion in certain ways may tell us something about what emotion is like and how it is used, but this does not mean that they are descriptively correct to characterize it in these terms. Rather they are performing communicative acts which are sometimes analogous to the communicative acts performed when people actually get emotional. On other occasions, representations of emotion serve instead as an ideologically derived moral commentary with only an indirect bearing on actual emotional conduct. In general, psychological theory needs to take common sense seriously but not unquestioningly. Some critical angle of independence must be maintained.

In order to approach emotion from a different trajectory I have taken a position defined by a rather different set of metaphors than those typically used by emotion theorists. Rather than seeing emotion as something inside that presses to get out, I take it to be something actually situated in the dynamic transactions between people that somehow gets inside, or at least attaches itself to certain subject locations.

I have used theoretical language derived from dramaturgical theories: relying on concepts of roles, scripts, actors, and audiences instead of the usual psychological vocabulary of stimuli, interpretations, and drives. Of course, it is possible to analyse whatever we agree to call emotion from either perspective, and retranslate explanations in both directions, but with respect to the problems that interest me at least, I think the new standpoint opens up the wider view. I see a whole new territory of social psychology waiting to be explored, into which I have taken only a few tentative steps.

References

Abelson, R. B., and Sermat, V. (1962). Multidimensional scaling of facial expressions. *Journal of Experimental Psychology, 63*, 546–64.

Abramson, L. Y., Seligman, M. E. P., and Teasdale, J. D. (1978). Learned helplessness in humans: Critique and reformulation. *Journal of Abnormal Psychology, 87*, 49–74.

Anderson, J. R., and Bower, G. H. (1973). *Human associative memory.* Washington DC: V. H. Winston.

Andrew, R. J. (1963). Evolution of facial expression. *Science, 142*, 1034–41.

Argyle, M., and Dean, J. (1965). Eye-contact, distance, and affiliation. *Sociometry, 28*, 289–304.

Aristotle (1909). *Rhetoric.* Trans. R. C. Jebb. Cambridge: Cambridge University Press.

Aristotle (1913). Physiognomica. In W. D. Ross (ed.), *The works of Aristotle* (pp. 805–13). Oxford: Clarendon Press.

Armon-Jones, C. (1986). The thesis of constructionism. In R. Harré (ed.), *The social construction of emotions* (pp. 32–56). Oxford: Blackwell.

Arnold, M. B. (1960). *Emotion and personality (volume 1): Psychological aspects.* New York: Columbia University Press.

Ashforth, B. E., and Humphrey, R. H. (1993). Emotional labor in service roles: The influence of identity. *Academy of Management Review, 18*, 88–115.

Austin, J. L. (1962). *How to do things with words.* Oxford: Clarendon Press.

Averill, J. R. (1969). Autonomic response patterns during sadness and mirth. *Psychophysiology, 5*, 399–414.

Averill, J. R. (1974). An analysis of psychophysiological symbolism and its influence on theories of emotion. *Journal for the Theory of Social Behavior, 4*, 147–90.

Averill, J. R. (1975). A semantic atlas of emotional concepts. *JSAS Catalog of Selected Documents in Psychology, 5*, 330 (ms. no. 421).

Averill, J. R. (1980). A constructivist view of emotion. In R. Plutchik and H. Kellerman (eds), *Theories of emotion* (pp. 305–40). New York: Academic Press

Averill, J. R. (1982). *Anger and aggression: An essay on emotion.* New York: Springer.

Averill, J. R. (1984). The acquisition of emotions during adulthood. In C. Z. Malatesta and C. Izard (eds), *Affective processes in adult development* (pp. 23–43). Beverly Hills, CA: Sage.

Averill, J. R. (1985). The social construction of emotion: With special reference to love. In K. J. Gergen and K. Davis (eds), *The social construction of the person* (pp. 89–109). New York: Springer.

Averill, J. R. (1987). The role of emotion and psychological defense in self-protective behavior. In N. Weinstein (ed.), *Taking care: Why people take precautions* (pp. 54–78). New York: Cambridge University Press.

Averill, J. R. (1992). The structural bases of emotional behavior: A metatheoretical analysis. In M. S. Clark (ed.), *Review of personality and social psychology 13: Emotion* (pp. 1–24). Newbury Park, CA: Sage.

Averill, J. R., Catlin, G., and Chon, K. K. (1990). *Rules of hope*. New York: Springer.

Averill, J. R., and Nunley, E. P. (1988). Grief as an emotion and as a disease. *Journal of Social Issues, 44,* 79–95.

Averill, J. R., and Nunley, E. P. (1992). *Voyages of the heart: Living an emotionally creative life*. New York: Macmillan.

Ax, A. F. (1953). The physiological differentiation between fear and anger in humans. *Psychosomatic Medicine, 15,* 433–42.

Bandler, R. J., Madaras, G. R., and Bem, D. J. (1968). Self-observation as a source of pain perception. *Journal of Personality and Social Psychology, 9,* 205–9.

Barefoot, J. C., and Straub, R. B. (1971). Opportunity for information-search and the effect of false heart-rate feedback. *Journal of Personality and Social Psychology, 17,* 154–7.

Barnard, P. (1985). Interacting cognitive subsystems: A psycholinguistic approach to short-term memory. In A. Ellis (ed.), *Progress in the psychology of language* (vol. 2, pp. 197–258). London: Lawrence Erlbaum Associates.

Barnard, P., and Teasdale, J. D. (1991). Interacting cognitive subsystems: A systemic approach to cognitive-affective interaction and change. *Cognition and Emotion, 5,* 1–39.

Baron, R. A., and Boudreau, L. A. (1987). An ecological perspective on integrating personality and social psychology. *Journal of Personality and Social Psychology, 53,* 1222–8.

Barrera, Jr., M. (1986). Distinctions between social support concepts, measures, and models. *American Journal of Community Psychology, 14,* 413–45.

Bassili, J. N. (1978). Facial motion in the perception of faces and of emotional expression. *Journal of Experimental Psychology, 4,* 373–9.

Bateman, T. S., and Organ, D. W. (1983). Job satisfaction and the good soldier: The relationship between affect and employee 'citizenship'. *Academy of Management Journal, 26,* 587–95.

Batson, C. D., Shaw, L. L., and Oleson, K. C. (1992). Differentiating affect, mood, and emotion: Toward functionally based conceptual distinctions. In M. S. Clark (ed.), *Review of personality and social psychology* 13: *Emotion* (pp. 294–326). Newbury Park, CA: Sage.

Bavelas, J. B., Black, A., Lemery, C. R., and Mullett, J. (1986). 'I *show* how you feel': Motor mimicry as a communicative act. *Journal of Personality and Social Psychology, 50,* 322–9.

Beck, A. T. (1976). *Cognitive therapy and the emotional disorders*. New York: International Universities Press.

Beck, A. T., Rush, A. J., Shaw, B. F., and Emery, G. (1979). *Cognitive therapy of depression*. New York: Guilford Press.

Becker, H. S. (1953). Becoming a marihuana user. *American Journal of Sociology, 59,* 235–42.

Bedford, E. (1957). Emotions. *Proceedings of the Aristotelian Society, 57,* 281–304.

Bem, D. J. (1972). Self-perception theory. In L. Festinger (ed.), *Advances in experimental social psychology* (vol. 5, pp. 1–62). New York: Academic Press.

Berger, P. L., and Luckmann, T. (1967). *The social construction of reality*. London: Allen Lane.

Berkowitz, L. (1993). *Aggression: Its causes, consequences, and control*. New York: McGraw-Hill.

Berkowitz, L., and Turner, C. W. (1974). Perceived anger level, instigating agent, and aggression. In H. London and R. E. Nisbett (eds), *Thought and feeling: Cognitive alteration of feeling states*. Chicago: Aldine.

Bermond, B., Nieuwenhuyse, B., Fasotti, L., and Schuerman, J. (1991). Spinal cord lesions, peripheral feedback, and intensities of emotional feelings. *Cognition and Emotions, 5,* 201–20.

Bernieri, F., Reznick, J. S., and Rosenthal, R. (1988). Synchrony, pseudo-synchrony, and dissynchrony: Measuring the entrainment process in mother–infant interactions. *Journal of Personality and Social Psychology, 54*, 243–353.

Bhaskar, R. (1989). *Reclaiming reality: A critical introduction to contemporary philosophy.* London: Verso.

Biglan, A., Hops, H., Sherman, L., Friedman, L., Arthur, J., and Osteen, V. (1985). Problem-solving interactions of depressed women and their husbands. *Behavior Therapy, 16,* 431–51.

Billig, M. (1987). *Arguing and thinking: A rhetorical approach to social psychology.* Cambridge: Cambridge University Press.

Birdwhistell, R. L. (1970). *Kinesics and context.* Philadelphia: University of Pennsylvania Press.

Bond, M. H. (1988) (ed.). *The cross-cultural challenge to social psychology.* Newbury Park, CA: Sage.

Bower, G. H. (1981). Mood and memory. *American Psychologist, 36,* 129–48.

Briggs, J. (1970). *Never in anger: Portrait of an Eskimo family.* Cambridge, MA: Harvard University Press.

Brockner, J., and Swap, W. C. (1983). Resolving the relationships between placebos, misattribution, and insomnia: An individual-differences perspective. *Journal of Personality and Social Psychology, 45,* 32–42.

Brown, G. W., and Harris, T. (1978). *Social origins of depression.* London: Tavistock Press.

Buck, R. (1979a). Measuring individual differences in the nonverbal communication of affect: The slide-viewing paradigm. *Human Communication Research, 6,* 47–57.

Buck, R. (1979b). Individual differences in nonverbal sending accuracy and electrodermal responding: The externalizing-internalizing dimension. In R. Rosenthal (ed.), *Skill in nonverbal communication: Individual differences* (pp. 140–70). Cambridge, MA: Oelgeschlager, Gunn & Hain.

Buck, R. (1984). *The communication of emotion.* New York: Guilford Press.

Buck, R. (1988). *Human motivation and emotion* (2nd edn). New York: Wiley.

Buck, R., Losow, J.I., Murphy, M. M., and Costanzo, P. (1992). Social facilitation and inhibition of emotional expression and communication. *Journal of Personality and Social Psychology, 63,* 962–8.

Buck, R., Savin, V. J., Miller, R. E., and Caul, W. F. (1972). Communication of affect through facial expressions in humans. *Journal of Personality and Social Psychology, 23,* 362–71.

Cacioppo, J. T., Berntson, G. G., and Klein, D. J. (1992). What is an emotion? The role of somatovisceral afference, with specific emphasis on somatovisceral 'illusions'. In M. S. Clark (ed.), *Review of Personality and Social Psychology 14: Emotion and Social Behavior* (pp. 63–98). Newbury Park, CA: Sage.

Calvert-Boyanowsky, J., and Leventhal, H. (1975). The role of information in attenuating behavioral responses to stress: A reinterpretation of the misattribution phenomenon. *Journal of Personality and Social Psychology, 32,* 214–21.

Campos, J.J. and Stenberg, C. (1981). Perception, appraisal, and emotion: The onset of social referencing. In M. E. Lamb and L. R. Sherrod (eds), *Infant social cognition: Empirical and theoretical contributions* (pp. 217–314). Hillsdale, NJ: Erlbaum.

Camras, L. A. (1992). Expressive development and basic emotions. *Cognition and Emotion, 6,* 269–83.

Camras, L. A., Malatesta, C., and Izard, C. E. (1991). The development of facial expression in infancy. In R. Feldman and B. Rimé (eds), *Fundamentals of nonverbal behavior* (pp. 73–105). New York: Cambridge University Press.

Camras, L. A., Oster, H., Campos, J. J., Miyake, K., and Bradshaw, D. (1992). Japanese and American children's responses to arm restraint. *Developmental Psychology, 28,* 578–83.

Cancian, F. M., and Gordon, S. L. (1988). Changing emotion norms in marriage: Love and anger in U.S. women's magazines since 1900. *Gender and Society, 2,* 308–41.

Candland, D. K. (1976). The persistent problems of emotion. In D. K. Candland, J. P. Fell, E. Keen, A. I. Leshner, R. Plutchik, and R. M. Tarpy (eds), *Emotion* (pp. 1–84). Monterey, CA: Brooks/Cole.

Cannon, W. B. (1927). The James-Lange theory of emotions: A critical examination and an alternative theory. *American Journal of Psychology, 39,* 106–24.

Cannon, W. B. (1929). *Bodily changes in pain, hunger, fear, and rage* (2nd edn). New York: Appleton.

Cantor, J. R., Zillmann, D., and Bryant, J. (1975). Enhancement of experienced sexual arousal in response to erotic stimuli through misattribution of unrelated residual activation. *Journal of Personality and Social Psychology, 32,* 69–75.

Carver, C. S., and Scheier, M. F. (1990). Origins and functions of positive and negative affect: A control-process view. *Psychological Review, 97,* 19–35.

Catanzaro, S. J., and Mearns, J. (1990). Measuring generalized expectancies for negative mood regulation: Initial scale development and implications. *Journal of Personality Assessment, 54,* 546–63.

Chapman, A. J. (1983). Humor and laughter in social interaction and some implications for humor research. In P. E. McGhee and J. H. Goldstein (eds), *Handbook of humor research volume 1: Basic Issues* (pp. 135–57). New York: Springer.

Chapman, A. J., and Wright, D. S. (1976). Social enhancement of laughter: An experimental analysis of some companion variables. *Journal of Experimental Child Psychology, 21,* 201–18.

Chovil, N. and Fridlund, A.J. (1991). Why emotionality cannot equal sociality: Reply to Buck. *Journal of Nonverbal Behavior, 15,* 163–7.

Chwalisz, K., Diener, E., and Gallagher, D. (1988). Autonomic arousal feedback and emotional experience: Evidence from the spinal cord injured. *Journal of Personality and Social Psychology, 54,* 820–8.

Clark, M. S., and Isen, A. M. (1982). Toward understanding the relationship between feeling states and social behavior. In A. H. Hastorf and A. M. Isen (eds), *Cognitive social psychology* (pp. 73–108). New York: Elsevier.

Clore, G. L., and Ortony, A. (1991). What more is there to emotion concepts than prototypes? *Journal of Personality and Social Psychology, 60,* 48–50.

Clore, G. L., Ortony, A., and Foss, M. A. (1987). The psychological foundation of the affective lexicon. *Journal of Personality and Social Psychology, 53,* 751–66.

Cohen, S., and Wills, T. A. (1985). Stress, social support, and the buffering hypothesis. *Psychological Bulletin, 98,* 310–57.

Collins, A. M., and Quillian, M. R. (1969). Retrieval time from semantic memory. *Journal of Verbal Learning and Verbal Behavior, 8,* 240–7.

Conway, M. A., and Bekerian, D. A. (1987). Situational knowledge and emotions. *Cognition and Emotion, 1,* 145–91.

Cooper, C. L., and Payne, R. (1988) (eds). *Causes, coping, and consequences of stress at work.* Chichester: Wiley.

Coyne, J. C. (1976). Toward an interactional description of depression. *Psychiatry, 39,* 28–40.

Coyne, J. C. (1982). A critique of cognitions as causal entities with particular reference to depression. *Cognitive Therapy and Research, 6,* 3–13.

Coyne, J. C., and Downey, G. (1991). Social factors and psychopathology: Stress, social support, and coping processes. *Annual Review of Psychology, 42,* 401–25.

Cupchik, G. C., and Leventhal, H. (1974). Consistency between expressive behavior and the evaluation of humorous stimuli. *Journal of Personality and Social Psychology, 30,* 429–42.

Daly, E. M., Lancee, W. J., and Polivy, J. (1983). A conical model for the taxonomy of emotional experience. *Journal of Personality and Social Psychology, 45,* 443–57.

Darwin, C. (1872). *The expression of the emotions in man and animals*. London: John Murray.

Dashiell, J. F. (1927). A new method of measuring reactions to facial expression of emotion. *Psychological Bulletin, 24*, 174–5.

Davis, M. H. (1983). Measuring individual differences in empathy: Evidence for a multidimensional approach. *Journal of Personality and Social Psychology, 44*, 113–26.

Davitz, J. R. (1969). *The language of emotion*. New York: Academic Press.

Davitz, J. R. (1970). A dictionary and grammar of emotion. In M. B. Arnold (ed.), *Feelings and emotions: The Loyola symposium* (pp. 251–8). New York: Academic Press.

de Rivera, J. H. (1984). The structure of emotional relationships. In P. Shaver (ed.), *Review of personality and social psychology 5: Emotions, relationships, and health* (pp. 116–45). Beverly Hills, CA: Sage.

de Rivera, J. H. (1992). Emotional climate: Social structure and emotional dynamics. In K. T. Strongman (ed.), *International review of studies on emotions* (vol. 2, pp. 197–218). Chichester: Wiley.

de Rivera, J. H., and Grinkis, C. (1986). Emotions as social relationships. *Motivation and Emotion, 10*, 95–108.

DeCasper, A. J., and Fifer, W. (1980). Of human bonding: Newborns prefer their mothers' voices. *Science, 208*, 1174–6.

DePaulo, B. M. (1992). Nonverbal behavior and self–presentation. *Psychological Bulletin, 111*, 203–43.

Descartes, R. (1649/1911). The passions of the soul. In E. S. Haldane and G. R. T. Ross (trans.), *The philosophical works of Descartes* (vol. 1, pp. 329–427). Cambridge: Cambridge University Press.

Douglas, M. (1971). Do dogs laugh? A cross-cultural approach to body symbolism. *Journal of Psychosomatic Research, 15*, 387–90.

Douglas, M. (1973). *Natural symbols: Explorations in cosmology*. Harmondsworth: Penguin.

Duffy, E. (1941). An explanation of 'emotional' phenomena without the use of the concept 'emotion'. *Journal of General Psychology, 25*, 283–93.

Duffy, E. (1962). *Activation and behavior*. New York: Wiley.

Dutton, D., and Aron, A. (1974). Some evidence for heightened sexual attraction under conditions of high anxiety. *Journal of Personality and Social Psychology, 30*, 510–17.

Edwards, D., and Potter, J. (1992). *Discursive psychology*. London: Sage.

Edwards, D., and Potter, J. (1993). Language and causation: A discursive action model of description and attribution. *Psychological Review, 100*, 23–41.

Eibl-Eibesfeldt, I. (1973). The expressive behavior of the deaf-and-blind-born. In M. von Cranach and I. Vine (eds), *Social communication and movement: Studies of interaction and expression in man and chimpanzees* (pp. 163–94). San Diego, CA: Academic Press.

Ekman, P. (1972). Universals and cultural differences in facial expressions of emotion. In J. K. Cole (ed.), *Nebraska symposium on motivation* (vol. 19, pp. 207–83). Lincoln, NE: University of Nebraska Press.

Ekman, P. (1979). About brows: Emotional and conversational signals. In M. von Cranach, K. Foppa, W. Lepenies and D. Ploog (eds), *Human ethology: Claims and limits of a new discipline* (pp. 169–202). New York: Cambridge University Press.

Ekman, P. (1984). Expression and the nature of emotion. In K. S. Scherer and P. Ekman (eds), *Approaches to emotion* (pp. 319–44). Hillsdale, NJ: Erlbaum.

Ekman, P. (1989). The argument and evidence about universals in facial expressions of emotion. In H. L. Wagner and A. S. R. Manstead (eds), *Handbook of social psychophysiology* (pp. 143–64). New York: Wiley.

Ekman, P. (1992). Are there basic emotions? *Psychological Review, 99*, 550–3.

Ekman, P. (1994). Strong evidence for universals in facial expressions: A reply to Russell's mistaken critique. *Psychological Bulletin, 115*, 268–87.

Ekman, P., and Friesen, W. V. (1969). The repertoire of nonverbal behavior. *Semiotica, 1,* 49–98.

Ekman, P., and Friesen, W. V. (1971). Constants across cultures in the face and emotion. *Journal of Personality and Social Psychology, 17,* 124–9.

Ekman, P., and Friesen, W. V. (1974). Detecting deception from the body or face. *Journal of Personality and Social Psychology, 29,* 288–98.

Ekman, P., Friesen, W. V., and Ellsworth, P. (1982). Does the face provide accurate information? In P. Ekman (ed.), *Emotion in the human face* (2nd edn) (pp. 56–97). Cambridge: Cambridge University Press.

Ekman, P., Friesen, W. V., and Simons, R. C. (1985). Is the startle reaction an emotion? *Journal of Personality and Social Psychology, 49,* 1416–26.

Ekman, P., Levenson, R. W., and Friesen, W. V. (1983). Autonomic nervous system activity distinguishing among emotions. *Science, 221,* 1208–10.

Ekman, P., Sorenson, E. R., and Friesen, W. V. (1969). Pan-cultural elements in the facial displays of emotion. *Science, 164,* 86–8.

Ellsworth, P. C. (1991). Some implications of cognitive appraisal theories of emotion. In K. T. Strongman (ed.), *International review of studies on emotion* (vol. 1, pp. 143–61). New York: Wiley.

Ellsworth, P. C. (1994). William James and emotion: Is a century of fame worth a century of misunderstanding? *Psychological Review, 101,* 222–9.

Ellsworth, P. C., and Smith, C. A. (1988). Shades of joy: Patterns of appraisal differentiating pleasant emotions. *Cognition and Emotion, 2,* 301–31.

Erdmann, G., and Janke, W. (1978). Interaction between physiological and cognitive determinants of emotions: Experimental studies on Schachter's theory of emotions. *Biological Psychology, 6,* 61–74.

Fantz, R. L. (1965). Visual perception from birth as shown by pattern selectivity. *Annals of the New York Academy of Sciences, 118,* 793–814.

Farr, R. M., and Moscovici, S. (1984) (eds). *Social representations.* Cambridge: Cambridge University Press.

Fazio, R. H. (1990). Multiple processes by which attitudes guide behavior: The MODE model as an integrative framework. In M. Zanna (ed.), *Advances in experimental social psychology* (vol. 23, pp. 75–109). New York: Academic Press.

Fehr, B., and Russell, J. A. (1984). Concept of emotion viewed from a prototype perspective. *Journal of Experimental Psychology: General, 113,* 464–86.

Fenigstein, A., Scheier, M. F., and Buss, A. H. (1975). Public and private self-consciousness: Assessment and theory. *Journal of Consulting and Clinical Psychology, 43,* 522–7.

Festinger, L., and Carlsmith, J. M. (1959). Cognitive consequences of forced compliance. *Journal of Abnormal and Social Psychology, 58,* 203–10.

Fineman, S. (1993) (ed.). *Emotion in organizations.* London: Sage.

Fischer, A. H. (1991). *Emotion scripts: A study of the social and cognitive facets of emotions.* Leiden: DSWO Press.

Fiske, S. T., and Taylor, S. E. (1991). *Social cognition* (2nd edn). New York: McGraw-Hill.

Fleming, J. H. (1994). Multiple audience problems, tactical communication, and social interaction: A relational-regulation perspective. In M. Zanna (ed.), *Advances in experimental social psychology* (vol. 26, pp. 215–92). New York: Academic Press.

Folkman, S., and Lazarus, R. S. (1980). An analysis of coping in a middle-aged community sample. *Journal of Health and Social Behavior, 21,* 219–39.

Foot, H. C., and Chapman, A. J. (1976). The social responsiveness of young children in humorous situations. In A. J. Chapman and H. C. Foot (eds), *Humour and laughter: Theory, research and applications* (pp. 187–214). Chichester: Wiley.

Forgas, J. P. (1991). Affective influences on partner choice: Role of mood in social decisions. *Journal of Personality and Social Psychology, 61,* 708–20.

Forgas, J. P. (1992). Affect in social judgments and decisions: A multiprocess model. In

M. Zanna (ed.), *Advances in experimental social psychology* (vol. 25, pp. 227–75). New York: Academic Press.

Forgas, J. P., and Bower, G. H. (1987). Mood effects on person perception judgments. *Journal of Personality and Social Psychology, 53*, 53–60.

Foucault, M. (1977). *Discipline and punish: The birth of the prison.* London: Allen Lane.

Freud, S. (1900). *The interpretation of dreams.* London: Hogarth Press.

Fridlund, A. J. (1991a). Evolution and facial action in reflex, social motive, and paralanguage. *Biological Psychology, 32*, 3–100.

Fridlund, A. J. (1991b). Sociality of solitary smiling: Potentiation by an implicit audience. *Journal of Personality and Social Psychology, 60*, 229–40.

Fridlund, A. J. (1992). The behavioral ecology and sociality of human faces. In M. S. Clark (ed.), *Review of personality and social psychology* 13: *Emotion* (pp. 90–121). Newbury Park, CA: Sage.

Frijda, N. H. (1986). *The emotions.* Cambridge: Cambridge University Press.

Frijda, N. H. (1987). Emotion, cognitive structure, and action tendency. *Cognition and Emotion, 1*, 115–43.

Frijda, N. H. (1993). The place of appraisal in emotion. *Cognition and Emotion, 7*, 357–87.

Frijda, N. H., Kuipers, P., and ter Schure, E. (1989). Relations among emotion, appraisal, and emotional action readiness. *Journal of Personality and Social Psychology, 57*, 212–28.

Frijda, N. H., Ortony, A., Sonnemans, J., and Clore, G. L. (1992). The complexity of intensity: Issues concerning the structure of emotion intensity. In M. S. Clark (ed.), *Review of Personality and Social Psychology 13: Emotion* (pp. 60–89). Newbury Park, CA: Sage.

Gabriel, Y. (1993). Organizational nostalgia: Reflections on 'the golden age'. In S. Fineman (ed.), *Emotion in organization* (pp. 118–41). London: Sage.

Garfinkel, H. (1967). *Studies in ethnomethodology.* New York: Prentice-Hall.

Geertz, C. (1984) 'From the native's point of view': On the nature of anthropological understanding. In R. A. Shweder and R. A. LeVine (eds), *Culture theory: Essays on mind, self, and emotion* (pp. 123–36). Cambridge: Cambridge University Press.

Gergen, K. J. (1987). Towards self as relationship. In K. M. Yardley and T. Honess (eds), *Self and identity: Psychosocial perspectives* (pp. 53–63). London: Wiley.

Gergen, K. J., and Davis, K. (1985) (eds). *The social construction of the person.* New York: Springer.

Gibson, J. J. (1979). *The ecological approach to visual perception.* Boston, MA: Houghton Mifflin.

Goffman, E. (1959). *The presentation of self in everyday life.* New York: Doubleday Anchor.

Goffman, E. (1961). *Encounters.* New York: Bobbs-Merrill.

Goffman, E. (1967). *Interaction ritual.* New York: Doubleday Anchor.

Goldberg, D. (1972). *The detection of psychiatric illness by questionnaire.* London: Oxford University Press.

Goody, J. (1962). *Death, property and the ancestors.* Stanford, CA: Stanford University Press.

Gordon, R. M. (1974). The aboutness of emotions. *American Philosophical Quarterly, 11*, 17–36.

Gotlib, I. H., and Colby, C. A. (1987). *Treatment of depression: An interpersonal systems approach.* New York: Pergamon Press.

Gottman, J. M. (1979). *Marital interaction: Experimental investigations.* New York: Academic Press.

Gottman, J. M., and Levenson, R. W. (1985). A valid procedure for obtaining self-report of affect in marital interaction. *Journal of Consulting and Clinical Psychology, 53*, 151–60.

Greenwood, J. D. (1994). *Realism, identity and emotion: Reclaiming* social *psychology.* London: Sage.

Grice, H. P. (1975). Logic and conversation. In P. Cole and J. Morgan (eds), *Syntax and semantics 3: Speech acts* (pp. 41–58). San Diego, CA: Academic Press.

Hamilton, D. L., and Trolier, T. K. (1986). Stereotypes and stereotyping: An overview of the cognitive approach. In J. F. Dovidio and L. Gaertner (eds), *Prejudice, discrimination, and racism* (pp. 127–63). Orlando, FL: Academic Press.

Harré, R. (1986) (ed.). *The social construction of emotions.* Oxford: Blackwell.

Harré, R., and Finlay-Jones, R. (1986). Emotion talk across cultures. In R. Harré (ed.), *The social construction of emotions* (pp. 220–33). Oxford: Blackwell.

Harré, R., and Secord, P. F. (1972). *The explanation of social behaviour.* Oxford: Blackwell.

Harter, S., and Whitesell, N. R. (1989). Developmental changes in children's understanding of single, multiple, and blended emotion concepts. In C. Saarni and P. L. Harris (eds), *Children's understanding of emotion* (pp. 81–116). Cambridge: Cambridge University Press.

Hatfield, E., Cacioppo, J. T., and Rapson, R. (1992). Primitive emotional contagion. In M. S. Clark (ed.), *Review of personality and social psychology 14: Emotion and social behavior* (pp. 151–77). Newbury Park, CA: Sage.

Hebb, D. O. (1949). *The organization of behavior.* New York: Wiley.

Heelas, P. (1986). Emotion talk across cultures. In R. Harré (ed.), *The social construction of emotions* (pp. 234–66). Oxford: Blackwell.

Heider, F. (1946). Attitudes and cognitive organization. *Journal of Psychology, 21,* 107–12.

Heider, F. (1958). *The psychology of interpersonal relations.* New York: Wiley.

Hempel, C. G. (1965). *Aspects of scientific explanation.* New York: Free Press.

Hilton, D. J. (1990). Conversational processes and causal attribution. *Psychological Bulletin, 107,* 65–81.

Hobson, R. P. (1993). *Autism and the development of mind.* Hove: Lawrence Erlbaum Associates.

Hochschild, A. R. (1983). *The managed heart: Commercialization of human feeling.* Berkeley, CA: University of California Press.

Hohmann, G. W. (1966). Some effects of spinal cord lesions on experienced emotional feelings. *Psychophysiology, 3,* 526–34.

Honkavaara, S. (1961). The psychology of expression. *British Journal of Psychology, 32* (Monograph Supplements).

Hunt, W. A. (1941). Recent developments in the field of emotion. *Psychological Bulletin, 38,* 249–76.

Hutchins, E. (1991). The social organization of distributed cognition. In. L. B. Resnick, J. M. Levine, and S. D. Teasley (eds), *Perspectives on socially shared cognition* (pp. 283–307). Washington DC: American Psychological Association.

Isen, A. M. (1970). Success, failure, attention and reactions to others: The warm glow of success. *Journal of Personality and Social Psychology, 15,* 294–301.

Isen, A. M. (1984). Toward understanding the role of affect in cognition. In. R. S. Wyer and T. K. Srull (eds), *Handbook of social cognition* (vol. 3, pp. 179–236). Hillsdale, NJ: Lawrence Erlbaum Associates.

Isen, A. M. (1987). Positive affect, cognitive processes, and social behavior. In M. Zanna (ed.), *Advances in experimental social psychology,* (vol. 20, pp. 203–53). New York: Academic Press.

Isen, A. M., Horn, N., and Rosenhan, D. (1973). Effects of success and failure on children's generosity. *Journal of Personality and Social Psychology, 27,* 239–47.

Isen, A. M., and Levin, P. F. (1972). The effect of feeling good on helping: Cookies and kindness. *Journal of Personality and Social Psychology, 21,* 384–8.

Isen, A. M., and Simmonds, S. F. (1978). The effect of feeling good on a helping task that is incompatible with good mood. *Social Psychology, 41,* 345–9.

Izard, C. E. (1969). The emotions and emotion constructs in personality and culture research. In R. B. Cattell and R. M. Dreger (eds), *Handbook of modern personality research* (pp. 496–510). New York: Wiley.

Izard, C. E. (1971). *The face of emotion*. New York: Appleton-Century-Crofts.

Izard, C. E. (1972). *Patterns of emotions: A new analysis of anxiety and depression*. San Diego, CA: Academic Press.

Izard, C. E. (1977). *Human emotions*. New York: Plenum Press.

Izard, C. E. (1981). Differential emotions theory and the facial feedback hypothesis of emotion activation: Comments on Tourangeau and Ellsworth's 'The role of facial response in the experience of emotion'. *Journal of Personality and Social Psychology, 40*, 350–4.

Izard, C. E., Kagan, J., and Zajonc, R. B. (1984) (eds). *Emotions, cognition, and behaviour*. New York: Cambridge University Press.

James, W. (1884). What is an emotion? *Mind, 9*, 188–205.

James, W. (1898). *The principles of psychology* (vol. 2). London: Macmillan.

Johnson, A. K., and Anderson, E. (1990). Stress and arousal. In J. T. Cacioppo and L. G. Tassinary (eds), *Principles of psychophysiology: Physical, social, and inferential elements* (pp. 216–52). New York: Cambridge University Press.

Johnson, E. J., and Tversky, A. (1983). Affect, generalization, and the perception of risk. *Journal of Personality and Social Psychology, 45*, 20–31.

Johnson, J. E., and Leventhal, H. (1974). Effects of accurate expectations and behavioural instructions on reactions during a noxious medical examination. *Journal of Personality and Social Psychology, 29*, 710–18.

Johnson, M. K. (1983). A multiple-entry, modular memory system. *The Psychology of Learning and Motivation, 17*, 81–123.

Jones, H. E. (1960). The longitudinal method in the study of personality. In I. Iscoe and H. W. Stevenson (eds), *Personality development in children* (pp. 3–27). Austin: University of Texas Press.

Jones, S. S., and Raag, T. (1989). Smile production in older infants: The importance of a social recipient for the facial signal. *Child Development, 60*, 811–18.

Kappas, A. (1991). The illusion of the neutral observer: On the communication of emotion. *Cahiers de Linguistique Française, 12*, 153–68.

Kelly, G. (1955). *The psychology of personal constructs*. New York: Norton.

Kelley, H. H. (1967). Attribution theory in social psychology. In D. Levine (ed.), *Nebraska symposium on motivation* (vol. 15, pp. 192–240). Lincoln, NE: University of Nebraska Press.

Kelley, H. H. (1992). Common-sense psychology and scientific psychology. *Annual Review of Psychology, 43*, 1–23.

Keltner, D., Ellsworth, P. C., and Edwards, K. (1993). Beyond simple pessimism: Effects of sadness and anger on social perception. *Journal of Personality and Social Psychology, 64*, 740–52.

Kemper, T. D. (1978). *A social interactional theory of emotions*. New York: Wiley.

Kemper, T. D. (1991). An introduction to the sociology of emotions. In K. T. Strongman (ed.), *International review of studies on emotion* (vol. 1, pp. 301–49). New York: Wiley.

Kihlstrom, J. F. (1987). The cognitive unconscious. *Science, 237*, 1445–52.

Kleinginna, P. R. Jr., and Kleinginna, A. M. (1981). A categorized list of emotion definitions with suggestions for a consensual definition. *Motivation and Emotion, 5*, 345–79.

Kövecses, Z. (1990). *Emotion concepts*. New York: Springer.

Kraut, R. E., and Johnston, R. E. (1979). Social and emotional messages of smiling: An ethological approach. *Journal of Personality and Social Psychology, 37*, 1539–53.

Kroon, R. M. (1988). *Aanleidingen en structuur van schuld gevoel*. Masters thesis, Psychology Department, University of Amsterdam. No. psy.11.8.88.225.

Kuhn, T. S. (1962). *The structure of scientific revolutions.* Chicago, IL: University of Chicago Press.

Lacey, J. I. (1967). Somatic response patterning and stress: Some revisions of activation theory. In M. H. Appley and R. Trumbull (eds), *Psychological stress* (pp. 14–42). New York: Appleton-Century-Crofts.

Lacey, J. I., and Lacey, B. C. (1958). Verification and extension of the principle of autonomic response stereotypy. *American Journal of Psychology, 71,* 50–78.

Laird, J. D. (1974). Self-attribution of emotion: The effects of expressive behavior on the quality of emotional experience. *Journal of Personality and Social Psychology, 29,* 473–86.

Laird, J. D., and Bresler, C. (1992). The process of emotional experience: A self-perception theory. In M. S. Clark (ed.), *Review of personality and social psychology 13: Emotion* (pp. 213–34). Newbury Park, CA: Sage.

Lakatos, I. (1970). Falsification and the methodology of scientific research programmes. In I. Lakatos and A. Musgrave (eds), *Criticism and the growth of knowledge* (pp. 91–196). Cambridge: Cambridge University Press.

Lakoff, G., and Kövecses, Z. (1987). The cognitive model of anger inherent in American English. In D. Holland and N. Quinn (eds), *Cultural models in language and thought* (pp. 195–221). Cambridge: Cambridge University Press.

Landis, C. (1924). Studies of emotional reactions II: General behavior and facial expression. *Journal of Comparative Psychology, 4,* 447–510.

Landis, C. (1929). The interpretation of facial expression in emotion. *Journal of General Psychology, 2,* 59–72.

Lanzetta, J. T., Cartwright-Smith, J., and Kleck, R. E. (1976). Effects of nonverbal dissimulation on emotional experience and autonomic arousal. *Journal of Personality and Social Psychology, 33,* 354–70.

Larsen, R. J., and Diener, E. (1992). Promises and problems with the circumplex model of emotion. In M. S. Clark, (ed.), *Review of Personality and Social Psychology 13: Emotion* (pp. 25–59). Newbury Park, CA: Sage.

Lazarus, R. S. (1966). *Psychological stress and the coping process.* New York: McGraw-Hill.

Lazarus, R. S. (1968). Emotions and adaptation. In W. J. Arnold (ed.), *Nebraska symposium on motivation* (vol. 16, pp. 175–265). Lincoln, NE: University of Nebraska Press.

Lazarus, R. S. (1982). Thoughts on the relations between emotion and cognition. *American Psychologist, 37,* 1019–24.

Lazarus, R. S. (1984). On the primacy of cognition. *American Psychologist, 39,* 124–9.

Lazarus, R. S. (1991a). *Emotion and adaptation.* New York: Oxford University Press.

Lazarus, R. S. (1991b). Cognition and motivation in emotion. *American Psychologist, 46,* 352–67.

Lazarus, R. S., and Alfert, E. (1964). Short circuiting of threat by experimentally altering cognitive appraisal. *Journal of Abnormal and Social Psychology, 69,* 195–205.

Lazarus, R. S., and Folkman, S. (1984). *Stress, appraisal, and coping.* New York: Springer.

Lazarus, R. S., Opton, E. M., Nomikos, M. S., and Rankin, N. O. (1965). The principle of short-circuiting of threat: Further evidence. *Journal of Personality, 33,* 622–35.

Lazarus, R. S., and Smith, C. A. (1988). Knowledge and appraisal in the cognition–emotion relationship. *Cognition and Emotion, 2,* 281–300.

Lazarus, R. S., Speisman, J. C., Mordkoff, A. M., and Davison, L. A. (1962). A laboratory study of psychological stress produced by a motion picture film. *Psychological Monographs, 76,* no. 34 (whole no. 553).

Levenson, R. W. (1988). Emotion and the autonomic nervous system: A prospectus for research on autonomic specificity. In H. L. Wagner (ed.), *Social psychophysiology and emotion: Theory and clinical applications* (pp. 17–42). Chichester: Wiley.

Levenson, R. W., Ekman, P., and Friesen, W. V. (1990). Voluntary facial action generates emotion-specific autonomic nervous system activity. *Psychophysiology, 27,* 363–84.

Levenson, R. W., and Gottman, J. M. (1983). Marital interaction: Physiological linkage and affective exchange. *Journal of Personality and Social Psychology*, *45*, 587–97.

Leventhal, H. (1974). Emotions: A basic problem for social psychology. In C. Nemeth (ed.), *Social psychology: Classic and contemporary integrations* (pp. 1–51). Chicago, IL: Rand McNally.

Leventhal, H. (1980). Toward a comprehensive theory of emotion. In L. Berkowitz (ed.), *Advances in experimental social psychology* (vol. 13, pp. 139–207). New York: Academic Press.

Leventhal, H. (1984). A perceptual-motor theory of emotion. In L. Berkowitz (ed.), *Advances in experimental social psychology* (vol. 17, pp. 117–82). New York: Academic Press.

Leventhal, H., Brown, D., Shacham, S., and Engquist, G. (1979). Effects of preparatory information about sensations, threat of pain, and attention on cold pressor distress. *Journal of Personality and Social Psychology*, *37*, 688–714.

Leventhal, H., and Mace, W. (1970). The effect of laughter on evaluation of a slapstick movie. *Journal of Personality*, *38*, 16–30.

Leventhal, H., and Scherer, K. R. (1987). The relationship of emotion and cognition: A functional approach to a semantic controversy. *Cognition and Emotion*, *1*, 3–28.

Lewin, K. (1935). *A dynamic theory of personality*. New York: McGraw-Hill.

Lutz, C. A. (1982). The domain of emotion words on Ifaluk. *American Ethnologist*, *9*, 113–28.

Lutz, C. A. (1988). *Unnatural emotions: Everyday sentiments on a micronesian atoll and their challenge to western theory*. Chicago, IL: University of Chicago Press.

Lutz, C. A., and White, G. M. (1986). The anthropology of emotions. *Annual Review of Anthropology*, *15*, 405–36.

Mandler, G. (1975). *Mind and emotion*. New York: Wiley.

Mandler, G. (1984). *Mind and body: The psychology of emotion and stress*. New York: Norton.

Manstead, A. S. R. (1991). Expressiveness as an individual difference. In R. S. Feldman and B. Rimé (eds), *Fundamentals of nonverbal behavior* (pp. 285–327). New York: Cambridge University Press.

Manstead, A. S. R., and Tetlock, P. E. (1989). Cognitive appraisals and emotional experience: Further evidence. *Cognition and Emotion*, *3*, 225–40.

Manstead, A. S. R., and Wagner, H. L. (1981). Arousal, cognition and emotion: An appraisal of two-factor theory. *Current Psychological Reviews*, *1*, 35–54.

Marañon, G. (1924). Contribution à l'étude de l'action émotive de l'adrenaline. *Revue Française d'Endocrinologie*, *2*, 301.

Markus, H. R., and Kitayama, S. (1991). Culture and the self: Implications for cognition, emotion, and motivation. *Psychological Review*, *98*, 224–53.

Marshall, G., and Zimbardo, P. G. (1979). Affective consequences of inadequately explained physiological arousal. *Journal of Personality and Social Psychology*, *37*, 970–88.

Maslach, C. (1979). Negative emotional biasing of unexplained arousal. *Journal of Personality and Social Psychology*, *37*, 953–69.

Mayer, J. D., and Gaschke, Y. N. (1988). The experience and meta-experience of mood. *Journal of Personality and Social Psychology*, *55*, 102–11.

Mayer, J. D., Salovey, P., Gomberg-Kaufman, S., and Blainey, K. (1991). A broader conception of mood experience. *Journal of Personality and Social Psychology*, *60*, 100–11.

McAllister, H. A. (1980). Self-disclosure and liking: Effects for senders and receivers. *Journal of Personality*, *48*, 409–18.

Mead, G. H. (1934). *Mind, self, and society*. Chicago, IL: University of Chicago Press.

Meltzoff, A. N., and Moore, M. K. (1977). Imitation of facial and manual gestures in human neonates. *Science*, *198*, 75–8.

Mesquita, B., and Frijda, N. H. (1992). Cultural variations in emotions: A review. *Psychological Bulletin, 112*, 179–204.

Meyer, G. J., and Shack, J. R. (1989). The structural convergence of mood and personality: Evidence for old and new 'directions'. *Journal of Personality and Social Psychology, 57*, 691–706.

Miller, N. E. (1969). Learning of visceral and glandular responses. *Science, 163*, 434–5.

Miller, R. E. (1974). Social and pharmacological influences on nonverbal communication in monkeys and man. In L. Krames, T. Alloway, and P. Pliner (eds), *Advances in the study of communication and affect: Nonverbal communication* (vol. 1, pp. 77–100). New York: Plenum.

Miller, R. E., Murphey, J. V., and Mirsky, I. A. (1959). Nonverbal communication of affect. *Journal of Clinical Psychology, 15*, 155–8.

Mills, J. (1993). The appeal of tragedy: An attitude interpretation. *Basic and Applied Social Psychology, 14*, 255–71.

Modigliani, A. (1971). Embarrassment, facework, and eye-contact: Testing a theory of embarrassment. *Journal of Personality and Social Psychology, 17*, 15–24.

Motley, M. T., and Camden, C. T. (1988). Facial expression of emotion: A comparison of posed expressions versus spontaneous expressions in an interpersonal communication setting. *Western Journal of Speech Communication, 52*, 1–22.

Munn, N. L. (1940). The effect of knowledge of the situation upon judgment of emotion from facial expressions. *Journal of Abnormal and Social Psychology, 35*, 324–38.

Murray, L., and Trevarthen, C. (1985). Emotional regulation of interactions between two-month-olds and their mothers. In T. M. Field and N. A. Fox (eds), *Social perception in infants* (pp. 177–97). Norwood, NJ: Ablex.

Nakamura, M., Buck, R., and Kenny, D. A. (1990). Relative contributions of expressive behavior and contextual information to the judgment of the emotional state of another. *Journal of Personality and Social Psychology, 59*, 1032–9.

Neisser, U. (1988). Five kinds of self-knowledge. *Philosophical Psychology, 1*, 35–59.

Nieuwenhuyse, B., Offenberg, L., and Frijda, N. H. (1987). Subjective emotion and reported body experience. *Motivation and Emotion, 11*, 169–82.

Nisbett, R., and Ross, L. (1980). *Human inference: Strategies and shortcomings of social judgment*. Englewood-Cliffs, NJ: Prentice-Hall.

Nisbett, R. E., and Wilson, T. D. (1977). Telling more than we can know: Verbal reports on mental processes. *Psychological Review, 84*, 231–59.

Oatley, K. (1990). Do emotional states produce irrational thinking? In K. J. Gilhooly, M. T. G. Keene, R. H. Logie, and G. Erdos (eds), *Lines of thinking* (vol. 2, pp. 121–31). New York: Wiley.

Oatley, K. (1992). *Best laid schemes: The psychology of emotions*. Cambridge: Cambridge University Press.

Oatley, K., and Johnson-Laird, P. N. (1987). Towards a cognitive theory of emotions. *Cognition and Emotion, 1*, 29–50.

Oatley, K., and Johnson-Laird, P. N. (1990). Semantic primitives for emotions: A reply to Ortony and Clore. *Cognition and Emotion, 4*, 129–43.

Organ, D. W. (1988). *Organizational citizenship behavior: The good soldier syndrome*. Lexington, MA: Lexington Books.

Organ, D. W., and Konovsky, M. (1989). Cognitive versus affective determinants of organizational citzenship behavior. *Journal of Applied Psychology, 74*, 157–64.

Ortony, A., Clore, G. L., and Collins, A. (1988). *The cognitive structure of emotions*. Cambridge: Cambridge University Press.

Ortony, A., and Turner, T. J. (1990). What's basic about basic emotions? *Psychological Review, 97*, 315–31.

Osgood, C. E., Suci, G. J., and Tannenbaum, P. H. (1957). *The measurement of meaning*. Urbana, IL: University of Illinois Press.

Ossorio, P. B. (1981). Explanation, falsifiability, and rule-following. *Advances in Descriptive Psychology*, *1*, 37–55.

Oster, H., Hegley, D., and Nagel, L. (1992). Adult judgments and fine-grained analysis of infant facial expressions: Testing the validity of a priori coding formulas. *Developmental Psychology*, *28*, 1115–31.

Panksepp, J. (1992). A critical role for 'affective neuroscience' in resolving what is basic about basic emotions. *Psychological Review*, *99*, 554–60.

Parkinson, B. (1983). *The attribution and misattribution of arousal information in emotion.* Unpublished PhD thesis, University of Manchester.

Parkinson, B. (1985). Emotional effects of false autonomic feedback. *Psychological Bulletin*, *98*, 471–94.

Parkinson, B. (1987a). The social construction of emotions. Ed. Rom Harré. *British Journal of Social Psychology*, *26*, 263–5.

Parkinson, B. (1987b). Emotion: Cognitive approaches. In A. M. Colman and H. Beloff (eds), *Psychology survey* (vol. 6, pp. 55–73). Leicester: British Psychological Society.

Parkinson, B. (1988). Arousal as a cause of emotion. In H. L. Wagner (ed.), *Social psychophysiology: Theory and clinical applications* (pp. 85–104). Chichester: Wiley.

Parkinson, B. (1990). Interrogating emotions: A dyadic task for exploring the common sense of feeling states. *European Journal of Social Psychology*, *20*, 171–9.

Parkinson, B. (1991). Emotional stylists: Strategies of expressive management among trainee hairdressers. *Cognition and Emotion*, *5*, 419–34.

Parkinson, B. (1993). Review of 'Emotion in Organizations'. Ed. Stephen Fineman. *The Occupational Psychologist*, *21* (December), 46–7.

Parkinson, B., and Colgan, L. (1988). False autonomic feedback: Effects of attention to feedback on ratings of pleasant and unpleasant target stimuli. *Motivation and Emotion*, *12*, 87–98.

Parkinson, B., and Lea, M. (1991). Investigating personal constructs of emotions. *British Journal of Psychology*, *82*, 73–86.

Parkinson, B., and Manstead, A.S.R. (1981). An examination of the roles played by meaning of feedback and attention to feedback in the 'Valins effect'. *Journal of Personality and Social Psychology*, *40*, 239–45.

Parkinson, B., and Manstead, A.S.R. (1986). False autonomic feedback: Effects of attention to feedback on ratings of erotic stimuli. *Motivation and Emotion*, *10*, 11–24.

Parkinson, B. and Manstead, A. S. R. (1992). Appraisal as a cause of emotion. In M. S. Clark (ed.), *Review of personality and social psychology 13: Emotion* (pp. 122–49). Newbury Park, CA: Sage.

Parkinson, B., and Manstead, A. S. R. (1993). Making sense of emotion in stories and social life. *Cognition and Emotion*, *7*, 295–323.

Parrott, W. G. (1993). Beyond hedonism: Motives for inhibiting good moods and for maintaining bad moods. In D. M. Wegner and J. W. Pennebaker (eds), *Handbook of mental control* (pp. 278–305). Englewood Cliffs, NJ: Prentice Hall.

Parrott, W. G., and Sabini, J. (1989). On the 'emotional' qualities of certain types of cognition: A reply to arguments for the independence of cognition and affect. *Cognitive Therapy and Research*, *13*, 49–65.

Paykel, E. S., Myers, J. K., Dienelt, M. N., Klerman, G. L., Lindenthal, J. J., and Pepper, M. P. (1969). Life events and depression: A controlled study. *Archives of General Psychiatry*, *21*, 753–60.

Peery, J. C. (1978). Magnification of affect using frame-by-frame film analysis. *Environmental Psychology and Nonverbal Behavior*, *3*, 58–61.

Pennebaker, J. W. (1982). *The psychology of physical symptoms.* New York: Springer.

Peters, T., and Austin, N. (1985). *A passion for excellence.* London: Collins.

Petty, R. E., and Cacioppo, J. T. (1986). The elaboration likelihood model of persuasion. In M. Zanna (ed.), *Advances in experimental social psychology* (vol. 19, pp. 123–205). New York: Academic Press.

Plutchik, R. (1980). *Emotion: A psychoevolutionary synthesis.* New York: Harper & Row.

Polanyi, M. (1958). *Personal knowledge: Towards a post-critical philosophy.* London: Routledge and Kegan Paul.

Pollock, K. (1988). On the nature of social stress: Production of a modern mythology. *Social Science and Medicine, 26,* 381–92.

Potter, J., and Wetherell, M. (1987). *Discourse and social psychology: Beyond attitudes and behaviour.* London: Sage.

Radley, A. (1988). The social form of feeling. *British Journal of Social Psychology, 27,* 5–18.

Rafaeli, A., and Sutton, R. I. (1987). Expression of emotion as part of the work role. *Academy of Management Review, 12,* 23–37.

Rafaeli, A., and Sutton, R. I. (1989). The expression of emotion in organizational life. In L. L. Cummings and B. M. Staw (eds), *Research in organizational behavior* (vol. 11, pp. 1–42). Greenwich, CT: JAI Press.

Read, S. J. (1983). Once is enough: Causal reasoning from a single instance. *Journal of Personality and Social Psychology, 45,* 323–34.

Reid, R. D. (1983). *Food service and restaurant marketing.* New York: Van Nostrand Reinhold.

Reisenzein, R. (1983). The Schachter theory of emotion: Two decades later. *Psychological Bulletin, 94,* 239–64.

Reisenzein, R. (1994). Pleasure-arousal theory and the intensity of emotions. *Journal of Personality and Social Psychology, 67,* 525–39.

Reisenzein, R., and Hofmann, T. (1990). An investigation of dimensions of cognitive appraisal in emotion using the repertory grid technique. *Motivation and Emotion, 14,* 1–26.

Reisenzein, R., and Schönpflug, W. (1992). Stumpf's cognitive-evaluative theory of emotion. *American Psychologist, 47,* 34–45.

Reiser, B. J., Black, J. B., and Abelson, R. P. (1985). Knowledge structures in the organization and retrieval of autobiographical memories. *Cognitive Psychology, 17,* 89–137.

Resnick, L. B., Levine, J. M., and Teasley, S. D. (1991) (eds). *Perspectives on socially shared cognition.* Washington DC: American Psychological Association.

Rimé, B., Mesquita, B., Philippot, P., and Boca, S. (1991). Beyond the emotional event: Six studies on the social sharing of emotion. *Cognition and Emotion, 5,* 435–65.

Rimé, B., Philippot, P., and Cisamolo, D. (1990). Social schemata of peripheral changes in emotion. *Journal of Personality and Social Psychology, 59,* 38–49.

Rippere, V. (1979). Scaling the helpfulness of antidepressive activities. *Behavior Research and Therapy, 17,* 439–49.

Rizzo, J. R., House, R. J., and Lirtzman, S. I. (1970). Role conflict and ambiguity in complex organizations. *Adminstrative Science Quarterly, 15,* 150–63.

Rosaldo, M. Z. (1984). Toward an anthropology of self and feeling. In R. A. Shweder and R. A. LeVine (eds), *Culture theory: Essays on mind, self, and emotion* (pp. 137–57). Cambridge: Cambridge University Press.

Rosch, E. (1978). Principles of categorization. In E. Rosch and B. B. Lloyd (eds), *Cognition and categorization* (pp. 27–48). Hillsdale, NJ: Lawrence Erlbaum Associates.

Roseman, I. J. (1979). *Cognitive aspects of emotion and emotional behavior.* Paper presented at the 87th annual convention of the American Psychological Association, New York City.

Roseman, I. J. (1984). Cognitive determinants of emotions: A structural theory. In P. Shaver (ed.), *Review of personality and social psychology 5: Emotions, relationships, and health* (pp. 11–36). Beverley Hills, CA: Sage.

Roseman, I. J. (1991). Appraisal determinants of discrete emotions. *Cognition and Emotion, 5,* 161–200.

Roseman, I. J., Spindel, M. S., and Jose, P. E. (1990). Appraisals of emotion-eliciting events: Testing a theory of discrete emotions. *Journal of Personality and Social Psychology, 59*, 899–915.

Roseman, I. J., Wiest, C., and Swartz, T. S. (1994). Phenomenology, behaviors, and goals discriminate discrete emotions. *Journal of Personality and Social Psychology, 67*, 206–21.

Rosenthal, R. (1966). *Experimenter effects in behavioral research.* New York: Appleton-Century-Crofts.

Ross, L., Rodin, J., and Zimbardo, P. G. (1969). Toward an attribution therapy: The reduction of fear through induced cognitive-emotional misattribution. *Journal of Personality and Social Psychology, 12*, 279–88.

Ruckmick, C. A. (1921). A preliminary study of the emotions. *Psychological Monographs, 30*, 30–5.

Ruckmick, C. A. (1936). *The psychology of feeling and emotion.* New York: McGraw-Hill.

Russell, J. A. (1980). A circumplex model of affect. *Journal of Personality and Social Psychology, 39*, 1161–78.

Russell, J. A. (1983). Pancultural aspects of the human conceptual organization of emotions. *Journal of Personality and Social Psychology, 45*, 1281–8.

Russell, J. A. (1987). Comments on articles by Frijda and by Conway and Bekerian. *Cognition and Emotion, 1*, 193–7.

Russell, J. A. (1991). In defense of a prototype approach to emotion concepts. *Journal of Personality and Social Psychology, 60*, 37–47.

Russell, J. A. (1994). Is there universal recognition of emotion from facial expression? A review of the cross-cultural studies. *Psychological Bulletin, 115*, 102–41.

Russell, J. A., and Fehr, B. (1994). Fuzzy concepts in a fuzzy hierarchy: Varieties of anger. *Journal of Personality and Social Psychology, 67*, 186–205.

Russell, J. A., Lewicka, M., and Niit, T. (1989). A cross-cultural study of a circumplex model of affect. *Journal of Personality and Social Psychology, 57*, 848–56.

Saarni, C. (1989). Children's understanding of strategic control of emotional expression in social transactions. In C. Saarni and P. L. Harris (eds), *Children's understanding of emotion* (pp. 181–208). Cambridge: Cambridge University Press.

Salovey, P., Hsee, C. K., and Mayer, J. D. (1993). Emotional intelligence and the self-regulation of affect. In D. M. Wegner and J. W. Pennebaker (eds), *Handbook of mental control* (pp. 278–305). Englewood Cliffs, NJ: Prentice Hall.

Sampson, E. E. (1977). Psychology and the American ideal. *Journal of Personality and Social Psychology, 35*, 767–82.

Sappington, A. A., and Russell, J. C. (1979). Self-efficacy and meaning: Candidates for a uniform theory of behavior. *Personality and Social Psychology Bulletin, 2*, 327.

Sarbin, T. R. (1986). Emotion and act: Roles and rhetoric. In R. Harré (ed.), *The social construction of emotions* (pp. 83–97). Oxford: Blackwell.

Sartre, J-P. (1962). *Sketch for a theory of the emotions.* London: Methuen.

Schachter, J. (1957). Pain, fear and anger in hypertensives: A psychophysiologic study. *Psychosomatic Medicine, 19*, 17–29.

Schachter, S. (1959). *The psychology of affiliation.* Stanford, CA: Stanford University Press.

Schachter, S. (1964). The interaction of cognitive and physiological determinants of emotional state. In L. Festinger (ed.), *Advances in experimental social psychology* (vol. 1, pp. 49–80). New York: Academic Press.

Schachter, S., and Singer, J. E. (1962). Cognitive, social, and physiological determinants of emotional state. *Psychological Review, 69*, 379–99.

Schank, R. (1982). *Dynamic memory: A theory of learning in computers and people.* Cambridge, MA: Harvard University Press.

Scherer, K. R. (1992). What does facial expression express? In K. T. Strongman (ed.), *International review of studies in emotion* (vol. 2, pp. 139–65). Chichester: Wiley.

Scherer, K. R. (1993). Studying the emotion-antecedent appraisal process: An expert systems approach. *Cognition and Emotion, 7*, 325–55.

Schlosberg, H. (1952). The description of facial expression in terms of two dimensions. *Journal of Experimental Psychology, 44*, 229–37.

Schwartz, B. (1974). Biological boundaries of learning. *Journal of the Experimental Analysis of Behavior, 21*, 183–98.

Schwarz, N., and Bless, H. (1991). Happy and mindless, but sad and smart? The impact of affective states on analytic reasoning. In J. P. Forgas (ed.), *Emotion and social judgments* (pp. 55–71). Oxford: Pergamon.

Schwarz, N., and Clore, G. L. (1983). Mood, misattribution, and judgments of well-being: Informative and directive functions of affective states. *Journal of Personality and Social Psychology, 45*, 513–23.

Shannon, C. E., and Weaver, W. (1949). *The mathematical theory of communication.* Urbana, IL: University of Illinois Press.

Shaver, P., Schwartz, J., Kirson, D, and O'Connor, C. (1987). Emotion knowledge: Further explorations of a prototype approach. *Journal of Personality and Social Psychology, 52*, 1061–86.

Sherrington, C. S. (1900). Experiments on the value of vascular and visceral factors for the genesis of emotion. *Proceedings of the Royal Society, 66*, 390–403.

Shields, S. A. (1984). Reports of bodily change in anxiety, sadness and anger. *Motivation and Emotion, 8*, 1–21.

Shields, S. A., and MacDowell, K. A. (1987). 'Appropriate' emotion in politics: Judgments of a televised debate. *Journal of Communication, 37*, 78–89.

Shiffrin, R. M., and Schneider, W. (1977). Controlled and automatic information processing II: Perceptual learning, automatic attending, and a general theory. *Psychological Review, 84*, 127–90.

Shotter, J. (1984). *Social accountability and selfhood.* Oxford: Blackwell.

Shotter, J. (1993). *Conversational realities: Constructing life through language.* New York: Sage.

Shweder, R. A., and LeVine, R. A. (1984) (eds). *Culture theory: Essays on mind, self, and emotion.* Cambridge: Cambridge University Press.

Simner, M. L. (1971). Newborn's response to the cry of another infant. *Developmental Psychology, 5*, 136–50.

Sjoberg, L., Svensson, E., and Persson, L. (1979). The measurement of mood. *Scandinavian Journal of Psychology, 20*, 1–18.

Skinner, B. F. (1953). *Science and human behavior.* New York: Macmillan.

Smith, C. A. (1989). Dimensions of appraisal and physiological response in emotion. *Journal of Personality and Social Psychology, 56*, 339–53.

Smith, C. A., and Ellsworth, P. C. (1985). Patterns of cognitive appraisal in emotion. *Journal of Personality and Social Psychology, 48*, 813–38.

Smith, C. A., and Ellsworth, P. C. (1987). Patterns of appraisal and emotion related to taking an exam. *Journal of Personality and Social Psychology, 52*, 475–88.

Smith, C. A., Haynes, K. N., Lazarus, R. S., and Pope, L. K. (1993). In search of the 'hot' cognitions: Attributions, appraisals, and their relation to emotion. *Journal of Personality and Social Psychology, 65*, 916–29.

Smith, C. A., and Lazarus, R. S. (1993). Appraisal components, core relational themes, and the emotions. *Cognition and Emotion, 7*, 233–69.

Smith, C. A., and Pope, L. K. (1992). Appraisal and emotion: The interactional contributions of dispositional and situational factors. In M. S. Clark (ed.), *Review of personality and social psychology 14: Emotion and social behavior* (pp. 32–62). Newbury Park, CA: Sage.

Smith, J. (1981). Self and experience in Maori culture. In P. Heelas and A. Lock (eds), *Indigenous psychologies* (pp. 145–60). London: Academic Press.

Snyder, M. (1974). Self-monitoring of expressive behavior. *Journal of Personality and Social Psychology*, *30*, 526–37.

Snyder, M. (1984). When belief creates reality. In L. Festinger (ed.), *Advances in experimental social psychology* (vol. 18, pp. 247–305). New York: Academic Press.

Sokolov, E. N. (1963). *Perception and the conditioned reflex*. New York: Macmillan.

Solomon, R. (1976). *The passions: The myth and nature of human emotions*. New York: Anchor/Doubleday.

Sommers, S. (1984). Adults evaluating their emotions. In C. Z. Malatesta and C. E. Izard (eds), *Emotion in adult development* (pp. 319–38). Beverly Hills, CA: Sage.

Sorenson, E. R. (1976). *The edge of the forest: Land, childhood and change in a New Guinea protoagricultural society*. Washington DC: Smithsonian Institute Press.

Spanos, N. P., and Chaves, J. F. (1989). Hypnotic analgesia and surgery: In defense of the social-psychological position. *British Journal of Experimental and Clinical Hypnosis*, *6*, 131–9.

Speisman, J. C., Lazarus, R. S., Mordkoff, A., and Davison, L. (1964). Experimental reduction of stress based on ego-defense theory. *Journal of Abnormal and Social Psychology*, *68*, 367–80.

Sroufe, L. A. (1979). The ontogenesis of emotion. In J. D. Osofsky (ed.), *Handbook of infant development* (1st edn, pp. 462–516). New York: Wiley.

Stanislavski, C. (1965). *An actor prepares*. New York: Theatre Art Books.

Stearns, C. Z., and Stearns, P. N. (1986). *Anger: The struggle for emotional control in America's history*. Chicago, IL: University of Chicago Press.

Stepper, S., and Strack, F. (1993). Proprioceptive determinants of emotional and nonemotional feelings. *Journal of Personality and Social Psychology*, *64*, 211–20.

Storms, M. D., and Nisbett, R. E. (1970). Insomnia and the attribution process. *Journal of Personality and Social Psychology*, *16*, 319–28.

Strack, F., Martin, L. L., and Stepper, S. (1988). Inhibiting and facilitating conditions of the human smile: A non-obtrusive test of the facial feedback hypothesis. *Journal of Personality and Social Psychology*, *54*, 768–77.

Strickland, L. H., Aboud, F. E., and Gergen, K. J. (1976) (eds). *Social psychology in transition*. New York: Plenum Press.

Surprenant, C. F., and Solomon, M. R. (1987). Predictability and personalization in the service encounter. *Journal of Marketing*, *51*, 86–96.

Sutton, R. I., and Rafaeli, A. (1988). Untangling the relationship between displayed emotions and organizational sales: The case of convenience stores. *Academy of Management Journal*, *31*, 461–87.

Tajfel, H., and Wilkes, A. L. (1963). Classification and quantitative judgement. *British Journal of Psychology*, *54*, 101–14.

Tavris, C. (1984). On the wisdom of counting to ten: Personal and social dangers of anger expression. In P. Shaver (ed.), *Review of personality and social psychology 5: Emotions, relationships, and health* (pp. 170–91). Beverley Hills, CA: Sage.

Taylor, S. E., and Fiske, S. T. (1978). Salience, attention, and attribution: Top of the head phenomena. In L. Festinger (ed.), *Advances in experimental social psychology* (vol. 11, pp. 249–88). New York: Academic Press.

Teasdale, J. D., and Barnard, P. J. (1993). *Affect, cognition, and change: Re-modelling depressive thought*. Hove: Lawrence Erlbaum Associates.

Tennant, L., and Bebbington, P. (1978). The social causation of depression: A critique of the work of Brown and his colleagues. *Psychological Medicine*, *8*, 565–78.

Tesser, A. (1990). Smith and Ellsworth's appraisal model of emotion: A replication, extension, and test. *Personality and Social Psychology Bulletin*, *16*, 210–23.

Thayer, R. E. (1989). *The biopsychology of mood and arousal*. New York: Oxford University Press.

Thoits, P. A. (1991). On merging identity theory and stress research. *Social Psychology Quarterly*, *54*, 101–12.

Tomkins, S. S. (1962). *Affect, imagery and consciousness (vol. 1: The positive affects)*. New York: Springer.

Tomkins, S. S. (1981). The role of facial response in the experience of emotion: A reply to Tourangeau and Ellsworth. *Journal of Personality and Social Psychology*, *40*, 355–7.

Tourangeau, R., and Ellsworth, P. C. (1979). The role of facial response in the experience of emotion. *Journal of Personality and Social Psychology*, *37*, 1519–31.

Trevarthen, C. (1984). Emotions in infancy: Regulators of contact and relationships with persons. In K. S. Scherer and P. Ekman (eds), *Approaches to emotion* (pp. 129–57). Hillsdale, NJ: Erlbaum.

Trevarthen, C. (1992). The functions of emotions in early infant communication and development. In J. Nadel and L. Camioni (eds), *New perspectives in early communication development* (pp. 48–61). London: Routledge.

Turner, J. C. (1982). Towards a cognitive redefinition of the social group. In H. Tajfel (ed.), *Social identity and intergroup relations* (pp. 15–40). Cambridge: Cambridge University Press.

Turner, J. C., Hogg, M. A., Oakes, P. J., Reicher, S. D., and Wetherell, M. (1987). *Rediscovering the social group: A self-categorization theory*. Oxford: Blackwell.

Turner, T. J., and Ortony, A. (1992). Basic emotions: Can conflicting criteria converge? *Psychological Review*, *99*, 566–71.

Valins, S. (1966). Cognitive effects of false heart rate feedback. *Journal of Personality and Social Psychology*, *4*, 400–8.

Vygotsky, L. S. (1986). *Thought and language*. Cambridge, MA: MIT Press.

Wagner, H. L. (1994). *Self-awareness of facial expression*. Paper presented at the British Psychological Society Social Section Conference, Downing College, Cambridge.

Wagner, H. L., MacDonald, C. J., and Manstead, A. S. R. (1986). Communication of individual emotions by spontaneous facial expressions. *Journal of Personality and Social Psychology*, *50*, 737–43.

Wallbott, H. G. (1988). In and out of context: Influences of facial expression and context information on emotion attributions. *British Journal of Social Psychology*, *27*, 357–69.

Wallbott, H. G., and Scherer, K. R. (1986). How universal and specific is emotional experience? Evidence from 27 countries on 5 continents. *Social Science Information*, *23*, 763–95.

Watson, D., Clark, L. A., and Tellegen, A. (1988). Development and validation of brief measures of positive and negative affect: The PANAS scales. *Journal of Personality and Social Psychology*, *54*, 1063–70.

Watson, D., and Tellegen, A. (1985). Toward a consensual structure of mood. *Psychological Bulletin*, *98*, 219–35.

Watson, J. B. (1929). *Psychology from the standpoint of a behaviorist* (3rd edn). Philadelphia: Lippincott.

Watson, J. B., and Rayner, R. (1920). Conditioned emotional reactions. *Journal of Experimental Psychology*, *3*, 1–14.

Weiner, B. (1985). An attributional theory of achievement motivation and emotion. *Psychological Review*, *92*, 548–73.

Weiner B., Amirkhan, J., Folkes, V. S., and Verette, J. A. (1987). An attributional analysis of excuse giving: Studies of a naive theory of emotion. *Journal of Personality and Social Psychology*, *52*, 316–24.

Weiner, B., Russell, D., and Lerman, D. (1978). Affective consequences of causal ascriptions. In J. H. Harvey, W. J. Ickes, and R. F. Kidd (eds). *New directions in attribution research* (vol. 2, pp. 59–88). Hillsdale, NJ: Erlbaum.

Wenger, M. A., and Cullen, T. D. (1958). ANS response patterns to fourteen stimuli. *American Psychologist*, *13*, 423–4.

Werner, H. (1956). Microgenesis and aphasia. *Journal of Abnormal and Social Psychology*, *52*, 347–52.

Wharton, A. S., and Erickson, R. J. (1993). Managing emotions on the job and at home: Understanding the consequences of multiple emotional rules. *Academy of Management Review*, *18*, 457–86.

White, P. A. (1984). A model of the layperson as pragmatist. *Personality and Social Psychology Bulletin*, *10*, 333–48.

Wittgenstein, L. (1953). *Philosophical investigations*. Oxford: Blackwell.

Wolff, P. H. (1969). The natural history of crying and other vocalizations in early infancy. In B. M. Foss (ed.), *Determinants of infant behaviour* (vol. 4, pp. 81–109). London: Methuen.

Wundt, W. (1897). *Outlines of psychology*. Leipzig: Wilhelm Engelmann.

Wynne, L. C., and Solomon, R. L. (1955). Traumatic avoidance learning: Acquisition and extinction in dogs deprived of normal peripheral autonomic function. *Genetic Psychological Monographs*, *52*, 241–84.

Zajonc, R. B. (1980). Feeling and thinking: Preferences need no inferences. *American Psychologist*, *35*, 151–75.

Zajonc, R. B. (1984). On the primacy of affect. *American Psychologist*, *39*, 117–23.

Zajonc, R. B. (1985). Feeling and facial efference: A theory reclaimed. *Science*, *228*, 15–21.

Zajonc, R. B., and McIntosh, D. N. (1992). Emotions research: Some promising questions and some questionable promises. *Psychological Science*, *3*, 70–4.

Zajonc, R. B., Murphy, S. T., and Inglehart, M. (1989). Feeling and facial efference: Implications of the vascular theory of emotion. *Psychological Review*, *96*, 395–416.

Zillmann, D. (1978). Attribution and misattribution of excitatory reactions. In J. H. Harvey, W. Ickes, and R. F. Kidd (eds), *New directions in attribution research* (vol. 2, pp. 335–68). Hillsdale, NJ: Lawrence Erlbaum Associates.

Zillmann, D., Weaver, J.B., Mundorf, N., and Aust, C.F. (1986). Effects of an opposite gender companion's affect to horror on distress, delight, and attraction. *Journal of Personality and Social Psychology*, *51*, 586–94.

Zimbardo, P. G., Ebbeson, E. B., and Maslach, C. (1977). *Influencing attitudes and changing behavior* (2nd edn). Reading, MA: Addison-Wesley.

Zuckerman, M., Hall, J. A., DeFrank, R. S., and Rosenthal, R. (1976). Encoding and decoding of spontaneous and posed facial expressions. *Journal of Personality and Social Psychology*, *34*, 966–77.

Name index

Subject index